The Post-Soviet Decline
of Central Asia

Sievers takes on the task of explaining the remarkable economic declines of the post-Soviet Central Asian states (Kazakhstan, Kyrgyzstan, Tajikistan, Turkmenistan and Uzbekistan) in the past decade, and the turn of these states toward despotism. In 1990–1992 optimistic hopes for achieving transition to free markets, democracy and sustainable development were voiced. Instead, there has been a continued worsening of the serious environmental problems of the Soviet era, and the region's track record on respect for civil, political and human rights is no better than, and in some cases worse than, that of the Soviet Union in its last decades.

Dismissing explanations of the decline as the result of "Asian" or "nomadic" values as simplistic and opportunistic, the author makes use of extensive field-work to explain this decline as the result of the region's unbalanced stocks of natural, physical, human, financial, organizational, and social capital, exacerbated by the influences of development agencies, environmental NGOs, scientists, corrupt local politicians, and the inequitable downside of globalization symbolized by the WTO. Drawing on recent developments in economics, law and political science, as well as a wealth of local sources, the book presents a compelling and unorthodox challenge to development agencies, scholars and human rights organizations to realize the implications of globalization and the challenges of sustainable development.

Eric W. Sievers is currently associated with Harvard University's Davis Center for Russian and Eurasian Studies and is an attorney in the Central Asian practice of LeBoeuf, Lamb, Greene & MacRae, L.L.P. He has managed and directed a number of development projects in Central Asia throughout the 1990s, and holds a PhD from MIT and a JD from Yale.

CENTRAL ASIA RESEARCH FORUM
Series Editor: Shirin Akiner
School of Oriental and African Studies, University of London

Other titles in the series:

SUSTAINABLE DEVELOPMENT IN CENTRAL ASIA
Edited by Shirin Akiner, Sander Tideman & John Hay

QAIDU AND THE RISE OF THE INDEPENDENT MONGOL STATE IN
CENTRAL ASIA
Michal Biran

TAJIKISTAN
Edited by Mohammad-Reza Djalili, Frederic Gare & Shirin Akiner

UZBEKISTAN ON THE THRESHOLD OF THE TWENTY-FIRST
CENTURY
Tradition and survival
Islam Karimov

TRADITION AND SOCIETY IN TURKMENISTAN
Gender, oral culture and song
Carole Blackwell

LIFE OF ALIMQUL
A native chronicle of nineteenth-century Central Asia
Edited and translated by Timur Beisembiev

CENTRAL ASIA
History, ethnicity, modernity
Edited by Tom Everrett-Heath

THE HEART OF ASIA
A history of Russian Turkestan and the Central Asian Khanates from the
earliest times
Frances Henry Skrine and Edward Denison Ross

THE CASPIAN
Politics, energy and security
Edited by Shirin Akiner & Anne Aldis

ISLAM AND COLONIALISM
Western Perspectives on Soviet Asia
Will Myer

AZERI WOMEN IN TRANSITION
Women in Soviet and Post-Soviet Azerbaijan
Farideh Heyat

THE POST-SOVIET DECLINE OF CENTRAL ASIA
Sustainable development and comprehensive capital
Eric W. Sievers

The Post-Soviet Decline of Central Asia

Sustainable development and comprehensive capital

Eric W. Sievers

RoutledgeCurzon
Taylor & Francis Group

LONDON AND NEW YORK

For Tatiana

First published 2003
by RoutledgeCurzon
11 New Fetter Lane, London EC4P 4EE

Simultaneously published in the USA and Canada
by RoutledgeCurzon
29 West 35th Street, New York, NY 10001

RoutledgeCurzon is an imprint of the Taylor & Francis Group

Transferred to Digital Printing 2003

© 2003 Eric W. Sievers

Typeset in Times by
Integra Software Services Pvt. Ltd, Pondicherry, India
Printed and bound in Great Britain by
Antony Rowe Ltd, Chippenham, Wiltshire

British Library Cataloguing in Publication Data
A catalogue record for this book is available from the British Library

Library of Congress Cataloging in Publication Data
Sievers, Eric, 1970–
   The post-Soviet decline of Central Asia : sustainable development
   and comprehensive capital / Eric Sievers.
      p.   cm.
   Simultaneously published in the USA and Canada.
   1. Asia, Central—Economic conditions—1991–   2. Sustainable
   development—Asia, Central.   3. Asia, Central—Social
   conditions—1991–   4. Post-communism—Asia, Central.
   I. Title.
HC420.3 .S53 2002
338.958′07′09049—dc21   2002069964

ISBN 0–7007–1660–2

Contents

Glossary of terms and abbreviations

1997 Treaty	United Nations Convention on the Law of Non-navigable Uses of International Watercourses
Aarhus Convention	1998 UNECE Convention on Access to Information, Public Participation in Decision-making and Access to Justice in Environmental Matters
ADB	Asian Development Bank
Aksaqal (Uzbek)	"White beard": (1) Head of a local community, (2) older man
AralGEF	Global Environment Facility funded project for the sustainable development of the Aral Sea basin
AZ	Azerbaijan
CATBP	Central Asia Transboundary Biodiversity Project
CBD	United Nations Convention on Biological Diversity
CCD	United Nations Convention to Combat Desertification in Countries Experiencing Serious Drought and/or Desertification, Particularly in Africa
CEP	Caspian Environment Programme
CIS	Commonwealth of Independent States
CITES	Convention to Regulate International Trade in Endangered Species of Flora and Fauna
CMS	Convention on the Conservation of Migratory Species of Animals
COP	Conference of the Parties
CRTC	Caspian Regional Thematic Center
Druzhiny (Russian)	Brigades: social associations that assume governmental functions
FCCS	Framework Convention to Protect the Marine Environment of the Caspian Sea
Gap (Uzbek)	"Talk": a social gathering involving rotating credit
GEF	Global Environment Facility
GONGO	Government Organized Non-Governmental Organization
Hashar (Uzbek)	Communal work or assistance
ICAS	Interstate Council on the Aral Sea
ICJ	International Court of Justice

ICWC	Interstate Commission for Water Coordination
IFAS	International Fund for the Aral Sea
IR	Iran
IUCN	World Conservation Union
Kengash (Uzbek)	Committee
KG	Kyrgyzstan
KZ	Kazakhstan
LRTAP	Convention on Long Range Transboundary Air Pollution
Mahalla (Uzbek)	Traditional neighborhood association
MARPOL	International Convention for the Prevention of Pollution from Ships
MedPlan	Mediterranean Action Plan
MOP	Meeting of the Parties
NABU	Naturschutzbund Deutschland
NEAP	National Environmental Action Plan
NGO	Non-Governmental Organization
NIC	Newly Industrialized Country
ODS	Ozone Depleting Substances
OECD	Organisation for Economic Co-operation and Development
OSCE	Organization for Security and Co-operation in Europe
Rais (Uzbek)	Chairperson
Ramsar	Convention on Wetlands of International Importance Especially as Waterfowl Habitat
RCA	Residential Community Association
REAP	Regional Environmental Action Plan
SSGO	Social Self-Government Organization
TACIS	European Union Programme for "Technical Assistance to the Commonwealth of Independent States"
TJ	Tajikistan
TM	Turkmenistan
Toi (Uzbek)	Celebratory event
UNDP	United Nations Development Programme
UNDP–GEF	UNDP unit charged with Global Environment Facility projects
UNECE	United Nations Economic Commission for Europe
UNEP	United Nations Environment Programme
UNESCO	United Nations Educational, Scientific and Cultural Organization
UNFCCC	United Nations Framework Convention on Climate Change
UNICEF	United Nation's Children's Fund
UNOPS	United Nations Office for Project Services
USAID	United States Agency for International Development

UZ	Uzbekistan
Viloyat (Uzbek)	Administrative unit subordinate to national state
Waqf	An Islamic trust or foundation
WHO	World Health Organization
WTO	World Trade Organization
WWF	World Wildlife Federation
Zapovednik (Russian)	Nature reserve

Introduction: Central Asia in transition – the capital of sustainable development

Central Asia[1] is an area of the planet poorly known beyond its own borders. Yet, Central Asia's contribution to the resolution of many global environmental problems will be critical in coming years, even as the region continues to venture to overcome the local environmental problems it inherited from the Soviet Union. In both endeavors, Central Asia's struggle is to embrace sustainable development. Central Asia as a whole, belying the optimism of reports (particularly previous to 1998) issued locally, by scholars, and by development organizations,[2] is in fact moving annually farther from embodying sustainable development.

The vast majority of the more than 55 million people in Central Asia were born Soviet. Only a little more than ten years ago, they overwhelmingly identified themselves as superpower citizens, as comparatively wealthy, and as distinct from their southern neighbors. Since then, three major changes transpired. First, these people have a new status as citizens of marginal states. Second, these citizens experience poverty typified by declines in annual salaries from thousands of dollars to, often, only 100 dollars, accompanied by a sharp decline in state programs providing welfare benefits, public education, and medical services. Moreover, the region suffered a severe economic shock in the wake of the 1998 Russian economic collapse, and in 1999 real income fell by half for a large proportion of the region's residents. The third change involves the appearance or realization of domestic problems and issues that make apparent the region's ties with other developing states in Asia and beyond, for example armed civil conflict, Islamicization as a challenge to secular state legitimacy, and efforts to appease China, Russia, and the IMF.

While newfound freedoms to use national languages, spotty and infrequent democratic reforms, and some possibilities for freedom of expression may somewhat offset these perceived trends of economic decline and global marginalization, increasingly, citizens of the region conclude that independence has not worked to their favor. Out-migration of scientists and specialists, fraying social safety nets, an aging and decaying, although appreciable, Soviet physical infrastructure, and a prevalence of elite authoritarianism over democratic rule of law all symbolize the decline of Central Asia and the region's difficulties in implementing reforms for sustainable development.

Illustrating the reticence of many in the region to accept the post-Soviet era, reactions to these components of decline, especially reactions from specialists and political leaders, more often produce suggestions appropriate to wealthy and/or very strong states than to the new realities of Central Asia. Exacerbating this situation, while assistance to Central Asia from developed countries consistently is at (comparatively) high levels, it is less than the states expected, is more targeted towards trade and markets than to environment and democratization, and is insufficient by itself to move the states into effective regimes of sustainable development.

None of this was expected. With its blend of endowments, Central Asia expected great improvements to follow from post-Soviet independence. Notwithstanding a variety of generally inarticulate negative voices, consensus within the region was that independence would bring economic growth, open and democratic societies, and rapid integration into Western economic, political, and social life. Western states, donors, and institutions, while somewhat more restrained in their enthusiasm, expected essentially similar outcomes. Internal and external commentators identified the risk of civil or regional armed conflict arising from Islamic renaissance, water disputes, hydrocarbon rents, or some sort of "clash of civilizations" as the greatest, and perhaps only, barriers to realization of a bright future in Central Asia.

Source: Adapted from Central Intelligence Agency, Map # 802410: Caucasus and Central Asia (Washington, D.C.: CIA, 1995).

Yet, the next 10 years in Central Asia did not usher in a bright future, and regional and civilizational conflict seem not to have had much to do with this disappointment. With the exception of Tajikistan (and Azerbaijan), wars have not materialized. Instead of war, the region has encountered pervasive stagnation. Perhaps the only kind of violence that has not appeared anywhere in Central Asia is civilizational violence; Christian/Islamic violence is actually far less common than virtually any other kind of violence and, if anything, has declined since 1992. Economies, societies, and institutions across contemporary Central Asia are in shambles, and each year brings more decline. Excepting the emerging and small elite classes, the people of Central Asia are every year looking more and more like impoverished post-colonial counterparts in Africa; their children are less literate, their lifespans are shortening, and their connections to political, social, and economic policies of their states are becoming increasingly tenuous.

PRE-SOVIET, SOVIET, AND POST-SOVIET CENTRAL ASIA

Central Asia's history is long and exceedingly complex. Likewise, the origins and heritage of its peoples are richly complex and open to heated controversy, both within and outside the region. Thus, the following effort to gloss this history is necessarily sparse and aims only to provide a useful context for readers who may not be familiar with the contours of the region's history and culture.

Indo-European peoples may have originated in areas of present-day southern Russian and Kazakhstan,[3] spreading from there southwards and westwards. Soon after agriculture blossomed in the Fertile Crescent, it took root in Central Asia. During the bronze age, as during most of Central Asia's history, the region was invaded repeatedly by steppe tribes from the north and kingdoms based in Persia, as well as infused culturally by civilizations to the south. Perhaps the first precise date in Central Asian history,[4] in 530 B.C., the Scythian queen Tomiris lured Kir II and his armies into an ambush within Central Asia to prevent expansion of the Persian Kingdom and avenge the death of her son. Nevertheless, for the next several centuries, southern Central Asia was under the control of Achaemenid rulers, known both for their harsh treatment and also for innovations such as introducing the first coins to the region. From this period until the advent of the global sea trade, Central Asia enjoyed the fruits of being at the crossroads of global trade. As a result, the region received wealth and cultural infusions.

When the Greeks defeated the Persians in 331 B.C., Alexander the Great began an advance to subjugate Persian lands. Experienced in fighting the Greeks as soldiers in Persian armies, the Sogdians of modern day Central Asia mounted fierce resistance to Alexander. However, through victories claiming hundreds of thousands of Central Asian lives and by marrying into the local nobility, Alexander brought Central Asia, with the partial exception of Khorezm (on the southern shores of the Aral Sea), into his empire, established new towns (such as Khujand in Tajikistan), and then returned home. After Alexander's death, a separate Seleucid Greek kingdom arose in Central Asia.

The Parthian state soon broke off from this kingdom. When, in 53 B.C. Parthia defeated Rome's armies, it settled captured Roman soldiers near Merv, in modern day Turkmenistan. Soon thereafter, a Buddhist Kushan state came to control much of Central Asia east of Turkmenistan. Earlier, Chinese armies temporarily captured areas in Kazakhstan and the Fergana Valley (present day KG, TJ, and UZ). Persian Sassanids also ruled parts of Central Asia and used Central Asian soldiers in both of their successful wars on Rome.

In A.D. 470, a wave of invasions from the north and east began. First, White Huns captured much of Central Asia, followed shortly thereafter by a series of Turkic invasions that led to establishment of the Turkic Kaganate, which at one time stretched from Korea to the Black Sea.

In 651, Arabs captured Merv and shortly thereafter began annual efforts to capture the Central Asian lands to the east of the Amudarya River. Beginning in 708, Arab armies took, lost, and gradually consolidated their hold on Bukhara and Khorezm. A Central Asian coalition formed to repel the Arabs failed, and by the middle of the eighth century, Islam had come to most of Central Asia. In 751, the khalifate's troops defeated Chinese armies sent to capture Central Asia.

While Central Asia flourished at this time, invasions, especially from the north, continued, as did internecine warfare. In the early thirteenth century, however, Chinggis Khan's armies descended from Mongolia, quickly subdued the entire region, and destroyed much of the region's impressive government, educational, and agricultural infrastructure. A century later, launching from the heritage of Chinggis Khan, Tamerlane established an empire based in Central Asia that controlled much of the civilized world. When Uzbek tribes[5] descended from the north two centuries later to capture the major cities of Central Asia, one of Tamerlane's heirs, Babur, fled to India, and there established the Moghul Empire.

From the seventeenth to nineteenth centuries, three states controlled much of Central Asia: Khorezm, Bukhara, and Kokand. Yet, much of Turkmenistan and Kazakhstan was under the control of nomadic tribes and many border areas were often controlled by neighboring states such as China, Balkh, Persia, and Russia. Importantly, none of the three established states within Central Asia developed strongly over this period, and all substantially lost power when compared to the development of neighboring states to the north, east, and south. By this time, Central Asia was no longer of any real importance to global trade, and it gradually receded into obscurity, even within the Islamic world.

Central Asia came under the control of the Russian Empire in stages. While northern Kazakhstan had mostly acceded to the Russian Empire by the end of the eighteenth century, the rest of Central Asia fell to Russian armies in a series of military campaigns in the second half of the nineteenth century, most notably in the 1860s. In 1887, delimiting their spheres of influence in Central Asia, Russia and Britain established the border between Central Asia and Afghanistan. The Russian Empire sought in Central Asia a consumer market for emerging Russian industries, a trade route to India, and a guaranteed supply of raw materials such as cotton. The Russian Empire settled its citizens in the region, built railroads, and embarked on plans to build the region into a major source of cotton.

After the October Revolution, the new leadership of Russia consolidated its control and embarked on the task of integrating Central Asia into the new state. Worried about Pan-Turkic or Pan-Islamic threats of revolution in the region (and similar movements in other parts of the realm), Soviet planners settled on a strategy of encouraging national consciousness and of building quasi-nation states as a bulwark against more widely appealing expressions of identity. It is this process that led to creation of the Kazakh (1936), Kyrgyz (1936), Tajik (1929), Turkmen (1924), and Uzbek (1924) Soviet Socialist republics as 5 of the 15 republics that constituted the Union of Soviet Socialist Republics (USSR).

At the beginning of the Soviet era, residents of Central Asia did not readily identify themselves as belonging to an ethnic group eponymous with these republics, nor could they readily discern by language to which group one should belong. A continuum of closely related languages (including a norm of multilingualism) and a diversity of primary associational loyalties (to city, to religion, to ethnic group, to tribe, etc.) made delineation of the region a largely arbitrary undertaking.

The experience of Central Asia under the Soviet Union was certainly ambivalent but not uneventful. In a relatively short period of time, the Soviet state quashed Islam and Islamic institutions, assigned citizens to ethnic groups, abolished religious trusts and schools, and redistributed land. In the second decade of Soviet rule, a rapid effort at collectivization of agriculture and animal husbandry led to a famine in which hundreds of thousands died or fled to neighboring states, such as China, Mongolia, and Afghanistan. Likewise, Stalinist repressions led to mass executions of prominent local leaders, intellectuals, and common folk alike.

Yet, at the same time, standards of living began to increase dramatically in the region, and basic infrastructure like schools, hospitals, and airports expanded dramatically. Of course, however, Central Asians did not enjoy extensive political freedoms. On the other hand, their educational opportunities were considerable, and over time, many Central Asians ascended to prominent positions within the Russian dominated political, scholarly, and economic communities of the Soviet Union, two even ascending to Politburo status. These improvements were especially notable when compared to the plight of the region's co-nationals residing at the time in Mongolia, China, and Afghanistan.

During the 1980s, life changed quickly in the Soviet Union after several decades of stability and slower growth under Leonid Brezhnev. In the 1980s, economic problems and shortfalls in meeting economic targets brought to light serious structural problems in the Soviet economy and society. The limitations of economic centralization, the cost of sustaining the military, the lack of appropriate incentives in the workplace, and a disconnect between technology innovation and industrial production were among the reasons why the USSR fell short of its own hopes for growth. However, enduring problems of lack of civic freedoms and corruption within government exacerbated these problems.

When Mikhail Gorbachev ascended to leadership of the USSR in 1985, all of these problems were already apparent. The economy had already begun to sour, and for the first time in its history the Soviet Union began to witness widespread declines in higher education matriculation, life expectancy, and similar social indicators. Gorbachev firmly believed that none of these problems, however, disproved the promise of the Soviet development enterprise. Rather, he saw in these problems errors of design and judgment that could be addressed effectively through decentralization of economic and political decisionmaking, greater civic freedoms, and an encouragement of public dialogue (Glasnost) to introduce accountability to political leadership. Accordingly, under Perestroika, Gorbachev replaced much of the top leadership in various republics, including in Central Asia, encouraged passage of new legislation to allow religious, entrepreneurial, and social freedoms, and sought to chart a new policy in Soviet foreign relations.

As a result, newspapers across the Soviet Union began to print letters to the editor and carry articles that diverged critically from the party line. Independent civic organizations, religious congregations, and private businesses sprouted up everywhere. Books on mysticism, training in martial arts, and exposes of every sort became hugely popular. More importantly, revisionist histories began to appear, and an open dialogue about Moscow's past and present actions and crimes gained momentum. Vehement resistance arose against state development projects, chemical factories, nuclear power plants, and the war in Afghanistan, where only a few years earlier few critical voices were heard. Free elections for republic and union legislative bodies in 1989 and 1990 further facilitated these reforms.

Moreover, with decentralization local governments began to reflect constituent concerns, or at least to leverage their own political aspirations with reference to such concerns. The formerly quiet republican governments began an open struggle with Moscow for greater power, funding, and autonomy. In the Baltic republics, which were only annexed into the USSR after World War II, true independence movements finally led to those republics declaring their independence and attempting to secede from the USSR, a right supposedly granted under the USSR Constitution. As part of their efforts to wrest power from Moscow, the Central Asian republics also asserted their sovereignty and independence, even though there is no serious indication that either the governments (beneficiaries of large subsidies from Moscow) or the citizenry desired separation from the USSR. Indeed, in a 1991 referendum on whether to preserve the Soviet Union, a large majority of voters across the USSR voted to prevent its disassembly, with the largest majorities coming from the Central Asian republics.

Accordingly, the Central Asian republics, unlike other Soviet republics, had little reason to want true independence. For the governments, Moscow subsidies were indisputably heftier than the promises of an independent local economy. For the populace, unlike in virtually every other USSR republic, Perestroika had brought no wars, no tanks in the street, and little expectation that a fundamental change was about to occur. Correspondingly, because of the region's reliance on Moscow subsidies and its isolation from the rest of the world, Central Asian was perhaps least prepared for liberation from the Soviet Union.

It is the uneven mix of its post-Soviet endowments that makes Central Asia's independence a more substantial event than mere liberation. While the region is now liberated from the atrocities of the Soviet era, from outside repression of civil and political rights, and from the economic limitations of Soviet development policies, it does not enter the independence era without history and without a unique heritage. While part of this history and heritage is grounded in the Islam, societies, and institutions of the pre-Russian era, a great deal of this heritage comes from the Soviet period as well and the educational and professional skills that the period offered today's Central Asian leaders. In other words, no matter the reaction of individuals in the region to the disassembly of the USSR, they greeted this independence as individuals distinctly Soviet.

Indeed, independence was a surprisingly casual event for the region. The actual physical infrastructure determining how people carry out their daily activities has remained virtually intact and much "reform" has frequently been little more than cosmetic, as the rise of the Democratic Party of Turkmenistan illustrates.

> The Turkmen [Communist] party had its last meeting on the morning of December 16, 1991. At that meeting the party faithful agreed to disband the party. The assembled then went to lunch together and reconvened afterward to establish the People's Democratic Party of Turkmenistan. Within months the Democratic Party had a membership of nearly 52,000, of whom 48,000 were former communists.[6]

CENTRAL ASIA EXPERIENCED AND ABSTRACTED

Central Asia's independence sparked a number of reactions beyond the borders of the region. Development organizations, spurred by European and American state commitments to assist the transition states, found opportunities to become active in the reason. Similarly, the scholarly world found reason to include Central Asia in surveys of late twentieth century expansions of democracy and markets. How both of these communities, development and scholarly, have approached the region is vital to understanding what has happened in Central Asia since independence.

Specifically, such an understanding is vital to understanding how these communities have failed the region in the past decade. In claiming that these communities have failed the region, I of necessity implicate myself, and thus this work is also infused with a personal investment. I spent almost all of the past decade, beginning even before the disassembly of the USSR, as a member of the development community on the ground in Central Asia or as a member of the academic community studying the region from abroad. Thus, to the extent that this work strongly criticizes the shortcomings of developers and scholars over the past decade, in neither case can I exempt myself from such criticism.

To begin with the abstract and academia, the main focus of comparative scholars is to categorize Central Asia into existing conceptions of states, societies, and transitions. Whether or not Central Asia is best characterized as post-colonial or simply post-Soviet is a matter of debate. Since the Soviet republics were contiguous, since they were constituents of a formally federal state, and since state subsidies arguably benefited the various republics more than Russia, it is probably incorrect to call Central Asia post-colonial, despite some similarities with other post-colonial areas. Perhaps most tellingly, the existence of Joseph Stalin and several other non-Russians among the USSR's top leadership separates Central Asia and other Soviet republics from the kind of "imagined communities"[7] that typify colonialism and the birth of nationalism.

While Central Asia's ambiguous status as colonial or merely newly independent provokes the expenditure of considerable scholarly effort and should (but does not) entail consequences for the states involved under international law,[8] this issue has little bearing on whether or not the region is moving in the direction of sustainable development. Moreover, given the contradictory experiences of post-colonial states in Latin America, Asia, and Africa in recent decades, the post-colonial label would provide much in the way of fueling claims of moral entitlement and little in the way of clarifying Central Asia's needs for the future or the sources of its current failures.

As a starting point, some possible explanations offer themselves as candidates for Central Asia's failures. These include, first, an explanation based on perverse inherent cultural attributes of Central Asia, as, alternately, Soviet, Asian, or Islamic. Easily the most popular thesis in the 1990s among the possibilities here listed, this first explanation resonates strongly with models such as the "Clash of Civilizations" of Samuel Huntington.[9]

A second possibility hinges on the structural alterations introduced in the global system by globalization; in short, the tighter commodity markets, increased personal mobility, and the isomorphic institutionalism of the era of globalization put any state that undergoes deep structural changes at a serious disadvantage. This possibility reflects some of the globalization and failed states ideas of thinkers such as Saskia Sassen[10] and Robert Kaplan.[11]

A third possibility is that Central Asia's decade of decline is only a temporary blip related to re-organization; Central Asia will inevitably reconstruct and resurrect itself to realize the advantages of free markets and democracy envisioned at the beginning of the decade.[12] This line of reasoning, increasingly tenuous, is proffered by a variety of donors inherently interested in continuing the status quo of aid programs in the region.

A fourth possibility is that donor policies and pressures from other states have weakened Central Asia. A strong form of this theory would assign this weakening to the purposeful planning of the West and would thus fit a hegemonic international relations theory. A weaker form, in which this weakening was not an intended result, suggests failures of international planning institutions of the kind that have sparked recent public protests at World Bank and World Trade Organization meetings.

Finally, a fifth possibility is that Central Asia's abandonment of the human capital emphases of the Soviet period and ideological emphases of Perestroika have rapidly driven it from the developed world to the third world. This final model resonates with ideas about social capital outlined by Robert Putnam,[13] as well as currently marginalized ideas about the role of science and technology in building strong economies.[14]

The goal of this book is, obliquely, to investigate the causation of Central Asia's 1990s decline. This investigation fits into a larger examination of the region's progress towards sustainable development generally and its preservation of natural capital specifically. Accordingly, the book begins by presenting a cognitive hurdle; it seems to suppose both the importance and interconnectedness of three very different topics: Central Asia, sustainable development, and natural capital.

While natural capital and sustainable development are indeed closely linked conceptions, pollution and natural resources are not the key to understanding modern Central Asia, and Central Asia does not hold special clues to understanding sustainable development. Moreover, while natural capital and sustainable development are globally important issues, Central Asia is not an area of special significance. Its importance pales compared with that of China, Russia, or Europe. Yet, partly for this reason, scholarly analyses and reliable data about Central Asia are notably not robust at present. Consequently, even if it promises no immediate application to policy, my effort to generate reliable data about and analyze the recent history of Central Asia facilitates the scholarly, if not the professional, mission of academia. Simply, "we can know more about ourselves."[15]

Yet, while Central Asia in itself may not be a key region in the world when measured with traditional metrics of size of population, military strength, importance for trade, wealth, and influence, it stands between some key regions, all of which are currently in transition. As scholars increasingly expand the depth of their analyses of transition successes and failures, comparative studies will need to become more sophisticated to explain the quite divergent experiences of Central Europe, Russia, China, and Vietnam. In this regard, the common general experience of the Central Asian states, even despite interesting differences among these states, may be indispensable to such scholarship in order to challenge the robustness of existing theories, which are based on extrapolations from events in a small number of world regions. Thus an important reason to study and understand the post-Soviet transition of Central Asia, and by extension to incorporate case studies of Central Asia into comparative studies, is that such an effort promises to enrich the insights of global analyses by challenging privileged assumptions, testing accepted ideas, opening avenues for new insights, and generally broadening scholarly horizons.

While the scholarly ideas and possibilities glossed above have found some expression in the policies of the development agencies that began arriving in Central Asia in 1992, on the whole development agencies exist as a separate community. Yet, like their academic colleagues, the policy staff of development organizations also endeavored as an initial task to identify Central Asia as an already familiar region, one either like Eastern Europe, like Latin America, or like other parts of Asia. Unlike their academic counterparts, however, developers injected themselves into Central Asian society and experienced it as a reality, albeit through the filter of the sheltered environs of development agency staff.

To illustrate how close the development community is to the scholarly community at times, the following relates a not unusual meeting between Harvard and Central Asia. In the early spring of 1997, Kazakhstan dispatched a dozen high ranking officials from its ministries and planning agencies to Harvard's John F. Kennedy School of Government for a week of training in strategic planning. One afternoon Galymzhan Zhakiyanov, the young new director of the Agency for Control over Strategic Natural Resources of the Republic of Kazakhstan, crossed the Kennedy School courtyard to the Harvard Institute for International Development (HIID) with me as his interpreter. Zhakiyanov, born close to the Semipalatinsk nuclear test site, thanks to the Soviet Union enjoyed social, human, and organization capital assets unknown to his parents. In the ensuing discussion, HIID attempted to sell its expertise to Zhakiyanov, and the two sides, as commonly occurs in development aid events, talked past each other.

HIID emphasized its current activities in dozens of developing countries, particularly its decades of success in Indonesia. Kazakhstan, HIID told Zhakiyanov, could learn much from Indonesia's successes. Zhakiyanov, a member of the technical intelligentsia of northern Kazakhstan, educated in Moscow and lured personally by President Nazarbaev out of a successful career in private business, replied that, having visited and studied Indonesia, he failed to see what Indonesia could offer Kazakhstan. After all, "Indonesia's per capita income is far below Kazakhstan's." Heading off further explanations from HIID, Zhakiyanov noted that much of Indonesia's international economic influence is the natural result of boasting such a large population. Since, Zhakiyanov continued, the majority of Indonesians live at the poverty line, Kazakhstan would have to do some regressing to arrive at an Indonesian model of development.

Not dissuaded, HIID then offered Korea as a development model for Kazakhstan. After all, being itself an Asian country, HIID reasoned, Kazakhstan could probably learn best from an Asian model. Zhakiyanov's retort expressed the opinion that both Korea and Indonesia treat their citizens in ways that not only the government of Kazakhstan finds unacceptable but that the citizens of Kazakhstan would actively resist. "There are no slaves in Kazakhstan," concluded Zhakiyanov. HIID then offered to help Kazakhstan chart an entirely new development path, eliciting Zhakiyanov's assurance that no novel path was justified; other postcommunist models, especially Poland, offered all the inspiration, warnings, and lessons that Kazakhstan would need.

The discussion then turned to Kazakhstan's natural resources. HIID outlined its current "environmental" initiatives in Kazakhstan, projects to improve the functionality of the extraction sector. In response, Zhakiyanov noted that while Kazakhstan faces some of the worst environmental problems on the planet, HIID had never once mentioned an environmental or ecological issue, only economic efficiency. HIID agreed that its projects were implemented by economists instead of ecologists, but posited that the core issue in any case was not whether

Kazakhstan's natural resources were going to be exploited, but how well. "As long as natural resources are going to be used, it would be illogical not to maximize their economic benefit for Kazakhstan," a young HIID economist volunteered. Such an approach should at least not be advertised as environmental, Zhakiyanov concluded.

Yet, what makes this exchange more interesting is to consider its relationship to development projects occurring on the ground in the former Soviet Union. Until soon after this exchange at Harvard, what most of the world knew about HIID's development work in the region came from HIID's own assessments or the assessments of HIID's funder, the United States Agency for International Development (USAID). In both cases, the self-interested norm was to advertise strong successes. Basically all USAID contractors and grantees, and USAID itself, achieved success in the early independence years, according to their own reports. These reports also had substantial impact on scholars tracking changes in the region, and as a result, most scholarly reports of the early transition period also glowed. My own experience has been, especially as someone who has been asked to pen such reports, that these reports have little connection to reality. As if to spite these reports on market and economic successes, all the region's economies tanked in 1998, and elections in the second half of independence have in virtually all cases been less free than their counterparts in the first years of independence.

Moreover, a U.S. federal criminal and civil investigation is now proceeding against HIID economists for their insider trading and other digressions in Russia.[16] Closer to home for Central Asia, USAID's prominent Central Asian American Enterprise Fund is now the subject of a potentially worse shortcoming. The FBI is now investigating allegations that two of its original American staff in Tashkent embezzled $10 million.[17] Not all development projects are failures and not all encourage criminal activity. Yet, as a corollary, no development project is a philanthropic panacea, and, once that point is accepted, no development project is beyond the reach of, or somehow entitled to exemption from, critical assessment.

SUSTAINABLE DEVELOPMENT

Putting aside for the moment the fact that there exists no consensus definition of sustainable development, Central Asia's leaders, the region's major international donors, and a variety of other stakeholders explicitly acclaim sustainable development as both a moral imperative and a rational long-term goal. It is this consensus that grounds the applicability of an analysis of the region's development within the framework of sustainable development instead of analyzing the region's economic development by sequestering it from concerns about environmental, social, and governance issues.

Outsiders are often puzzled about why Central Asian policymakers devote considerable attention to and valorize biodiversity and carbon emissions concerns. Although the modeled effects of global warming promise comparatively little dislocation to Central Asia (and a few models even hint at better conditions for agriculture through increased precipitation), nowhere in the region does one encounter any substantive opposition to the assertion that a global effort is needed to limit global warming and that all states must lower carbon emissions. This global outlook is just one of the peculiarities of Central Asia that sets the region apart from paradigm transition states like China.[18]

Sustainable development, in its early and concise definition, "is development that meets the needs of the present without compromising the ability of future generations to meet their own needs."[19] In the practice of development, this definition is unworkable for two reasons. First, its straightforward implementation implies a level of reform and action that is a radical departure from development policy norms and values. Namely, it would require raising the development bar, a bar whose upper limits are usually set at the levels of Western states' democracies, governments, schools, and financial systems. In other words, for sustainable development, Westernization is patently insufficient. Second, sustainable development's employment of the term "needs" does not provide a context for natural capital as distinct from other forms of capital. Of the needs of humanity, some can be met by assets of natural capital, some by assets of physical capital, and some others by assets of human capital.

In other words, for their needs, human societies depend on and revolve around more than just natural capital. Consequently, other forms of capital also claim relevance to any discussion of reform possibilities and objectives. Such other forms of capital include financial capital, human capital, physical capital, social capital, and organizational capital.[20] The relevance of other forms of capital to sustainable development hinges on three considerations, explained briefly below and also analyzed in Chart 1.

First, sustainable development involves more than just conservation of natural resources; it implicitly assumes the continuation of human communities and human life. So, if general sustainable development "success" could involve extinction of some species, it could not involve extinction of *Homo sapiens*. The "needs of future generations" means the needs of future humans. Even were it shown that gradual elimination of the human species was the only means of achieving sustainable development's objective of preventing the collapse of global ecosystems, there is no chance that such a program would be approved.

Second, to a certain degree forms of capital are fungible. For example, better technology (human capital plus physical capital) can reduce carbon emissions (natural capital improvement), increased education (human capital) can facilitate a wider involvement in networks of secondary associations (social capital), and better government (organizational capital) can spark creations of economic wealth (financial capital). Given the broad complementarity of forms of capital, proponents of improvement in the stock of any kind of capital can frame their efforts as not only related to sustainable development but, opportunistically, as intrinsic to achievement of sustainable development. In practice, the complementarity of capital has provided a platform for human rights advocates to emphasize freedom from torture as the key to sustainable development, all the while that women's organizations, poverty alleviation organizations, and any number of other advocacy

Chart 1 Conceiving sustainable development (SD)

(A) *Carrying capacity* SD success implies the indefinitely continued existence of *Homo sapiens*. Long-term survival requires not overshooting carrying capacity, as each overshoot of carrying capacity erodes potential for sustainable development. Liebig's Law (LL) states that carrying capacity is always determined by a limiting factor.* Accordingly, carrying capacity for humanity (locally or globally) at any one time is determined by the more restrictive of:	(B) *Fungible capital* LLS, LLI, and PCN are not static. Their values can be changed through application of capital assets in any form, such as, *inter alia*, technology to filter water, discoveries of new deposits of natural resources, lifestyle changes, improvements in allocation of resources.
$$\frac{LLS}{PCN} \quad \text{or} \quad \frac{LLI}{PCN},$$ where LLS is LL applied to a critical natural resource (i.e. fuel), LLI is LL applied to a critical resource flow (i.e. potable water), and PCN is per-capita need. As PCN is the denominator, population control concerns are not separable from SD.	(C) *Comprehensive capital* There can be no laissez-faire SD. As SD cannot occur spontaneously given the current abilities of humanity, there will need to be a conscious and non-market coordinated application of diverse capital assets to effect reform. In this enterprise, all stocks of capital in its various forms will be applicable and relevant to prospects for and possible types of reforms for sustainability.

Note
* William R. Catton, Jr, *Overshoot: The Ecological Basis of Revolutionary Change* (Urbana, IL: University of Illinois Press, 1982), p. 158.

and reform camps make similar, and ultimately irreconcilable, claims. For just this reason, sustainable development has become a "dump for everyone's environmental and social wish lists."[21]

Third, as the old adage posits, "wealth begets wealth." Perhaps the only thing on which proponents of sustainable development can agree is that reform is both imminent and necessary. Even if and after desired or acceptable reforms are envisioned, their realization will rely on mobilization and expenditure of other forms of capital. Some reforms may require large financial outlays, others changes in legal regimes or eating habits, still others a rethinking of education. In this regard, larger (or more robust) stocks of physical, financial, social, human, and organizational capital may be key to realizing ambitions to safeguard stocks of natural capital. It is the importance of this combination of forms of capital that underpins my urging of "comprehensive capital" as a benchmark for the potential of states to achieve sustainable development, or any other development objective.

Despite the relationships and mutual dependencies that exist between the various forms of capital, there is something of special importance about natural capital, both in its own right and with regard to human communities. Human experience, especially the American and the immigrant American experience, shows that improvements in and recoveries of physical, financial, human, organizational and, probably, social capital require little time.[22] These forms of capital can be built almost as quickly as they can be destroyed; while it is by no means easy to build these forms of capital quickly, it is possible.

The same thing cannot be said of natural capital. The land, the atmosphere, and sources of water cannot be restored within either human lifetimes or with equivalent expenditures of other forms of capital. Given enough will to expend its collected financial, organizational, and physical capital, humanity could build Sierra Leone in one or two generations into a model of democracy and human welfare.[23] Even mobilizing all its various forms of capital, humanity probably cannot prevent mass extinctions, reduce concentrations of carbon in the atmosphere, or remove polychlorinated biphenyls in the oceans by the end of the twenty-first century.[24]

Thus, while my analysis sustains a general concern with other forms of capital, it privileges the implications of natural capital. This emphasis on natural capital and attention to other forms of capital comes at a time when economists are beginning to agree that post-Soviet reforms failed largely because development agency economists *en masse* (the "Washington Consensus") pursued too narrow a definition of capital and too neoclassical a conception of the relationship between kinds of capital.[25] Through surveying the various forms of capital, I conclude not only that Central Asia's stock of natural capital is degrading,[26] but that so are its stocks of other forms of capital. To the extent that Central Asia faces a Sisyphian task in moving from Soviet practices to sustainable development, the post-Soviet period has involved reforms that make the hill it faces ever higher. Ironically, almost all forms of capital were higher in the twilight of the Soviet era that at any time under the celebratory glow of the alleged free markets, democracy, and freedom that, as the teleological tale goes, killed communism.

The following sections of this Chapter expand upon and define the forms of capital glossed above. Subsequent chapters explore, first, stocks of these various forms of capital in Central Asia and, second, case studies that confirm that the region's post-Soviet trajectory has been one moving it away from, instead of towards, hopes of realizing sustainable development.

The use of various forms of capital to frame a study into the environment and society of Central Asia, especially by a non-economist, is the result of the singular influences on and in Central Asia in the past decade. The 1990s were the decade of reform (even if reform did not occur) in Central Asia, and the language of reform in the 1990s was economics, despite the existence of more economic reform failures than successes. Despite nearly a decade of victorious reports about independence released by both state governments and development agencies alike, the development failures of Central Asia are now finding scholarly appreciation. Lacking still, however, is a robust scholarly explanation to account for Central Asia's decline and to reconcile how the myopic successes of individual development projects have aggregated into manifest regional failures.

The usual suspects guilty of intra-regional differences find little application in Central Asia; despite clear differences between the Central Asian states, they have shared a post-Soviet fate. States that have experienced war (TJ and AZ) only slightly trail their more peaceful neighbors in human development indicators. States that have embraced free trade and embraced wholesale the policy prescriptions of international financial institutions (Kyrgyzstan and, to a lesser extent, Kazakhstan) are not better off than the more isolationist states. States that have embraced human rights also show no economic or other advantages a decade after independence. Likewise, the states with the most abundant natural resources also have failed to leap ahead of their neighbors. In short, the Clinton administration's panacea of free trade finds no support in Central Asia, but neither do propositions that human rights, democracy, or structural readjustment hold the key to economic prosperity and human welfare.

Concurrently, environmental issues suffuse and run parallel to larger issues of political governance, legal reform, economic management, social solidarity, and many other developmental concerns. Upon independence, environmental issues rated among the top three or five concerns of Central Asia's citizens. Governments, groups of scientists, and NGOs predicted that Western assistance, matched with local scientific strength, would effect rapid and durable environmental improvements in the region, including the clean-up of the Semipalatinsk nuclear and other test sites, the restoration of the Aral Sea, and the re-fitting of the industrial sector to more efficient and environmentally friendly technology. So pervasive was this belief that it was echoed in virtually every presidential speech, political party platform, donor prospectus, and NGO newsletter of 1992.

Encouraging these statements, beginning this decade, international environment and development organizations began the difficult task of establishing programs within these states to help them adjust to markets and effect a transition to sustainable development. Yet, both society and the political establishment were blindsided by unexpected and sharp economic declines that displaced general environmental programs to the far edges of popular concern and political action. Consequently, environmental management reforms and initiatives struggle to win support from political and other leaders as a priority for these states, despite a wave of environmental interest and activism that emerged in the twilight years of the USSR.

The economic analysis that follows explicitly assumes that, in all cases, higher stocks of each type of capital are preferable and, of themselves, public goods.[27] "Stock" implies a purely quantitative assessment, but because of globalization and the nature of certain kinds of capital, it carries in this discussion a strong qualitative character as well.[28]

In economic terms, the ideal of "sustainability" narrowly defined is "maintenance of capital."[29] My argument assumes that all economic activity, save the most primitive, relies on the simultaneous drawdown of (and possible accretion to) stocks of all types of capital, and, therefore, the continuous interaction of all kinds of capital. Sustainability, then, would depend upon maintenance of an aggregate stock of comprehensive capital instead of rigorous maintenance of each stock of capital in isolation.[30]

While capital is inherently an economic term, it is not alien to other social sciences. In defining forms of capital and their relationship to sustainable development, the following discussion relies primarily on economic theory to provide a model of how these divergent forms of capital complement each other. However, it relies equally strongly on symmetry, a mode of social science inquiry poorly represented in economics. By symmetry, I mean that social scientists must not dismiss "false" ideas according to one criterion and accept "true" ideas by another; unless a social science theory can be and is applicable to both successes and failures, bad and good, and us and them, it should be eschewed. While there is a wealth of literature about symmetry, the core concerns behind symmetry find little application in scholarship about the USSR or post-Soviet world. Instead of approaching such issues from an appropriately scholarly stance, many writers base their work on assumptions about the immorality, inferiority, and unacceptability of communism and all things Soviet.[31]

In contrast, I note both that the failings of the USSR were numerous and that democratic and capitalist societies are also not perfect. Moreover, from a methodological and epistemic standpoint, I note that the failure of various communist governments does not in any way justify or validate democracy or capitalism. In part, my approach is based on an appreciation that both of these systems are fallible because they are human and complex, and in part on an appreciation that communist governments have strayed far from communism and capitalist governments far from free markets. Religious, political, or ideological commitments are certainly valuable and justifiable, but they cloud social science research, and I explicitly attempt to distance myself from such commitments. Social science conclusions are not necessarily more valuable than other conclusions, but, I contend, very little social science "research" currently being pursued on Central Asia, development, or the former Soviet Union really qualifies as social science from the standpoint of the requirement of symmetry.

Stocks of capital are comprised of capital assets, which leads to a quandary. Colloquially, an asset is an unqualified positive. In other languages, French and Russian are most applicable, asset is expressed as "acquisition" or "active," respectively, which in both cases are less misleading terms. When an object of capital is "active," at least such an expression does not connote that it produces only positive externalities, which is the case with "asset." For example, a gun, which is a physical capital asset, is still an asset in strict economic terms even if held in the hand of a bank robber. Likewise, mafia solidarity is, despite subjective opinions about the phenomenon, a form of active social capital. Thus, the mere fact of a large stock of a certain kind of capital is important and significant, but the composition of the capital stock is also important. Accordingly, as a primary task, I inquire into the raw stocks of capital in Central Asia, but as a secondary task am interested in the composition of these stocks.

METHODOLOGY: THE DILEMMA OF STATISTICS

Intentionally, this book relies on data of questionable authority for statistical support. Reliable statistical information about Central Asia is sparse, but a diverse set of possible sources exist. For example, in addition to statistical information from development agencies, Central Asian governmental statistical agencies, nongovernmental organizations, and independent scholars all provide statistical references. Except where development agencies have either not compiled statistical information (such as for science in Central Asia and for some environmental problems) or where I have been personally able to undertake original research (such as in social capital and international environmental policy), I prefer development agency statistics to alternative sources, even if the alternative sources seem more credible.

Preferring World Bank and International Monetary Fund publications (when possible penned by World Bank and IMF staff) and eschewing more radical thinkers and other disciplinary voices is an intentional discursive strategy. This strategy is based on anticipated resistance from an important component of the audience intended to be reached through this work. I believe that, to the extent that my work may be considered by the development community, it would be easily dismissed if it relied on diverse statistical sources, but taken much more seriously if it remains within the parameters of development discussions already underway. What this strategy sacrifices in foreclosing presentation of some of the more dramatic local stories and interpretations of post-Soviet decline it makes up for in opening opportunities for critical deconstruction of development community assumptions.

Not an abstract strategy, this decision is a direct result of my own frustrating affiliation with the development community. Employed in USAID projects in Central Asia from 1992–1995, I consistently, yet futilely, protested counterproductive efforts by USAID, World Bank, and others. I saw (and participated in) environmental aid projects that demoralized the environmental community, a result of surprisingly little concern to technical environmental development specialists. I saw (and participated in) rule of law development projects that rejected promising Perestroika reform trajectories because of their "communist taint." I saw (and participated in) civil society development programs that eagerly awaited dynamic 20-somethings who never arrived, all the while pushing aside middle-aged Ph.D.s with long resumes of social action on the curious, but USAID-mandated, assumption that over-40 is synonymous with civic obsolescence.[32]

And I saw (and participated in) dozens of training programs premised on the notion that Central Asians are ignorant or cannot read training materials on their own, programs that drove away the best participants in disgust and boredom and rewarded the convivial smiles of their less impressive cohorts who remained, often for lack of anything better to do. Based on these experiences, I predicted failure at a time when faith in development economics (as it was practiced in the early 1990s) was strong and when that faith easily pushed aside critical voices much stronger than my own.[33]

Looking back on these disheartening experiences, I believe that my failure to explain convincingly then why development projects were not destined to succeed in Central Asia was not because I did not clearly state my arguments. Rather, this failure was because I expressed my arguments outside of the dominant discourse of the development community (namely, economics [34]). Within this community, the strongest arguments are those expressed within the shared intellectual foundations and practices of the community itself.

Curiously, far more people in 2000 claimed to have predicted decline in 1995 than was in fact the case in 1995. As a result, while decline is now almost universally acknowledged and pessimists may now outnumber optimists in Central Asian development circles, no one has yet explained this decline in a robust manner. The simplistic explanations (i.e. "laws were not enforced" or "corruption") are remarkably similar to the simplistic panaceas (i.e. "privatize" or "remove subsidies") that failed. Thus, I believe these new explanations to be similarly flawed, and, consequently, I believe that revisionist development programs based on such explanations will also fail.

PHYSICAL AND FINANCIAL CAPITAL

Physical (or man-made) capital refers to artifacts available to human communities. These include housing, transportation networks, factories, clothes and televisions, and other tangible goods. Any item of physical capital is usually (comparatively) easily expressed in terms of financial capital, and for this reason it is not necessary to distinguish between the two forms of capital. Financial capital involves nontangible savings, investments, and other goods related to monetary systems. Objects of both physical and financial capital are (comparatively) straightforward to catalog, aggregate, and measure. They, along with natural and human capital, are the traditional units of capital, and they are the two units most often emphasized in analyses of economic well-being.

Because the bulk of the work pursued on Central Asia by economists and political scientists, as well as the bulk of the reports of donors like the World Bank, USAID, and the International Monetary Fund, chose physical and financial capital as their major concerns, my analysis devotes no special effort to compiling inventories of these forms of capital in later chapters. Rather, it is well-settled that levels of physical and financial capital in Central Asia have been steadily on the decline. Just how much they have declined is an issue I leave to the economists.

Most likely, none of the values in Table 1 is accurate. Most indicators, except life expectancy, can vary by as much as an order of magnitude depending on source consulted.[35] The low reliability of and lack of standardization of economic statistics on Central Asia precludes much reliance on such statistics. However, in the aggregate, these statistics do converge on two salient facts: the region boasts non-GDP (infrastructure and consumer goods) figures exorbitantly high by developing country standards, and the high standards of the Soviet era are in decline.

It is easy for commentators to belittle Soviet accomplishments in Central Asia by pointing out that other Soviet republics exhibited much higher per capita GDP, as if that alone relegates the area to Third World status or precludes investigating progress from the 1917 local baseline. However, in reality, the regional discrepancies in the Soviet Union were no more severe than those in contemporary Italy,[36] or even the United States. What's more, in terms of both absolute and percentage gains, for some indicators Central Asia led the USSR, and in ownership of many consumer goods (especially cars and televisions), it led all republics save the Baltics.[37] While per capita numbers of cars, refrigerators, and televisions have increased since independence, especially in Uzbekistan, there is now little upkeep of apartment and other buildings. Many families, perhaps even most families, continue to rely primarily on clothes and books purchased during the Soviet period, or on inferior Chinese imports. Of course, a few families have also become much better off.

But the numbers of such families are few. In fact, what is striking from an economics point of view is that the former Soviet Union has virtually overturned a tenet of development economics. Increases in inequality are supposed to be the price paid for economic growth. The tide that raises all ships is expected to raise the ships very unevenly. The former Soviet Union has achieved the inequality of growth, without any of the benefits of growth. The receding tide, it seems, also lowers ships unevenly.

Beyond the figures in Table 1, in every republic, exports have declined, foreign debt continues to soar, balance of payments figures elicit concern, and the occasional signs of hope shown by some statistics in some years disappear when factored into a time line longer than 1 or 2 years. Over the past decade, annual GNP has fallen by an average of 4.4 per cent per year.[38]

As unreliable and misleading as current economic statistics on Central Asia are, they are far more accurate and accessible than assessments of the region's other kinds of capital. With the partial exception of human capital, Soviet-era statistics (from the centralized State Statistical Committee) related to other forms of capital have no or very weak counterparts in the independence period.[39] For social and organizational capital, there may indeed be no data at all upon which to base a rigorous, or at least a credible, assessment. Chapters 3 and 4 attempt to address this vacuum.

NATURAL CAPITAL

Natural capital refers to natural resource stocks, natural resource flows, pollution of such stocks and flows, and sinks for such pollution. While natural capital could (and perhaps should) be measured from the perspective of its relation to the sustainability of non-human species, within the framework of sustainable development, it primarily relates to human communities. In this regard it refers not only to the ability of these communities to extract and use available resources, but also to the impact of the natural environment on human health and welfare. In other words, as with all other forms of capital, natural capital evidences impact on and by other forms of capital; an extractive enterprise that enriches a local

Table 1 Various physical and financial indicators in Central Asia*

	KZ		KG		TJ		TM		UZ	
	Pre-1999	1999	Pre-1999	1999	Pre-1999	1999	Pre-1999	1999	Pre-1999	1999
Percentage of population below poverty line†	35% (1996)	35%	40% (1993)	51%	N/A	>50%	20.9% (1993)	48%	3.3% (1993)	29%
GNP	$42.3b	$19.4b	$7.1b	$1.7b	$6b	$2.1b	$6.8b	$3.1b	$29.3b	$20.9b
Per capita GDP	$2470	$965	$1550	$380	$1050	$344	$1700	$654	$1350	$673
Televisions per 100 people	28	23	20–23	4–5	15–19	29	18–19	20	18	27–28

Notes

  Decline in capital;

  Increase in or maintenance of capital.

* Figures taken from most current World Bank Group Country Reports (http://www.worldbank.org). Where figures were unavailable from this source in dollars, information was taken from as similarly conservative sources as possible. 1991 GDP figures from Alexander Akimov, "Central Asia as a Region in the World Economy," in Roald Z. Sagdeev and Susan Eisenhower (eds), *Central Asia: Conflict, Resolution, and Change* (Baltimore: CPSS Press, 1995), p. 279. Data on consumer goods from UNDP, *2000 World Development Indicators* (UNDP: New York, 2000), pp. 301–302; T. Koichuev et al. (eds), *Istoriya Kyrgyzov i Kyrgyzstana* (Bishkek: Ilim, 998), p. 282; UNDP, *Human Development Report 2000* (New York: UNDP, 2000), pp. 199–200; and Emine Gurgen, "Central Asia: Achievements and Prospects", *Finance & Development* 37 (September, 2000), p. 41.

† World Bank Vice President Stiglitz posits a forty-fold increase in poverty. Stiglitz, "Whither Reform: Ten Years of the Transition", p. 1.

community may also pollute the water and lead to increased morbidity, while subsequent financial outlays to purify sources of drinking water may lead to increased local human health.

Accordingly, in assessing natural capital, a traditional economic analysis would restrict attention to the availability and quantities of scarce natural resources valuable for various processes of producing physical capital. According to traditional economic modes, extraction and use of natural resources could not, by definition, deplete stocks of capital, but would only increase them. "Prevailing modes of economic analysis tend to treat consumption of natural capital as income, and therefore tend to promote patterns of economic activity that are unsustainable."[40]

However, an analysis that recognizes natural capital asks whether use of natural resources depletes stocks of natural capital and whether the result of this use balances or exceeds the costs of depleted natural capital.[41] Likewise, such an analysis concerns itself with the impacts of pollution, and it would consider such results as improved water quality in a river, rebounded populations of endangered species, and newly discovered reserves of natural resources to be accessions to wealth from increased natural capital.

Such an approach is especially warranted since countries essentially do not differ with regard to their potential natural capital, meaning the potential return in terms of financial capital from utilization of their forests, croplands, minerals, waters, and other natural assets. Across dozens of states, this potential financial capital return from present natural capital evidences a 3:1 ratio between the richest and poorest states. In contrast, ratios based on differences in human or financial capital are roughly 20:1.[42]

Accordingly, my analysis appreciates that Central Asia enjoys a wealth of natural assets valued by financial capitalists, but also appreciates that their value is diminished because of transportation and other problems. It also appreciates that much of the region's forests and croplands are far less impressive, although these are, consistently, the most significant contributors of natural capital throughout the world. Central Asia's general potential financial wealth contained in natural assets is probably, given the peculiarities and structure of financial systems, near the average for world states.

While on a global scale considering climate change, what happens with Central Asia's hydrocarbon reserves is at the core of global sustainable development, locally sustainable development depends greatly on the ability of humans to inhabit the environment of Central Asia, and this concern dominates the following Chapter on natural capital. Despite the fact that clear causal chains between environmental conditions and morbidity are lacking, the assumption that poor environmental conditions degrades human capital is, by now, generally and broadly accepted. Accordingly, accepting that Central Asia boasts appreciable stocks of natural resources, the component of natural capital of most interest in this analysis concerns the environmental health risks faced by the population of Central Asia and their access to the most basic natural resources (potable water, adequate food, etc.) needed for human life.

HUMAN CAPITAL

Human capital refers to the non-tangible elements of knowledge (educational capital) and health possessed by members of human communities. These translate into information, technology, physical labor, and other inputs and components of production processes and other economic activities.

Indicators of human capital related to the mind involve literacy rates, levels of completion of various stages of formal education, numbers of scientists, and investments in research and development. Indicators of human capital related to the body include life expectancy, morbidity rates, and nutrition. Not only building human capital is important; maintaining it is also important. Illustrating the connection between natural capital and human capital, in Chile, every ton of reduced air pollution results in an estimated $18,000 in public health benefits.[43]

Human capital issues are an especially rich topic for a study of the comprehensive capital stock of the former Soviet Union. At the beginning of the Soviet period, Soviet Central Asians were illiterate and unhealthy. By Perestroika, they enjoyed European levels of education, universal literacy, and health indicators superior to almost any part of the developing world. The task of the independence era, thus, was to maintain this high level of human capital, and the hopes were that it would be increased through improvements in the educational system, especially the social sciences, and overdue reforms, such as removal of lead from gasoline.

However, that has just not happened. Life expectancies have declined. Sanitation services have disappeared even in capital cities. Physicians have emigrated. Years of required schooling have decreased, and the quality of education has plummeted. Illiteracy is on the rise. Students who once would have studied engineering or physics and pioneered the kind of innovation that builds economies now study the social sciences. Infectious diseases, like typhus, thought locally eradicated are reappearing.

A number of experts posit that the single most important form of capital for economic growth and high returns on investments is human capital, especially investments in increasing years of formal education. "Natural resources count, but people count for more."[44] Drawing on 1990 U.S. Census figures, Robert Ellickson argues that 75 per cent of wealth in the United States takes the form of human capital.[45] In a complementary study, rates of return on investments in human capital in the form of expenditures on scientific research and development have consistently far exceeded the private rate of return.[46]

ORGANIZATIONAL CAPITAL

Organizational capital, the least appreciated and recognized of the types of capital presented here, refers to the set of governing rules and organizations of a community. Organizational capital embraces both laws and state agencies, but it also accords central importance to social norms, structures of families, and other

Table 2 Axes of organizational capital

	Formal	*Informal*
Organizations	Administrative state: expert agencies, courts, police, schools, hospitals, armies	Families and civil society: friendship cohorts, families, NGOs, non-state employers
Rules	Laws: constitutions, laws, sublegal acts, city ordinances, tax codes, court-made laws	Social capital and other social norms: playground rules, club rules, civic values, norms of participation, norms of trust, obedience to authority

elements of organization or regulation of behavior not dictated formally or by the state.

Accordingly, organizational capital consists of four definable poles: (1) formal rules, (2) formal organizations, (3) informal rules, and (4) informal organizations. In the conceptual language of sociology (institutions) or political science (regimes), only two poles would require explication since both concepts embrace the interplay between rules and organizations. In a simplified explication of the four poles of organizational capital, formal rules consist of both laws and the extent to which laws and other administrative processes are or are not enforced. Formal organizations, actually inseparable from formal rules, involve the structure and composition of courts, state agencies, local agencies, legislatures, and other organizations. Informal rules connote customs, conventions, norms, and other acculturated rules of behavior not fully reflected by law, uniform, or even recognized cognitively. Informal organizations relate to the range of forms of organization, such as, *inter alia*, families, friendship cohorts, and ad hoc clubs, that are to a degree beyond the realm of attempted or actual state regulation (Table 2).

Organizational capital is important because different rules and organizations produce different effects. Legalization of abortion (a change in a rule) has led to lowered crime rates in the United States.[47] Similarly, the federal organization of the United States has allowed contradictory human rights regimes (for the most part North/South) throughout much of the country's history. Likewise, a preference for boys in some cultures underlies patterns of abortion and child abuse linked to social norms, while increasing expectations in industrializing cultures of parental obligations to provide for all children until late in life partially explain reductions in average fertility.

At the beginning of the twenty-first century, an unspoken consensus has emerged about organizational capital. The state, despite valorization of free markets, must be an administrative state, engaged in a great many activities requiring a kind of capacity, even in the smallest states, far beyond the imagination of even developed states at the beginning of this century.[48] No state without courts, environmental protection agencies, or schools can even be imagined today, although, empirically, a great many states lacked all of these at the beginning of this century and, theoretically, none of these is necessary for human life.

Similarly, laws are universally accepted and valorized. No authority would seriously propose regulation of a modern state through informal norms such as universal respect, love, or the golden rule, despite the fact that, throughout human history cherished philosophers have argued for just such a condition.[49] Likewise, especially after the demise of communism and other utopian ideas, there prevails a global consensus that children should be raised in families and that independent associations are preferable to corporatist formations. All of these consensus positions contain tremendous, if under-appreciated, significance. Only in the realm of informal rules is there still a great amount of flexibility in labeling the normative content of modern society. Some scholars suggest that social norms are merely the content of normatively desirable future laws, but others suggest, theoretically and empirically, that this "law from order" approach will often lead to failures of both formal and informal rules.[50]

Both rules and organizations impact and shape transaction costs, information economics, incentives, and the ease with which self-interested actors can achieve efficient allocations of resources while limiting the negative externalities produced from free-riding, adverse selection, moral hazard, and defection. The entire current debate on corruption would in fact be best framed as an investigation into a shortfall in organizational capital.[51] Likewise, an emphasis on only one element of organizational capital (i.e. an anti-corruption law) will surely fail if such a reform does not resonate with the other formal and informal organizations and rules in a society. Similarly, a concept such as rule of law is not contained within just one axis of organizational capital, but depends upon the interaction between the formal content of laws, formal organizational enforcement of law, informal norms of lawfulness, and the impact of informal organizations on incentives to obey the law.

All other capital stocks being equal, a society with a more robust stock of organizational capital may be at a distinct advantage. Many states, including many NICs, with poor endowments of natural capital and very little physical (or financial) capital, have nonetheless experienced dynamic growth in recent years. Conversely, some states with abundant natural and human capital, including most post-Soviet states, have experienced decline over the same period.

Consequently, in recent years, major international lenders, especially the Bretton Woods institutions, have begun to devote considerable attention to shortfalls in organizational capital, but using a terminology different than that employed here.[52] Under a set of concerns labeled "governance," these institutions have broadened their conception of the necessary precursors of development from physical, natural, and human capital to also include organizational capital. However, they have yet to formulate a workable understanding or nuanced approach to the task of developing organizational capital.

In surveying stocks of organizational capital in Central Asia, my analysis concentrates on disaggregating Central Asian society into formal and informal organizations and rules in order to produce a rough survey of the assets and shortfalls of Central Asian organizational capital in the pre-independence and post-Soviet eras.

SOCIAL CAPITAL

Social capital is only vaguely defined in existing literature; social capital's presence is inferred in many works, but no where it is defined with either the language of economics or with internal consistency. As Francis Fukuyama notes: "While social capital has been given a number of different definitions, most of them refer to manifestations of social capital rather than to social capital itself."[53] To date, no definition of social capital allows the term the two core elements of any other form of capital: the ability to disaggregate the stock into discrete assets and the ability to link deployment of such assets to externalities, both negative and positive.

I posit that social capital can be defined concisely with reference to game theory and that its full explication will depend on its integration into information economics.[54] Social capital consists of two necessary but independently insufficient conditions. First, social capital requires a dense network of social interaction; it requires that individuals be enmeshed in multiple social networks. These social networks are the loci of the repetitive interactions that constitute social capital assets; they are, to paraphrase Durkheim, the social facts that are the things that lend themselves to social science inquiry.[55] For example, a person who has a family, is employed, and belongs to a number of clubs has more potential social capital than an unemployed single person who spends most of the day in front of a television. Second, social capital requires that these social networks fulfill two quite different functions: reduce information transaction costs and provide signals about propensities to cooperate or defect.

Social capital facilitates the reduction of information transaction costs by providing alternate channels for information flow. Persons with high social capital often rely on their informal knowledge about potential business partners, investors, and service providers, and in doing so eliminate costs associated with investigation of and search for such information. Persistent data from a variety of sources in the United States suggest that most people find employment through such social networks instead of through formal employment procedures.

Social capital also provides information and signals about other people's tendencies to cooperate or defect. In their economic and game theory contexts, these terms refer to individuals' decisions to honor agreements or break agreements (when there is some payoff for doing so). Individuals may tend to cooperate either because of some predisposition to do so generally (some internal morality or standard) or because the payoff from defection is lowered because an interaction (a "period" in game-theory terms) is not one-time but "iterated." In iterated games, a player will encounter the other player again, at least many or an indefinite number of times, in the future and will be disadvantaged by that other player's refusal to cooperate.[56] While this phenomenon clearly applies to villages where reputation and frequent interaction are central elements of life, given dense enough social networks, it can also apply to towns, segments of cities, or professional cohorts.

Generally speaking, individuals are involved in two broad types of social networks. Their primary associations are largely non-voluntary and hierarchically organized (vertical) and include family, residence, school, and work. Their secondary associations are voluntary and less hierarchical (horizontal) and involve civic organizations, sports leagues, and similar associations. While no clear boundary exists between primary and secondary associations (neighborhood watch groups, school alumni associations, and professional societies all combine elements of both), the distinction between the two is important because of evidence about the ambiguous externalities that stem from social capital. "Bonding" social capital based primarily on primary associations tends often to produce negative societal externalities and inefficient resource allocation.[57] Examples include old boys' networks, the Mafia, and nepotism. "Bridging" social capital, in contrast, relies less on the phenomenon of (and disadvantages of) cartel loyalty and more on the gains to efficiency produced by reduced transaction costs in information. Moreover, bridging social capital can displace some of the inefficient aspects of bonding social capital. Thus, while bonding social capital is not (by any means) an unqualified bad, all other things equal it is preferable to have at least a large part of a society's stock of social capital in bridging social capital. More concisely and importantly, the lack of bridging social capital can be a serious developmental disadvantage.[58]

All of the foregoing builds up to a definition of social capital. A social capital asset is a social network (primary or secondary) combining two or more people. The sum of such networks and the breadth of such networks constitute a society's social capital. The relevant composition of these networks between bonding and bridging social capital directly shapes the kinds of negative and positive externalities flowing from a society's social capital.

In so defining social capital, I also concede that social capital is a subset of organizational capital. Its place as a separate category of capital is contestable, but is useful in the present analysis because it complements analyses of organizational capital and confronts, directly, the past decade's simultaneously confused and exuberant fascination with social capital.

Expanding the discussion above to focus more explicitly on economic issues, one's social capital refers to the sum of one's involvement in iterated games. The result is that one's social capital reflects reputation and reduces certain transaction costs. Reputation allows other players to gauge in advance what your game strategy will be what your skills are, and how likely it is that you will cooperate or defect. Expanding critique of the Arrow–Debreu model begun by the information economists that prices do not convey all relevant information, social capital hones in on the information contained in reputation, information valuable for such core economic activities as forming a partnership.

Likewise, the information forcing and sharing elements of social interactions reduce general societal transaction costs of information. As social capital relates to democracy, to the extent that social capital is a barometer of how active or passive individuals are generally, it is directly proportional to democratic participation. As social capital relates to economics, while reducing transaction costs of information facilitates general economic well-being, some cooperative game strategies (like cartels) have negative economic externalities.

Accordingly, social capital is generally coterminous with civil society, but it is not identical. A vibrant civil society assumes high levels of social capital within many secondary associations, but it also highlights the organizational capital character of social capital by connecting the latter to a variety of political functions, such as expression of diverse values, ensuring accountability, and providing alternatives to state services. Nevertheless, given the lack of viable alternatives, in surveying stocks of social capital in Central Asia, I employ civil society second-ary associations, as well as residence associations and simple economic transac-tions, as a proxy for social capital.

SUSTAINABLE DEVELOPMENT AND INTERNATIONAL ENVIRONMENTAL LAW

Thus far, my assumption has been that the concerns behind adopting a mode of analysis based on comprehensive capital relate directly to sustainable develop-ment. This assumption implies that physical, natural, human, and organizational capital all will be needed in a transition from Soviet-era practices to sustainable development. It thus rejects the non-organizational capital and indirect means of achieving sustainable development that can be imagined under scenarios initiated by disaster, war, or disease. The implication of this rejection is a commitment to the idea that sustainable development is primarily an organizational and intentional endeavor; as such it cannot be achieved without law, institutions, or related feats of social engineering.

Perhaps no social science agenda more complex and demanding can be imagined than the one suggested by this chapter. Assessing stocks of all relevant kinds of capital, cataloging how these stocks are currently deployed and impacted, and pro-jecting how these stocks can and will be deployed in the future to, alternately, fail or succeed to attain sustainable development is an ambitious, and unworkable, agenda.

At some risk of irrelevance and running afoul of a fallacy of composition, I choose international environmental law as a lens through which to frame a work-able investigation into how Central Asia's comprehensive capital relates to aspir-ations for sustainable development. By international environmental law, I mean the existing range of policies and institutions that currently relate to efforts to manage transboundary environmental problems. These include, *inter alia*, multi-lateral treaties (such as the Convention on Biological Diversity), multilateral institutions (such as the Global Environment Facility), bilateral donors (such as USAID), international NGOs, and local NGOs. In the aggregate, the policies and practices that form the heart of current international environmental law display the advantage of addressing directly key issues for natural, physical, human, and organizational capital. It is this implicit embrace of comprehensive capital and explicit efforts by actors in international environmental law to change strategies and practices of deploying these forms of capital that rest at the heart of the decision to view trends through the lens of international environmental law.

Moreover, justification for a focus on international environmental law stands on two observations. First, these five states have been unusually active in ratifying international environmental conventions; the story of their integration alone provides case studies that challenge and support a number of current debates within the field of international environmental politics. Second, these environmental conventions, in both theory and practice, create a meaningful and unusually dynamic framework in which to study interactions between sectors of societies (state, science/research, and NGO) and between important conflicting aspects of national policies (*inter alia*, economics, environment, and nationalism).

Thus, the nature of Central Asia's relationship to international environmental law is my proxy for evaluating the region's movement towards or away from sustainable development. The following chapters follow the emphases of this Introduction in assessing the region's rising and declining stocks of natural, human, organizational, and social capital through three broad periods (pre-Soviet, Soviet, post-Soviet). Complementing this assessment of stocks, I then examine realizations of current comprehensive capital within case studies of ongoing international environmental law projects in Central Asia. Disappointingly, I conclude that modern Central Asia may now lack the comprehensive capital necessary to pursue a viable transition to sustainable development.

Table 3 Complementarity of capital: perverse effects of poor stocks of one type of capital on other forms (emphasizing experiences of the former Soviet Union)

	Physical/Financial (P)	Natural (N)	Human (H)	Organizational (O)	Social (S)
Physical/Financial (P)		N: Lack of infrastructure forces local populations to deforest and harm local biodiversity	H: Low salaries for physicians lead to inadequate provision of medical care	O: State unable to enforce against or monitor opportunistic behavior, enforce laws	S: Even when they work longer hours than poorer counterparts, high earning individuals tend to be engaged in more bridging social capital networks
Natural (N)	P: Salinized lands, lands showing trends of desertification less productive		H: Pollution causes increased morbidity and mortality	O: As pollution levels increase, threat to stability increases	S: As pollution increases, survival threats elevate bonding social capital over bridging
Human (H)	P: Healthier and more-well-educated individuals are more productive	N: Loss of strong infrastructure in science and technology precludes innovation in pollution abatement and energy saving technologies		O: As scale of government increases and complexity of management functions increases, need increases for skilled technical managers	S: Within states, individuals with less education tend to have less bridging social capital
Organizational (O)	P: Local political instability causes capital flight	N: Poor enforcement of environmental laws frustrates attempts to control or abate pollution	H: Corruption changes preferences in state expenditures. Officials prefer rent-seeking options (large projects, licensed activities) to support of schools		S: Where protections for nongovernmental organizations, foundations, and the press are lacking or decline (or are precluded by corporatism), bridging social capital also declines
Social (S)	P: Low social trust inhibits access to credit	N: A community low in social capital falls prey to a "tragedy of the commons"	H: Reduced transaction costs of information facilitated by bridging social capital facilitate better individual choices in selection of educational and health opportunities	O: Areas low in social capital evidence low levels of tax compliance, frustrate creation of independent watchdogs, and offer few "training grounds" to build leadership skills	

1 Natural capital: the Central Asian human and natural environment

With northern taiga forests and large southern deserts, as well as the largest mountains in the former Soviet Union, Central Asia exhibits a tremendous diversity of ecosystems. Central Asia contains the world's fourth deepest lake (Issyk-kul) and borders the largest inland body of water in the world (the Caspian Sea). Central Asia also holds some of the USSR's principal nuclear, chemical, and biological weapons production and testing sites, and one of the world's worst environmental disasters, the desiccation of the Aral Sea, once both the planet's fourth largest lake and a thriving fishery. Bequeathed substantial and highly polluting industry from the remarkable Soviet development enterprise, the region also boasts important reserves of hydrocarbons and precious metals. At over 4 million km², Central Asia covers an area larger in size than India, Pakistan, and Bangladesh combined, but with less than 5 per cent of their population.

The major environmental event of the twentieth century in Central Asia was the reign of the Soviet Union. Just as in the West, Soviet economic, accounting and planning ideology for most of this century assumed that natural resource stocks were not scarce and underestimated the costs resulting from pollution of natural resource flows. In other words, environmental management was, for most of its existence, not a concern of the Soviet Union. Soviet factories produced tremendous amounts of pollution, and the environmental consequences of this pollution were easy to ignore considering the heavy winds of many industrial areas and the immense flow of such rivers as the Irtysh in northern Kazakhstan. With development and industrial progress enjoying sacred status in the Soviet political establishment, the state placed few restraints or safeguards on industrial development. Given the social and political context of the USSR, criticism of Soviet development policies was rare, and it only gained momentum in the 1980s, later than analogous voicings in the West.

At the same time, population expanded rapidly in Central Asia after the famines and purges of the pre-World War II era. This population, coupled with ambitious educational programs favoring the natural and technical sciences and the USSR's early integration of women into the labor force, served dynamically to facilitate the Soviet development enterprise. Collective and mechanized agriculture, especially cotton (with great reliance on chemical fertilizers and pesticides), dominated the fertile valleys of Central Asia. Industry, research, and economic planning came to absorb much of the population freed from subsistence agriculture. The contributions to the Soviet economy from this new professional class resulted in many of the weapons, factories, and infrastructure innovations whose deployment lies at the heart of the unsustainability of modern Central Asia.

To reiterate, this assumed unsustainability of natural capital in Central Asia refers not to stocks of exploitable resources (like hydrocarbons) of the type that could be used to generate physical capital through export to world commodity markets. This unsustainability of natural capital is related not to the magnitude of stocks of natural resources, but to the integrity of these stocks from the standpoint of biological organisms, specifically people.

Whereas Central Asia may currently have as much water as a century ago and therefore just as great a raw stock of this natural resource, untreated potable water is now relatively rare in the region (Table 1.1). Similarly, while the region now

Table 1.1 Central Asian environmental problems

Environmental issue	Examples
Soviet military legacy	1999 rocket explosions (heptyl fuel pollution) in Kazakhstan Runoff from Kyrgyzstan and Tajikistan uranium mines into regional rivers Clean-up of dozens of chemical, biological, and nuclear testing and production sites in Kazakhstan and Uzbekistan
Water management	Aral Sea desiccation Chinese diversion of Black Irtysh River from Kazakhstan Lack of potable water in Turkmenistan and Uzbekistan
Land degradation	Most of region already covered by deserts and semi-deserts Salinization and topsoil erosion reducing yields throughout region Connected to and exacerbated by biodiversity, water, poverty issues
Biodiversity	Loss in past 50 years of both cheetah and tiger from region Inability/unwillingness of state agencies to control illegal trade and poaching Loss of critical habitat due to expanding population
Industrial pollution	Chronic disease and high cancer rates in most industrial cities High levels of lead in soils Air quality very low in most capital cities due to expanding automobile use and Soviet industry
Caspian Sea	Caviar industry crash Threats to ecosystems from hydrocarbon production and transport Region's only nuclear power plant (providing heat and de-salinization in Kazakhstan) on Caspian shore
Oil, Gold, etc.	1998 cyanide/chlorine spill in Issyk-kul related to Kumtor gold mine Drilling in Caspian Sea for oil Still poorly understood consequences of Soviet era nuclear-assisted mining

has equivalently as much ore containing potentially valuable radioactive isotopes as a century ago, previously less of this ore was openly exposed to air or water. Currently, mining waste tailings leach radioactive elements into the air, water, and agricultural soils of Central Asia. Added to such "natural" contaminants are an abundance of anthropogenic pollutants. The effects on human health of drinking water saturated with various kinds of salts, of eating plants containing radionucleides, and of consuming meat suffused with concentrated amounts of persistent organic pollutants are not beneficial. This pollution, degradation of the natural resource flows upon which human populations depend, directly impacts possibilities for sustainable development. Other natural resource flows, arguably not as directly or no longer as vital to human health (such as levels of flow in small mountain streams) nevertheless directly influence the viability of other species and, hence, larger ecosystems.

In addition to stocks of natural resources and flows of natural resources, the environment also contains sinks. Forests are a carbon sink, meaning that they reduce concentrations of carbon dioxide in the atmosphere. Sinks for various, but not all, types of pollutants frame possibilities for sustainability; when emissions of pollutants exceed rates at which sinks (natural or artificial) remove these pollutants from the environment, sustainability is threatened. For example, notwithstanding the appreciable size of carbon sinks such as forests and the ocean, industrial era emissions of carbon dioxide far exceeding the capacity of such sinks, explaining the rapidly increasing concentrations of carbon dioxide in the atmosphere.

Currently, seven major problems involving natural resource flows and sinks afflict Central Asia. These are: (1) the lingering effects of the Soviet military establishment, (2) problems of water management, (3) desertification and land degradation, (4) loss of biodiversity and habitat, (5) industrial pollution, (6) preservation of the Caspian Sea, and (7) dangers from hydrocarbon production and mining activities (see Table 1.1).

In addition, another natural condition related directly to development aspirations afflicts Central Asia: an abundance of threats from natural disasters. In recent years, devastating earthquakes have ringed the borders of Central Asia, specifically in Afghanistan, Iran, and Turkey. In the past century, massive quakes, ten times larger than the summer 1999 Turkish earthquake, killed tens of thousands of residents of Almaty, Tashkent, Ashgabat, Turkmenbashi (TM), and Armenia. In many cities of Central Asia, the population lives in desperate fear of imminent quakes, and even of the delayed results of pre-Soviet earthquakes. On February 18, 1911, a quake 50 times stronger than the 1999 Turkish quake "caused a $2.2\,km^3$ piece of the Muzkol Range...to fall off, closing off the entire width of the Murgab Valley" in Tajikistan and creating the Sarez Lake.[1] Experts in the region are now warning that this natural dam is weakening and could break, releasing more than $17,000\,m^3$ of water and endangering more than five million people.

LINGERING EFFECTS OF THE SOVIET MILITARY ESTABLISHMENT

In July 1999, a Russian Proton rocket launched from the Baikenour Launch Facility in Kazakhstan exploded five minutes after take-off, spreading debris and fuel (dimethyl hydrazine) over parts of the Karaganda Region. Russia leases this principal Soviet launch facility from Kazakhstan. While no one was killed in the incident, and while the incident resulted in only a temporary suspension of launches and a small compensation payment by Russia, it served to remind residents of Central Asia that their region was an important participant in the entire Soviet military enterprise. As another reminder, in October 1999, a second Proton rocket exploded over the Karaganda region.

Hundreds of nuclear, chemical, and biological weapons tests were conducted at the Semipalatinsk/Kurchatov (KZ) nuclear test area, the Naryn (KZ) testing area, and on Resurrection Island (KZ/UZ) in the Aral Sea. In many of these tests, radiation and chemicals escaped the test ranges to intrude upon nearby human settlements. Moreover, much of the uranium mined for Soviet nuclear weapons came from open mines near Atbasar (KZ), Chkalovsk (TJ), and Maili Su (KG), among other places. An installation to recover uranium from the waters of Lake Issyk-kul also operated in Kyrgyzstan for nearly 40 years.[2] In addition, principal chemical and biological weapon production facilities, including for the production of anthrax, were located in Stepnogorsk (KZ) and Karakalpakstan (UZ). Accompanying all these inherently dangerous activities were a range of still little known military accidents in the region, such as a very large late Soviet spill of kerosene into the Irtysh River from an airbase in Kazakhstan. While the Soviet army no longer exists, the national militaries still control vast swaths of the region.

Since 1991, Kazakhstan has voluntarily relinquished all of its nuclear armaments, a unique accomplishment in Asia, especially in counterpoint to India and Pakistan. While all of the Central Asian states have nuclear capability, none has essayed to become a nuclear power. Likewise, none of the states in the region attempts to continue Soviet military production in chemical and biological weapons, despite wars involving Azerbaijan and Tajikistan. Turkmenistan has even declared itself a neutral state.

Nevertheless, Soviet military past practices plague Central Asia. Radiation pollution around Semipalatinsk from testing and around many mining areas causes high levels of morbidity. Radioactive tailings in Kyrgyzstan and Tajikistan threaten the entire region if run-off or all-too-frequent (due to land degradation and seismic activity) landslides wash these materials into regional rivers. Moreover, although Kazakhstan is currently decommissioning its sole large Soviet-era nuclear reactor (research reactors exist in every republic), it is also developing plans to construct several new nuclear power plants.

Despite the scale and importance of these environmental problems, no state in the region independently assumes responsibility for addressing these problems. International funding is at the heart of all the major military clean-up efforts in Central Asia, from Semipalatinsk to nuclear plant decommissioning, to safeguarding and dismantling the materials and technology contained in remaining anthrax production facilities.

WATER MANAGEMENT

At the beginning of the Soviet era, the Aral Sea, the fourth largest lake on the planet, occupied the center of Central Asia, and its two main feeder rivers, the

Amudarya and Syrdarya, carried flow of well over $100\,km^3$. The climate around the Aral Sea, especially on the southern and eastern shores, was very habitable, the land agriculturally productive, and the Aral Sea itself one of the most productive and major fisheries of the Soviet Union. Tigers roamed the tugai forests along the major tributaries. At the end of the Soviet era, the Amudarya no longer emptied into the Aral Sea; it ran out of water before reaching the sea. The Syrdarya only emptied into the Aral in good years. Most of the volume of the sea had already disappeared, the fishery was dead and all native fish species extirpated, and agricultural productivity had been reduced to less than its pre-Soviet levels. Where once tugai forests abounded, the land was denuded, desertified, and devoid of most life.

In contrast to many other arid areas of the world, Central Asia's problems with water management rarely are as simple as lack of water. In fact, the region has a great amount of water. Kazakhstan, for example, claims more than 85,000 rivers and streams,[3] and 57,000 lakes.[4] The four largest rivers in the region alone (the Syrdarya, Amudarya, Ural, and Irtysh), even despite greatly reduced levels due to irrigation diversion, carry more than $100\,km^3$ of water annually. Serious problems, however, stem from unsound practices of irrigation, pollution, and coordination. Distribution, not availability, is the principal problem in Central Asia.

Symptomatically, crude over-irrigation leading to salinization of soils is perhaps the most appropriate snapshot of the root of Central Asia's water problems. Most of the region's agriculture is now based on irrigated lands, three times the area that was irrigated at the beginning of Soviet collectivization efforts. As one expert on the Central Asian environment observes, "a sustainable future in Central Asia begins and ends with improving irrigation and water management".[5]

Most irrigation canals are unlined, and these canals are especially prone to choke with weeds when not maintained. Throughout the region, it is common to see such canals so choked with weeds as to be virtually closed. Local communities lack plausible incentives to maintain these canals since the state still controls selling prices of agricultural goods in many areas and/or is still the major consumer of water for agriculture. As a result, large pools of standing water, instead of being directed towards replenishing the Aral Sea, gradually evaporate, ruining the land in the process. Indeed, 30 per cent of the Aral's "missing" water has been driven underground, mobilizing deep salt reserves, raising the water table, and waterlogging fields.[6] As a counterpoint, many lined or maintained canals divert far more water than needed. In either case, the roots of the Aral Sea crisis are not widely debated. Because of poorly designed irrigation canals and the Soviet tradition of payment-free use of water, 50–90 per cent of water diverted for irrigation never reaches crops.[7]

Moreover, drainage water does not flow back towards the sea as it should. While the Aral Sea has all but disappeared as the result of irrigation, the Aidar-Arnasai Lake System, a 300 km by 60 km body of water, appeared after 1960 primarily as the result of excess irrigation flows diverted from the Syrdarya River, and its level continues to rise.[8] The Amudarya River counterpoint to the Aidar is Lake Sarykamysh in northern Turkmenistan, which is also expanding and already covers several thousand square kilometers. Despite all these well-known consequences of Soviet practices, Turkmenistan announced in 2000 plans to create a 150 km^3 lake in the middle of the Kara-Kum Desert using drainage waters;[9] this "Lake of the Golden Century" would only exacerbate the region's water problems.

Along the lower reaches of the Amudarya and Syrdarya rivers, which both empty into and are the source of the Aral Sea, these water management practices have had devastating effect on human lives and the environment. Beginning in the latter half of the nineteenth century, cotton cultivation expanded rapidly along these two river basins; since 1960 the Aral Sea itself has been shrinking. The Aral Sea is a dead sea, desiccated now to a discontiguous fraction of its former size of almost 70,000 km^2; all 24 native species of fish in the sea are now extirpated.[10] In all, an area of the Aral seabed substantially larger than Taiwan has been exposed in the last two decades. Cities near the sea, such as Tashauz (TM), Nukus (UZ), and Kzyl-Orda (KZ), not to mention dozens of towns near the shore, saw quality of life and life expectancy plummet as a result of lack of clean drinking water and failed agriculture. Ninety-seven per cent of women in the hardest hit area, Karakalpakstan, are anemic,[11] and levels of infant mortality, cancer, and respiratory diseases have skyrocketed in recent decades.

The environmental situation in Central Asia is so desperate that for many problems solutions are no longer pursued. Instead, mitigation is the only response possible given economic and technological constraints. The paradigm case to illustrate this point is the Aral Sea. In the first years of independence, states and donors, especially USAID and the World Bank, asked what would be needed to restore the sea. In fact, United States political leaders and diplomatic staff pledged in 1992 to provide the funds and expertise needed to help the basin states restore the sea. However, as estimates of the costs of this undertaking increased to well over a billion dollars, U.S. and other donors began to recede quietly from their enthusiastic promises to facilitate restoration of the sea. Plans turned to mitigation, to a plan to stabilize the region as a set of discontiguous lakes and wetlands capable of supporting some agriculture and fisheries. The agriculture and fisheries envisioned under this new plan will produce only a fraction of what the Aral Sea once produced, even as population in the region continues to grow.

Water management issues likewise trouble the areas of Central Asia not contained in the Aral Sea basin. For example, recent activities in China will divert portions of the flow of the Ili and Irtysh rivers, two of Kazakhstan's most important rivers. The Irtysh, the fifth largest river in the world, flows through Kazakhstan on its way to Russia where it joins the Ob and eventually flows into the Arctic Sea. How Kazakhstan will react to these Chinese efforts to increase irrigation in Xinjiang Province will prove to be of great importance to the economic and ecological future of northern and eastern Kazakhstan. However, despite public outcry, Kazakhstan has yet to take any substantive measures to either attempt to restrain China or to mitigate the consequences of this project, although the project would ravage the agricultural and animal husbandry industry of northern Kazakhstan and make several key hydroelectric and shipping installations untenable to operate.[12]

Soviet policies encouraged liberal application of pesticides and chemical fertilizers on crops in Central Asia, and levels of these chemicals per hectare, even DDT, which while supposedly banned was nonetheless used widely, were perhaps the highest in the world before the dissolution of the USSR. While the Central Asian states have roughly halved their pesticide use since independence, DDT is still highly concentrated in the soils of residential areas far from centers of agriculture.[13] Little consideration was paid to the environment's ability to absorb these chemicals, which has led, among other things, to high concentrations of these chemicals in both the water and wildlife of the region. Agricultural pesticides also highlight the linkages between environmental problems, especially the close link between land and water in Central Asia.

LAND DEGRADATION

No environmental issue in Central Asia enjoys more consensus than that of desertification and related forms of land degradation. The Central Asian republics were among the very first states in the world to sign and ratify the 1994 United Nations Convention to Combat Desertification. Moreover, the large numbers of geographers, soil scientists, and other specialists in the region do not diverge appreciably in their qualitative or quantitative assessments of the causes and consequences of desertification in Central Asia. A recent UNDP report states that losses in "natural potential" in Kazakhstan stemming from desertification could "already be comparable to the country's GDP."[14]

Within the Central Asian republics, diverse factors cause and exacerbate desertification and land degradation. These are loss of vegetative cover (i.e. from over-grazing, expanding human populations, and pollution), erosion (both wind and water), depletion of soil resources (i.e. from non-rotation of crops), waterlogging of soils and salinization (from substandard irrigation practices), and, of course, the desiccation of the Aral Sea. Consequently, land degradation in Central Asia is a concern equally of settlements at the edge of existing deserts and semi-deserts in Turkmenistan, of agriculturists in Uzbekistan's valleys, and of populations living at high altitudes in the Tien-Shan and Pamir mountains of the Kyrgyz Republic and Tajikistan.

The largest states of Central Asia are already largely desert; roughly 60 per cent of Kazakhstan's territory is covered by deserts or semi-deserts, compared to 80 per cent of Turkmenistan and Uzbekistan. The remaining states also contain arid and desert areas, but are also more mountainous. All the states of the region utilize deserts and semi-deserts extensively for agriculture and animal husbandry, despite the sensitivity of these lands and the expense of reclamation.

The arable lands of Central Asia are heavily degraded. For example, in Turkmenistan, 95 per cent of irrigated lands suffer from salinization,[15] 40 per cent from extensive degradation, and only 17 per cent are in acceptable condition.[16] Approximately 30 per cent of Kazakhstan's agricultural lands are salinated, waterlogged, or at-risk.[17] In Tajikistan, 16 per cent of irrigated lands suffer to some degree from salinization,[18] another eight per cent are otherwise degraded,[19] and soil erosion affects most areas of the republic not used directly for agriculture.[20] In their adverse impacts on Central Asia, desertification and land degradation reach levels similar to those of Africa.[21]

The transition period exacerbates these trends. While total numbers of livestock have decreased, thereby allowing some natural restoration,[22] control and regulation of where livestock graze has become lax and contributes to degraded local carrying capacity. As a result, many sensitive areas, especially in mountainous areas, are overgrazed, leading to land degradation. Likewise, wartime conditions in Tajikistan that have forced refugees to new areas, impoverishment that forces villagers to cut slow-growing critical species like saksaul (*Haloxylon*) and juniper for fuel,[23] and trade in species like soaproot, for local subsistence and Asian medical markets, explain loss of vegetation.[24]

While the root causes of land degradation in Central Asia are not actively disputed, to date almost no effort has been made to address these root causes, and there is little political will to do so. While it is no secret that extensive cultivation of cotton is a prime culprit in degradation, the governments of the major cotton export states (TM/UZ) show no intention to abandon the reduced but considerable foreign currency to be gained from "white gold."

Ten years into independence, discussions about the need to reinvent the economy still abound. Yet, while these states are actively interested in mitigation of the effects on the land of cotton and other agriculture, they balk at the idea of more serious reforms and more substantive revisions of their economic foundations. They also remain committed to untenable practices (such as the overgrazing that is connected to the livestock industry or the population expansion connected with policies that encourage high birth rates) despite the medium and long-term erosion of natural capital that results from such practices.

BIODIVERSITY

Central Asia boasts considerable biological diversity, including more than 7000 flowering species of plants; in some areas up to 20 per cent of plant species are endemic.[25] Similarly, the region has nearly a thousand species of vertebrates, including more than a hundred reptile species.[26] Notable species include snow leopard, Caspian seal, Karatau argali, Severtsov urial, MacQueen's bustard, bearded vulture, Ship sturgeon, Menzbir's groundhog, and Striped hyena. Complementing these species are numerous rare and endangered ecosystems, such as feathergrass steppes, walnut and pistachio forests, and high altitude (above 10,000 feet) lakes. Other species (Turan tiger, Near Eastern cheetah, and honey badger) and ecosystems (tugai forests) have either completely disappeared or declined by more than 90 per cent over the past 100 years.

Central Asia is substantially more biodiverse than its neighbors to the north and west. This wealth of biodiversity and its continued existence are important for both global reasons (as sinks and as the common heritage and concern of humanity) and local reasons (as an indicator of the health of the human environment, as a source of tourism revenue, and as local heritage).

While the region now possesses only limited capacity to reverse or mitigate its other environmental problems, it boasts established mechanisms to protect biodiversity. Central Asia contains a developed network of nature reserves inherited from the Soviet Union. Roughly 3 per cent of the region existed as conservation land in the late Soviet era,[27] the bulk primarily in strict reserves (*zapovedniki*), temporary or less strict, at times even only nominally conservationist, reserves (*zakazniki*), and newly emerging national parks. Complicating analysis, there is overlap between these lands; in most states, a zakaznik can be part of a zapovednik, which itself can be part of a national park. Azerbaijan and Turkmenistan have over 2 per cent of their territory in zapovedniki, and the other states roughly 0.5 per cent. Today, 2.5 per cent of Central Asia, or 100,000 km^2, is in some sort of conservation regime. For perspective, the aggregate size of the parts of Central Asia set aside as conservation land slightly exceeds the total area of the Democratic People's Republic of Korea. These various conservation lands directly protect the viability of Central Asian ecosystems to sustain agriculture, supply fresh water, and buffer an increasingly harsh climate (Table 1.2).

The post-communist fate of these reserves remains unclear. After independence governments permitted previously unthinkable assaults on these reserves. These assaults took the form of military activities (TJ/AZ), widespread appropriation or lease of reserve lands for fishing and agriculture (KZ/TM), and parties of Arabs and Europeans taking trophies of endangered species such as argali and urial in reserves (KG/UZ/TM).[28] Indirectly, similar damage was inflicted to the reserve system because of the collapse of science in all six states, the out-migration of scientists, and the remarkably severe impoverishment of park rangers, leaving the latter understandably prone to participate in or ignore violations of environmental laws.

However, the states in the region and their activist communities of conservation and research biologists deserve special recognition for taking steps toward the preservation and even revitalization of the system of nature reserves. Tajikistan plans to complete its pre-independence steps toward creation of a Pamir National Park covering much of the eastern part of the country, in effect creating one of the largest parks in the world.[29] Also notable, Kazakhstan created the Eastern Kazakhstan Zapovednik in 1992 and the Alakol Zapovednik in 1998, and it recently formed the Ili-Alatau National Park in the mountains bordering the former capital, Almaty. Similarly, Kyrgyzstan is establishing the Issyk-kul area as a biosphere reserve, and Turkmenistan is also on the verge of creating a new zapovednik. Yet, while the situation with regard to reserves provides some basis for optimism, most of the region's biodiversity, of course, is located outside of the boundaries of these reserves. Most activities relating to biodiversity protection in the region nevertheless focus exclusively on reserves.

In summary, current efforts to protect biodiversity in Central Asia have two major failings due to the over-use of reserves as proxies for preservation. First, a comparatively minor effort is directed towards general enforcement of the region's adequate laws on wildlife protection; legal efforts are limited to drafting new laws instead of enforcing existing laws. Second, local communities are often very

Table 1.2 Rough overview of protected lands in Central Asia*

State	#	km²
Azerbaijan		
Zapovedniki	14	2,000
Kazakhstan		
Zapovedniki	9	9,000
National Parks	4	3,000
Zakazniki	60	60,000
Kyrgyzstan		
Zapovedniki	4	1,000
National Parks	3	600
Zakazniki	70+	4,000+
Tajikistan		
Zapovedniki	4	1,000
National Parks	1	300
Zakazniki	11	5,000+
Turkmenistan		
Zapovedniki	7	11,000
Zakazniki	14	5,000
Uzbekistan		
Zapovedniki	9	2,000
National Parks	5	300
Zakazniki	2	1,000
Total	≈200	≈100,000

Notes
* Derived from Eric W. Sievers *et al.*, "National Parks, Snow Leopards, and Poppy Plantations: The Development and Degradation of Central Asia's Preserved Lands," in *Central Asia Monitor* 2 (1995): 23–30 and 3 (1995): 17–26; I. Kh. Mirkhashimov (ed.), *Biologicheskoe i landshaftnoe raznoobrazie Kazakhstana* (Almaty: Ministry of Ecology and Natural Resources of the Republic of Kazakhstan, 1997), I. Kh. Mirkhashimov *et al.*, "Osobo okhranyaemye prirodnye territorii Kazakstana," in V. I. Drobzhev *et al.* (eds), *Novosti nauki Kazakhstana* (Almaty: Ministry of Science-Academy of Sciences of the Republic of Kazakhstan, 1997); Kh. Atamuradov, "Osobo okhranyaemye prirodnye territorii i buduschie zapovednye zony" (unpublished map of Turkmenistan Ministry of Nature Use and Environmental Protection, 1999).

hostile to the assignment of lands to conservation regimes,[30] especially zapovedniki that, by law, prevent even physical access to their territories by non-scientific personnel. The consequences are that Central Asia's stocks of important biodiversity are on the decline, conditions for recovery are diminishing, and, although field science is not supported enough to report them, rates of extinction have probably increased in the post-independence period.

INDUSTRIAL POLLUTION

Energy and water are comparable components of Central Asian life. The massively inefficient irrigation practices of Central Asia match massively inefficient patterns of energy use. Kazakhstan's Ekibastuz coal power plant was the most polluting power plant in the USSR.[31] While hydropower and natural gas meet an appreciable amount of the region's energy needs, reliance on coal and inefficient power plants drives levels of tons of carbon emission per unit GDP to extraordinary levels. Kazakhstan's levels even surpass those of the United States,[32] as probably do Azerbaijan's.

One of the most significant reforms of the post-Soviet period has been the separation of Central Asia's energy grid into two districts; this process, ongoing since 1997, will reverse the trends towards nationalization of energy transmission networks that dominated the early independence period. Under this effort, all of Central Asia except northern Kazakhstan will be part of a single electricity and gas network, while northern Kazakhstan and Siberia will form a separate grid. This scheme promises savings in both costs and efficiency and is a major concession of each state's sovereignty since disputes over electricity and gas have been among the largest tensions between the governments of Kazakhstan, Kyrgyzstan and Uzbekistan in recent years. Notably, the northern Kazakhstan grid hopes to reduce its reliance on local high-ash coal by emphasizing the hydroelectric assets that it already contains; Kazakhstan currently exploits only 10 per cent of its hydroelectric potential.[33] For Central Asia as a whole, electricity consumption, while still massively inefficient, is only half what it was during the late Soviet era.[34]

Because Central Asia is already heavily degraded environmentally and since much of the region is situated in environmentally sensitive xeric territories, the link between economic activities and environmental sustainability is accentuated. The sensitive ecosystems of the area are for the reasons stated above less able to absorb and mitigate pollution than are ecosystems in other areas of heavy industrial development, and this situation elevates the marginal environmental and health costs of industrial activities and development in the region. In other words, Central Asia's environmental sinks are compromised from the start, with the consequence that resource flows are prone to degrade faster than in other areas of the planet.

Since 1990, levels of pollution have decreased because of the economic crash in the region; many factories closed or operate at greatly reduced capacity. Nevertheless, every state in the region pins hopes for the future on restoration of and, then, expansion and diversification of the level of industrial output reached by the end of the Soviet era. Thus, the region's uncertain industrial future presents both regional and global environmental issues, global primarily because of carbon emissions related to highly inefficient industry, and regional because of air, soil, and water pollution related to this inefficient industry.

Because the Soviet state situated so many industrial enterprises close to or (especially those established before the end of World War II) in cities, many heavily populated areas contain substantial soil pollution. For example, in Leninogorsk (KZ), lead and cadmium levels around apartment buildings exceed maximum allowable concentrations by nearly 100 times.[35] In Batken (KG), the Kyrgyzstan Medical Ecology Research Institute recorded soil concentrations of mercury and antimony in 2000 at levels that exceeded maximum allowable concentrations by several hundred times.[36] While Leninogorsk and Batken are uniquely heavily polluted, levels of heavy metal pollution exceeding allowable norms can be found in every major city in Central Asia.

Given the region's geography, transboundary river pollution can be easily divided into regional (little or no flow outside the region) and interregional categories. Within the region, the internal transboundary rivers are not the most polluted industrially. Salts and agricultural chemicals are the major, although not exclusive, concerns associated with rivers such as the Amudarya and Syrdarya. However, these concerns are not trivial. A recent report claims that 98 per cent of women in northern Turkmenistan have reproductive disorders and that 35 per cent of children born to women exposed regularly to pesticides are partially herma-phroditic.[37]

The major water borne flows of industrial pollutants are through interregional watercourses such as the Ural River (phenols, petroleum byproducts, and boron) as it flows from Russia to Kazakhstan and in the Irtysh (ammonium nitrate, zinc, phenols) as it flows from Kazakhstan to Russia.[38] These two rivers are the most polluted of Kazakhstan's large rivers.[39]

Notable exceptions to this general rule include the Chu, Mailisu, and Surkhandarya rivers. The Chu flows into Kazakhstan from Kyrgyzstan, where a Chinese joint venture paper mill operates on the border. Kyrgyzstan NGOs claim that this mill violates environmental laws, uses polluting technology, and was only approved due to political influence.[40] The Surkhandarya is heavily polluted by the Tursunzade Aluminum Works (with a half million ton per year capacity, one of Asia's largest) in Tajikistan on its way into Uzbekistan, a situation that Uzbekistan protests often. The Mailisu, which receives runoff from several Kyrgyzstan mines with large waste piles of radioactive tailings, is of similar concern to Uzbekistan.

An analogous situation holds for transboundary air pollution. Much of the region's air pollution comes from sources in Russia and beyond. For example, Russia received 4×10^6 g of sulfur deposition from Kazakhstan in 1994, but Kazakhstan received 74×10^6 g from Russia, accounting for 28 per cent of the Kazakhstan total.[41] However, Kazakhstan and Uzbekistan both also send high levels of airborne particulate pollution to their neighbors within the region.

In summary, Central Asia currently possesses, even after post-Soviet collapses, an unusually high level of industrial infrastructure. This infrastructure is, per unit output, far more environmentally devastating than is the global norm. As a consequence, even a slashing of industrial output in Central Asia of the type that has occurred since 1991 has not been able to effect a reversal of trends in industrial pollution. Rather, economic decline has merely resulted in more modest rates of environmental degradation, but rates still in excess of what would be considered catastrophic in other parts of the world. Environmental gains from reductions in industrial output are partly offset by the increasing obsolescence of industrial infrastructure. For example, in the energy sector, "over 90 per cent of gas turbines, 57 per cent of steam turbines, and 33 per cent of steam boilers have been in place for 20 years or more."[42] Therefore, stated aspirations by all states in the region to resurrect industrial output and expand industries only promise to further degrade the natural resource flows and sinks of the region. They are not coupled to any viable or known technologies (or sources of funding) to restrict emissions of pollutants into the air or water to levels within regional or global carrying capacities.

CASPIAN SEA

The Caspian Sea, covering more than $370,000\,km^2$, is, by far, the planet's largest inland body of water and is roughly the size of the Lao People's Democratic Republic and Thailand combined or the size of New York State alone. Its littoral states are Azerbaijan, Iran, Kazakhstan, Russia, and Turkmenistan, meaning that half of the states of Central Asia have a direct interest in the sea. This interest extends to communities living near the sea, as well as to the sea's traditional provision of appreciable income from caviar exports and the sea's potential status as a major source of hydrocarbons. The Kashagan Field off Kazakhstan's Caspian coast may be the second or third largest hydrocarbon deposit in the world.

However, the Caspian is already afflicted by massive amounts of pollution, primarily brought into the sea from the more than 100 rivers that feed into it, as well as by oil refining operations on the coast in Azerbaijan. The Volga River is the major Caspian tributary, contributing 80 per cent of the Caspian's inflow and draining a watershed that includes the bulk of the Russian Federation's industry. In July 1996, an oil spill from an Azerbaijan offshore drilling operation covered $1000\,km^2$ of the sea;[43] oil is the major pollutant in the sea.[44] In early 2000, the Russian press reported widely about several million tons of oil released into Caspian tributaries due to hostilities in Chechnya.

Perhaps partly due to this pollution, the Caspian's annual yield of sturgeon plummeted from tens of thousands of tons per year to under ten thousand tons. Yet, since the planet's other sturgeon fisheries have also collapsed, the Caspian still yields 90 per cent of the world's sturgeon.[45] Other primary reasons for sturgeon decline are overfishing, dams, and pollution of rivers used for spawning, especially the Volga. In 1988, almost no sturgeon spawned successfully in the Volga River due to heavy metal poisoning.[46]

More recently, resolution of these problems and the success of conservation programs have been frustrated by a precipitous rise in poaching. A 1999 TRAFFIC report argues that the majority of government officials in the Republic of Kalmykia in Russia are involved in sturgeon poaching.[47] A 2000 report prepared for TRAFFIC on Kazakhstan and Turkmenistan also revealed previously unknown levels of poaching and state corruption in those republics.[48] In a needed but insufficient move, the Interstate Commission for Conservation of the Biological Resources of the Caspian Sea reduced its 2000 national quotas to only 70 per cent of 1999 quotas,[49] which themselves were only a fraction of late Soviet production figures. The littoral states' state fisheries cannot even meet these small quotas, and as a result Russia has announced that it may suspend all exports of caviar in order to preserve a commercially viable stock of sturgeon. Kazakhstan expected to export in 2000 only one-sixth of its 1999 caviar exports.

In recent decades another major environmental issue involving the Caspian has been the rising level of the sea. Before World War II, the sea's level fell to such a great degree that ports and other coastal installations had difficulties operating. However, beginning two decades ago, the sea began to rise dramatically and by 1995 had flooded over 12,000 km^2 of coastal areas.[50] However, 1999, saw a slight decline in the level of the sea and consequent hopes that this environmental problem is abating.

Beyond sturgeon and other species connected to Caspian fisheries, biodiversity concerns are also relevant to the Caspian. The sea's unique seal population has in recent years been subject to mass die-offs. Moreover, the seals are primarily in the northern Caspian shelf area, the very shallow but highly biologically productive area shared by Kazakhstan and Russia; it is here that Kazakhstan began drilling for hydrocarbons in 1999. To wit, in spring 2000, 10 per cent of the entire population of Caspian seals perished under unresolved conditions in the Kazakhstan and Russian sectors of the Caspian Sea. Also, several important nature reserves lie on the shores of the Caspian and embrace parts of the sea. In Central Asia, these are Kyzylagach Zapovednik (AZ, 88,360 ha) and Khazar Zapovednik (TM, 262,000 ha). Both are important nesting areas for migratory birds and waterfowl, like flamingo, herons, and francolins.

Finally, the only nuclear power plant in Central Asia lies on the shores of the Caspian in Aktau (KZ). The plant is so close to the shore that the rising sea subsumed a cooling pond. Constructed in the early 1970s, this BN-350 heat and de-salinization plant was the first of its kind in the world. Due to be decommissioned in 1996,[51] the Mangystau reactor may remain operational until at least 2002.[52]

HYDROCARBONS AND MINING

On May 20, 1998, a truck carrying 20 tons of sodium cyanide veered off a bridge in Kyrgyzstan, spilling 1760 kg of the chemical into the Barskoon River, which empties into Issyk-kul. Several deaths in the nearby eponymous village and a localized fish kill in Issyk-kul were blamed on the accident.

Despite widespread hysteria from political groups, NGOs, and the foreign press, it is likely that no human died as a result of cyanide, especially considering the flow of the Barskoon river, the immense volume of Lake Issyk-kul, and the rapidity of the dissolution of the toxin as documented by chemical analyses immediately following the accident.[53] Most damage tied to this incident probably occurred as a result of the Ministry of Health's decision to dump calcium compounds into the river, an event not well-publicized[54] and which, inexplicably, continued for a week after the accident.[55] The truck was owned by a Canadian–Kyrgyz joint venture operating the Kumtor gold mine; this mine produces a sizeable portion of Kyrgyzstan's GNP. Likewise, gold mines in Tajikistan and

Radiation and human health[56]

We studied several indicators of health in the town of Atbasar (Akmola region in central Kazakhstan). The town itself is located in a depression and lacks central heating; coal containing radionucleides is used for fuel. For the past 40 years, uranium ore has been transported through the town without regard to human safety. There is one river that flows through the town, and it is saturated with radionucleides as the result of dumpings 100 km upstream at the uranium mines. There is also a chemical fertilizer plant in the town. In addition, atomic tests were carried out in the region at a rocket test site not far from the town. In 1992, the average life expectancy was 62 years; in the first half of 1993 it was 59 years. Infant mortality is 37 in 1000.

After researching several population groups with an average age of 36, it was revealed that 100 per cent had dental pathologies and a quarter had lost more than four teeth. Cardiograms of 90 per cent of the group evidenced abnormalities. Psychological disorders among adults are increasing by almost 5 per cent a year, and by almost 7 per cent a year among children. Over the past 10 years, the incidence of ectopic pregnancies has increased by over ten times. Seventy per cent of tenth grade boys have evidenced serious morphological abnormalities in their sperm. Morbidity rates for malignant tumors are increasing by 3 per cent each year. Radiation and heavy metal pollution have been documented in the soil, air, flora, and water of Atbasar. We looked at human leukocytes and found that 16 per cent evidenced abnormalities.

Uzbekistan, not to mention hydrocarbon sources in Azerbaijan, Kazakhstan, and Turkmenistan, account for large portions of their respective state's GNP.

Kyrgyzstan's accident never really threatened to halt the work of the Kumtor Operating Company. Because of the economic scale of hydrocarbon and mining activities in Central Asia, companies involved in these activities and the activities themselves are not scrupulously monitored. This situation is exacerbated by the fact that every mining and drilling operation is distant from densely populated areas. Increasingly, multinationals are assuming management of extractive activities from Soviet-era state concerns, with the exception of coal mining, a major activity only in Kazakhstan.

NGOs and newspapers often accuse governments of approving mining and hydrocarbon projects without legally appropriate environmental impact statements or liability guarantees. In response, states in the region rightly point out that transnational corporations employ technology that is both more efficient and less polluting than its Soviet counterparts. Yet, as the scale of activity increases, and as emerging pipelines to Europe, China, Pakistan, and Iran increase the chances that accidents will occur near areas of denser human population or more environmental sensitivity, hydrocarbon development is emerging as a potential source of massive transboundary and regional environmental damage.

For example, TengizChevroil allowed a sizable hydrocarbon spill in 1998 that worked its way into the Caspian watershed leading to deaths of local wildlife (seals and waterfowl), and the Kazakhstan government complains that Chevron consistently violates Kazakhstan maximum allowable emissions of pollutants.[57] Moreover, without adequate environmental impact statements, it is hard to gauge the extent to which extractive enterprises are polluting the environment in Central Asia with the kind of dangerous and persistent radioactive and hydrocarbon byproducts that gold mining and hydrocarbon extraction produce. It is the persistence of these pollutants in the environment that explains why parents in southern Kyrgyzstan in 2000 were still advised against breast-feeding; very high levels of radionucleides in human milk pose a potent health threat to children.[58] What is still more striking is that information is still gradually emerging about the non-military uses of nuclear explosions during the Soviet period to facilitate mining efforts in Central Asia; no fewer than 32 underground explosions were conducted outside of military areas for scientific research and industrial purposes.[59]

Moreover, gold (and other metal) and hydrocarbon (but not coal) production in Central Asia is almost entirely for export. The bulk of the region's several hundred billion barrel reserves of oil and several hundred trillion cubic feet of gas reserves are destined for markets in Asia and Europe. Most states in the region rely on coal, natural gas, and hydropower for their domestic needs, although some are considering nuclear and oil for the future. They all also have had research programs on and limited use of solar, wind, and other alternative sources of power. Needless to say, local funding and support for environmentally less damaging sources of energy has dissipated or all but disappeared in the independence period.

EVALUATING THE ERAS OF NATURAL CAPITAL IN CENTRAL ASIA

Painted in broad strokes, the history of natural capital in Central Asia is that natural capital was steadily but modestly reduced in the centuries before Russian conquest, seriously compromised during the Soviet-era, and further still degraded after independence.

Even though Central Asia was a center of technology, agriculture, education, culture, and trade for millennia prior to the advent of the global sea trade, the environmental impacts of these activities did not rise to the scale of those of modern industrial endeavors and may not have even exceeded the carrying capacity of the region.

At worst, human activities compromised biodiversity and exacerbated desertification. There is some evidence that human settlements may have been a factor in the extirpation centuries ago of lion and other species.[60] Later, the Chingissid era saw the permanent demise of what had been one of the world's most efficient irrigation systems in the Zeravshan Valley (UZ/TM),[61] and it also saw a reduction in population. Expansion of the region's deserts probably preceded and was exacerbated by these and later human agricultural and grazing activities.

Nevertheless, population in Central Asia did not expand during the pre-Russian era at rates comparable to other parts of the world, and the delayed entry of the industrial revolution into Central Asia meant that pollution of the region's natural capital flows occurred primarily after the region lost its independence.

The pollution of the present is primarily linked to the past. Economic and industrial development, measured traditionally, was the yardstick of Soviet progress. The natural world, the environment, and quality of life concerns usually took back seats to objectives of factory construction, resource extraction, and GNP expansion. Enforcement of environmental laws was lax; and concern for the welfare of future generations was expressed through bequests of large amounts of human and physical capital, rather than preservation of natural capital. As Central Asia so recently gained independence from the USSR, most reasons for unsustainable development in the region are linked to the Soviet past. These include, *inter alia*, inefficient and ineffective policies typical of world experience (among others, overuse of agricultural chemicals, lack of catalytic converters for automobiles, and inappropriate storage procedures for mining tailings). They also include elements inherent to the Soviet system (such as elevation of development concerns, traditionally formulated, to the level of a state religion) and the scale of the Soviet system (which emphasized giganticism).

In response to these environmental problems, Soviet culture and government remained largely uninterested in imposing restraints on industry, or on preserving the viability of natural resource flows and sinks. Rather, a culture of mitigation arose in which folk remedies like vodka were believed to cleanse the body of any and all pollutants. This culture of mitigation fails to capture the whole picture of Soviet society, however; the Ala-Tal farm in Kazakhstan was one of several farms that turned to organic agriculture and aquaculture in the late Soviet period.[62] Unfortunately, such examples are few and far between.

Once environmental problems became a serious public issue in the USSR, the region's set of responses was typical and largely a failure. Namely, the Soviet Union embraced a variety of command and control mechanisms, such as scrubbers in factories and cooling ponds to prevent heat pollution, but the effectiveness and availability of such mitigation technologies was questionable. Azerbaijan and Kazakhstan had fulfilled only 2 and 1 per cent, respectively, of their mandates to implement such technology as of 1988.[63] Beyond best available technology approaches, the Soviet Union also made wide use of standards, like "maximum allowable concentrations" for industrial effluents and discharges. Yet, legend in the region abounds of nighttime violations, clandestine dumping, and other practices well-known in other parts of the world through which dedicated polluters sidestep such regulations. The region also experimented with quasi-market mechanisms to encourage environmental responsibility, but the budgetary system of Soviet industry only with great difficulty accommodated such reforms, and so these, too, produced few notable or durable successes.

These attempts encouraged moving the Soviet economy towards better environmental management, but without major dislocations to the economy. A full assessment of the performance of these efforts is precluded by the fact that the

Soviet environmental *gestalt* occurred later than in the West and lasted only a few years before the USSR crumbled. Hence, Central Asia inherited a range of destructive (but economically vital) practices and policies from the USSR, but only a protean set of responsive mechanisms to these destructive influences.

Upon disassembly of the USSR, Western environmental donors, especially American, offered to share with Central Asia the experience of states that had, they said, solved environmental problems. The explicit implication of early programs and exchanges was that the West had achieved sustainable development, and that Central Asia would be allowed to copy this Western model. One reason why this overstatement by Western donors found ready acceptance in the region is because of the uniquely technophilic nature of Soviet society. Soviet ideology predicted that there were, echoing similar American leanings, essentially no limits to the capabilities of human societies *if* science and technology were allowed their full development. Accordingly, by this logic, technological solutions to all problems both exist and are always the best solutions. The dissolution of the USSR did not discredit this ideology, and since most governments in the region are composed primarily of individuals trained in the technical sciences, the effects of this singular aspect of post-Soviet society frustrate transition to a more sustainable future. Ideas such as appropriate technology or modest lifestyles are essentially immiscible with this ideology, especially when the American lifestyle is the tangible dream that has replaced Soviet ambitions.

Central Asia's factories and agricultural systems are based on technologies and techniques that still rely on massive resource throughput, low efficiency, and high levels of pollution. Because of the reduction of the private sphere under communism and the technological giganticism of Soviet planning, Central Asia's development did not embrace small and medium sized enterprises. Rather, it included several of the largest tractor factories, smelting operations, mining facilities, and weapons facilities on the planet. When such enterprises taxed the ability of local electricity grids, the Soviet response was not so much to increase efficiency, but to increase capacity of the grids. The Soviet system prized output, whereas efficiency had little practical relevance in a system in which valuations of inputs were clouded by the lack of markets.

It is this lack of clear pricing and preference for immensity that explains the scale of efforts in the region. These factors explain Soviet policies for pushing cotton production in Central Asia through construction of the massively inefficient Kara-Kum Canal (TM), building a torpedo plant in Kazakhstan's capital city, and expecting northern Kazakhstan's semi-deserts to become a major source of wheat under Khruschev's Virgin Lands scheme.

As a result, Central Asian economies appear undiversified. Tajikistan's Tursunzade aluminum factory consumes the bulk of all electricity used in the entire country. While such enterprises are inefficient, they are also the foundations of their states' economies, which explains why the transition to sustainable development in the region may be particularly difficult.

Thus, Central Asia's nonsustainable development rests on its Soviet past and impoverished and economically inviable present. However, capturing the effects of Central Asia's environmental degradation on other forms of capital is unusually difficult. The area is not the subject of any large-scale environmental health studies, nor does it offer any reliable raw economic data amenable to an economic analysis of the region's environmental problems and their effect on GNP. Even if such data did exist, they would embrace only recent years, making any conclusions suspect for lack of a meaningful time comparison. Global surveys, such as WHO's *The World Health Report 1999*, provide unusually scant information about the Central Asian states.

While life expectancy increased in Central Asia steadily this century, after 1990 it fell in all states by several years, and unlike the sad picture of other Soviet republics like Russia, in parts of Central Asia life expectancy has fallen for both men and women, not just for men. However, the situation in Central Asia is not simply that the old are dying at a younger age, infant and child mortality is also noticeably on the rise in the region.[64] This mortality is partly explained by increases in morbidity for a variety of diseases and conditions in Central Asia. In the industrial cities of Eastern Kazakhstan, life expectancies are up to a decade shorter than in the rest of Kazakhstan, and morbidity rates per 1000 for a standard list of afflictions actually exceed 1000. In the Aral Sea region, nearly 99 per cent of women are anemic, and several forms of cancer have become 25–200 per cent more common over the last generation.[65] In fact, reports from newspapers in virtually every city of the region and from virtually every epidemiologist in the region, as well as from a limited number of development studies, assert across the board increases (sometimes doubling or trebling) in morbidity rates. These rates are for respiratory ailments, cancers, and infectious diseases that are widely suspected by the medical sciences to be linked in part to environmental conditions.[66] More sensationalist accounts appearing in the years immediately following the disassembly of the USSR reported that in areas of Central Asia environmental conditions caused viral hepatitis rates to increase by 700 per cent, typhoid fever by 3000 per cent, and stomach cancer by 1000 per cent.[67]

While reliable statistical evidence is lacking, this increased morbidity is assumed to be largely due to lack of access to potable water, worsening air quality in cities, various sources of radiation, and the effects of land degradation. All of these sources of risk relate directly to degradation of the natural resource flows and sinks in Central Asia. Recent World Bank-funded emergency food supply programs in Kyrgyzstan, Tajikistan, and Turkmenistan explicitly state that environmental factors in large part explain these states' inability to produce enough food for their citizens.

In addition to refugees, possibly up to 100,000 from the Aral Sea region alone, environmental degradation is also demanding changes in the lifestyles of the region's residents. Fishermen can no longer fish for a living. Many children cannot swim in local ponds and lakes. Turkmen traditions of taming cheetahs disappeared a generation ago when cheetah were extirpated. Families across the region prefer to grow their own food so as to be guaranteed produce free of pesticides and nitrates, or to be guaranteed food at all. These and other changes in the social fabric and modes of life of the region's residents impose burdens on the population that tax both family budgets and social cohesiveness. In other words, they inveigh perversely on the region's stocks of physical, human, and organizational capital.

While a poor area, Central Asia has already substantially drawn down its reserve of natural capital and ended the era when subsistence inputs, such as fresh water, could be secured in the absence of state programs. Since all the states of the region already face chronic inability to meet the spending needs of their social programs, environmentally exacerbated needs for food, medical attention, and water help drive the governments of the region into deeper insolvency and frustrate their efforts to structurally adjust their economies. In this context, added expenditures for environmental protection face little chance of realization, which means that environmental control devices for industry pioneered in the late Soviet era that are now wearing out or worn out will not be replaced.

2　Human capital: health, education, and science in Central Asia

Central Asia and Azerbaijan's 60 million population differs from previous post-colonial populations, and it differs remarkably from other post-colonial Islamic populations. Whereas other states have boasted highly educated elites at the moment of independence, Central Asia differs in that such a large percentage of its population, and not just select elites, was homogeneously educated, modern, and integrated into the state. At the moment of independence, Central Asia boasted per capita rates of university education on a par with the West, comparable per capita numbers of scientists and engineers, and life expectancies nearing developed country levels. However, the post-Soviet period has witnessed declines in most of the region's human capital assets. The people of the region are sub-stantially less healthy and less educated than even a decade ago, and this lack of health and education will frustrate attainment of sustainable development.

However, as with natural capital issues, the newly independent states frequently invoke the USSR as a scapegoat for current declines, stating that they represent the continuing consequences of bad Soviet practices. There is indeed an argument to be made for the delayed consequences of environmental pollution created in the Soviet period, as well as for the legacy of Soviet disregard for individual rights. Yet, while the assertion that Soviet inertia troubles the region is valid, it fails to consider the positive aspects of Soviet inertia, particularly as regional counterfactuals (i.e. Iran, Afghanistan, and China) highlight the comparative developmental successes of Central Asia.

Moreover, frequent emphases of negative Soviet endowments alone mask the serious contemporary shortcomings of the human capital policies of the newly independent states, such as Kyrgyzstan's recent plans to reduce wheat production in order to make tobacco its primary export.[1] In scapegoating the USSR, critics imply that the region enjoyed something other than dismal social indicators prior to the Soviet era. Yet, Central Asia was indeed an area of particularly poor health and poor learning in the middle of the nineteenth century and at the beginning of the twentieth century.

The following sections disaggregate human capital into two broad categories: health and education. Human capital in health refers to a variety of impacts on human capital that occur through the medium of the physical body. In the roughest understanding, human capital in health could refer to a population's enjoyment of enough health to engage in economically productive undertakings as diverse as farming and computer programming. However, beyond workplaces, human capital in health is also a significant proxy for quality of life and human happiness.[2] Better daily diets, lower morbidity rates, and declining mortality rates suggest higher levels of human capital in health that are important both to economic productivity and to quality of life.

Educational human capital refers, also roughly, to the ability of a population to manipulate and manage its physical and social environments so as to achieve better economic productivity and efficiency. As with human capital in health, beyond manipulation of the environment, educational capital may also be a proxy for quality of life; if this was not true in a more pastoral time, under current trends of globalization it is at least a more forceful argument. Rates of educational attainment, infrastructure for the pursuit and implementation of science and technology, newspaper readership, and migration rates are all fundamental indicators of levels of and changes in levels of the educational human capital of a society.

HUMAN CAPITAL IN HEALTH

During the Soviet period life expectancies increased by several decades in each republic, although data for accurate pre-revolutionary life expectancies is lacking.[3] For the USSR as a whole, official sources claimed that the increase was from 32 years to 70 years by 1985.[4]

By the late Soviet era, Central Asia enjoyed levels of health care and security from disease at levels that placed the region only slightly behind Russia. Accordingly, the region occupied a position intermediary between the West and the developing world and substantially ahead of any of Central Asia's neighbors to the east or south. To quantify this position, extrapolating from various UNDP Human Development Reports, the Central Asian republics would have been ranked among the top 50 states in the world according to current WHO criteria.[5]

By 2000, the region had not merely slipped in the rankings; it plummeted, even considering the sizable number of new developing world states that have appeared in recent years. According to *The World Health Report 2000*, the average ranking in Central Asia put the area towards the bottom of the world's states in 1997 (Table 2.1), as a region closely equivalent to Pakistan.[6] The situation has probably deteriorated further in the intervening years. This deterioration is best viewed through mortality and morbidity rates in the region.

Both morbidity and mortality rates relate dynamically to endowments of the two types of capital whose decline has been charted so far, physical capital and natural capital. As they relate to physical capital, elevated morbidity and mortality rates are results of poverty. Morbidity and mortality rates rise because of insufficient or declining availability of adequate preventative and curative medical care. This shortfall in availability can arise because of, *inter alia*, a result of poor state infrastructure (hospitals/equipment), lack of private funds (for medicines or hospitalization), lack of funds for adequate sanitation (a deficiency in organizational capital resulting from a low stock of physical capital), and lack of qualified medical personnel (educational human capital).[7] Because medical budgets, municipal sanitation services, doctors' salaries, and per capita incomes in Central Asia would all be higher now were it not for the region's crash in stocks of physical capital, morbidity and mortality rates exemplify the impact of physical capital on human capital.

Natural capital exhibits a similar relationship to human capital in health, one partly glossed in Chapter 1. As the integrity of natural resource flows deteriorates (such as happens when a river becomes polluted[8]), absent some sort of mitigation strategy (i.e. a municipal water treatment facility), declining stocks of natural capital effect a decline in stocks of human capital in health through increases in incidences of such diseases as cancers. In the developing world in general, 20 per cent of all death and disease arises from exposure to the risks created by environmental degradation.[9] Accordingly, it is of no small consequence for public health that by 1997, 70 per cent of Kyrgyzstan's pollution mitigation technology was in disrepair.[10]

By the end of the Soviet era, life expectancies in Central Asia had risen, depending on the republic, to between 65 and 70 years, comparing favorably with levels for developed states. Since that time, life expectancies have been falling in every republic and morbidity rates have been rising. While data from international agencies varies from year to year, the sources presenting panel data document decreases in life expectancies from 3 to 5 years in the past decade in all the Central Asian states except Uzbekistan.[11]

Even though Uzbekistan has been generally more successful than its neighbors in preventing post-Soviet human capital decline, by 1996 its adult morbidity rates had increased by 18 per cent and its teen morbidity rates by 66 per cent.[12] The previous chapter presented examples of the kinds of increases in morbidity from non-infectious diseases that in part explain this increasing mortality. In many cases it is nearly impossible to distinguish between the physical and natural capital causes of declines in human health, such as, for example in cases where

Table 2.1 Health in Central Asia and comparison states in 1997 out of 191 World States*

	Overall health ranking	Ranking of health system
AZ	65	109
Chile	32	33
China	81	144
KZ	122	64
KG	123	151
Russia	91	130
TJ	120	154
TM	128	153
UZ	100	117

Note
* Derived from World Health Organization, *The World Health Report 2000: Health Systems* (Geneva: World Health Organization, 2000), pp. 152–155.

environmental pollution weakens human immune systems leaving them vulnerable to infectious diseases. In recent years, compromised human capital from disease has become a major explanation of the persistent economic troubles of many developing countries. In particular, malaria and AIDS have attracted academic and policy attention from the World Bank and other major development agencies.[13] Although neither of these diseases is yet currently prevalent in Central Asia, at least to an appreciable degree, the region's increases in morbidity rates for other infectious diseases, like tuberculosis and hepatitis, stem not only from worsening sanitation, but also from such compromised immunity.

EDUCATIONAL HUMAN CAPITAL: BASIC LITERACY

The Soviet Union demanded and mandated ambitious improvements in literacy and education in every single part of its territory. With the establishment of the Soviet Union in 1922, Soviet human development policies gained momentum in Central Asia. At the core of the Soviet development philosophy was the idea that social environments could trump factors such as race, culture, and language in human communities. To a large degree, Soviet policymakers saw in education the future transcendence (as opposed to the more dramatic interim control measures for which the period is well known as one of terror) of divisive elements within Soviet society such as nationality and class. More precisely, they planned this transcendence to unfold through a combination of education and exposure to a common set of institutions and experiences.

Accordingly, the USSR attempted to level the playing field between its capital and its more remote territories. While the Soviet Union had neither the capacity, and probably in many ways lacked the will, to carry these policies to conclusion, the actual impacts of these policies strongly shaped Central Asia. Within a few years, most school age children were literate. Moreover, almost every child went through similar (despite linguistic differences) experiences with extracurricular activities, Pioneer camps, consumer goods, and hundreds of other institutional influences. All of these policies affected rural Russia in much the same way they affected Central Asia, and thus it is the case that these policies were not merely an extension of development opportunities to Central Asia, but the participation of Central Asia in the building of Soviet society.

Two decades into the past century, a very small number of people in Central Asia were literate; starting from a literacy rate of only around 5 per cent in 1917,[14] Central Asia enjoyed nearly universal literacy by the 1970s.[15] Most of those literate prior to 1917 were emigrants from Russia. For example, prior to 1917, only half a per cent of Kyrgyz were literate.[16] What makes this accomplishment even more notable is that the 60-year span within which this feat was achieved did not see the USSR blessed with wealth or peace, or even a tradition of universal education that could be extrapolated from Russia.[17] Nevertheless, Central Asia exited the Soviet era with a primary education system in which over 90 per cent of all teachers had university degrees. This was, moreover, a system in which roughly 95 per cent of teachers in math and science held degrees in the discipline they taught (not rarely, in the case of female high school teachers, Ph.D.s).

So important was the educational mission of the USSR that Soviet culture developed a word for "the state campaign to eradicate illiteracy": Likbez. At exactly the same time that the early Soviet police state was forcing citizens to alter behavior in ways that made it infamous, it also forced children into schools, and forced them to stay there. This aspect of the history of the application of state force in the USSR receives little scholarly attention; yet, in context, it was ahead of its time. Major humanitarian donors (i.e. World Bank, UNDP, and UNICEF) now argue that states should remove possibilities (in reality – freedoms) for even poor students to drop out of schools and should keep all students in schools for a longer number of years.[18]

Since the 1980s, real per-capita spending on education has increased across the planet, with the glaring exception of the transition states.[19] Since the communist states had much higher than average expenditures for education, through one lens their reductions are expected regressions to the mean and do not risk the standings of these states as educationally superior to developing states in Africa and Asia. However, through another lens, the poor economic performance of these states may be directly connected with the forces that reduced these states' emphases on development of human capital.

Current research suggests that literacy rates in the post-Soviet period are falling. Kazakhstan's Geller Institute regularly issues warnings that the generations in Kazakhstan currently coming up through the educational system may exhibit functional illiteracy at rates of up to 40 per cent. Even in the state with the best conditions for study, Uzbekistan, university enrollment fell by 41 per cent in the years after the disassembly of the USSR.[20] At the other end of the spectrum, Turkmenistan slashed opportunities for university education by roughly an order of magnitude; it limited the number of first year university students to only 3340 in 2000.[21]

EDUCATIONAL HUMAN CAPITAL: SCIENCE AND TECHNOLOGY

Until the conquests of Chinggis Khan in the early thirteenth century, Central Asians made substantial contributions to mathematics, engineering, and the natural sciences. Indeed, one source claims that more than half of all the scholars at the Baghdad Academy in the ninth and tenth centuries were from Central Asia.[22] A number of the works of Central Asian scientists were translated into Latin and laid the foundation for later European advances. Examples of such scientists include Ibn Sino (Avicenna) in the fields of medicine and physics in the eleventh century, Abu Nasr Muhammad al-Farabi in the field of chemistry (distillation) in the tenth century, and Muhammad b. Musa al-Khuwarazmi in the field of mathematics (algebra and trigonometry) in the ninth century.[23] Similarly, Abu 'Abd Allah al-Khwarazmi wrote an important encyclopedia of the sciences in the eleventh century. Finally, al-Biruni (physics), often recognized as the greatest Islamic scientist, was born 1000 years ago in what is now Uzbekistan.

After the thirteenth century, the contributions of Central Asia to science began to dissipate. By the Russian conquest, Central Asia was one of the most technologically backward areas of the Islamic world. While many educational institutions continued to thrive thanks to the Islamic institution of waqf (charitable endowments),[24] state interest in the sciences or technology was notably low, as evidenced by the accounts of a variety of local scholars educated abroad whose plans for local technological enterprises were shunned by political leaders.[25]

However, the Soviet Union quickly established scientific committees in each republic. These committees were followed by affiliate institutions of the USSR Academy of Sciences and the expansion of institutions of higher education. While scientific committees and affiliate institutions employed Slavic and Jewish directors, the next step in the institutionalization of science in a Soviet republic required a qualitatively different set of resources. The availability of individuals of the eponymous nationality with substantial scientific credentials or achievements, as well as the establishment of a mass of scientific institutions large enough to justify a separate academy were clear requirements. These twin foundations of any nascent academy served the purpose of establishing "adult" instead of "infant" or "young" peak scientific institutions.[26]

It is in the dual nature of a national academy of sciences, that it was meant to be an expression of both national and scientific development, that we begin to glimpse the ways in which the discourse of science and the discourse of Soviet politics intersected in Central Asia. In the Soviet political ideology, scientific and technological development equated to national strength and progress. Accordingly, scientists were often, especially in the early years of the USSR, elevated to far more visible and influential levels in the USSR than were their peers in other countries. The Central Asian republics subscribed fully to this Soviet adoration of science, and Kazakhstan's most enduring political leader, geologist Dinmuhammed Kunaev, was the President of the Kazakh Academy of Sciences before serving 30 years as leader of the Kazakh SSR and member of the USSR Politburo.

Consequently, scientists assumed primary responsibility for engineering and fostering the scientific development of the Soviet Union. One explicit goal of Soviet politics was to erase the gulf that existed economically, socially, and culturally between rural and urban areas of the country. Accordingly, scientists were asked to develop science not along the centralized pathways seen in the rest of world, but so as to create a scientific infrastructure with centers of research and education in every part of the country.

However, the logic of the Academy of Sciences plans for scientific development, a logic that placed primary emphasis on natural resources and population centers, was in the end mediated by another current of Soviet development policies, the "nationality" factor. Indeed, the original plans for the scientific development of the country largely ignored the division of the USSR into national republics.

Accordingly, the two foci for development were imagined as Siberia and Central Asia, with Siberia as clearly the more important area.

In 1931, the Academy endorsed plans to create Academy affiliates throughout the USSR, with emphases on "those districts, where in compliance with a unified plan, particularly intensive construction is being implemented."[27] To coordinate these efforts, the Academy created a Commission on Bases.[28] The ten priority areas for development in the 1931 plan included five Siberian cities, four Central Asian capitals, and Tiflis.[29] The nationality factor helped republican capitals, especially in Central Asia, gain precedence over other city candidates for development, most notably over several large cities in Russia.

At this time, when scientists discussed the creation of affiliate institutions, the language they employed treated "base," "department (*filial*)," "station," "department (*otdelenie*)," and "institution" as largely interchangeable terms. However, as with other aspects of Soviet development, legal organizational terms soon cemented these discussions in the specific (Figure 2.1). "Base" and "Department (*filial*)" became the two official types of proto-academy structures. Both structures were governed by presidia, the nomenklatura bodies that replaced democratic decision making in the Academy. These presidia were directly accountable not to republican bodies, but to the Academy and its Commission on Bases, which in 1935 was renamed the Base and Department Management Committee.[30] When, in 1942, this body was again renamed to the Council of Departments and Bases,

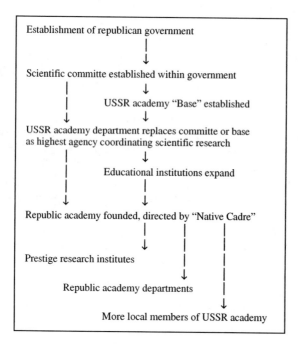

Figure 2.1 Flow chart of Soviet continuum of development of scientific infrastructure.

its only non-academician members were from Central Asia: the Kazakh geologist Satpaev and the Uzbek mathematician Kary-Niyazov.[31]

Bases, the less developed form, envisioned the establishment of institutions working on a set of integrated research issues related primarily to local natural resources, economics, and culture. Departments were assumed to pursue a more cosmopolitan and substantial research agenda (often as active partners of central Academy institutions), and, in addition to publishing, assumed the right to open graduate programs. The Academy was divided into both thematic departments (*otdeleniya*) and geographic departments (*filialy*). By 1940, 38 per cent of Academy institutions were located in and 20 per cent of Academy staff were employed in local bases and departments, and more than half the departments were in Central Asia.[32]

For its part, the Academy took these bases and departments seriously, and it sent many of those who just completed one of its graduate programs to become permanent staff in these emergent institutions. These personnel transfers were extremely important since department graduate programs were institutionally weak. The department graduate programs were, effectively, all in technical and scientific disciplines. The first Uzbek Department programs were in math, chemistry, geology, botany, soil sciences, and zoology.[33]

Of over a dozen generic major fields used by Soviet statisticians to group undergraduates and researchers, roughly half belonged to the sciences. Always, four to six of the most populous categories belonged to the sciences.[34] Similarly, the most populous graduate programs were almost all in the sciences,[35] this even considering that the best physics students, for example, traveled to study in Moscow and Leningrad, while the best Uzbek literature students probably stayed home. Accordingly, while Figure 2.2 shows aggregate numbers of Ph.D.s (equivalents) in Central Asia, the majority were awarded in the natural and technical sciences.

A full assessment of the quality of Soviet science in Central Asia exceeds the scope of this book. However, its quality was, ignoring issues of access to funding and equipment, remarkably close to European and American levels. By this I mean that the education of students and the general quality of their later research programs and methods (in terms of human capital, not funding or equipment) was closer to the level of Russia, Japan, and the United States[36] than to the norm in the developing world. From a global perspective, there exists a tremendous gap between the West and the Third World in science. While Central Asia certainly fit somewhere in this gap, the simple fact of the dearth of scientists and scientific infrastructure in most states of the world is what allows Central Asia to boast "Western" levels of scientific development. Evidence of the scale and intensity of the scientific enterprise in Central Asia can be seen in the large numbers of scientific workers (the majority of them holding undergraduate science degrees) employed in research institutions (Figure 2.3).

What does science mean for Central Asia? Recent efforts to ask the analogous question of the USSR in general led one group of scholars to conclude that "Western analysts of the Soviet Union have usually ignored or underestimated

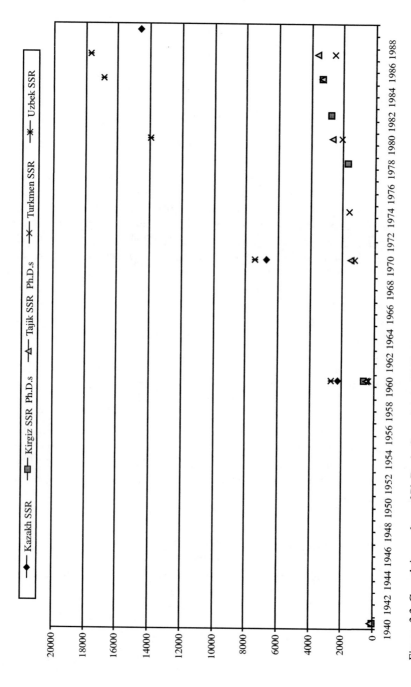

Figure 2.2 Growth in numbers of Ph.D.s in Central Asia (1940–1989).

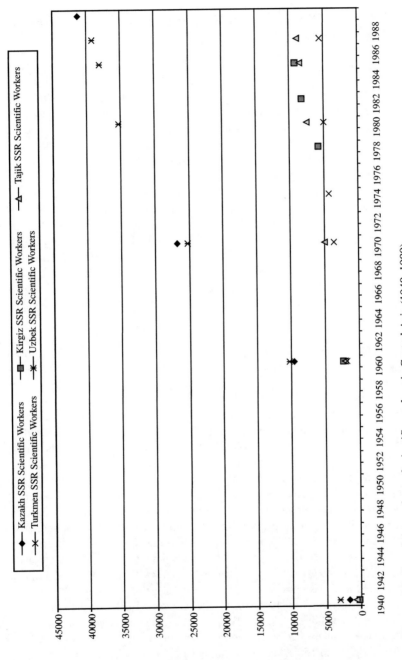

Figure 2.3 Growth in numbers of scientific workers in Central Asia (1940–1989).

science and technology in their efforts to understand the evolution of Soviet society."[37] Indeed, a review of the evolution of scientific infrastructures in Central Asia reveals much about its Soviet era changes.

Within Central Asia, every republic experienced a singular but impressive growth of its scientific infrastructure. The Kazakh Academy opened in June 1946. Over 300 academicians were elected to the academy during its first 45 years, and 354 by the date of its 50th anniversary.[38] When the Kazakhstan Base of the USSR Academy of Sciences was established on March 8, 1932, it consisted of only two sections: zoology and botany.[39] A. D. Arkhangelsky, a hydrocarbon geologist, directed the department, and his legacy is detectable in the prominence of geologists in the Kazakhstan Academy in later years. I. M. Gubkin (another hydrocarbon geologist) was also on the governing board, and he went on to be a founder of the oil industry in Azerbaijan.[40] When the Kazakhstan Academy was founded, it consisted of four departments, one of which was for the humanities and social sciences. The other three were for physics/mathematics, geological sciences, and life sciences. By 1978, only one more department had been added, chemical/technical sciences,[41] partly in recognition of Kazakhstan's development of a particularly notable school in chemistry led by Yesen Bekturov. By the 1980s, Kazakhstan's science and technology community boasted a cyclotron and a nuclear reactor devoted to desalinization on the shores of the Caspian Sea.[42] Kazakhstan also boasted experimental reactors, the largest per capita concentration in the USSR of chemical, biological, and nuclear weapons facilities, and the immense Bukhtarma Hydroelectric Station.

The Kyrgyz Academy was established on December 20, 1954. The Kyrgyz Department of the USSR Academy was founded on August 13, 1943; and the Kyrgyz State University opened in 1951. The Kyrgyz Department chair was Konstantin Ivanovich Skryabin,[43] a biologist and leading scholar of helminths. However, when Skryabin stepped down 2 years before the establishment of the Kyrgyz Academy, instead of a member of the Soviet Academy, Isa Akhunbaev, a heart surgeon, ascended to this top post.[44] The fivefold mission of the Kyrgyz Academy was to investigate the biological and geological resources of the region, build local capacity, exploit "productive forces," conduct fundamental research, and facilitate nation and union building.

Tajikistan (which gained Soviet republic status only in 1929) established an Academic Council within its Central Executive Committee in 1930, and in the same year the Academy formed a Tajik Scientific Commission.[45] Tajikistan boasted 13 research institutions by 1932, including an observatory established in that year. The 1930s also saw the opening of pedagogical and medical institutes in Dushanbe and Khojand. In 1932, the Tajikistan Base of the USSR Academy of Sciences was founded and was comprised of three sectors: geology/chemistry, biological sciences, and the arts.[46] In 1940, the USSR Academy finally established a Tajik Department, headed by Ye. N. Pavlovsky, a pioneer in parasitology and one of the first leading Russian scientists to join the Communist Party.[47] By 1950, the Tajik Department boasted 150 scientists, including 11 doctors and 71 candidates of science.[48] Finally, on April 14, 1951, the Tajik SSR Academy of Sciences opened.

The institutional history of the Turkmen Academy began in 1925 with the formation of the State Academic Council of the People's Enlightenment Commissariat.[49] In 1929, the Academy created a Turkmen SSR Research Commission.[50] During the 1930s, pedagogical, medical, and agriculture institutes were the first higher education institutions to appear in Turkmenistan. In 1937, a Scientific Affairs Committee, charged with coordinating all scientific issues in Turkmenistan, was formed under the Council of People's Commissariats of the Turkmen SSR.[51] On June 29, 1951, the Turkmenistan Academy formally opened.

Finally, in 1932, the Uzbek SSR government formed the Committee to Manage Scientific Research Institutions, which later became the Science Committee. In 1940, the USSR Academy of Sciences created an Uzbek Department, and on November 4, 1943 (ahead of Kazakhstan), the Uzbek SSR Academy of Sciences emerged. By 1983, the Uzbek Academy claimed 34 research institutes (including one the largest cybernetics institutions in the USSR; Kibernetika employed 16,000 people), 41 academicians, and 57 corresponding members.[52]

While the tenths of a per cent of each state's population engaged in the sciences (Figure 2.4) may seem too small a figure to merit attention, it should be kept in mind that this figure does not include several things. It does not include several other institutional settings for scientific research, does not include many engineers (of whom the USSR had the highest per capita level in the world), and excludes both future and retired scientists. The scope of these omissions can begin to be understood if one considers that the number of undergraduates in Tajikistan in 1985 receiving engineering degrees was 1322. While this class was not aberrantly large, the total number of engineers contained in the "scientific employees" category for that year in Tajikistan was 1197 (and in the next year it only rose to 1237).[53] Accordingly, the actual figure could be two or three (or more) times as high, something that only further research could elucidate. However, for comparison, the most developed states do not boast levels of scientists much higher than those cited above for Central Asia.

Indeed, while Central Asia boasted a Ph.D. level of between 0.015 and 0.05 per cent of the population, the comparable figure for the United States is only 0.021 per cent according to a 1995 National Science Foundation study.[54] Of course, large number of these U.S. Ph.D.s are immigrants to the United States, a benefit that Central Asia does not enjoy.

Moreover, investigating these same communities from a critical sociological perspective also yields surprisingly favorable interpretations of Central Asian science. Whereas scientific communities in the United States are seemingly constantly embattled over their inabilities to attract or include representative numbers of women and minorities in their ranks, Central Asia largely overcame this problem in the Soviet era. One recent National Research Council report states that women comprised only 16 per cent of the scientific labor force in the United States in 1988, and only 30 per cent of those receiving advanced degrees in the sciences were women.[55]

By contrast, while women have historically not commonly held second-tier leadership positions (i.e. institute directors) and have never held an academy

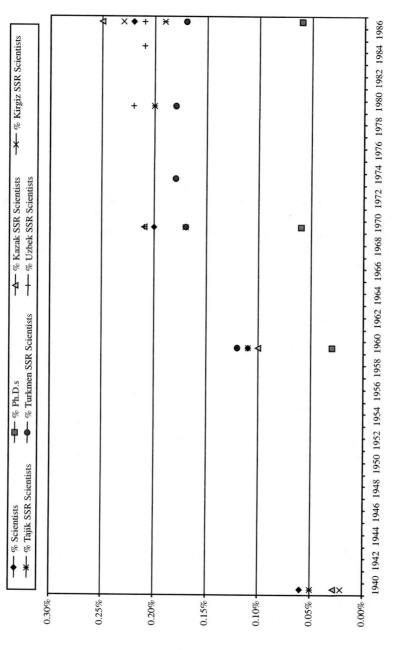

Figure 2.4 Per cent of population in the sciences (1940–1989).

presidency in Central Asia, their representative levels of employment and educational attainment exceed those of their peers in the United States. In Kazakhstan, in 1960, women already made up 36 per cent of the scientific labor force, and by 1970, they had increased their level of participation to 40 per cent.[56] While figures are not available for how many women received advanced degrees in Central Asia, the number of women in the group of people holding advanced degrees is available. In Kazakhstan, this figure grew from 24 per cent in 1960 to 27 per cent in 1970.[57] In Kyrgyzstan, where statistics are available over a more comparable period, the picture is even more impressive. From 1960 to 1986, the employment of women increased steadily, from 38 per cent in 1960 to 44 per cent in 1986, and in terms of holders of advanced degrees from 25 per cent to 32 per cent.[58]

In the more "conservative" and "Islamic" republics of the south, even better records are available, and the results they yield illustrate a Soviet society, at least in the sciences, quite different from what most scholars would expect and much more professionally egalitarian than its Western counterparts of the same period. In Tajikistan, while in 1939, 42 per cent of the scientific labor force was composed of women, by 1970 this figure fell to 36 per cent. However, from 1970 to 1985, this figure again rose steadily, finally reaching 40 per cent.[59] Also, its contingent of women among those holding advanced degrees increased from 23 per cent to 26 per cent between 1970 and 1980.[60] Even the worst results from Central Asia are impressive; from 1970 to 1988, the percentage of women scientists in Turkmenistan grew from 37 per cent to 40 per cent before falling again to 39 per cent.[62] Similarly, Uzbekistan's figures remain between 36 per cent and 37 per cent for the entire period between 1970 and 1987.[63] In both of these latter republics, the percentage of women among advanced degree holders held steady after 1970 at roughly 24 per cent.[64]

Moreover, in advancing women in the sciences, the Soviet system drew explicit attention to the issue. For example, in addition to fostering the development of the republican academies of science in Central Asia, Academician Nalivkin was also the author of a 1979 monograph *Our First Women Geologists*.[65] Thus, without making any claims about the actual level of Central Asian science, the gains made by Central Asia in a half century remain astounding.

Notably, the penultimate president of the Kyrgyz SSR Academy, Askar Akaev, became the first President of the Kyrgyz Republic. Four of the five Central Asian presidents hold Ph.D. level graduate degrees, primarily from Russian educational institutions, and all are multilingual. Yet, instead of affirming the importance of science in Central Asia, these leaders allowed independence to mark the beginning of a remarkable dismantling of scientific potential. Akaev was quick to marginalize the importance of the Kyrgyz Academy. On March 2, 1994, President Nazarbaev of Kazakhstan conducted the largest purge in the history of the Kazakhstan Academy, replacing its entire leadership. Two years later, he ended the academy's history as a semi-self-regulating and autonomous institution by folding the academy into the Ministry of Science and adding the academy presidency to the ministerial portfolio.

That same year, the UNDP Human Development Report for Kazakhstan, in its small section on science, estimated that levels of research and science in Kazakhstan would probably level off at 20 per cent of their Soviet level, with fundamental research at less than 7 per cent of its former scale.[66] The Kazakhstan government itself provides figures suggesting that it awarded funds for basic research in the sciences in 1997 that totaled far less than $1 million.[67]

In its 1997 report before the United Nations Commission on Sustainable Development, Uzbekistan frankly documented the effect of the transition period on human capital within its borders; it admitted to losing 10 per cent of its research and development scientific population every year for the first 4 years of independence.[68]

Perhaps most distressing, in December 1997, President Niyazov of Turkmenistan began an 8-month siege on the Turkmen Academy with massive reductions of technical staff and a new building for an Institute of Religion. Both *Nesil* (Turkmen language) and *Turkmenskaya iskra* (Russian language) state newspapers carried a very large article on June 26, 1998 by A. Poladov, editor of *Nesil*. In "Who Ruled the Soviet System?" Poladov attacks the "pseudohypothesis" that humans arose from apes and links communism and evolution together as foundations of the Soviet ideological brainwashing of the Turkmen people.[69] Later that day Niyazov ended his siege on the Turkmen Academy by issuing a terse resolution, with the effect of a coup de grace, to "abolish the central apparatus of the Academy of Sciences of Turkmenistan."[70]

While hopeful signs do spring up, like the 1997 award of the UNESCO Niels Bohr medal for fundamental research to Kazakhstan's outstanding physical chemist Yesen Abikenovich Bekturov, such incidents are on closer inspection no more than recognition of accomplishments that belong to the Soviet past.

However, in response to calls from the scientific community, long-range plans for recovery of the sciences are regularly proposed and adopted. For example, Kazakhstan's "Strategic Goals and Priorities for the Development of the Sciences until 2030" calls for four stages. Under this plan, adopted in 1998, Kazakhstan will come out of crisis by 2000, attain sustainable development by 2010, claim sustainable economic growth by 2020, and during the next decade will become "competitive,"[71] but that merely means that only then does the government envision increased funding for the sciences. Needless to say, such a long-term plan is a political way of abandoning the sciences.

Scientific communities in Central Asia did not universally equate the attainment of republic sovereignty with the decline of science. Yet, large numbers of them recognized that separation from Russia would mean a dramatic cut in funding, and many feared that brewing nationalist ambitions would result in a loss of interest in fundamental research (and a renaissance in revisionist history and linguistics). However, many of them also thought that joint research projects with the West, better access to scientific peers in other states, and Western support would actually improve conditions for science. A considerable number believed independence would facilitate local projects in hydrocarbon development, environmentally safer technology, and even the diversion of Siberian rivers to the Aral Sea. Finally, appreciable numbers of scientists could simply not imagine that any modern government would not support its scientists.

Accordingly, independence saw not only major declines in the scientific infrastructure. It also witnessed attempts to continue regional progress along the Soviet continuum of scientific development. For example, in 1992, the Kazakhstan Academy of Sciences founded a Western Kazakhstan Department (since closed), and in 1993 an Eastern Department to complement its Soviet-era Southern and Central departments. The Western Department was created in recognition of the support needed by the hydrocarbon industry of this sparsely populated region's two academicians, 38 doctors, and 200 candidates, as well as its six institutions of higher education and 47 research facilities.[72]

While the actions of local scientists may not have been enough to stem the decline of science, the influence of foreign donors and governments may have facilitated the political marginalization of science. Every large[73] state donor and foundation that provided funds or experts to Central Asia in this decade, with the exception of the Soros Foundation, did so within the framework of or building on the experience of existing programs for post-colonial developing states. Such programs arrived in Central Asia eager to conduct literacy programs, initiate municipal sewage works, and bring civilization to Central Asia. Despite initial reinforcement, in the form of a lack of English speakers who act as an easy barometer of development in other places, of the presupposition that Central Asia was essentially the same as other postcolonial areas, the singularities of Central Asia reduced the relevance of many development programs.

Although "capacity-building"[74] is a cornerstone of development programs, in Central Asia virtually no funds went to support the maintenance of scientific capacity. Support of the impressive educational and research structure in Central Asia failed to materialize, because of donor discomfort in acknowledging the successes of the USSR and because such a developed system was beyond the pale of development agency paradigms. In either case, prejudices against a USSR that no longer existed or an Asian Muslim area beyond the experience of the developers left the development (or even simple maintenance) of science in the lurch in Central Asia. In turbulent fields such as genetics, ignoring the scientific infrastructure for even 2 years had the effect of making that part of the scientific community virtually obsolescent from a global perspective. In less turbulent fields, a decade of disrepair has effected a similar outcome.

In the many consultations representatives of foundation and state donors organized with Central Asian governments, the focus of "development" was squarely on democratization and market reforms. The message of these Westerners (and, to a lesser extent, Japanese) was that political and economic reform would create wealth and stability in Central Asia. The concentration of virtually all attention (both verbal and monetary) on these two aspects of society (law and economics) implicitly led to the devaluation of the productive and knowledge sectors of society. Non-economics education and science/technology became tertiary concerns of both the state and of large and influential parts of society.

This sea change in attitude overhauled the educational landscape. In qualitative terms, it meant that international relations, law, and various manifestations of business administration (economics, marketing, and management) began to attract the most talented youth, thereby replacing math, physics, and other sciences as the prestige disciplines. Quantitatively, it meant a sharp decline in numbers of students in the sciences and scientists overall. During the Soviet era (and the late Russian Empire as well) politicization of the social sciences consistently drove talented students with primary interests in the humanities into the relative academic freedom of the natural sciences.[75]

Numbers of practicing physicists, mathematicians, biologists, chemists, engineers, and agricultural scientists all declined by roughly 50 per cent between 1990 and 1996 in Kazakhstan, that on the heels of less dramatic declines from 1985 to 1990. Better off sciences, such as geology and medicine, saw declines of only 40 per cent during the same period, while numbers of literature scholars increased by 7 per cent, veterinarians by 14 per cent and lawyers by 50 per cent over the same period.[76]

THE BRAIN DRAIN

The Turkmenistan government shut down Ariana, that state's largest Internet service provider in summer 2000, in order to lessen competition for the state-run Turkmentelecom. As a result, Ariana's managers, who were simultaneously the holders of multiple technical graduate degrees and leaders in Turkmenistan's most well-known environmental NGO (Catena), initiated plans to emigrate to Canada.[77].

While it is well accepted that capital flight is a major reason for the crippling effects of transition in the former Soviet Union, largely ignored is the fact that this capital flight is not restricted to physical capital. Human capital flight may be of greater import for the future of the region than flights of dollars. In general, flows of capital are always accompanied by flows of people, flows of human capital.[78] This has certainly been the case, the extreme case, with the former Soviet Union, whose two largest republics (Russia and Kazakhstan) are depopulating due to emigration. Post-Soviet emigrants generally represent the more highly educated sectors of the former USSR, a trend that only adheres to, and probably exceeds, the global norm.[79] Despite devalorization of immigrants in the popular mind as disadvantaged and disempowered, naturalized U.S. citizens earn 40 per cent more than native-born Americans.[80] However, not only financial opportunities coax former Soviets to emigrate. One important reason for emigration is also schooling, a reaction against the decline in the quality of local schools.

Trends such as high birth rates and high suicide rates, the latter especially applicable to Kazakhstan,[81] can exacerbate the effects of brain drain. Except in Kazakhstan, which lost 10 per cent of its population, the region shows distressingly high birth rates[82] and increasing death rates. Accordingly, in this decade the demographic structure of the Central Asian states has skewed remarkably in the direction of having a majority of the population under 18 years old. However, while the birth rates throughout Central Asia are high, they are declining. Taking the five country region as a whole, the weighted average fertility rate has dropped from 3.8 in 1990 to 3.1 in 1999,[83] which, ignoring emigration, represents 39 per cent of the birthrate reduction needed to stabilize population in the region.

Through one lens, this reduction in birthrates is a hopeful sign for sustainability. However, by definition, every child born in Central Asia is uneducated. Substantial resources will need to be invested to build that child's human capital. In contrast, also virtually by definition, every emigrant from Central Asia is well educated. On July 10, 2000, BBC analyst Stephen Dalziel reported that the reason London's former Soviet population has skyrocketed is because educated former Soviets have such an easy time finding high-paying jobs in the United Kingdom.[84]

Part of the region's experience with emigration and brain drain echoes what is now expected of foreign aid programs.[85] By opening doors between societies, such programs now as a rule provoke increased emigration from the developing state to the developed state. While foreign aid was envisioned primarily as a means to build the capacities of the recipient states, it has partially had the opposite effect. Foreign aid has also exacerbated emigration from Central Asia in general, and to the United States in particular.[86] Accordingly, notwithstanding good intentions, the effects of Western advice and aid in Central Asia have lowered the region's stock of human capital.

EVALUATING THE ERAS OF HUMAN CAPITAL IN CENTRAL ASIA

> Today, Kazakhstan provides qualified scientific and technical assistance to peoples in countries of Asia and Africa, Europe and Latin America. Every year the republic sends hundreds of specialists to dozens of countries.[87]

These words, written almost 20 years ago by Kazakhstan's current president, when read in the present encapsulate the fate of human capital in Central Asia. Ironically, when Western donors claim development successes in the developing world, the kinds of accomplishments of which they are especially proud are along the lines of those produced by the Soviet Union in human capital.

Figure 2.5 illustrates the declines in human capital now underway as part of the transition period. The sad reversal of human capital fortunes in Central Asia is exemplified in the fate of the Declaration of Alma-Ata, one of the key, if not the key, documents in the modern global movement for public health spearheaded by the World Health Organization. In 1978, the USSR hosted an International Conference on Primary Health Care in Alma-Ata specifically because it considered the Kazak SSR's capital to be a showcase of development triumph. Given the current situation, it is sadly ironic to look back two decades, especially since the central achievement of the Declaration of Alma-Ata is its aspiration for "the attainment by all peoples of the world by the year 2000 of a level of health that will permit them to lead a socially and economically productive life."[88] Compared

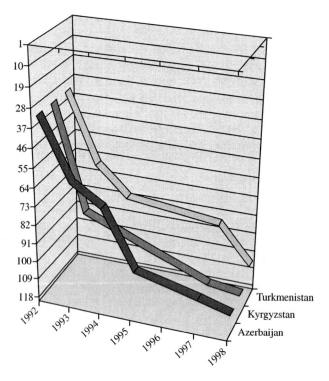

Figure 2.5 Decline in human development indicators in three Central Asian states since independence: rankings out of 174 states.

Source: Author's modeling of data from UNDP Human Development Reports.

to 1978, few places on earth have realized less progress towards the aspirations of the 1978 Declaration of Alma-Ata than Almaty, Kazakhstan.

While poverty is not new in Central Asia, Soviet poverty, especially as experienced by post-World War II generations, possessed a character different than post-Soviet poverty. Despite its justifiably famous failings, the Soviet state was proud, and with remarkable consistency, it mobilized resources to ensure that its citizens did not die of hunger and did enjoy a minimum level of state services. In the post-Soviet era, the fundamental character and mission of the state changed. With abandonment of the totalizing ideology of the USSR, the new states of the region also accept the worst human consequences of poverty with greater complacency. This poverty connects to non-sustainable development because of the potent way in which it exacerbates other social and environmental problems. Poverty goes far in explaining why endangered species are extirpated, why corruption is so difficult to eradicate, and why regional competition for foreign investment may be leading to a "race to the bottom" in environmental standards and corporate accountability.

Jeffrey Sachs recently lamented that a third of the world is disconnected from technological innovation, and he explicitly includes Central Asia in that disadvantaged third of the world.[89] He is probably correct. However, he is correct at least in substantial part because, in 1991, development organizations, influenced in no small part by the efforts of Jeffrey Sachs himself, decided to ignore the scientific potential of the former Soviet Union. Were Sachs to have the opportunity now to retread the 1990s, he would, judging by his recent work, exclaim the importance of two things at which he explicitly scoffed previously. These are the rule of law and the wonderful opportunities that existed in 1991 when Central Asia was full of molecular biologists, computer programmers, engineers, and physicists. At that time, the Soviet scientific and technology establishment did essay to point these conditions out to their governments and donors. Led by confident Western advisors like Sachs, governments chastised them for not understanding economics.

In 1991, the states of Central Asia may have been capable of making investments that would have allowed them to create high-technology islands of expertise for their economy (the kind that most economists now recognize as crucial in separating the developed and NIC economies from the rest of the world). However, the success of any such investments would have depended on applying the scientific and technology endowments of Central Asia to economic applications in a way capable of overcoming the shortcomings of Soviet science. These shortcomings included, among other things, a lack of incentives to develop a culture or practice of innovation, a stark separation between research and teaching, and a stark separation between fundamental science and technological applications.

While even the most successful transition of the science and technology sector from the Soviet to a market economy would certainly have involved substantial dislocations, the best mentors in this process would probably have been the Americans, the Europeans, and the Japanese. Yet, outside of conversion of military installations and modest efforts to provide research funding to scientists to prevent emigration to developing state weapons programs, little effort was made by donors to effect such a transition, and certainly no effort even remotely the scale of that targeting restructuring of the financial systems of the post-Soviet states. At decade's end, with the loss of the best personnel, the loss of ten years, the loss of equipment (much sold abroad on the gray market), and the decimation of educational pathways for young scholars, these areas are no longer in the same position to secure economically significant places in global science and technology markets.[90]

3   Formal organizational capital: governments and markets

> ...it would be much wiser to manage the processes of liberalization and privatization at a pace compatible with the speed of human capital development.... We speak of building institutions, but in reality, they must be learned.[1]

As described in the Introduction, of the types of capital analyzed in this work, organizational capital is the least appreciated and least recognized in scholarly circles. Yet, this lack of scholarly deference is purely semantic; it does not mean that little is known about organizational capital. Indeed, key catchwords of contemporary ideologies – capitalism, communism, democracy, rule of law, subsidiarity – are, primarily, issues of organizational capital.[2] That scholars conflate, at least in the case of the former USSR, these catchwords with stocks of other kinds of capital is largely a consequence of two trends. First, non-economics scholarship rarely frames governments and markets as systems in which decision making is impacted by implicit pricing systems. Second, as is still true of the bulk of English language work about the former Soviet world, ideological allegiances inevitably produce distorted depictions of the complex relationships between stocks of capital. Indeed, only as a second order question, and therefore by no means of necessity, does democracy have much to do with human rights, communism much to do with environmental degradation, or capitalism much to do with amassed wealth.

So, we require a clearer definition of organizational capital in order to tease apart its assets and impacts from the normative aspirations (i.e. sustainability, human rights, and eradication of poverty) of both scholars and policymakers. As the first step towards creating such a definition, I omit democracy from this list of normative aspirations for the reason that "democracy" is probably not a normative aspiration, despite its rhetorical deployment as such. Democracy may be, empirically and theoretically, a very good way to achieve compliance with human rights, but this situation is of itself not sufficient for deployment of democracy as a proxy for human rights, for "black-boxing" the link between democracy and human rights.[3] To wit, democracy and communism are not only not the only possible types of government – they are also not uniformly practiced.[4] Proponents of democracy, read closely, rarely argue for democracy for democracy's sake but rather for democracy as a proxy for some other aspiration, a confusion that rests at the core of a justification for a clearer recognition of the importance of organizational capital. This confusion also explains why democracy advocates so readily disregard democratic outcomes that they do not like (i.e. Hitler's 1933 election or the Soviet electorate's 1991 vote to preserve the USSR[5]) as somehow non-democratic. It also explains why they consider it appropriate to nullify such decisions using undemocratic means as diverse as war, courts,[6] and embargoes.

Democracy, like all other expressions of organizational capital is a means of organization alone; without belittling the importance of process, limits exist to efforts to imbue process with either moral significance or infallibility. Accordingly, as a working definition, organizational capital refers expressively to the governing rules and various organizations within a community and refers functionally to the ways in which these rules and organizations shape incentives related to actions intended to impact and shape the social and natural environment.

Instead of being a trivial or avocational aspect of humanity, because of the limitations imposed by scarcity and the laws of thermodynamics, such actions (reflexive and unreflexive) epitomize the material dimension of human existence. Thus, human lives proceed through a succession of efforts to manipulate the natural environment, and human lives in communities proceed through a succession of efforts to manipulate both natural and social environments. At the risk of sounding tautological, it should be stressed that human survival (at the level of either individuals or communities) largely depends upon the consequences of these efforts. Moving from topography to action, we can define assets of organizational capital as the various incentives at play on individuals to engage in or abstain from specific actions aimed at manipulating the natural or social environment.

However, this definition is only half-complete without an appreciation of the interplay between individual perceptions and organizational rules.[7] While the general premises of a rational approach to human behavior[8] do not preclude nor are they disproved by the concept of bounded rationality (arising from incomplete information) or alleged examples of irrational behavior,[9] they have been more deeply challenged by the fact that rationality is linked to context.[10] Divergent contexts trace their roots to the divergent organizations and rules of communities, and, hence, contextual rationality is a concept at the heart of an understanding of organizational capital. Accordingly, the dynamic feedback between, on the one hand, actual and perceived human options on courses of action and, on the other hand, the rules and organizations of the social environment constitute the core assets of a stock of organizational capital.[11] This feedback also helps explain both the limits to and foundation for social science approaches based on assumptions of rationality.[12] When it comes to human behavior, for the purposes of the social sciences, all evaluations of rationality should ideally be weighed with all organizational capital assets on the scale.

Consequently, we should be able, theoretically, to evaluate a stock of organizational capital as the aggregate of these assets/incentives, keeping in mind the Introduction's admonition to define asset in an agnostic manner. As the "active" or "acquired" constituents of capital, assets may readily be liabilities or, phrased colloquially, bad incentives. In this conception, a degraded stock of organizational capital need not necessarily be one in which the variety of incentives and options at play are fewer, only one in which "bad" incentives assume precedence.

Yet, in a modern society, the converse is not necessarily true. Merely "good" incentives are probably insufficient to meet the organizational demands of complex modern societies; a certain amount of complexity and diversity of incentives is a requirement for the demands of such a society. At the very least, the diverse externalities produced by high resource-throughput modern industries and narrow employment specializations demand complex sets of incentives.[13] Proceeding from this assertion, despite the difficult questions arising about how to evaluate and aggregately assess organizational capital assets, three qualitative components of a stock of organizational capital are relevant to comprehensive capital: efficiency, power, and spillover. Efficiency refers to the degree to which organizational assets prevent deadweight losses, the degree to which resources are utilized without waste. Power refers to the impact of technology and organizational complexity in increasing the scale of human potential to impact natural and social environments. Finally, spillover refers to the impacts of organizational capital on other capital stocks, such as the effects of a nationwide system of school testing on human capital, of stock markets on physical capital, and of free trade guarantees on natural capital.

While efficiency, power, and spillover constitute benchmarks for evaluating a stock of organizational capital, they do not speak to the nature of the incentives that vivify organizational capital. As stated above, these incentives relate generally to actions intended to impact the social and natural environments. More specifically, these incentives are what shape reactions to, channel incentives to engage in or desist from, and engender predictability about the consequences of such actions. While the previous paragraphs suggest obliquely how these reactions are related to rationality and the relationship between modern societies and the need for a broad array of incentives, thus far this analysis has not touched on the critical role of predictability.

To illustrate the importance of predictability, people would never have engaged consistently in (relied on) agriculture, if they were not convinced of the predictability of their efforts, both in terms of climate and in terms of risks of appropriation from other people and animals. Similarly, people engage in non-agricultural endeavors only when provided with organizational guarantees (contracts, food distribution networks, stable currencies, etc.) that other people will, directly or indirectly, provide them with sustenance. Amartya Sen revealed that the great famines of recent centuries occurred largely due to hoarding (a breakdown in faith in predictability), not because of failed crops.[14] "[S]ome of the worst famines have taken place with no significant decline in food availability per head."[15] Thus, the very nature of human hunger has changed over the course of human civilization from an event illustrating the degradation or stochasticity of flows of natural capital to one of degradation of organizational capital assets. In other words, modern famines occur primarily due to breakdowns in organizational capital, not natural capital.

This example highlights the fact that, in modern societies organizational capital does not consist alone of elegant Weberian structural frameworks for administrative governments or corporations. If people within these structures lack faith in the predictability of future payoffs, and if people in these structures do not expect that deviations from the rules of these structures will be punished, the elegance of the structures will not impart functional viability. Thus, predictability is a core component of organizational capital that links organizations and rules.

Predictability occurs in two forms, sure good things and sure bad things. If I know my crop will be appropriated by a neighbor who promises that no such event will occur, I enjoy the benefit of my knowledge. I am better off with this knowledge than without it. In counterpoint, a person who can rely on the promises of her neighbor enjoys the benefit of having more personal and economic choices of action. Moreover, not only is she better off, but her neighbor probably is as well for reasons connected to comparative advantage.[16] Accordingly, predictability in the form of knowing that another person will act cooperatively is probably more important economically than is knowing which potential joint venturers will not act cooperatively. This kind of predictability is described in various disciplines as morality, trust,[17] or the key to solving the Prisoners' Dilemma when Nash equilibrium rests in payoff representations whose sum is lower than the best possible aggregate payoff.[18]

While predictability and trust are important, without appropriate incentives organizational capital will still fail to reach its full potential. An agreement between two neighbors to cooperate in principle is hollow; both want to know how exactly the fruits of cooperation will be split. Incentives speak to the quantities and qualities of the payoffs of cooperation, and the establishment of proper incentives is important since the flip side to any cooperation payoff is a defection payoff. Even the most "moral" neighbor may essay to undermine an agreement that is patently unfair or whose breach gives him a winning lottery ticket.

North employs a complementary analytic framework in his work in economic history; central to his work is the assertion that organizations reduce uncertainty by providing dependable and efficient frameworks for economic exchange.[19] Viewing the Soviet period through such a lens, I argue that one of the reasons why the Soviet Union worked as well as it did is because its post World War II era enjoyed a feeling of predictability unknown under Lenin or Stalin. Sovietologists labeled this emergence of stronger organizational capital as the appearance of an unwritten social contract, beginning under Nikita Khrushchev, between the state and the citizens.[20] In return for government legitimacy, the state would abandon Stalinist scale repression and provide social guarantees to society. However, one of the reasons why the Soviet Union worked as poorly as it did is because the incentives it provided to its citizens were not appropriate to produce either economic dynamism or efficiency. Unmotivated workers and little innovation were hallmarks of the Soviet economy.

Continuing this mode of analysis, this Chapter reviews elements of formal organizational capital in modern Central Asia in an attempt to recast the corrupt, authoritarian, and oligarchic failures of the reform period. It essays to recast them from events of high human drama rooted in murky cultural traits to events stemming from rational behavior and leading to degraded organizational capital. The

Chapter roughly divides formal organizational capital into its public and private aspects, its relationship to public goods and to private goods. While the boundaries between public and private goods are far from clearly marked, this rough dichotomy captures the essence of the consensus aspirations of international donors to build organizational capital in the developing world, to improve governance and to free markets.

Salient differences between approaches appear when one turns to the question of how to ensure the integrity of the organizations responsible for managing public and private goods, but these differences, importantly, do not spill outside the consensus described above. Thus, while Europeans praise parliaments, Americans valorize a different set of democratic institutions. While Americans praise deregulation, Europeans are more hesitant to expose people to risks of market failure. However, in both cases, whatever specific tactics are chosen to ensure the integrity of organizations, law is the instrument through which integrity is (allegedly) ensured. Therefore, market failures in the United States are often violations of antitrust or securities laws, and corruption scandals in European states are most frequently framed likewise as violations of the law. The explicit universal appeal of law and the implicit universal acceptance of organizations as components of modern societies undergird this Chapter's argument that the true currency of both effective governments and effective markets is to be found in strong organizational capital assets.

KALDOR-HICKS AND GLOBALIZATION

Returning to the efficiency, power, and spillover criteria for evaluating stocks of organizational capital, I largely leave an analysis of spillover to the final section of this Chapter. Accordingly, much of this Chapter restricts itself to the efficiency of current organizations in Central Asia and the question of whether efficiency has improved in the reform period. I take for granted the raw power of organizational capital in Central Asia.

After all, the republics in question survived and were shaped by Stalinist-era dislocations and were constituent parts of one of the world's major industrial, military, and agricultural states. Despite the problems of the Soviet state, despite ideological considerations, the USSR operated in general as a modernist administrative state. It did not operate as a "failed state," like those seen in many parts of the developing world. Many important decisions came as the result of the efforts of a variety of specialized expert state agencies, and implementation of these decisions occurred through a system of local governments, courts, and law enforcement agencies. Extensive information about state activities (yet, misleading and selective information) was contained in the pages of state newspapers and other media outlets. Every day this state managed to feed, clothe, educate and care for its citizens. Starvation, illiteracy, and gross poverty had largely disappeared by the time of the USSR's demise. In counterpoint to its deserved reputation for inflicting serious burdens on its citizens, especially its more politically active citizens, the Soviet state also mobilized frequently to mitigate natural disasters and prevent human suffering from material deprivation. At the heart of the success of these efforts was an appreciable level of organizational capital.

Theorists of institutions strive to effect reforms that make participants in systems better off. Such reforms are called Pareto efficiency. A Pareto improvement in which each participant is better off would be a Pareto superior improvement. However, especially when systems involve many or heterogeneous participants, very few reforms will or could actually meet the criterion of leaving all participants better off. Thus, potential Pareto improvements are changes that increase aggregate welfare, even though some participants may be left worse off than before. The challenge in pursuing potential Pareto improvements is to design incentives for those made better off to compensate those made worse off, in effect engineering Pareto efficiency. Lawyers and economists refer to a potential Pareto improvement as Kaldor-Hicks efficiency; in reform shorthand Kaldor-Hicks allows reformers to satisfy themselves with potential Pareto improvements. Kaldor-Hicks is the "black box" of the economics and legal community that this section seeks to open. The reasons for challenging the viability of this development black box concern not only the empirical failures of the post-Soviet transition; rather, this black box is simply no longer viable for state-level analyses in an increasingly globalized world. In a world in which both capital and people are mobile, many Kaldor-Hicks assumptions for state-level welfare unravel.

The implications of this mobility of people and capital (and not just goods) reveal the fundamental errors of reason of those who embrace free trade as a moral imperative or as a proven key to wealth. The theories of comparative advantage behind free trade correctly describe free trade as a mechanism through which to increase the aggregate physical capital of humanity. In the language of this essay, free trade promises a potential Pareto improvement, ignoring spillover. Remembering spillover, free trade (more correctly and insightfully called deregulated international commerce[21]) also encourages, even demands, increased resource throughput and increased depletion of stocks of natural capital, even if free trade practices result in increases in efficiency of use of natural capital. Thus, even at a global scale and even before considering the implication of the assumptions concerning the "potential" side of Kaldor-Hicks efficiency, free trade is at least a challenge to, if not a clear barrier to, achievement of sustainability. For the same reasons that we would choose to regulate power utilities or chemical factories, we should be wary about the consequences of free trade at the global level.

However, more pertinent to this discussion, free trade rests upon the oft-explicit assumption that all states will benefit from free trade; this assumption is a fallacy of composition. There exists no evidence that this paradigm example of the conflation of Kaldor-Hicks efficiency with Pareto efficiency is actually the case, theoretical or otherwise. "Otherwise," in recent years leaders of developing states have essayed to make it abundantly clear to Western leaders that globalization has not yielded benefits to the most needy. Indeed, globalization contains no guarantees of equitable distribution among states. So, free trade proponents may accurately predict that Uzbekistan will increase world stocks of physical capital if it abandons production of certain foodstuffs and consumer goods in order to concentrate on exports of gold and oil. However, that does not preclude the chance that Uzbekistan's citizens will become impoverished as a result. No economic law dictates that this move will lower food prices in Uzbekistan, especially in cases where dozens of developing states compete to sell the same commodity to monopsistic developed states and where capital is mobile. Mobile capital can be (and frequently is) invested or stored in less volatile or more auspicious corporations and banks in Western states.

Accordingly, globalization is altering the efficacy of development interventions. Development programs that were a success two decades ago may be untenable today, and such concerns find considerable support in the recent experience of Central Asia. For example a natural resource export strategy successful two decades ago would now face quite a different environment; margins are lower and competition among sellers more fierce than before. Especially for landlocked states emerging from an autarkic economy, globalization and free trade are not panaceas. The classical free trade paradigm, assumes that people and capital are not mobile. Thus, if international migration ceased and capital was restrained within national borders, free trade's promise of reducing global poverty would be more viable.

Yet, ironically, free trade proponents also advocate (often as fundamental rights) freedom of movement for capital and people, movements that undermine the theoretical underpinnings of comparative advantage's relationship to the transition from Kaldor-Hicks to true Pareto efficiency. To illustrate, as Kazakhstan's best assets of human capital emigrate and its revenues from hydrocarbons sit in the foreign personal bank accounts and stock portfolios of its ruling elite, where is globalization's benefit to Kazakhstanis? The situation would be different if the country now contained both all of its highly educated native population and stockpiles of revenue (even if held by a corrupt nomenklatura) from foreign trade that had to be invested or held within Kazakhstan.

Indeed, emigrants from Kazakhstan (and most other developing states) are more highly educated than the country average, and autocratic leaders and oligarchs of developing countries tend not to keep their wealth in country. There are few private investments within Kazakhstan known to have been made by President Nazarbaev, whose personal wealth is enormous,[22] alleged widely in the former USSR to reach into the billions of dollars. Similar situations hold for Uzbekistan's Karimov and Turkmenistan's Niyazov, both of whom may be, personally, billionaires and both of whose most talented compatriots continue to flee to the West.

Accordingly, without contesting the aggregate potential economic benefits of globalization, it is theoretically possible for a country or society to lose much more to globalization than would be gained by either a controlled exposure to global free trade or by remaining in a state of autarky.[23] Ironically, stock market holdings, levels (and kinds) of immigration, and the general economy of the United States in the past decade suggest that globalization even works to further enrich the richest states. The relationships between the poles of globalism (autarky and free trade), on the one hand, and between the poles of post-Kaldor-Hicks reforms (equitable distribution and arrogation), on the other hand, are the lenses through which the following pages examine recent events impacting the governments and markets of Central Asia.

FORMAL ORGANIZATIONS: THE DEMOCRATIC ADMINISTRATIVE STATE

An irony of constitutional democracy (participatory governance and rule of law) is that its elevation to the status of a normative ideal, most recently in the *United Nations Millennium Declaration*,[24] coincides with the virtual disappearance of what Bruce Ackerman calls constitutional politics.[25] Rarely anymore are constitutions expressions of a national voice or aspirations or the product of the transformative impact of a popular movement as much as they are an administrative act whose genesis and negotiation differs little from that of any other law. Perhaps nowhere is this more true than in Central Asia; constitutions have appeared in Central Asia, but nowhere have they evolved as an expression of national consensus or meaningfully been impacted by non-governmental forces.

One example is Kazakhstan, where Nursultan Nazarbaev came to power in 1988. Kazakhstan's 1993 constitution was both not the product of public dialogue and, simultaneously, it was a generally fair blueprint for a democratic state with separation of powers.[26] However, this very separation of powers vexed Nazarbaev's administration, and, gradually, Nazarbaev's administration cultivated enmity towards the other constitutional organs of the state. Twice in the early years of independence, Nazarbaev dismissed the legislature for failing to endorse the government's policies. In 1995, with his power consolidating, Nazarbaev managed, prior to the dismissal of the sitting legislature, to convince the legislature to confer on the president the power to adopt acts having the force of law, even to adopt, unilaterally, the "constitutional laws" that required supermajorities for passage in the Kazakhstan legislature. Subsequently, Nazarbaev illegally put forward a new constitution. This new constitution abolished the Constitutional Court (and thereby judicial review of presidential acts), and it established a legislature institutionally incapable of acting as a check on presidential power (and therefore really capable only of serving as an "advisory committee"[27] to the president). Nazarbaev became the functional equivalent of an autocrat with this constitution; accordingly, the 1995 Kazakhstan Constitution is one of the darkest moments in organizational design in post-Soviet Central Asia. Figure 3.1 illustrates the textual failure of the Central Asian republics to establish meaningful balance of powers within their constitutions.

Outside of Kazakhstan, in no other Central Asian republic has a second post-Soviet constitution appeared; however, if it were to appear, it would almost certainly now copy in large part the autocratic tendencies of the Kazakhstan Constitution. In all the republics, the current constitution arose in the period

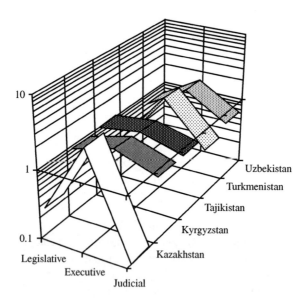

Figure 3.1 Separation of powers in Central Asian constitutions as of 1996.

between 1992 and 1994 without substantial public input.[28] Amendments to these constitutions have likewise been engineered and discussed without much public input, and their usual purpose has been to insulate the administrations of sitting presidents from the limitations imposed by constitutional regimes. In other words, constitutional reform in Central Asia is a synonym for the legalization of authoritarianism. One of the great ironies of the reform and transition period is that, despite the facade of turbulence and re-engineering, there has been little turnover among the members of the governing elite. The average Central Asian head of state has been in office for more years than his country has existed.

The durability of the sitting presidents has relied on attacks on the integrity of core democratic institutions, such as elections and constitutions. A review of post-Soviet constitutions and elections in Central Asia reveals the extent to which the integrity of governmental organizational capital may have declined even below that of general Soviet times, much less the Perestroika period. For example, in Kazakhstan, Nazarbaev's proposal of the 1995 Constitution coincided with his illegal[29] Referendum on the President, asking the electorate whether they wanted Nazarbaev to continue as president.

During the tense period during which Nazarbaev orchestrated this disenfranchisement of all non-presidential political components of the Kazakhstan state, Western development agencies and embassies tacitly supported Nazarbaev and even threatened to deport their nationals who spoke out against Nazarbaev.[30] Western interests in both (perceived) guarantees of stability and in hydrocarbon investments lay behind this culpability.[31] Through this referendum and the new constitution, Nazarbaev avoided holding a presidential election and could claim in 1999 that he was standing for the first time for election as president, despite the 1993 and 1995 constitutions' identical limitation of two 5-year terms in office for the president. Nazarbaev counts his 1991 Soviet-era election and his 1995 referendum mandate as grandfathered into the status of null acts under the 1995 Constitution. Through such manipulation, Nazarbaev will likely sit in office until 2009.

Similarly an early darling of the West, coming into office in 1990 and winning a popular election in 1991, Askar Akaev has employed constitutional amendments in order to extend his term. Akaev was nearly universally celebrated by Westerners in the early 1990s as possessing an unbending commitment to democracy and rule of law. Yet, when faced with local opposition Akaev also disbanded the legislature in 1994 and followed this act with a weakening of the judiciary and an illegal[32] referendum on amendments to the constitution. These amendments substantially weakened the powers and structure of the legislature. As would be the case in Kazakhstan a year later, "the international community colluded" to head off criticism of Akaev's policies or his government as anti-democratic.[33] Akaev will also sit in office well into the twenty-first century. In a vivid illustration of the perceived durability of the authoritarian regimes in Kazakhstan and Kyrgyzstan, the 1998 wedding between the children of Nazarbaev and Akaev was called, throughout the former Soviet Union, Central Asia's "royal wedding."

Turkmenistan's Saparmurat Niyazov (a.k.a. Turkmenbashi), in power since 1985, is not tainted by such a track record of disdain for the constitution of his state. The Turkmenistan Constitution, from the beginning, never offered the legislative or judicial branches any real powers to act as checks or balances, reflecting the level of Niyazov's consolidation of power by 1991. Akaev and Nazarbaev only attained equivalent levels of consolidation in the mid-1990s. While the Turkmenistan judiciary is patently weak, the legislature is made ineffectual because so many of the powers traditionally conceived of as legislative really rest in a constitutional meta-structure called the People's Council[34] that is controlled by the president and that is in form and practice substantially indistinguishable from a feudal royal court.

The early basis of Niyazov's popular support was his re-invention of the Soviet social contract; in exchange for support, Niyazov's "Ten Years to Prosperity" program promised the citizenry that the end of the decade would bring them Western levels of wealth, including a Mercedes in every driveway. Now that the decade is over, it is clear that the Soviet social contract actually delivered more than did the Turkmenbashi social contract. *Prima facie*, Turkmenistan has no strong claim to being a constitutional democracy, and practice within Turkmenistan only confirms this conclusion.

Off to a more rocky start than the other Central Asian authoritarians, Islam Karimov faced palpable opposition during the December 1991 presidential election, especially from a collection of popular movements, the most powerful of which was Birlik ("Unity"). He had been in power only 2 years at the time of this election, becoming First Secretary in 1989 and being appointed President by the legislature in 1990. However, since Karimov was popular and since opposition candidates found their efforts frustrated at every turn by the government, Karimov won by a large margin and then set out to dismantle or co-opt these opposition movements. As with his peers in the other republics, Karimov had consolidated power by the mid-1990s; in 1995 a referendum extended his term in office from 1997–2000, obviating the scheduled 1997 presidential elections and violating the Uzbekistan Constitution's provisions on presidential elections. In 2000, Karimov again won re-election; although, as with Nazarbaev, this third popular election counts as only the first under the 1992 Constitution. Karimov may actually remain in office 21 years, until 2010.

While each Central Asian republic now advertises itself as a constitutional democracy, no state, with the outside exception of Tajikistan, amassed over its first decade of existence a credible claim to either the respect for constitutions or deference to popular sovereignty that symbolizes constitutional democracy. Only in Tajikistan is the current president a relative neophyte; Emomali Rakhmonov has only been in office since 1993, and he is the third post-Soviet leader in Tajikistan, succeeding Rakhman Nabiev and Akbarsho Iskandarov. Similarly, only in Tajikistan is the transition period invested with meaningful symbols of a break with the Soviet past; unfortunately these have come at the high cost of a lengthy civil war. However, the national consensus around the need for peace and an actual national government that since 1998 shares power between the warring sides infuses Tajikistan political life with a kind of democracy and dialogue almost entirely missing in the other states. Unlike his peers, Rakhmonov was elected under the current constitution in 1994 and in 1999, in problematic and, the second time, uncontested elections, meaning that he should leave office in 2004.[35]

The foregoing falls far short of cataloguing the quality of elections (local, parliamentary, and presidential), the strength of the judiciary, the efficacy of checks and balances, and the place of administrative agencies in the political systems of the Central Asian states. Such an accounting would be quite long and quite tilted toward a listing of failures of process and the law; as such, the foregoing sets the tone of and is symptomatic of such a more nuanced accounting. For example, many of the tendencies leading to disruption of organizational capital show up in the environmental administrative sphere.

Perhaps the best example is Kazakhstan's state environmental community, which has been so much in organizational turmoil that it has been unable to operate as an effective part of the administrative state. Upon attaining independence, Kazakhstan boasted a Ministry of Ecology and Bioresources; in the past decade this ministry has been renamed, re-organized, re-located, or merged with other ministries on average once a year. For recent examples, in 1997 the Ministry of Ecology and Bioresources merged with remnants of the Ministry of Energy and Natural Resources and its Minister Nikolai Baev was replaced with the geologist head of the latter ministry; the new ministry carried the name Ministry of Ecology and Natural Resources. In 1998, the ministry moved to Kokshetau. In 1999, its portfolio expanded substantially at the expense of the Ministry of

Agriculture and the ministry's name changed to the Ministry of Natural Resources and Environmental Protection. Finally, in late 2000, responsibility for mineral resources was removed from the ministry and vested in a resuscitated Ministry of Energy and Mineral Resources; Andar Shukputov replaced Serikbek Daukeev as minister.

In Kokshetau, the current Ministry of Natural Resources and Environmental Protection is far from either of Kazakhstan's "capitals" (Almaty and Astana), has lost most of its staff, and is now charged simultaneously and contradictorily both with exploiting and conserving natural resources. Analogous ministries and state committees in the other republics share similar, sometimes even more dramatic, histories. As if to outdo Kazakhstan, in January 2001, Kyrgyzstan slashed the staff of its environmental ministry, canned the existing minister, and exiled the institution and newly appointed Minister Eshmambetov from Bishkek to Osh, but not before combining the ministry with another one to create, aptly enough for the declines tracked herin, a Ministry of Ecology and States of Emergency.[36] Despite this organizational flux, in each state there exists an appreciable corpus of environmental laws and regulations, but resources for enforcement have been particularly slim in recent years.

In my interviews with them, officials, scientists, and NGOs within central Asia broadly agreed that the administrative capacity and efficacy of environmental institutions had declined drastically over the past decade. Some of these respondents did harbor hope that the situation would soon improve. Yet, it is not unimportant that the respondents who overwhelmingly believed that this component of the modern administrative state had improved since independence were foreigners employed by development agencies.

Post-Soviet Central Asia's governments, from their constitutional organs to their most basic administrative agencies, are a failure when measured with Western standards of accountability, rule of law, democracy, and efficacy.

However, this observation can be viewed historically in two lights; either as a betrayal of Perestroika reforms or as the inevitable inertia of sinister Soviet practices. While most readers are familiar with the shortfalls of the Soviet Union that could be implicated here (i.e. lack of human rights, ideological monism, lack of transparency, etc.), readers may not be as familiar with the impact of the Perestroika period in directly confronting and partially overcoming just such shortfalls. Accordingly, an overview of Perestroika's connection to organizational capital may be needed.

Perestroika in this regard had two contradictory manifestations: statist and discursive. As a state program, its mandates to attack local corruption and otherwise improve Soviet society cannot meaningfully be separated from the entirety of the government of the USSR. Through this lens, Perestroika may have been an interesting and remarkable undertaking, but its claims to validity and importance are largely undercut. They are undercut by the fact that by the mid-1980s the Soviet economy was largely untenable and the government's totality of policies during the Perestroika period produced no reason to believe that the USSR was able to ensure the security or prosperity of its citizens in the future. Through this statist lens, Perestroika was not distinct from the state, and, consequently, any contemporary laments that Perestroika policies ended are synonymous with appeals to reinstate the Soviet state.

However, when I refer to Perestroika, I intend to invoke instead its discursive nature, and, by implication, a project composed not of agents of the state, but of individuals in a polity. In this regard, Perestroika participants included a wide range of actors (most notably, officials, dissidents, NGOs, newspaper editors, and independent politicians) and "Perestroika" could have continued in the independence period. The fundamental substance of discursive Perestroika, Perestroika dialogues (tracked on the pages of newspapers and other periodicals and through statements of Perestroika actors) concentrated most attention on the meaning of rule of law, on the nature and value of individual liberties, on defining democracy, on exposing corruption and nepotism, on wondering about the meaning of civil society, and on debating distribution of powers in a federal state. As dialogue, discursive Perestroika contained many viewpoints, ranging from liberal democracy to communism to nationalism; accordingly, while the dialogues did not point to prescription, they encouraged participation, reflection, and critical thinking.

These dialogues attracted substantial attention, and the diversity and strength of minority and other views put into discursive play during this period shocked both locals and Sovietologists used to the party line's previous tight grip on the substance of public dialogue. Beyond novelty, these dialogues also attracted attention because of their depth, a depth that has rarely been matched in post-Soviet public dialogues on transition, nationalism, Russian chauvinism, and the other themes that now dominate even where the press is free.

With this perspective, we can revisit whether post-Soviet declines in organizational capital are a betrayal of Perestroika reforms or as the inevitable inertia of sinister Soviet practices by considering the fate of discursive Perestroika after independence. The USSR's disassembly shook apart Perestroika by removing Moscow's checks on the republics, by allowing economic crisis to subvert governance aspirations, and by permitting Western voices to muddy and subvert the democratic and law-based agendas and priorities of reform movements. For example, notwithstanding the extensive references to democracy in the Soviet legal system and several actual practices, the popular American conception of the fall of the Soviet Union is of democracy over communism.

This image persists despite a strong democratic element in theoretical communism and in disregard for the myriad ways in which Western states fall short of democratic ideals. Western embassies and programs, especially American, continued (destructively) to fight the straw man of communism instead of to endeavor (constructively) to support democratic and rule of law aspirations wherever they did in fact exist. In other words, paradoxically, discursive Perestroika founded on critical dialogue was not nurtured by the West, but summarily ignored or discredited. Paradoxically, discursive Perestroika birthed critical dialogue as a challenge to the blind ideology of the Communist Party, but in successfully unshackling society from one uncritical ideology it opened the door to its own demise through, the valorization of the ideology of the West. Western donors and development agents did not know about (and lacked the linguistic and cultural skills to lean about) and did not want to learn about (since they equated everything pre-independence with communism) discursive Perestroika, and they therefore forcefully urged on communities a break with everything from the Soviet era and an uncritical acceptance of donor prescriptions.

Thus, Western influence contributed to post-Soviet decline by undermining a powerful venue for public education and consensus. Neither hegemonic Western prescriptions nor the imported pamphlets and programs of Western agencies managed to create a viable substitute, and so public efforts to participate in, shape, and monitor reform declined quickly. As a result, the disassembly created ideal conditions for ruling local politicians to maximize their rational political ambitions; just as capitalists seek to maximize profits instead of to ensure competitive markets, politicians seek to maximize their terms in office instead of to ensure the integrity of the political process.

However, the alternate viewpoint is also convincing. Under this line of reasoning, the bloodlessness of the demise of the USSR is a mixed blessing; that the structures and modes of the USSR existed intact the day after communism may be to the long-term detriment of the region. On the first day of markets, independence, and democracy in Central Asia in 1991, everyone reported to the same job, in the same building, to the same boss, and at the same salary as the day before. While the names and labels of the region changed dramatically, below the surface the communist society remained intact. Reconstruction does not face the same challenges of bureaucratic inertia as "transition." This bureaucratic inertia in Central Asia, symbolized in the resistance of the region to rule of law reforms, this "old vodka in new bottles," is one of the region's enduring causes of unsustainable development.

While bureaucratic inertia in Central Asia is certainly a problem, that Perestroika reforms, practices, and rhetoric were not supported by influential foreign embassies and donors (but instead often dismissed as atavistic or tainted) certainly did facilitate the region's slide towards autocracy. Although the Soviet Union in practice fit no serious scholar's ideal of democracy, towards its end it exhibited a startling embrace of democracy and a dynamic federalism. National referenda and the emergence of checks and balances among political subdivisions effected tremendous changes in the USSR, including the demise of the Soviet Union. More than any ideological divisions, the problems generated by the struggles for power between the central Soviet structures and their republican counterparts lay at the heart of the disassembly of the USSR. In Central Asia, none of the republics actually expected or even desired sovereign status,[37] despite deployment of rhetoric of independence and sovereignty as tools to wrest more power from Moscow.

The roots of independence aside, the link between the public and private failures of organizational capital in Central Asia is to be found in the "nomenklatura," the oligarchy in the region whose defining characteristics are its Soviet pedigree and its simultaneous attention to economic and political power as two sides of the same coin. This group, equivalent but distinct in each republic, has been the primary blocker of change and co-opter of reforms. In fact, at times this group has actively supported certain reforms to the extent that such reforms have facilitated further consolidation of political or economic power. As even IMF staff have finally recognized, "economic reform has been thwarted by rent-seeking vested interests who have the most to gain if reforms stall halfway between the central planning of the past and a well-functioning, open, and competitive market economy."[38] More specifically, it seems that these "vested interests" have supported financial stabilization and privatization, while resisting the equally important objectives of liberalization of markets and rule of law.[39]

Feared originally as a reactionary group that had everything to lose from independence, the nomenklatura actually had everything to gain from a controlled transition from the Soviet system of generous but limited social and economic entitlements for the nomenklatura. By, in each republic, working to remove the upper limits of such entitlements (through privatization, access to global markets, language laws, etc.) while restraining risks to such entitlements (popular sovereignty, free press, independent judiciaries, etc.) this group managed to turn itself into the principal beneficiary of the fruits of independence. While sacrificing symbolic or small amounts of its political hegemony through facilitation of Western development programs, this group also used such programs to gain economic advantages, in effect trading political for economic power. In simpler terms, the nomenklatura was and is corrupt,[40] but it is corrupt not because of any peculiar cultural or ethnic traits, but because its members are, in their own context, rational maximizers of their own welfare.

ASSET STRIPPING: THE POST-SOVIET MARKET GAME

> When reform began 10 years ago … output was expected to fall as a result of economic stabilization programs and the reallocation of resources from unproductive to productive sectors. The view was that, as reform policies took hold and new sectors began to develop, aggregate output would begin to grow. Output was expected to grow more rapidly in the less advanced economies, and there would be a closing of income gaps or even, eventually, convergence.[41]

It took me many years to reconcile the fact that Kazakhstan was supposed to be a major hydrocarbon producer and was supposed to possess immense industrial potential with the fact that so many of my acquaintances were involved in international trade and that so many of them described their activities as "metals trading." Metals trading, it turns out, was a euphemism. It did not mean so much the sale of any of Kazakhstan's extensive deposits of ore, nor did it mean trading in the production output from Karaganda's Karmet steel factory, one of the largest in the world. It actually meant the export of finished goods made of metal to foreign purchasers, usually in Iran, Pakistan, China, or Russia. However, these finished goods were not consumer goods, but the physical capital of the productive sector, either scrap metal (including parts of the infrastructure) from Kazakhstan factories or machines for making consumer goods. Some of this trade was legal, in that the sellers were the legal managers of the enterprises from which these goods were obtained. Some was illegal, in that these goods were stolen from ill-monitored enterprises. Perhaps the worst, but most appropriate, snapshot of these practices is the all-too-common news broadcast about unfortunate young men electrocuted while attempting to steal active power lines from remote areas to sell to scrap metal brokers.[42]

Privatization, no less than democracy, was and continues to be an ideological cornerstone of almost all internal and foreign development scholars interested in Central Asia's future. This consensus around privatization attaches to privatization's multiple benefits. The classic goals of all economic policy are to facilitate economic efficiency (and growth) and, highlighting the laudable humanistic core of economics as a discipline, just and equitable distribution (both to eliminate poverty and to increase equality among citizens).[43] Theoretically, privatization facilitates efficiency by transferring assets (usually physical and natural capital assets) to actors better able than the state to manage these assets productively. The advantages of these non-state managers arise from a combination of decentralization, a convergence of interests between managers and owners, rewards to efficient managers, and relief from the perverse impacts of state planning. Just as theoretically, mass privatization facilitates just distribution by giving citizens a formal and financial stake in the productive assets of the state; effectively mass privatization is a dividend payment to citizens as stakeholders in society.

This metals trading described above, while illegal or only semi-legal, is one form of privatization. Indeed, the transfer of state assets into private hands can take many different forms; "privatization programs" stress only a few of these forms. The main kinds of privatization in post-Soviet Central Asia are informal privatization (of the kind illustrated above), formal privatization (the type embraced in most development programs), privatization of sovereign rights, and privatization of human and organizational capital assets. In each case, as practiced in the last decade in Central Asia, each form of privatization has failed to yield Pareto efficiency. Since property rights are a core, if not the core, component of modern organizational capital's incentive structure, privatization in Central Asia has thus sometimes contributed to the degradation of organizational capital. More disturbingly, privatization has also largely failed to produce intranational Kaldor-Hicks efficiency, a failure which poses a special challenge to the validity of the current consensus around the need for privatization.

Ironically, informal privatization, while often patently illegal, may come the closest to effecting a Pareto improvement, in part because it is the only type of privatization available to most people. Despite its theoretical promise, formal privatization has yielded effectively no direct financial rewards to the citizenry of Central Asia. Kazakhstan's privatization efforts embraced the norm for post-communism, an effort to distribute state assets to all citizens as shareholders. All Kazakhstan citizens were issued "private investment coupons" (PIKs) in 1994, and they could choose from roughly a hundred investment privatization funds in which to deposit these coupons. Thus, in contrast to Russia, where similar coupons were transferable and could be used to acquire shares in specific enterprises or investment funds, Kazakhstan constrained its citizens. Kazakhstanis now joke about PIKs, and almost no one expects any financial return on this investment. PIKs are already part of Kazakhstan's past.

Kazakhstan's PIKs and Kyrgyzstan's privatization coupons have, for the most part, disappeared into murky management funds, and the managers of these funds have not been held accountable enough for their holdings. More specifically, they have managed in large part to informally privatize for themselves the assets they were entrusted to privatize formally for their fiduciaries. While vague, but convincing, accounts of the alleged mechanics of these deals circulate as rumors and in occasional newspaper accounts in the Russian language, to date no details about privatization swindles from Central Asia (as opposed to from the Czech Republic, Azerbaijan, Russia, and Ukraine) have been explored by reliable sources.[44]

Privatization of sovereign assets is a less appreciated, potentially more devastating perversion of the humanistic aspirations of privatization. Sovereign states enjoy both rights of seignorage (coinage) and rights of credit. Private parties may appropriate both rights, with the effect, directly apposite from the goals of equitable distribution, of a tax on citizenship. For example, the continued lack of convertibility of Uzbekistan's sum (despite promises by Karimov to institute convertibility by January 2000), and the enduring disparity between official and black market exchange rates (in 2000 still roughly 200 and 700 sum to the dollar) operates as a windfall to those privileged few in Uzbekistan upon whom is conferred the right to convert sum into dollars at the official rate. Likewise, when states in the region secure dollars from the IMF and other lenders, the state assumes a debt; when these funds find their way to private accounts, the fortuitously enriched oligarchs have in effect levied a private tax on future taxpayers.

Finally, because individuals in the Soviet Union were more subjects than citizens, independence created curious conditions for the privatization of human capital assets. Taking their futures in their own hands, many Central Asians quickly abandoned the region, and the effect of their private decisions was to remove human capital assets formerly at the disposal of the state and relocate them to foreign states. Likewise, the staying power of the nomenklatura has meant that state entities (like the office of the President) that should not be privatized and were never meant to be privatized have remained in private hands instead of reverting to public control and management.

FORMAL RULES: THE RULE OF LAW STATE

No authority would seriously propose regulation of a modern state through informal norms such as universal respect, love, or the golden rule, despite the fact that, throughout human history cherished philosophers have argued for just such a condition.[45] Assuming that Central Asia will not find encouragement to pioneer a strategy for sustainable development employing and encouraging nepotism and patronage networks as frameworks for environmental incentives, the lack of rule of law in Central Asia is a potent barrier to effective environmental management. At the threshold of the past decade, it was virtually axiomatic that the key to a successful transition from communism was a rapid transfer of management of assets into private hands: to private businessmen for private goods and to electorates for government. In a new decade, there exists far less enthusiasm for either transfer. Yet, inasmuch as the development community grasps at new panaceas as old ones fail, it is now just as axiomatic that a successful transition must involve a deep commitment to rule of law.[46]

This new consensus around the need for rule of law presents an unreal counterfactual. Nowhere in the former Soviet Union did development efforts in the last decade put at their core a commitment to the finer points of rule of law, namely enforcement, courts, and accountability. The vast bulk of "legal" work by developers centered on the task of writing legislation, and at that only laws, not the instructions upon which regulators and law enforcement agencies rely. Correspondingly, most legal "assessments" ended with a review of the texts of laws. Given the gulf between written laws and actual implementation and enforcement, past legal development work was often meaningless. Accordingly, there is no counterfactual to justify, or sink, the new belief that the reform period would have progressed much more favorably if rule of law had been accorded more importance.

Yet, during the Perestroika period, the concept of rule of law (*pravovoe gosudarstvo*) lay at the core of reform aspirations.[47] Rule of law was the consensus aspiration that conjoined Perestroika-era social movements as diverse as those representing victims of Stalinist repression, environmental groups, human rights organizations, and cultural associations. During Perestroika, some of Central Asia's better and more effective laws were adopted,[48] the region's most daring public interest environmental lawsuits were filed,[49] non-governmental parties introduced draft legislation, and independent candidates were elected to all levels of legislatures. The post-Soviet era has paled in comparison.

The reason why the post-Soviet era has paled in comparison has been suggested in previous sections, but not directly addressed. In all republics, certain "Washington Consensus" reforms have been supported, and certain of these reforms have been systematically blocked; especially the reforms related to rule of law have found little support at high levels of government. Thus, the governing elite's transformation from the communist vanguard to signatories of the *United Nations Millennium Declaration* has not been entire. It has been a transformation that has stressed the elements of rule of law that maintain public order, but that has belittled those elements that encourage participatory government and accountability. For example, again turning to the environmental sphere, inasmuch as sustainable management depends on the rule of law, the current situation in Central Asia is not laudable. Aspects of rule of law applicable to sustainable development include clear liability regimes, jurisdiction over polluters, incentives against pollution, public oversight, and transparency guarantees like public access to information.

None of these is developed in the region. Instead, their antitheses – political protection, secrecy, corruption, and exemptions from liability and laws – are the norm in the extractive sector.[50] This particular transformation is what I call a state of apostasy.

The state of apostasy is actually a kind of rule of law, although it is not Pareto optimal. Because of its socialist foundations, it does not provide efficient incentives for economic actors, nor does it take advantage of the benefits of policies for decentralized decision making. However, it boasts all or most of the institutions of a rule of law society, including courts, elected political representatives, and a culture of the printed word. It boasts a highly developed criminal law system, high levels of social rights, and a secular conception of justice and authority. As it is a modern state, it also devotes central authority to administrative and special-ized agencies in the management of economic, social, and welfare programs. In all of these aspects, the apostate state is an isomorph of the basic structure of the state apparatuses of Europe and North America, or at least no more different than these states are between themselves.

Yet, the apostate state lacks as least three key attributes of democratic rule of law, and all of these focus attention not on the state or government itself, but on authority outside the state sector. The first of these attributes is the equal capacity or rights of all citizens, regardless of their position within the state structure. The second attribute is an organizational pluralism that includes independent organ-izations and limits the density of corporatist or parastatal organizations. The third attribute is the ability of non-state actors to call at will upon the legal mechanisms of the state, without prior state approval or monitoring, to enforce individual rights.

The transition from the apostate state to democratic rule of law is not reducible in terms of needs and challenges to the paradigm transition from a state of nature to rule of law glossed or assumed by law and economics scholars.[51] Moreover, were one to catalog the challenges faced under other transitions in this century, the transition of apostate states to democratic rule of law may not have much in common with the experience of Germany or Japan as defeated powers either.[52] Nor would there be confluence with the post-communist states that are not apostate, such as the Czech Republic. Perhaps, from a transition perspective, Kazakhstan is more like potential other apostate states, like China or Chile, than it is to its western post-communist peers, at least as far as democracy (as opposed to economic reform) is concerned. Naturally, the apostate transition is also sepa-rable from the transitions occasioned by any of the revolutions of this century or past centuries, such as occurred in Russia, China, or the United States. In broad strokes, the states of nature, revolution, defeat, and apostasy are four discernible states from which theory and practice can imagine a transition to democratic rule of law. Each initial state has discrete implications for both theory and develop-ment interventions as these seek to build strong stocks of organizational capital.

Finally, in considering the limits of rule of law, the changes being effected by globalization are striking. The massive movements of people, capital, and infor-mation systems that comprise what is colloquially known as globalization challenge the belief that a stronger commitment to rule of law would have warded off post-Soviet decline. Imagine reactions of the global community to what I term autarkic rule of law, an attempt by a state to bring flows of people, flows of capital, flows of information, flows of public goods, and flows of private goods firmly under national control for the benefit of the national policy. Judging by the reactions of the world community to efforts by Bulgaria to charge emigres for the costs of their schooling, efforts by Turkmenistan to forbid its nationals to hold accounts in foreign banks, efforts by Germany to block access to Internet pornography, efforts by Russia to deny sovereignty to Chechnya, and efforts by Kazakhstan to discourage "bubble-gum" traders, autarkic rule of law is disfavored by the West. Autarkic policies may even be violations of emerging norms of international public law.

EVALUATING THE ERAS OF ORGANIZATIONAL CAPITAL IN CENTRAL ASIA

Beyond the problems for sustainability created by depletion of Central Asia's late Soviet-era organizational capital, an important aspect of international organizational capital has also been degraded in the region. At the start of independence, international institutions enjoyed both popular legitimacy and substantial influence in Central Asia as a reflection of the USSR's strong public respect for both the United Nations and international law, a topic addressed in Chapter 6. Now however turning to the environmental sphere, residents of the desiccated Aral Sea region often quip sarcastically that if only each World Bank and UNDP expert who has been sent to investigate the Aral Sea had merely brought a glass of fresh water, there would be no more Aral Sea disaster.

Conditions are not now ideal for Western development efforts, even well considered efforts, to rebuild organizational capital in Central Asia. Donor failures are more notable than successes, and these failures or perceived failures inform a widespread social pessimism about the goals and efficacy of Western projects. A lauded 60 per cent recovery of output[53] only exacerbates this local pessimism. Indeed this Washington spin conveniently obscures the facts that this output's dollar value is now far lower than in 1990 and that the gap between the former Soviet Union and a West that boomed in the 1990s has widened by far more than 40 per cent. Indeed, a state experiencing 5 per cent annual growth in the past decade would now have a 60 per cent larger economy than in 1990, meaning that a 40 per cent absolute decline in output in the 1990s is equivalent to a 60+ per cent comparative decline, even before considering the devaluation of this output because of depressed raw commodity markets and obsolescence. So, in counterpoint to Washington spin, the obverse of this local pessimism is a growing popular nostalgia for the USSR, particularly for those social and economic modalities of the USSR that were existentially better than the conditions experienced by the populace in the post-Soviet era.

As a result of the degradation of organizational capital in Central Asia, the region has been unable to protect, manage, and maximize returns on its stocks of natural capital. It has likewise been unable to protect, nurture, and win the loyalty of its citizens. It has been unable to enforce laws. It has been unable to practice popular sovereignty. Thus, through the lens of sustainability, the degradation of the region's stocks of formal organizational capital has had destructive spillover effects. These disappointments have been mediated only by the region's successes in pioneering relative fiscal stability, partial privatization, occasionally competitive markets, and the institutional semblance of constitutional democracy.

4 Social capital: civil society and solidarity

Rounding out the types of capital and their manifestations in Central Asia, I return now to the underpinnings of a concern for social capital. Social capital is appropriately defined as a manifestation of organizational capital; its assets are composed of similar elements of rules and organizations, and the same dynamic feedback between perceived and actual options. However, social capital deserves separate treatment here for the reasons that it is currently in vogue, that it is still largely undefined, and that there exist almost no available data about its history or manifestations in Central Asia.

The development community has reacted to the failures of recent years by seeking a new panacea. Together with rule of law,[1] social capital's reputation has benefited from this search. Portes and Landolt note that "the popular view now portrays social capital as wholly beneficial with no significant downside."[2] Tellingly, social capital now even has its own homepage on the World Bank website.[3] Likewise, the IMF supports Francis Fukuyama's effort to connect social capital policy to efforts of international lending institutions.[4] There is probably no development agency in existence that has not partially reconceived its orientations in recent years to integrate social capital concerns into its programs.

However, this embrace of social capital occurs in the continued absence of a clear definition of social capital, understanding of the origins of social capital, clear conception of the implications of social capital, or even an explicit effort to connect social capital to social capital assets. Without reiterating in full the section on social capital in the Introduction, the need for a working definition of social capital demands some repetition.

To date, no prominent definition of social capital allows the term the two core elements of any other form of capital: the ability to disaggregate a stock into discrete assets and the ability to link deployment of assets to externalities, both negative and positive. I posit that social capital should be defined concisely with reference to game theory and that its full explication will depend on its integration into information economics. Social capital consists of two necessary but independently insufficient conditions. First, social capital requires a dense network of social interaction; it requires that individuals be enmeshed in multiple social networks. Second, social capital requires that these social networks fulfill two quite different functions: reduce information transaction costs and provide signals about propensities to cooperate or defect where market failures preclude inclusion of such information in implicit pricing systems.

Social capital facilitates the reduction of information transaction costs by providing alternate channels for information flow. Persons with high social capital often rely on their informal knowledge about potential business partners, investors, and service providers, and in doing so eliminate costs associated with investigation of and search for such information. Social capital also provides information and signals about other people's tendencies to cooperate or defect. In their economic and game theory contexts, these terms refer to individuals' decisions to honor agreements or break agreements (when there is some payoff for doing so). Individuals may tend to cooperate either because of some predisposition to do so generally (some internal morality or standard) or because the payoff from defection is lowered because an interaction (a "period" in game-theory terms) is not one-time but "iterated." In iterated games, a player will encounter the other player again, at least many or an indefinite number of times, and will be disadvantaged by that other player's future refusal to cooperate.[5] While this phenomenon clearly applies to villages where reputation and frequent interaction are central elements of life, given dense enough social networks, it can also apply to towns or segments of cities.

Generally speaking, individuals are involved in two broad types of social networks. Their primary associations are largely non-voluntary and hierarchically organized (vertical) and include family, residence, school, and work. Their secondary associations are voluntary and less hierarchical (horizontal) and involve formal civic organizations, sports leagues, and like ad hoc associations. While no clear boundary exists between primary and secondary associations (neighborhood watch groups, school alumni associations, and professional societies all combine elements of both), the distinction between the two is important because of evidence about the ambiguous externalities that stem from social capital.

"Bonding" social capital based primarily on primary associations tends often to produce negative societal externalities and inefficient resource allocation.[6] Examples include old boys' networks, the Mafia, and nepotism. "Bridging" social capital, in contrast, relies less on the phenomenon of (and disadvantages of) cartel loyalty and more on the gains to efficiency produced by reduced transaction costs in information. Moreover, bridging social capital can displace some of the inefficient aspects of bonding social capital. Thus, while bonding social capital is not an unqualified bad (it is a potent means of insurance), all other things equal it is preferable to have at least a large part of a society's stock of social capital in bridging social capital. More concisely and importantly, the lack of bridging social capital can be a serious developmental disadvantage.

All of the foregoing builds up to a definition of social capital. A social capital asset is a social network (primary or secondary) combining two or more people. The sum of such networks and the breadth of such networks constitute a society's stock of social capital.[7] The relevant composition of these networks between bonding and bridging social capital directly shapes the kinds of negative and positive externalities flowing from a society's social capital.

Little fieldwork has been conducted to test existing pluralist conceptions of social capital with empirical data. Outside of limited work in a variety of locales throughout the world, the only comprehensive effort at an empirical investigation of social capital is Robert Putnam's *Bowling Alone*,[8] which limits itself to the United States. While several efforts to survey social capital in Russia are in progress, I know of no fieldwork in any part of Central Asia, other than my own, to survey social capital. Accordingly, in surveying social capital in Central Asia, this chapter departs from the bias of Chapters 1, 2 and 3 of preferring World Bank, IMF, and similar "conservative" sources. Such sources simply do not exist. However, this chapter draws on a similarly narrow set of sources, primarily my own fieldwork within Central Asia.[9]

In order to survey social capital in Central Asia, I choose three proxies: simple economic transactions between strangers, social associations, and residential community associations. These by no means exhaust the range of proxies suggested by economists, sociologists, and other scholars for similar purposes. Among the proxies suggested have been, *inter alia*, numbers of independent associations, hours spent visiting neighbors, newspaper readership, means used to secure jobs, the existence of rotating credit associations, and neighborhood watch groups. Few, if any, of these proxies are unproblematic or generally accepted, which is inevitable if one remembers that social capital has no consensus definition. Given the great gulfs between the World Bank's "social cohesion," Fukuyama's ambivalent privileging of transaction cost reduction through "trust," Putnam's bonding and bridging social capital, Coleman's reduced costs of contracting,[10] and the myriad other definitions of social capital, this lack of consensus about how social capital manifests itself is inescapable.

However, some of the most popular social capital proxies contradict the fundamental definitions pursued in this book. Accepting social capital as a component of organizational capital exposes certain popular measures of social capital as at worst no more than wishful thinking and at best multicollinear with truer estimators of social capital. For example, throughout his works, Putnam relies heavily on voter turnout and membership in political parties, which relate to social capital, but contradict my definition of social capital as the nonstate aspect of organizational capital. Similarly, Fukuyama relies heavily on data regarding trust in government, which may be collinear with social capital in a robust understanding of organizational capital, but has nothing directly to do with social capital itself. Fukuyama's emphasis on crime rates is similarly misdirected; it relies on a perfect confluence between positive law and the concerns of social norms.

Partly for these reasons, I employ three, instead of only one, proxies. While each of these proxies could be accepted under any of the schools of social capital listed above, their selection is purely linked to the definition of social capital I outline in the Introduction. Specifically, embracing the symmetric insight that active social networks may produce both positive and negative externalities, I examine the game theoretical aspect of these social networks as well as their information economy aspects. Symmetry in the first instance is contained within the payout possibilities for cooperation and defection in the simple economic transactions that I examine. Deference to symmetry in the second instance comes through attention to the variable externalities of social (bridging) associations and residential (bonding) associations.

ONE-SHOT GAMES

Expanding the discussion above to focus more explicitly on economic issues and ignoring for the moment the economic effects of social capital's role in reducing transaction costs in information, we can redefine a person's individual stock of social capital to be the sum of his involvement in the iterated games that we alternately call social networks. The result is that his social capital simultaneously reflects his individual reputation and reduces certain transaction costs connected to economic bargaining, particularly those costs that are involved in contracting. However, reputation and transaction costs are intimately connected. Reputation allows other players to gauge in advance what his game strategy will be and how likely it is that he will cooperate or defect. Expanding the critique of the Arrow–Debreu model that was initiated by the information economists, prices indeed do not convey all relevant information. Social capital conveys reputation, whose reliability for assessing the viability of a joint venturer is not infallible, but is both relevant and even determinative for many joint venturers given the absence of a market solution.

The significance of this use of reputation is that it reduces the costs of pursuing economic activities. Since not all contractual relations are enforceable through the law, and since it is usually cheaper to arrange contractual relations outside the formal requirements of the law, social capital avoids costs both in deadweight losses and in transaction costs. In other words, social capital functions to further economic efficiency both through reducing the information costs of selecting reliable partners and through allowing joint venturers to avoid the costly process (notarizations, lawyer fees, etc.) that accrue to the formalization of contractual arrangements.

Such a description almost captures the basic confluence between game theory in economics and the broader social science embrace of social capital. In the finer points of their expression, however, these two camps have not so readily agreed on the bases for why many economic actors engaged in non-iterated games act as though they are engaged in iterated games; some actors comport themselves as if there is something at stake. They act as if they care what strangers think of them, or, just as "irrationally," simply desire not to cheat a stranger. For non-economists, culture and values offer themselves as explanations; for game theorists this explanation is too facile and lacks theoretical rigor. Yet, simultaneously, game theorists do seek an explanation for such empirically verifiable human behavior and are willing to accept its occurrence as a manifestation of social capital. Accordingly, perhaps the only social capital proxy elemental enough to fit the tastes of all scholars concerns the actions of unacquainted individuals involved in one-shot economic transactions. Given the opportunity to cheat without a readily discernible chance of punishment, will a member of a given community betray the trust of another?

Of course, for the purposes of this discussion this question is embedded within the context of the former Soviet Union, moreover its Central Asian republics. The region is notorious for unaccountable business practices. The Western business community constantly complains that its local counterparts are untrustworthy, dishonest, and sneaky. What hope can one have of finding social capital in such an environment? Notwithstanding the merits of conventional wisdom, this reasoning lacks a social science foundation. It implies that economic actors in the West are uniquely trustworthy, which is a suspect implication, and it assumes that there is only one proxy for and manifestation of social capital, which is, at best, an unproven suggestion. Moreover, it assumes that local dealings with foreigners capture fundamental truths about social capital, which may not be true. Accordingly, I concentrate in this section on social capital as it actually exists within the region, not as it is experienced by foreigners. In such situations, a number of practices and norms in Central Asia do suggest high levels of social capital, and levels that are, in my experience, largely unchanged since the Soviet era.

The absence of cheating in the situations described below hint, whatever one's definition of it, the prevalence of social capital. In game theoretic terms, a community permeated by enough social networks leaves a rational actor rationally to conclude that her perceived anonymity in such a transaction is unlikely to be real; sooner or later the community will identify her transgression and her as its perpetrator. In vaguer social capital terms, the generalized norm of trust penetrates very deeply into the community. Bridging these two approaches, the law and economics explanation of such a condition is that the social networks of the community are robust enough so as to make it economically unproductive for an individual actor to weigh the risks involved in defection in such a situation. The efficient rule of thumb, the default rule, which saves individuals the (transaction) costs associated with calculating risks and benefits over and over again in each new instance, is to treat all countrymen reciprocally. It is this law and economics view of the efficient rule (the rule that minimizes the sum of transaction costs and opportunity costs) that frames the following discussion of two largely anonymous economic transactions in Central Asia's largest (and hence assumedly its most anonymous) city, Tashkent. These two transactions, among the most common in the city, are the processes of waiting in lines and riding in private taxis.

Of course, the former Soviet Union is famous for its lines, but these lines are also the setting for a rich set of cultural norms; an identifiable set of rules guides the behavior of participants in these lines. At first sight, many of these lines appear to Western observers to be chaotic mobbings; no single-file construction meets the eye. However, quite outside the law, or at least the reach of the law should a transgression occur, these mobbings contain a large complement of social order. For example, most participants in the line can easily point to the three or four people in front and in back of them. Accordingly, in the event that someone breaks ahead in line, several line participants can identify such a transgression.

Pure rational actor theory predicts that, in such instances, those waiting in line behind the transgression will have a reason to expel rule-breakers, while those ahead of the link in the line under question will be indifferent. However, in actual cases of rule infraction, participants on both sides of the line take active part in re-establishing order. In many cases, honest mistake lies at the heart of line arguments; newcomers are expected to seek out and find the last person in "line" and inform that individual that she or he is assuming the next position. Because the line's occupants are scattered and conditions for communication often less than ideal, two people often believe they are directly behind the same person. In such cases, persons immediately in front of and behind this confusion take equal part in determining the correct order of the line; in almost all circumstances anterior participants take the opinions of those in front of the confusion as authoritative determinations. The observation relevant here to an observation about the reciprocity aspects of social capital is that the people in forward positions in the line simply do not ignore what is happening in the anterior parts of the line when appeals are made to them. That they do not is a partial suggestion that the region boasts a healthy stock of some social capital assets.

Soviet practices also, through both law and norms, allowed certain persons the option of moving towards the front of the line. The very elderly, those with infants, World War II veterans, and, occasionally, average citizens offering impassioned reasons for being unable to wait were allowed to move ahead in the line. While signs often outlined rules for such privileges in the Soviet period, such signs have become increasingly uncommon in the post-Soviet period. In stark contrast to what scholars like Fukuyama predict to follow in the wake of the removal of authoritarian rules,[11] the loss of these signs has not ended the authority of these special privileges in practice. If anything, in recent years in Tashkent such privileges have experienced a renewed vigor with these Soviet-era privileged categories trumping other possible privileged categories, such as the category that comprises foreigners.

This phenomenon of persistent line privileges also suggests a strong stock of certain social capital assets. Although pure self-interest can explain why people monitor lines (every person spends equal amount of time in the front and end parts of lines every day), such an explanation does not go far in explaining why these privileges maintain intact. Large numbers of people will never, or believe they will never, carry infants, be war veterans, or be disabled. The reason why they nevertheless adhere to the social norms described above in anonymous situations is best illustrated through the following discussion of taxis; the reason is the same reason that explains the maintenance of taxi social norms throughout Central Asia.

The practice of using private cars as taxis remains the province of very informal bargaining and generalized trust. To get from one place to another in any Central Asian city, most people are indifferent as to whether the car that they flag down is a taxi or a private automobile. During Soviet times, whereas official taxis were expensive, drivers of private automobiles offered fair odds of refusing payment, especially for passengers with interesting stories, attractive figures, or destinations that required no detours. One result of the disassembly of the USSR is that such free rides are now a rarity, and virtually all private cars charge fares. Over the years, police in every republic have periodically attempted to discourage such private entrepreneurs, but both riders and drivers have quickly found ways to work around such efforts; at present the practice is generally tolerated everywhere. Except in Kyrgyzstan, the vast majority of trips take place in private cars, and there is no real difference in price between cars and taxis. Sometimes riders or drivers negotiate fares in advance; just as often no such advance negotiation occurs. Almost as universally known as the current dollar/local currency rate of exchange, city residents know current taxi fares.

That strangers so regularly pick up strangers, especially when riders always have the option of waiting for formal taxis, hints at a certain level of trust. Likewise, that both drivers and riders so often fail to negotiate fares in advance also suggests a certain level of trust. Perhaps most telling, when fares are not negotiated *ex ante*, disagreements frequently break out at destination points. However, these disagreements almost never last long, and they virtually never result in any violence; they are contained by a set of informal rules, and a mutually agreeable fare usually only requires less than a minute to negotiate.

Further, both taxis and private cars can easily be hired for more complex services. Upon arrival at a destination, you can ask a driver to wait while you run an errand. What makes the driver's agreement of interest for social capital is that, if the driver agrees, only in rare circumstances will you be asked to pay for the trip just taken or leave possessions in the car as insurance. Drivers are relatively unconcerned that riders will use such a request as a pretext to avoid paying a fare. Of course, some riders do welch on their obligations in this manner; drivers readily remember numerous such incidents when queried on the subject. Yet, these situations have nevertheless not coaxed drivers into demanding security payments from their riders, while drivers make such demands in places like Moscow.

Both taxi and line norms in Central Asia raise a number of interesting questions. Why would people risk confrontation in a line for the sake of strangers? Why would drivers and riders so often fail to negotiate fares in advance when doing so is a simple affair? Why do drivers leave them themselves so open to cheating passengers? How can one reconcile this trusting behavior with true stories about graft, extortion, and the fleecing of gullible Western business people in the region? I find answers to all these questions by arguing that an appreciation of how social capital operates on the ground in Central Asia emphasizes and refines three aspects of social capital assets. Namely, these aspects are their positive information externalities, their role in redefining community bonds in even large groups, and their fundamental nature as operative assets instead of moral imperatives.

First, the information economics of social capital are an intrinsic element of social capital. In both lines and in taxis, Central Asians talk and share information. From both sources, individuals gather valuable information about where to (or where one can) secure certain goods and services and at what prices, learn what jobs are available, and learn about current events in their cities. That this information is valuable creates incentives for Central Asians to facilitate the cooperative atmosphere in which this information exchange occurs, for example even if this means paying the price of risking loss of a taxi fare. While the information externalities of such interactions between strangers could theoretically be negative, within Central Asia they are overwhelmingly positive.

Second, during the course of such communication, people quite often discover that, although apparently strangers, they have acquaintances in common. Whereas in the English speaking world, it is a popular myth that the lives of any two people are separated by no more than six other people, in no Central Asian city is that true. Three degrees of separation are all that separate most people in even the largest cities; most people know by name and face a thousand or more of their urban compatriots. In such an environment, anonymity is more apparent than actual and the boundaries of community membership are greatly expanded.

Finally, the transactions detailed above belong to a cadre of interpersonal relations in Central Asia that define the core of one's social being, that define what kind of person one is both personally and in the community. These low-stake transactions, characterized by strong positive externalities of information, contrast sharply with the kind of perverse business dealings that make the region's investment climate suspect in the eyes of foreign investors. The high-payoffs of business dealings help explain how the same driver who is unconcerned with whether a passenger will pay his fare would be well advised against entrusting a large investment with his passenger.

This description resonates with the stark contrast Robert Kaplan describes existing between Africa and Central Asia. Kaplan praises the extent of social order in Central Asia, while describing Africa as a place in which exactly the kinds of low-stakes transactions described above deserve no amount of trust.[12]

In summary, for economic relations, there are two worlds of social capital in Central Asia. In the first world, a world of unusual trust in which information sharing and low stakes prevail, the game strategy of most participants is to cooperate. In the other world, one of little trust in which high stakes trump the positive information externalities of the business social network, the risk of defection is much greater.

BRIDGING SOCIAL CAPITAL: SOCIAL ASSOCIATIONS AND CIVIL SOCIETY

Social capital is generally coterminous with civil society, but the two should not be confused. A vibrant civil society assumes high levels of social capital within a variety of secondary associations, but it also highlights the organizational capital character of social capital by connecting the latter to a variety of political functions, such as expression of diverse values, ensuring the accountability of state agencies, and providing alternatives to state services. These organizational capital functions of civil society actors need not by definition take place within secondary associations that are engaged in using and creating social capital. For instance, neither a rigidly hierarchical NGO that employs its only workers full time, nor a one-person organization, even if both organizations are highly successful, resonates with the social capital idealistic view of NGOs as voluntary, secondary associations that expand the density of a community's social networks and build trust. As a corollary, the lack of civil society is by no means dispositive of the absence of social capital, even though it does speak to the lack of important connections between social capital and organizational capital.[13]

Accordingly, a strong stock of social capital is neither a sufficient nor a necessary component of a vibrant civil society. That said, social capital is probably a very important component of strong civil societies. It may be especially important for any civil society whose strength is in part built on organizational diversity, for instance with formal primary association organizations (i.e. the Washington, D.C. corporate office of Sierra Club) complementing the efforts of more informal secondary associations (local volunteer Sierra Club chapters). Likewise, all other things being equal, a civil society infused with a large stock of social capital is probably more effective in its organizational missions and produces more positive externalities than one weak in social capital.

These observations highlight the assumptions behind the use of NGOs by scholars as a convenient proxy for social capital, and the serious limitations behind these assumptions. The social capital relevance of quantitative measurements of members, numbers of organizations, and rates of growth of both membership or organizations depends on the qualitative horizontality, secondariness, and social penetration of these members and organizations. This section thus attempts to survey the history of NGOs in Central Asia, with an emphasis on environmental civil society, from both quantitative and qualitative perspectives.

For roughly a century, Russia and Central Asia answered to the same sovereign authority. During that time, both the legal system that bred the first Russian NGOs and some of those Russian NGOs themselves heavily influenced Central Asia. Current Western development efforts in the former Soviet Union emphasize the need to develop a local language for NGOs and expand the number of indigenous NGOs. These efforts are curiously unaware that terms such as "private voluntary organizations" were in use in Russia a century ago, long before they became popular in the United States. There were, in fact, hundreds of thousands of NGOs in Tsarist Russia.

The first such NGO, the Friendly Learned Society, was formed in 1782.[14] In the 5 years from 1896–1900, more than 1000 charitable poverty relief societies were formed in the Russian Empire.[15] The spectrum of NGOs also included at least five credit unions by 1868, such as the Petersburg Mutual Credit Society whose insolvency in 1869 was due to over-liberal lending standards.[16] By 1868, non-profit banks had also appeared.[17]

In addition to charitable organizations, the Russian Empire also boasted a large number of academic and advocacy organizations. The Mineralogical Society (1816), the Russian Geographical Society, and the Russian Archaeological Society (both 1840s) grew into large institutions. Yet, their formation and continued control by foreign scientists (usually German), as well as their unambiguous ties to the autocracy, argue against accepting these organizations as great leaps forward for civil society and social capital in Russia.

In contrast, a host of learned societies that sprang up after Russia's defeat in the Crimean War did encourage civil society and social capital formation. The Chemical Society, the Moscow Mathematical Society, the Moscow Society for the Dissemination of Technical Knowledge, and the Juridical Society are some of the dozens of organizations that appeared in the 1860s to occupy new ground between private life and the state. Often peopled by scientists eager to encourage the economic and cultural development of the state, the projects and agendas of these groups regularly challenged the conservative entrenched policies of the autocracy. Moreover, unlike their predecessors, lacking the financial backing of the state, these organizations had fewer problems reconciling their goals with those of their financial backers.

For example, of more than two dozen such societies recognized by the Ministry of National Education in 1865, only seven received continuous financial support from the Russian state.[18] By the 1870s, literacy committees under a variety of names offered courses of instruction to women in university cities. They also attracted the volunteer time of Russia's greatest scientists and scores of progressive students in active constructive protest against continued state resistance to opening the doors of institutions of higher education to women and minorities.

Several of these academic societies have great historical importance.[19] The Ledentsov Society for the Advancement of the Exact Sciences and Their Practical Applications began in 1903. When roughly half of Russian university science professors lost or resigned their posts in a conflict with the government in 1911, the Ledentsov Society provided salaries, stipends, and research facilities for many of them. Without the Ledentsov Society, many of these scientists, some of whom later garnered international acclaim, would have emigrated from Russia, a curious observation considering the current mass emigration to Russia from Central Asia of scientists (as well as from Russia to the West).

The Pirogov Medical Society was founded in the 1880s in honor of Nikolai Pirogov, a famous surgeon who supported the autocracy. Despite its namesake's politics, the Pirogov Society eventually outraged the Tsarist regime through its grassroots efforts to address medical problems as social problems. By the 1905 Revolution, the Pirogov Society, virtually an umbrella association of practicing Russian physicians, had to manage its campaign to fight a cholera epidemic covertly; at the same time, it overtly encouraged all physicians to fight the autocracy in the name of democratic reforms.[20]

On the eve of the 1905 Revolution, foreshadowing the politics of the post-Soviet era, the regime attempted to undermine the power of independent associations by creating and fostering state-sponsored quasi-NGOs. Ironically, it was one of these quasi-trade unions, the Assembly of Factory Workers, that sparked the outbreak of the 1905 Revolution in St Petersburg.[21] After the revolution, in March 1906 a new NGO decree, "On Temporary Rules About Societies and Unions," passed. It restricted state officials from participation in any organization with political goals, and gave the Ministry of Internal Affairs the power to close organizations whose activities threatened the social order.[22]

Concurrent to the outbreak of the 1905 Revolution, several quasi-NGO structures endeavored to facilitate independence and self-government in Central Asia. Most of these organizations embraced either direct or implicit appeals to the authority of Islam and were innately political. While they often worked at odds with one another, the Islamic Council, the Council of Religious Scholars, the Association of Working Muslims, the Society of Turkistanian Federalists, and the Society of Turkic Federalists[23] adopted names and organizational principles that clearly displayed the influence of Russian culture and Russian norms of mobilizing political power, despite the fact that their membership was non-Russian. These organizations existed alongside other local organizations that are usually ignored in scholarship since they are more often considered as traditions, rather than as organizations. For example, ancient chivalric organizations of middle class citizens and trade corporations existed in a variety of Central Asian cities.[24]

The immigrant Russian-speaking population also established its own organizations, primarily in urban areas such as Tashkent, Samarkand, and Ashgabad. These organizations, or at least the ones that garnered attention at the time or, later, the attention of academic writers, boasted similar political motivations; perhaps, outside of church related associations, only a handful of these organizations could really be considered nonpartisan charities.

> One of the first and the most important of these groups was the Pushkin Society…whose avowed aim was to conduct schools on Sunday for workers, open public reading rooms, and give lectures. Until 1904–1905 all the opposition groups flocked around this society without worrying about the divergencies expressed then in Russia between the parties. The activities of the society very quickly disturbed the local authorities, and the military commander of Tashkent pointed out in 1905 that "the Pushkin Society for cultural dissemination has long since been transformed into a social-democratic and revolutionary society."[25]

Jadid (reformist Islamic) groups became especially influential in this period, both on their own merits and thanks to support from Russia. However, eventually, the Empire's administrators in Central Asia interpreted the growing involvement of the local population in revolutionary activities (and some Jadid newspapers, especially after 1905, were considered revolutionary) as substantially more threatening than the activities of orthodox religious organizations. For example, in the first years of the twentieth century, the Union of Holy Bukhara, a Jadidist association, eventually led to the creation of the Young Bukharan Party,[26] and secret societies such as Marifat, Barakat, and the Society for the Education of Youth appeared.[27] Accordingly, twentieth century Russian attempts to co-exist with or control Islam in Central Asia gradually developed into policies aimed at protecting Islam in its "most rigid, hardened forms" in the belief that doing so would impede the development of potentially more reactionary social movements.[28]

It should be noted here that the organizations listed above, despite their fame among scholars, often boasted far less than 100 members, often fewer than 20.[29] This point will become important when Glasnost and independence era organizations are reviewed below since one of the main criticisms of the new NGOs of Central Asia is that they often have fewer than 20 members.

A core concept in civil society literature is that a private sector exists as a counterweight to the state; thus, civil society precludes absolutism. Thus, it is of no small importance that, contrary to popular Western beliefs, destatization was a cornerstone of late Soviet development policy. The evolution of this policy during the middle decades of the USSR should be understood as the enabler of the explosion of Glasnost civil society.

In theory, the establishment of the Soviet state and the nationalization of economic activity (in order to eradicate the perverse influences of private ownership of the means of production) were supposed to be followed by a devolution of state power into nongovernmental hands. By Stalin's death, the Soviet state had progressed far in eradicating private initiative and concentrating state power. Khruschev in turn, in repudiating Stalin's excesses at the Twentieth Party Congress in 1956 and in the 1961 Party Program, placed devolution of state power and functions onto social associations as a primary mission of the next stage of communist development, leading to the eventual withering of the state. *Druzhiny* (brigades) of citizen police, comrades' courts, and other social associations were meant to handle the basic governmental functions of securing public order, while a variety of more charitable associations, like the Red Cross and the Knowledge Society, were hoped to advance public health, education, and related fields. Not truly nongovernmental, these parastatal organizations were nevertheless somewhat independent.

Soviet law recognized three types of social associations: social organizations, social movement organizations, and social self-government organizations (SSGOs).[30] The first two types relate to horizontal (bridging) expressions of social capital. Social organizations, like trade unions and the Red Cross/Red Crescent, displayed (ideally) four legally identifying elements: voluntary membership, a charter, property, and self-government. Social movement organizations, typified by the Soviet Peace Committee, were more informal and lacked membership. Since membership was meaningless anyway in the Soviet context of state funding, there were, for our present purposes, few salient differences between social organizations and social movements.

Soviet social associations during this period enjoyed a special relationship with the state. The Soviet state was envisioned as democratically holding property in trust and acting as a fiduciary for citizens consonant with the idea of popular sovereignty. Social associations were envisioned as subsidiary organizations, more efficient since subsidiary, but with essentially identical fiduciary duties. This conception of fiduciary duties, resting on both subsidiarity and popular sovereignty,[31] explains much of the structure of Soviet society. It explains why Soviet architects scoffed at the utility of separation of powers,[32] why Soviet doctrinaire political scientists could not acknowledge social or environmental problems,[33] why Soviet civil society was parastatal,[34] and why nongovernmental organizations were corporatist.[35]

This curious intellectual tradition and policy framework set the stage for an enormous amount of growth among noncorporatist and independent NGOs in Central Asia beginning in 1987 (Table 4.1). However, roughly a year before the USSR disassembled, grassroots NGOs began to decrease their activities and disband. Two of the reasons why NGOs up to this time could operate in Central Asia may have been because most people, especially in urban areas, had significant leisure time (without television[36]) and because the cost of basic office supplies and communications (mail, telephone, transportation) was low enough to be funded out of one or more members' pockets. A fundamental change in way of life began previous to 1990, but by 1990 it strongly affected people's behavior and outlook. Rising prices and second jobs slaughtered small NGOs that united five or six people and were run out of someone's kitchen. Those small NGOs that did survive had to change their basic structure and operations to become more like a primary association employer and less like a secondary association club.

Unfortunately, we will never know how many NGOs formed and dissolved in Central Asia during Perestroika. The only directory prepared during this period is an analysis that is not interested in NGOs as components of civil society, but only in NGOs (including political parties) as nascent political forces. This directory indicates that in Kazakhstan from 1987 to 1991 (for 11 of Kazakhstan's 19 regions) over 151 NGOs and 24 independent publications formed. These formations were more common in the north than in the south (with the exception of Alma-Ata) and 90 per cent of them were located in the republican or regional capitals.[37] The same directory lists 27 NGOs (more than 18 of them existing at the end of 1990) and 6 independent publications for Bishkek, and a very conservative estimate of more than 53 NGOs formed (and more than 36 operating in 1991[38]) and 8 independent publications for all of Kyrgyzstan.

However, Ponomarev's research, prepared from justice ministry lists and concerning only politically active[39] NGOs, does not identify smaller or less political

Table 4.1 Number of NGOs active at end of year in Kazakh SSR

Region	1986	1987	1988	1989	1990	Total formed
Alma-Ata	0	2	10	33	44	64
Djambul	0	0	1	2	2	4
Dzhezkazgan	0	0	0	2	2	2
Karaganda	0	0	1	5	8	8
Kokchetav	1	1	1	2	2	3
Pavlodar	1	2	1	2	6	10
Northern-Kazakhstan	0	0	0	2	7	9
Semipalatinsk	0	0	1	5	8	9
Taldy-Kurgan	0	0	2	2	3	5
Tselinograd	1	2	3	6	8	11
Chimkent	0	0	2	5	6	16
Total	3	7	22	66	96	141

Source: Adapted from Ponomarev, *Obschestvennye organizatsii v Kazakhstane i Kyrgyzstane 1987–1991*.

NGO initiatives in smaller towns. At the other extreme, a deputy prosecutor in Kazakhstan in September 1988, probably through subjective overestimation of quasi-political groups and certainly inclusive of non-registered organizations, estimated 300 NGOs in Kazakhstan with roughly 3000 members.[40] Returning to Ponomarev, despite his understated number of NGOs, exclusion of 8 regions of Kazakhstan, and exclusion of ethnic centers and Kazakh Tili (a very large nationalist NGO), he estimates that roughly 10,000 people were moderately politically active and 1500 were very active in Kazakhstan through NGOs during Glasnost.[41] He similarly estimates, excluding Ashar, Democratic Movement of Kyrgyzstan, and the national culture centers, 1200 moderately politically active and 300 very active individuals in Kyrgyzstan NGOs during the summer of 1990.[42]

Ponomarev's estimates are certainly conservative. While he lists only 100 very active members and more than 700 members total for Nevada-Semipalatinsk, the organization advertised itself as comprised of over one million members. It collected over one million signatures for a petition to close the Semipalatinsk nuclear test-site. Similar situations exist for Edinstvo, Zheltoksan, and other political NGOs in Kazakhstan.[43] Moreover, while Ponomarev lists only 22 NGOs active at the end of 1988, *Kazakhstanskaya Pravda* posited more than 100 in November 1988.[44]

Asserting that 70 per cent of these early NGOs in Kazakhstan were effectively local independent NGOs (thus engaged in building bridging social capital), Ponomarev also, somewhat confusingly, divides Kazakhstan's NGOs into interest categories: 35 per cent are partisan political, 30 per cent are environmental or peace, 15 per cent are national cultural (ethnic), 10 per cent are historical educational (and, ostensibly, human rights), and 10 per cent are "other."[45] While this general compositional dissociation holds true for the other republics, in Uzbekistan and Turkmenistan far fewer NGOs formed, perhaps an order of magnitude fewer. Tajikistan, while less vibrant than Kazakhstan or Kyrgyzstan, boasted an NGO community and civil society more active than that of Turkmenistan or Uzbekistan.

Outside of numbers, across the region during this period existing environmental NGOs in Central Asia had teeth. Green Salvation (KZ) illustrates the unusual abilities expressed by environmental NGOs. In a case that went up to the Procurator General of the USSR on the eve of the disassembly of the Soviet Union (and therefore a case that simply died), Green Salvation sued Alma-Ata's mayor for gross professional and criminal negligence in performing his duties in a previous post. The group alleged that Mayor Nurkadilov willfully failed to enforce environmental and safety standards. They alleged, *inter alia*, a dereliction of duty that on one count resulted in an explosion at an illegally situated, but officially approved, railway fuel station in Alma-Ata that killed 16 people, including five children.[46] The fact that five average citizens could bring an individual symbolic of the political and economic elite of Kazakhstan to court and potentially win is testimony to the seriousness of the early Gorbachev reforms and the promise of NGOs. Almost as important, Green Salvation's financing came from the income that the group received from a consulting business to banks engaged in automating their operations and from the 1 per cent of their gross incomes that group members gave the organization in membership dues.

FELLOW CITIZENS!

Leaflet copied and distributed in Alma-Ata during the 1991 coup.

A coup has taken place in the USSR. The legal President of the country has been unconstitutionally removed from power.

Maybe Mikhail Gorbachev foreordained his own removal through his inconsistent and contradictory domestic policies, but *this* kind of removal from power by *this* kind of people is a state crime, and the people who have removed him are state criminals.

The sovereignty of the republics is being trampled; political parties and democratic social organizations are being dispersed; freedom of the press is being liquidated; and the country has been driven to the brink of civil war.

Those in the State Committee for States of Emergency promise to restore order, but can they really do so through criminal means? We say – no way! Therefore, any support for their activities or any submission to criminal orders is being an accessory to a crime.

Kazakhstanis, let's not be accessories to this crime!

We, the signers of this appeal, demand that legal government in the USSR be restored and that the coup organizers be brought to trial.

In the event that the actions of the State Emergency are extended into the territory of Kazakhstan, we call upon the public to begin a campaign of civil disobedience, and specifically: on the grounds of anticonstitutionality and illegality, to refuse to submit to the orders of the self-appointed committee, and at places of work and residence to form civil disobedience committees.

We call on the government of sovereign Kazakhstan to arrogate in full all governmental powers in the republic for itself, excluding any execution on our territory of the self-appointed "Center."

We call on all political powers of Kazakhstan to forget yesterday's disagreements. Today, something else is more important: the younger generation accuses the older for its lack of resistance to the forces of Stalinism and Brezhnevism. We'll do everything we can to ensure the future generation does not so accuse us!

Azat Citizen Movement of Kazakhstan
Azamat Youth Organization of Kazakhstan*
Alash Party of National Independence of Kazakhstan
Zheltoksan National Democratic Party of Kazakhstan
Unity Interethnic Movement of Kazakhstan*
Nevada-Semei Anti-Nuclear Movement of Kazakhstan
Memorial Historical Enlightenment and Human Rights Society
Public Committee Alma-Ata–Helsinki–Paris
Public Committee Aral-Asia
Social Democratic Party of Kazakhstan
Helsinki Group
Adilet Historical Enlightenment and Human Rights Society
Democratic Union
Birlesu Trade Union
Transnational Radical Party
Green Salvation Ecological Society
Association for Resistance to Violence
Parasat Society

denotes that no signature recorded for an organization.

Concurrently the nascent Dashkhovuz Ecological Guardians (TM) ran a computer programming business to help finance its anti-poaching efforts. The Guardians won the right from local law enforcement agencies to make citizen arrests for violations of environmental law. And they exercised this right by, at times violently, preventing would-be poachers from shooting and capturing native fauna. The physical scars displayed by some members of this NGO attest to the level of commitment of this organization, while the technological prowess and wide talents of the organization's members enabled the organization to give full expression to that commitment.

At the time of the disassembly of the Soviet Union, two general types of non-profit organizations existed: the independent NGOs described above and their more lackluster communist corporatist peers. The latter type of organization was more affected by the breakup. Usually completely dependent on the state for funding, often disinterested in public opinion, and too frequently lacking in clear purposes, the communist-era organizations were ill suited for existence independent of state support. In some cases, especially for critical welfare programs, reduced state assistance did continue after 1991, but it was often delayed and small. The recipient of immense subsidies from the Soviet state for so many years, independent Central Asia was stymied by the problem of where to find new sources of funding for social programs and state-sponsored non-profits. Initial hopes of international support, especially among the region's environmentalists, were quelled when actual amounts of foreign assistance became evident.

However, most of the more visible organizations were not so directly threatened in the first year or two of independence. Very often, these organizations, forming the core of residual corporatism, possessed large offices in the center of cities and were directed by individuals with direct and intimate connections with the local political and economic elites, in other words with elite social capital. These resources allowed them to remain visible, lowered their operating costs, and gave them the option of renting out office space for cash. It also enabled possibilities for special governmental consideration, exposure to foreign funders, and insulation from enforcement of tax and other legal obligations. Nevertheless, even with these considerable advantages, many communist non-profits withered away. There are three reasons for this, two of which are internal. First, governments have been less willing to provide these organizations with resources. Second, the elites in these organizations fled to positions in emerging commercial structures, where ministry contacts and family names turned out to be no less important. Finally, the vast majority of communist organizations failed to reorganize themselves into viable NGOs with clear missions.

> As a typical example of the operations of a voluntary society [communist non-profit], one can take the work of the Kazakhstan Nature Protection Society (NPS). The Society was organized in 1962 by a decision of the Council of Ministers of the republic for the purposes of providing popular environmental education. Despite quickly changing economic and socio-political conditions, NPS's work is still formulated on the basis of unfulfillable five year plans. The leadership of the society essentially ignores the problems

stemming from the difficult environmental conditions in various regions of Kazakhstan. The only large action of the NPS in the past two years was a "popular mobilization" to green the streets in honor of the Society's thirtieth anniversary. The organization suffers chronic financial problems, because of which a number of regional affiliates have been forced to involve themselves in agricultural projects: in Kzyl-Orda Region a small rice growing business, in Northern Kazakhstan Region grain, in Kokchetav Region potatoes, etc. The NPS does not cooperate with native or foreign environmental organizations.[47]

Those organizations that lacked a mission rarely found one. By the end of 1995, the dust had largely settled. Most communist non-profits had disappeared. Some had become, although somewhat stilted, NGOs. The vast majority of those that survived found a way to plug in either to state political needs, often connected with state-building, or to become attractive to businesses. While some businesses did and do contribute to charities, the most important connections between businesses and non-profits are popularly suspected as stemming from the ability of non-profits to avoid taxes or act as holding companies.

Similarly, grassroots NGOs encountered massive setbacks during this period. The challenges of meeting basic operational costs that slowed their growth in 1990–1991 intensified as the prices of basics, such as telephone calls, skyrocketed. While regular mail was less expensive, it also became unreliable. Membership and volunteer participation plummeted as formerly active individuals channeled their activism into private businesses, took second jobs to make ends meet, lost faith in their organization's ability to effect change, or emigrated. Many NGOs were not able to muster the time and resources necessary to re-register their organizations within the 1 year grace period after enactment of national laws on social associations. The impressive regional and union-wide communication networks that had developed only a year or two earlier fell apart. International contacts floundered as fax costs were impossible to meet, even for incoming faxes. Worse, beginning in 1993, even those local groups that secured access to e-mail found that their potential partners, especially in Europe, were dependent on faxes and unconnected to e-mail.

They also found that they had, somewhere, lost a generation. During the very difficult 1992–1994 years, the vast majority of dedicated grassroots activists were between 35 and 65. People in their twenties were rarities, despite the fact that, according to Ponomarev, at the end of the Soviet period, almost one-quarter of associations were comprised only of youth (65 per cent in Kyrgyzstan) and young adults, and one half of all NGO activists were under 30.[48] Thus, for example, Pavlodar's Ecology and Public Opinion (KZ), arguably the oldest continuously active registered NGO in Central Asia, has based its work on a full time staff person and roughly 30 active members, over 75 per cent of whom are over 50. What happened is that, where possible, youth fled to the allure of the private sector, which considering its novelty, its brandishment as a panacea for social ills, and the promise of the fruits of a market economy, could be considered as an activist decision. Throughout Central Asia, in the environmental sector, the emigration of scientists and the exodus of younger activists led to an observable increase in numbers of the "pleasantly insane and scientifically illiterate."[49]

Furthermore, independence knocked the wind out of many NGOs. At the time, some environmental groups, especially Nevada-Semipalatinsk, had built thriving constituencies by blaming Moscow for local ecological disasters. By adapting their discourse to complement the "ascending spiral of local assertiveness,"[50] they accrued nationalist backing, while maintaining their environmental constituency. However, in an independent Kazakhstan, demands that Moscow restore degraded areas lost political force. Suddenly, the movement's demands could only be directed to republican structures that did not appreciate being saddled with additional problems. Moreover, in the case of Nevada-Semipalatinsk, the nuclear testing ground that was the rallying cry for the organization's activities was closed.[51] Similar situations held for organizations of deported ethnic groups lobbying to be allowed to return to their homelands and Islamic revivalist groups. Whereas they were previously primary beneficiaries of the struggle between the union republics and the center, after independence, they became gadflies to the newly independent states.

While gadflies to new governments, these same organizations were and are the darlings of international donors. Several foreign programs, channeling in total roughly $25,000,000 to local NGOs, have existed in Central Asia over the past decade. The largest, most influential, and most well-known of these is Counterpart Consortium, funded by USAID. Whatever Counterpart's successes (and they are scant given the organization's lack of case studies similar to those of Green Salvation and Dashkhovuz Ecological Guardians above), the emphases of its grants belie both the civil society and the social capital aspects of NGOs. By focusing almost exclusively in its early years on NGOs as alternative, but state-funded, providers of social services, Counterpart has largely disregarded the organizational capital promise of NGOs in democracies and market economies. By emphasizing a later vision of NGOs as full-time employers, Counterpart has similarly ignored the importance of NGOs as secondary associations that enrich the density of a community's social networks. Since other donor programs are similar to Counterpart, foreign aid to Central Asian civil society may not actually be helping to build the social capital of the region.

Likewise, in response to the availability of donor funds, government organized NGOs (GONGOs) sprang up across the region. Whereas Soviet nonprofits served to push policy goals of the Communist Party, GONGOs exist to absorb funds and soften the democratizing impacts of civil society. Uzbekistan has been the most prolific founder of GONGOs, with ECOSAN in the environmental sphere an excellent example. Most of the 2300 NGOs UNDP cites as having been created in Uzbekistan since 1991[52] are either mahalla or GONGOs.

I estimate that there are currently at least 2000 grassroots NGOs in Central Asia that explicitly or implicitly have the goal of facilitating the development of civil society. However, this number is conservative and only refers to actual grassroots NGOs, a label not applicable to the vast majority of social associations and informal associations. Of these, perhaps only a hundred or so are really very active or composed of more than one or two people. On the other hand, I expect that the total number of existing social associations, using the Soviet definitions and categories, of various types must be well over 25,000. For example, while there has usually been only one grassroots environmental NGO in the Khorog area of Tajikistan, the Pamir EcoCenter, there are a large number of other environmental groups that can be classified as social associations in Khorog:

> In 315 grammar schools, 21 extracurricular institutions, and 18 kindergartens, there are 52.7 thousand students and a teaching collective of 6600 teachers and 124 kindergarten instructors. The schoolchildren have 30 hectares of arable land for scientific experiments and work, and 70 hectares are employed by schoolchildren working brigades from 152 schools. There are roughly 200 functioning voluntary nature protection societies, more than 150 nature lovers' and young ecologist clubs, and roughly 30 young forester clubs.[53]

All of this information leads to an ambiguous assessment of social capital and NGOs in Central Asia's civil society. On the one hand, there were and are an appreciable number of non-profits working throughout Central Asia, far more in fact than in most other developing regions. In absolute numbers, there are more NGOs now, especially in Uzbekistan and Tajikistan, than in 1990. On the other hand, more pessimistically, there are no longer any massive membership NGOs in the region to compare to Kazak Tili or Nevada-Semipalatinsk. Furthermore, there may be no more NGO members today than there were a decade ago.

Also, there is a nagging suggestion that the organizations that exist today, quite apart from the likelihood that they contribute less dynamically to civil society development, do a substandard job of creating social capital. Because of economic crisis, failures within the NGO community, and the perverse priorities of donors, there are almost certainly fewer people who are volunteers and participants in NGOs as secondary associations than there were even 10 years ago. By trading in this aspect of civil society and formalizing their structures (while failing to maintain new voluntary structures), the NGOs of Central Asia are gradually decreasing their claim to be incubators of social capital.

BONDING SOCIAL CAPITAL: MAHALLA COMMUNITY ASSOCIATIONS[54]

SSGOs, the third type of Soviet social association defined in the last section, date back to the earliest days of the regime in legal acts establishing institutions like the 1920 library committees,[55] the 1918 police support brigades and the 1919 comrades' courts.[56] In later years they more commonly took the form of druzhiny, residential committees, agricultural committees, and parents' committees for schools. They in general served as the locus of civil society in its closest connection to primary associations. Activities of SSGOs included presenting state agencies with the opinions and ideas of constituents and facilitating rights of citizens to participate in managing the state and society. They were intended to, and did, assume quasi-governmental powers,[57] even police powers in the case of druzhiny members' authority to make arrests. SSGOs were formed by decrees of state agencies and, unlike social organizations, did not have paid staff or status as legal persons.

By focusing on mahalla, the dominant form of post-Soviet SSGO, we can illustrate one aspect of "bonding" social capital in primary associations; the externalities of such social capital are expected theoretically to differ from those attaching to bridging social capital. In particular, a form of insular "familism" is expected to be common of such social capital. I take it for granted that mahalla do, indeed, produce such negative externalities, but they also do produce positive externalities. The positive externalities of insular communities have long been believed to be most important during crises; as the current situation in Central Asia is a crisis situation for the residents of the region, the primary concern of this section is to connect crisis concerns with the externalities of bonding social capital and to ask whether such bonding capital is currently being transformed in the post-Soviet period.

Roughly half of Central Asians live in traditional residential community associations (RCAs), informal obligatory organizations that provide services to and demand contributions from residents. These "mahalla" are known by various names and exhibit tremendous diversity throughout the region. Four basic types of mahalla exist in post-Soviet Uzbekistan. In rural areas, former state and collective farms comprise mahalla ("rural mahalla"). In cities, mahalla encompass modern apartment complexes ("apartment mahalla"), blocks of relatively spread-out single-family dwellings ("new mahalla"), and blocks of densely organized pre-Soviet single-family dwellings ("traditional mahalla"). These last two types of RCAs are the focus of this section; until 1992 no Uzbekistani would have called a kolkhoz or a high-rise apartment a mahalla.[58]

Fundamental mahalla divisions include family, sex, and status. While each of these divisions holds significance, family possesses the most significance for the organization of space in a mahalla, and mahalla themselves probably evolved out of family groupings within expanding cities. In new and old mahalla, teahouses, markets, mosques, and stores are public and quasi-public spaces. The private spaces in a mahalla consist of family dwellings, although in some mahalla community members (especially children) feel free to wander in off the street into the courtyards of family dwellings. They are not as free to enter the rooms off this courtyard.

The entire perimeter of a mahalla property lot is usually walled-in, and abutting houses either share a wall or have walls built snug against each other. Newer or more ostentatious houses may boast small lawns or orchards separating a house from the street. One or more sides of this walled perimeter contain living quarters, and a courtyard always occupies a sizable portion of the area of the home. Most windows face in towards this courtyard, and the defining characteristic of any house is its courtyard. Many courtyards are dedicated to complex gardens that yield a good part of a family's food from a few square yards of soil, while others combine more decorative gardens with a pool, decorative brick pathways, an *aivan* (enclosed porch), or a pen for livestock. The courtyard is a barometer of wealth and status.

Traditional mahalla are, topographically, face blocks in which streets are not boundaries but medians of communities.[59] In contrast, in new mahalla, streets (often major streets) constitute the boundaries delimiting the edges of mahalla. In either case, mahalla often include some central *guzar* collection of institutions, like a bazaar, a mosque, a barbershop, a tea house, or a store. Mahalla are named, sometimes for people, sometimes for events, and sometimes with monikers whose meaning is now lost to its residents. While most female socializing occurs within family courtyards and on streets, men (especially older men) also socialize in a *choikhana* (tearoom) or in cafes run out of private courtyards. In the past, where a choikhana did not serve as a social center, a mosque or market did. Children socialize primarily on streets.

One is a member of a mahalla by virtue of residency, not choice. While one can maintain an association with a close relative's mahalla, one cannot renounce one's own mahalla except by moving out. Non-Uzbeks (i.e. Russians) living within mahalla are often not expected to contribute work and services, or even to participate in mahalla events, but the mahalla usually still provides them with services and expects them to acknowledge the mahalla as a primary social force.[60] Even as a theoretical possibility, most Uzbeks reject the possibility of divorcing oneself from a mahalla. However, while voluntary secession from a mahalla is virtually unknown, some individuals do become separated from mahalla by becoming outcasts. The devastating effect of such exclusion is captured by several Uzbek sayings that equate internal mahalla exile with death. Uzbekistan society brandishes a robust set of non-legal punishments for those who defect from the requirements of mahalla life. Yet, once a family moves to another mahalla, ties to the old mahalla are greatly attenuated, and the family is expected to reorient its social life to the new neighborhood. Similarly, when a woman marries, she settles in her husband's mahalla (usually in a house shared with her in-laws) and is discouraged from maintaining strong ties with her former mahalla.

A norm of a right of first refusal is conferred on mahalla members in the event a member sells a home. In many Islamic areas, only an abutting neighbor enjoys this right, but in Central Asia it extends to all mahalla members.[61] In the event that no intra-mahalla buyer comes forward, a seller may still not be able simply to sell to the highest bidder. Without the formality of a New York co-op, but with equivalent scrutiny, the blessing of mahalla leadership is often sought before final sale. While law does not require this blessing, a family taking up residence against the wishes of mahalla leaders could be subject to unpleasantries. Savvy immigrants usually seek such a blessing or, at least, make sure that their immediate neighbors are amenable.

Modern mahalla leadership draws on four distinct sources of authority. Under formal authority: a chairperson (*rais*) leads the mahalla committee (*kengash*). Second, under informal authority, an *aksaqal* (whitebeard) is an older male selected by consensus from his generational cohort for his wisdom, clout, and managerial finesse. As wealth engenders respect, the wealthy comprise a third authority. Finally, under female authority, a senior woman (*kaivoni*) assumes informal leadership roles, often in tandem with formal service on a mahalla women's committee.

In clientalistic Uzbekistan, state power, gerontocracy, wealth, and female status are usually not diffused throughout the mahalla. Usually a few families capture the bulk of mahalla leadership positions or alter the comparative weight of these positions so as to capture *de facto* power,[62] notwithstanding formal legal entitlements (a straightforward apportionment of votes according to population). Yet, the structures, public demands on, and internal composition of mahalla across Uzbekistan produce a great diversity of allocations of mahalla power.

Mahalla channel several institutions that mediate between mahalla and family, mahalla and culture, mahalla and survival, and mahalla and commerce. Mahalla even externalize the most meaningful and intimate relations of nuclear families. Families must (at great expense) mark births, male circumcision, weddings, and deaths with formalities, called, generically, *toi*. Some toi are open to the community at large, but a number are restricted to more parochial identity groups, such as adult males. Often, the mahalla owns or possesses a supply of tables, chairs, cooking supplies, and other implements for such events that it lends or leases to community members for such occasions.

Among the Uzbek traditions that bring mahalla or large parts of a mahalla together are births (*sunnat toi* and *beshik toi*),[63] *khudoii* (prayer),[64] *toi* (weddings), four funeral events spread over a year,[65] post-Soviet celebrations (*Novruz* and *Mustakillik*[66]), and *gap* (mutual aid).[67] In a mahalla of 2000 people, excluding the rituals that happen more often than once a year, the annual and once in a lifetime rituals alone create roughly 200 occasions for community or partial community gathering in a year.[68] On average, the mahalla community comes together once a week, although the warmer months actually see more activity.

Even outside of these formal occasions, mahalla are a primary source of social services for residents. In some Soviet era mahalla, this aspect of mahalla life declined due to the Soviet welfare state, while under post-Soviet decline, some mahalla have again superceded the state as the primary provider of social guarantees. Mahalla residents call on each other to provide labor for house repairs, hand-me-downs to children, and a variety of informal services that are easily described as neighborliness. Uzbeks have a well-developed practice of mutual assistance called *hashar* that transcends bilateral relations. Mahalla rais and members draw on hashar to motivate residents to, *inter alia*, maintain the cleanliness of streets and gutters and improve the look of their mahalla on the eve of celebrations and state holidays. Mahalla frequently also provide substantial support to the elderly, intercede in cases of domestic abuse (and deter divorce), provide adjudication to quell disputes between neighbors and, in the converse, pressure more wealthy residents to share some of their wealth with the wider community.[69]

Finally, with the collapse of employment opportunities after the disassembly of the USSR, mahalla have in many cases become primary centers of economic activity. During the Soviet period, large parts of Uzbekistan's fabled gray economy also rested on mahalla foundations. With the collapse of the state's ability to provide even subsistence employment, the economic significance of mahalla has shifted from being a vehicle through which to amass additional wealth to a vehicle for survival. Much of Uzbekistan's foreign trade has been conducted by mahalla-based groups of traders.

Perhaps the most universal aspect of mahalla is that no member is, for class, profession, or religious reasons, excluded from community events. Without idealizing mahalla into areas of social harmony (which, of course, they are not), mahalla are traditionally the only places where some kinds of people (i.e. Sunni/Shiite, merchants/laborers, rich/poor) interact with each other.

Moreover, the mahalla system may have historically created a mechanism through which the services of Islamic charitable institutions (*waqf*) reached a social cross-section of the population. Olga Sukhareva, an anthropologist who studied mahalla in Bukhara, posits that residents of mahalla possessed the right to use all social institutions in their mahalla, including mosques, large cooking areas and supplies, water supply (for cooking, drinking, and ablutions), and materials for transporting the deceased to a cemetery.[70]

The foregoing discussion relates to a modern analysis of Uzbekistan's mahalla because it establishes a history of public goods in Uzbekistan communities similar to the kinds of modern public goods important to Uzbekistan citizens and the Uzbek state. At the risk of presenting an overly simplified picture, public goods in medieval Central Asian cities flowed primarily from the community and waqf, and only marginally from the state. Mahalla provided the framework for important social and professional networks, coordinated defense, implemented social insurance strategies, and facilitated communication with the government.[71] Complementing mahalla, waqf provided spiritual public goods and, with less complete coverage, public goods such as water, education, medical care, libraries, and charitable assistance.[72]

When the USSR began uprooting native social institutions to replace them with isomorphic Soviet institutions, as a glaring exception to this policy, mahalla were incorporated into the Soviet system rather than targeted for dissolution. Whether Moscow developers primarily saw mahalla as impossible to eradicate without risking revolt or whether these developers primarily saw the institutions as complementing development and ideological goals is not clear, nor is it important to assign primacy to either of these reasons. In the final assessment, Moscow decided that the benefits of subversion of mahalla outweighed the costs of abolishing it.

The Soviet government retained mahalla as self-governing (in name) RCAs. The mahalla aksaqal became a symbolically elected chairperson, whose appointment was controlled by the local party apparatus. Instead of informal advisors, he now could rely on a committee to advise him, and certain issues were managed by separate committees, such as a women's committee. By the late Soviet period, the room occupied by the mahalla committee often looked like any Soviet office, decorated with Soviet symbols and graced with portraits of Soviet leaders, and most residents did not distinguish between the bureaucratic and informal aspects of mahalla.[73]

Over its lifespan, the Soviet state steadily razed neighborhoods of traditional mahalla with their narrow streets providing shelter from the summer sun and replaced them with apartment complexes or new mahalla. Residents could choose to take apartments in these buildings or move away to areas reserved for new mahalla,[74] with the effect that the composition of mahalla changed. By 1989, only a third of Tashkent citizens lived in new or traditional mahalla.[75] Those who remained in mahalla nevertheless shared increasingly little in common with pre-Soviet predecessors. While Soviet-era mahalla carried the same name as their eighteenth century predecessors, and while these mahalla looked similar on the surface, they had changed into fundamentally different institutions.[76] Most important for the present discussion, whereas pre-Russian mahalla residents expected almost nothing from the state in the way of public goods, late Soviet mahalla residents imagined that the only way to good schools, adequate medical care, potable water, and crime prevention was through a strong state.

A process of state "mahallization" further distances mahalla from its roots in social norms despite the fact that most current legal reforms primarily codify the heretofore informal working of mahalla. By law, a "citizen gathering"[77] now governs mahalla, but day to day governance is in the hands of its agents: the *kengash* (composed of the rais, his advisors, commission chairs, and a secretary). While all mahalla residents 18 and older ostensibly elect these agents in a direct vote, in fact the district government is the principal power broker.

These changes and the mahallization of farms and apartment buildings are measures taken in shallow rejection of the USSR and as a bulkhead against Islam. The appeal of mahallization from the state's perspective is that it introduces homogeneity into the governing structure of the state, can be portrayed as Uzbek without reference to Islam, and can Uzbekify an ethnically diverse population.[78] It is such a foundation of mahallization that explains how the state can trumpet mahalla as the cornerstone of Uzbekistan society and at the same time accelerate Soviet projects to raze traditional mahalla, ignore protests from local residents, and erect modern apartment buildings. In this process, the state views mahalla as secular, foundational political subdivisions that facilitate communalistic values, and it would appear to assume that mahalla are inevitable, immutable, and stable.

Uzbekistan is eager to harvest the fruits of social norms, but unconcerned about their roots. State policies assume mahalla norms to be static and stable and, therefore, manipulable. For example, the state advocates the creation of mahalla *posbonlari* (guards) as neighborhood patrol groups. These groups are formally citizen self-government organizations (CSGOs) like Soviet SSGOs. Through mahallization they are expected to draw on *hashar* norms of noncompensated work and produce results consistent with the fact that during the Soviet and early post-Soviet period new and traditional mahalla reported lower crime rates than other areas.

When it comes to management, the state views mahalla purely as CSGOs, not as a balance of social norms. For example, kengash now include, by law, non-resident representatives of state welfare agencies. In response, in many mahalla, an unofficial aksaqal has arisen parallel to the official rais and kengash. Through one lens, this parallel power structure can be viewed as a form of resistance to state arrogation of mahalla.

The irony, of course, is that civil society presupposes spheres of public life autonomous from the state. Leaving aside concerns about democracy for the moment, it is impossible to reconcile efforts by the state to consolidate control at the expense of autonomous associations with development of civil society and social capital. At best, Uzbekistan's current trajectory is towards an, albeit organizationally pluralistic, parastatal civil society.

Time and again in Uzbekistan, policymakers list the alleged traditional benefits of mahalla, add new responsibilities to mahalla, and then laud mahalla for providing both traditional and new public goods. The implicit assumption is that mahalla will retain local authority and will continue to provide traditional public goods, all while integrating themselves into the new administrative system of sovereign Uzbekistan.

Is this assumption defensible? Might *administrative mahalla* turn out to be immiscible with *social mahalla*? Might this result erode the positive externalities of mahalla? Might expanding administrative functions and state salaries gradually effect a change in perceptions, gradually transforming mahalla into state agencies unable to mobilize the local community without dangling funds and no longer allowed authoritatively to mediate neighborhood affairs?[79]

To research how mahalla are changing, we surveyed mahalla resident attitudes toward mahalla and aspects of contemporary life in Uzbekistan. We introduced regional disaggregation to illustrate the degree to which regions of Uzbekistan exhibit persistent differences despite uniform national laws. We also introduced resident disaggregation in order to understand better how the role of mahalla is changing in light of the administrative reforms of the 1990s.

Two thousand respondents in seven of Uzbekistan's 12 viloyatlar provided information to my colleagues[80] on the importance of mahalla in their lives. In this survey, divorcees valued mahalla less than did their married or widowed neighbors. Also, the more children in a family, the more it values mahalla. The richer a family is, the less it values mahalla, with the caveat that the richest families either highly value (at levels substantially higher than the merely rich) or essentially resent mahalla. Of critical interest, among the services most appreciated and valued by residents is spousal dispute resolution. By surveying mahalla homebuyers[81] in three cities,[82] we found that the presence of relatives in a mahalla shapes attitudes as strongly as does number of children (Figure 4.1).[83]

	Nearby Extended Family	No Nearby Extended Family
Few Children	Low	Medium
More Children	Medium	High

Figure 4.1 Mahalla importance.

We found substantial differences between respondents who inquire into the identities and characters of rais and aksaqal before purchase and those who do not (Table 4.2). While these differences include variables such as what region of Uzbekistan one inhabits, they also include a proxy for social capital,[84] the desire to avoid environmental risks, individual risk averseness, the desire to live near family, and when respondents moved. The dividing line between the 71 per cent of home buyers who learn about rais before purchasing and the 29 per cent who do not is in large part explained through these variables.

At statistically significant levels, prospective buyers who do not seek advice outside the family on whether or not to purchase a given house also tend not to inquire into rais and aksaqal. Likewise, buyers without family in their prospective mahalla and more risk averse buyers more frequently make inquiries about aksaqal and rais. While 71 per cent of homebuyers inquired into rais, only 39 per cent inquired into aksaqal. However, also at statistically significant levels, the more recent homebuyers[85] were more likely to inquire into aksaqal, suggesting that as the effects of the transition period penetrate society, the aksaqal is gaining importance again.

While the influence of environmental concerns is not statistically significant, the variable's coefficient is positive for aksaqal and negative for rais. Under transition reforms, mahalla have been endowed with extensive rights and duties regarding environmental protection and assessment. This curious difference in coefficients may reflect some early effects of state efforts to establish mahalla as local environmental agencies. New residents concerned about environment health may see *administrative mahalla* as relevant and *social mahalla* as irrelevant. Education, surprisingly, is a poor predictor of environmental concern. Rather, women, older respondents, and those who emphasize prestige of a mahalla in

Table 4.2 What sparks concern about rais and aksaqal?

$N=72$	$Prob.>chi^2=0.00$		$Pseudo\ R^2=0.48$	
	Coef.	*Std. Err*	z	$P>|z|$
Rais				
Advice	4.7	1.8	2.6	0.01
Family	−4.4	1.7	−2.7	0.01
Ecology	−3.9	3.8	−1.0	0.30
Risk	−4.0	1.2	−3.2	0.001
City	0.82	0.64	1.3	0.20
Time	.0.12	0.27	0.46	0.65
Aksaqal				
Advice	1.4	0.78	1.8	0.07
City	1.2	0.44	2.8	0.01
Risk	−1.5	0.76	−2.0	0.05
Ecology	2.9	3.2	0.92	0.36
Family	−1.5	0.87	−1.7	0.08
Time	0.41	0.22	1.8	0.07

Table 4.3 What predicts environmental concern?

Ecology (N=78)	Prob. > F = 0.00		Adjusted R^2 = 0.27	
	Coef.	Std. Err	t	P > |t|
Sex	−0.059	0.026	−2.3	0.026
Age	0.0065	0.0013	5.1	0.000
Image	0.059	0.025	2.3	0.024
Intercept	−0.028	0.054	−0.52	0.61

house selection are more concerned with environmental health (Table 4.3). Disaggregating the data by sex or education fails to produce statistically significant divergent populations with regard to attitudes about rais, aksaqal, and most other aspects of mahalla life. Similarly, the bifurcation between city and country is not a significant source of divergent attitudes in the dataset.[86]

The general conclusion relevant to evolving mahalla is that family characteristics remain central to understanding individual attitudes. The role of the family comes into clearer focus within the framework of understanding both mahalla and family as insurance mechanisms. Table 4.4 outlines some of the characteristics of those who emphasize the importance of living in a mahalla that contains close relatives. Those who are unconcerned with aksaqal, are younger, are less concerned with the material comforts of a given home, or are less likely to turn to friends for advice are more likely to be seeking out a house in a mahalla with family.

In contrast, as illustrated in Table 4.5, those who simply looked for the best house at the best price were more likely to be moving from another city or viloyat than from one mahalla to another. They were also less likely to be interested in the distribution of power in a mahalla, were more likely to be younger, less likely to be interested in home gardening, less concerned about environmental health, and less likely to have family in their prospective new mahalla.

Table 4.4 What predicts desire to live near relatives?

Family (N=72)	Prob. > F = 0.00		Adjusted R^2 = 0.32	
	Coef.	Std. Err	t	P > |t|
Rais	−0.37	0.11	−3.4	0.001
Age	−0.011	0.004	−3.0	0.004
Risk	−0.18	0.092	−2.0	0.05
Utilities	0.22	0.087	2.5	0.02
Advice	0.15	0.089	1.6	0.11
Intercept	1.0	0.21	4.9	0.000

Table 4.5 What predicts emphasis on price alone?

Price (N=75)	Prob. > F = 0.00		Adjusted R² = 0.23	
	Coef.	*Std. Err*	*t*	*P > |t|*
Immigrant	0.09	0.07	1.3	0.20
Aksaqal	0.19	0.08	2.3	0.022
Age	−0.010	0.004	−2.7	0.009
Price/Services	0.10	0.075	1.4	0.17
Utilities	−0.11	0.087	−1.3	0.19
Price/Ag	−0.16	0.077	−2.1	0.041
Price/Ecology	0.21	0.075	2.7	0.008
Family	0.14	0.080	1.8	0.077
Intercept	0.61	0.18	3.4	0.001

A great number of Uzbekistanis today look beyond primary family and employment associations to ensure the future. Uzbekistan currently offers three general risk-spreading institutions: extended family, social mahalla, and administrative mahalla. Given the critical importance of risk-spreading institutions in the lives of Uzbekistanis, fundamental disruptions in any institution could produce misfortune for many. Family may still be sacred in Uzbekistan. The state has lost much of its capacity in the past decade. It remains an open question how traditional mahalla functions of providing social insurance will weather the transition.

In the present, mahalla residents may enjoy an advantage over apartment mahalla peers. The failed economy of Uzbekistan and the inadequate social insurance programs of the post-Soviet period create insurance needs that reinvigorate mahalla, and may possibly provide a foundation for the appearance of mahalla functions in apartment mahalla. In modern Uzbekistan, few weddings, emergency medical operations, university matriculations, house repairs, or funerals take place in the life of the average mahalla resident without some community financial support.

Property scholars usually look to the productivity of agricultural land as the metric to compare property regimes. However, such analyses offer little to those interested in urban areas in states with large service sectors, like Uzbekistan. The connection between alternative property regimes and wealth in Uzbekistan's cities depends little on which regimes foster better agricultural productivity. Wealth in urban land regimes depends more on issues such as security, location, aesthetics, and transportation. In contemporary Uzbekistan, wealth in land regimes may largely depend on social insurance institutions, and the bonding social capital foundations of these institutions.

Since they are now at the heart of elections, at the heart of executive government, at the heart of much employment, administer most social programs, notarize wills, collect taxes, act as a monitor against the appearance of enemies of the state, organize community events, and are the conduits for foreign efforts for human rights, family planning, and microcredit, mahalla are suddenly no longer mere residential associations. Elegantly employing the very rhetoric of development agencies in the process of defeating the objectives of these agencies, Uzbekistan is transforming post-Soviet mahalla into the main agencies of an emerging absolutist state.

The majority of mahalla residents, and probably the majority of rais, are unaware of the normative provisions of recent mahalla legislation. Despite major changes in the laws, for the most part, mahalla change slowly. In most mahalla, most social organization and most problem solving proceeds from the same bases as 10 years ago, often in contravention of these new laws. However, it would be premature to conclude from this situation that mahalla will resist legislative restructuring. More likely, mahalla will, over time, increasingly conform to the provisions of the new laws. Accordingly, the warning signs and trends provoked by the 1993 mahalla reforms are probably only minor compared to what will result from the 1999 Mahalla Law, which is far more ambitious in its demands on these local associations to assume new roles.

Just as mahalla begin to capture scholarly attention, much of their charm and promise may be disappearing. Despite Western awe of the scale of clientalism in Uzbekistan, somehow all parties (except mahalla residents, who are already complaining) assume that the hallowed status of mahalla limits corruption, the need for monitoring of agents, and the need for increased oversight of mahalla by institutions such as courts and auditors.[87] In contrast, it is nearly a truism of politics in general and RCAs in particular that they warrant "more and more external checks as [their] power grows."[88]

This need is exacerbated given new rights of rais to lease land, collect rents, and engage in commerce. It is no surprise that rais are well-off and that mahalla are increasingly the objects of popular resentment; they may soon be as healthily resented as any other unit of government. Even in connection with the supposed charitable functions of mahalla, the new power to disburse funds challenges and erodes mahalla norms of using community resources to address welfare cases poorly decided by state welfare agencies.[89] It also creates opportunities for corruption.[90]

Current residential regime reforms threaten to disrupt and dislocate local communities across Uzbekistan, all in the name of harnessing the promise of local communities. Since this process is already well under way and broadly supported by foreign donors, one can only hope that social norms of community celebration, hashar, and gap will migrate to new settings sheltered from state regulation and beneficence. Notwithstanding the undeniable benefits to be gained by harnessing the power of mahalla, these benefits pale in comparison to what stands to be lost in the form of conflict resolution, social insurance, and strong communities.

But, while the state continues to try to move mahalla from the province of *gemeinschaft* to the rule of *gesellschaft*, one trend provides some hope for the continuance of a strong stock of social capital at the residential level. The individualistic foundations of *gesellschaft* are being fundamentally rejected by grass-roots Uzbekistani community, and this rejection is building a new set of mahalla social norms (i.e. the reinvigoration of the aqsakal's role) and a new variety of mahalla social networks (i.e. connected to new employment and mosques). While neither of these trends finds favor with the Uzbek ruling elite, they do create an appreciation for both the stock and the staying power of social capital in an important segment of Central Asian society.

EVALUATING THE ERAS OF SOCIAL CAPITAL IN CENTRAL ASIA

[L]evels of social capital were low or depleted under communism to begin with. This should not surprise us, since the objective of Marxist-Leninism was to stamp out an independent civil society and the ties between citizens on which civil society was based.[91]

Asked about the historical spread of social capital in Central Asia, recent generations of scholars, especially economists and political scientists, would likely answer that the region had low stocks of social capital in both the pre-Soviet and the Soviet eras. The continued social science dominance of simple and statist depictions of Asian societies, as despotic and hydraulic,[92] is only very gradually giving way to the effects of more nuanced histories.[93] I believe that, eventually,. a careful review of medieval Central Asian communities will produce a picture of a society in which most public goods and most complex coordination problems were solved through social norms and social coordination, not through the offices of the state. Nevertheless, coupling Orientalism's biases with American scholarship's ambitions to reiterate and expand the failures of the Soviet Union, existing scholarship related to past social capital is very weak and very pessimistic. For example, the scholarly world has missed out on the fact that the USSR, which allegedly was in the Orientalist tradition indifferent to internal public opinion and lacking in any civil society, abandoned its budgeted and approved program to divert Siberian rivers to the Aral Sea basin for the sole reason that the public rejected that plan.[94]

Likewise, much of the current international research that specifically targets country-level studies of social capital rests on highly suspect foundations. The current consensus about social capital is that it is of critical importance to economic development, as well as to many other public goods. Therefore, in areas experiencing economic booms, researchers implicitly seek social capital; in areas of less fortunate economic times, researchers seek the absence of social capital. It is to this trend that Portes and Landolt point when they write that when "social capital and the benefits derived from it are confused, the term merely says that the successful succeed."[95] Francis Fukuyama exemplifies this trend in the passage above.

Fukuyama proceeds from the assumption, presented as a conclusion, that the Soviet Union possessed little social capital. Interestingly, in *The Great Disruption*, he pursues this point through a contrast between Boston's North End since the 1950s and a generalized description of community in the "former communist world."[96] For Fukuyama, this simultaneous deterioration of community (and hence social capital) was epitomized through a loss of the streets of Boston as communal areas: "The adults retreated from sidewalks to their high-rise apartments, and as a result, crime rates began to soar."[97]

Unlike Fukuyama, for me a comparison between the North End and the former communist world is not an abstract inquiry; as a full-time resident of the North End and frequent resident of the former communist world, I find Fukuyama's descriptions inverted. While Fukuyama cites Jane Jacobs for his description of the North End, he cites nothing for his picture of the decline of or absence of community in the communist world. In reality, the Central Asian communities during the period that he cites (1950–1990) experienced many problems, but not those ascribed to them by Fukuyama. These neighborhoods, even those, to a lesser degree, characterized by high-rise apartments, experienced exactly the kind of watchful street life valorized by Fukuyama and described in passing in the section above on mahalla.

Indeed, Fukuyama's concurrent celebration of social capital and castigation of the USSR is discursively compelling but factually self-defeating. He celebrates as social capital the fact that, when in trouble, America's Nucor Corporation cut back on hours instead of laying off staff;[98] rare in America, this practice has been the norm in the entire post-Soviet world in the past decade. He suggests that the USSR was a place of weak families, no secondary associations (and he defines such as non-kinship associations for rich countries but, asymmetrically, as non-state in the Soviet context), and rampant organized crime,[99] while no serious study would support any of these findings. He explains why Korea is successful and China is not by citing five Korean practices (allegedly) without analogs in China: extended kinship, regionalism, a university class, universal conscription, and hobby groups.[100] These are the same things that differentiate the USSR (and its successor states) from China,[101] which, to follow Fukuyama's logic, implies either that the USSR had high social capital or that Korea has no trust; Fukuyama, because of his ideological predispositions, denies either result.

Similarly, Fukuyama emphasizes as proof of the existence of social capital in suburban Washington, D.C. the appearance of "slugs," commuters who ride in the cars of complete strangers.[102] Without denying the validity of Fukuyama's conclusions regarding the social capital consequences of such carpooling, his own work would seem to suggest that Washington, D.C. may now be moving towards levels of trust typical of the USSR during the height of its existence as an Evil Empire.

Given these observations, that crime rates soared after the disassembly of the USSR is not as telling a symptom of low social capital as Fukuyama suggests. Rather, given the concurrent spread of heavy out-migration, rising unemployment, and a destroyed economy, it seems curiously ambitious to ascribe rising crime rates in an area so much in turmoil to something as obscure as social capital. Moreover, even if social capital plays a role, social capital use and formation occur on many different levels. Given that the Internet is a minor presence in Central Asia, and therefore not a mitigating factor, the spread of televisions and non-educational programming throughout Central Asia is probably as large a factor as anything else in degrading levels of social capital. Extended families and individuals do socialize less often than before specifically because of the spread of televisions, satellite dishes, knock-off cassettes of Hollywood block-busters, and the expense of cafes, restaurants, and other non-home recreational venues.

The danger of work such as that pursued by Fukuyama exists on two levels. On one level, since Fukuyama bases his efforts on a false data set and just is not getting the story right, his writings work against a deeper understanding of the former Soviet Union. He is, in other words, misleading. Yet, on the other hand, Fukuyama's work has a darker consequence. By reducing moments of great suffering and tragedy to simplistic explanations, explanations that are false, Fukuyama suggests that social capital is a panacea. That is the implicit message of *The Great Disruption*, and it is the natural corollary to his assertion in *Trust* that a deficiency of social capital is what explains the downfall of the Soviet Union.[103] Fukuyama's message is unmistakable: if the former communist world or any developing state only had social capital, it would quickly ascend to the level of a developed state.[104] This kind of scholarship only sets the stage for a new wave of ill-considered and disastrous development interventions.

Soviet society, very much a civil society in terms of its bounty of crosscutting interests and vectors of possible identity expression, was more vibrant and more complex than Fukuyama imagines. What's more, this civil society and its diverse manifestations of social capital built on pre-Soviet forms of social capital and civil society. Of course, Stalinism may have been the antithesis of social capital development, but, curiously, World War II may have been one of the major facilitators of Stalin-era social capital. Simple descriptions and explanations of the strengths and weaknesses of Central Asia's historical and current levels of social capital and civil society are destined to fail given the actual complexity of the region.

Accordingly, the disassembly of the USSR had multiple impacts on social capital. It probably weakened levels of general social capital, although these may be rebounding and never reached the low levels that characterize parts of Africa or, for that matter, the United States. However, indicators from the region suggest that levels of bridging social capital have fallen in the last 10 years. In contrast, bonding social capital experienced less degradation during the transition period. Yet, what has transpired with bonding social capital in the region has substantial implications for social capital's context for development interventions. Some scholars suggest that social norms are merely the content of normatively desirable future laws,[105] but others suggest, theoretically, that this "law from order" approach will often lead to failures of both formal and informal rules.[106] The case of mahalla provides interesting empirical support for a large theoretical reservation about social norms.

5 International environmental regimes and international environmental law

The international environmental arena is now thematically crowded; few unaddressed themes can be found among thousands of environmental treaties,[1] several dozen specialized international environmental institutions, and the tens of thousands of NGOs with interests in international environmental law and politics. Yet, despite this expansion of raw organizational capital in the international environment, very few of the principles, objectives, or commitments contained within these treaties, institutions, and associations can readily be considered law. In other words, a shortfall exists between the organizational capital aspirations of the international environmental community and the reality that the organizational capital assets that this community commands display a pervasive lack of robustness. At a global level, the current era of environmental law has not produced a halt in the degradation of biodiversity, a reversal of carbon concentration in the atmosphere, a stopping of the advance of deserts, or an aggregate decline in water pollution. For successes, the era can boast little more than a projected decline in ozone depleting substances and scattered local improvements.

Nevertheless, the organizational capital assets of environmental regimes, contained for the most part in a pantheon of treaties and organizations, illustrate the aspirations of a growing international community. This community endeavors to bring the international environment under strict regulation (whether through market or command and control mechanisms) and secure the reign of international environmental rule of law. Yet, while these assets and their attendant aspirations hold legal content and speak in legal language, they lack several key features of a democratic system of rule of law.[2] Specifically, they do not root themselves in the authority of a representative legislative body, boast almost no law enforcement agencies, and lack a judicial system with broad jurisdiction.

In domestic legal systems, a sovereign possesses the exclusive right to declare law; where a state embraces the emerging international norm of popular sovereignty, as is the case in all the Central Asian republics,[3] the "sovereign" is constituted through elected representatives. In contrast, the genesis of international law only appears democratic; new rules of international law can only arise through the consent of states. However, for several reasons, this process falls short of both the democratic and legislative ideals of popular sovereignty. First, democracy involves people, and states are imperfect proxies for human individuals, especially considering the number of states not ruled democratically and the fact that foreign policy decisions are rarely the issues around which internal democratic elections revolve. Second, the international legislative process remains murky; while international law can and is created through explicit treaty-making, this process rarely involves, or even invites, the involvement of all the states of the world. Finally, international law also largely arises from the custom of states, and no scholars or states have developed a test to determine custom that does not leave wide latitude for manipulation and coercion.[4]

Moving to the second general failing of the international legal system, no environmental regime possesses efficacious law enforcement agents. Where states should perform this function, they often either do not or, by necessity, constrain this enforcement to their own borders. While international bodies such as the UN Security Council could essay to assume such environmental law enforcement functions, to date they have infrequently done so. There simply is not formal enforcement of international environmental law as such. Moreover, despite provisions of the United Nations Charter[5] meant to establish an effective law enforcement arm for international law, states ignore (and effectively disobey) requirements to contribute forces, equipment, and authority to the United Nations. Thus, the failings of international environmental law enforcement reflect general limits of international law enforcement.

Finally, despite the existence of an International Court of Justice (ICJ) created under the United Nations Charter and the more recent emergence of a plan for an International Criminal Court, there is no effective judicial arm of international environmental law. To wit, despite early willingness by states to give the ICJ a wide degree of jurisdiction,[6] currently the ICJ finds itself with a narrow jurisdiction over international disputes. The Environmental Chamber of the ICJ has, in fact, never once been used. Similarly, there is almost no precedent for, and there are numerous treaty prohibitions against, the use of domestic courts to adjudicate allegations of the violation of international environmental law.

All of these organizational weaknesses find expression in international environmental regimes, and many are exacerbated because, to date, few environmental problems elicit excited expressions of state interest on the scale of those elicited by concerns over governing ideologies, nonproliferation, ethnic cleansing, or even trade. As a result, international environmental regimes lack equivalents to NATO, the World Trade Organization, or the International Atomic Energy Association.

Yet, that does not mean that environmental regimes are not moving in the direction of establishing strong international bodies and the institutional arsenal of an effective system of rule of law. Over the past 30 years, environmental regimes have expanded their scope dramatically. Nevertheless, at present in those cases when states implement, enforce, and effectuate international environmental law, it is rarely because of the autonomous imperative of an environmental rule of law, but rather because of the fortuitous confluence of diverse organizational, physical, human, and social capital assets mobilized for non-environmental concerns.

The history of Soviet environmental diplomacy illustrates this trend. Prior to the 1970s, while environmental treaties, especially for the conservation of wildlife, were not uncommon, these treaties were, except for the International Convention for the Regulation of Whaling (1946), not global in scope and not part of a broader environmental agenda. However, in the 1970s a wave of global environmental accords appeared, including, the 1971 Convention on Wetlands of International Importance Especially as Waterfowl Habitat (Ramsar), the 1973 Convention to Regulate International Trade in Endangered Species of Flora and Fauna (CITES), and the 1973 International Convention for the Prevention of Pollution from Ships (MARPOL). Although more generalized environmental concerns did gain attention in the 1970s, wildlife conservation continued to be the major focus of formal lawmaking.

While largely dismissive of these early 1970s initiatives, by the end of the decade the Soviet Union actively participated in numerous environmental agreements. However, for the most part, these agreements were European in scale and motivated in large part by the USSR's efforts at detente in order to attract Western capital.[7] For example, the USSR ratified the 1974 Convention on the Protection of the Marine Environment of the Baltic Sea, the 1979 United Nations Economic Commission for Europe (UNECE), Convention on the Conservation of Migratory Species of Animals (CMS), and the 1979 UNECE Convention on Long-Range Transboundary Air Pollution (LRTAP), but was not an original party to either CITES or Ramsar, acceding to both in 1976. It did not accede to MARPOL until 1983.

In the 1980s, international environmental law greatly expanded the scope of its ambitions, although it did not appreciably increase the number of global environmental conventions. The 1980s saw major global agreements on protection of the ozone layer and on movements of hazardous waste, both of which the USSR signed and helped negotiate.[8] While the decade's efforts to create agreements for other issues did not come to fruition until the 1990s, the Soviet Union remained a central and active player in international environmental diplomacy. In no small part as the result of this activity, the international response to the Soviet Union's disassembly has involved substantial attention to the environmental legacy of the USSR and the need to assist the successor states to make a transition to both democratic free markets and sustainability.

The early 1990s not only saw the appearance of global climate change, biodiversity, and desertification conventions, but also of the Global Environment Facility (GEF), the first major environmental financial mechanism, jointly managed by UNDP, UNEP, and the World Bank. In addition to these innovations, the 1990s also witnessed a large number of additional protocols for, *inter alia*, the ozone regime, CMS, and LRTAP, as well as two major conventions regulating the use of transboundary watercourses. Matching these trends, state donors and private foundations also dramatically increased their international environmental assistance, often for projects explicitly connected to the expansion of international environmental law.

Accordingly, the implementation of international environmental laws now interests not only treaty secretariats and state parties to treaties; in recent years it has also come to involve the full panoply of development agencies and global civil society.[9] On their heels, it also captures substantial academic attention. Moreover, as these environmental regimes expand, they increasingly intersect with, and at times challenge, other international regimes regulating issues such as human rights, trade, intellectual property protection, and boundary delimitation.

Given this evolving nature, participatory richness and increasing reach of environmental regimes, an analysis of environmental treaties in terms of their operation in individual states and regions promises to yield valuable information about local societies, as these societies adapt to and act to shape such regimes. This lens promises to provide a rich set of insights to complement and challenge analyses based entirely on internal factors.[10] Considering an emerging consensus about the importance of globalization as an influence on people the world over, such an effort to connect the culture of international regimes with Central Asian culture promises to highlight forces impacting changes in the region.

The region will not and cannot (evidenced most especially by Turkmenistan) seal itself off against globalization and the global culture. Despite Turkmenistan's isolationist efforts,[11] the government of Turkmenistan constantly frets about its international image, monitors international markets, and essays to impact geopolitical alliances. Likewise, the people of Turkmenistan, even if deprived of many outside contacts, boast a high rate of satellite television ownership, listen to popular music, and display tastes and preferences deeply impacted by other global media.

This chapter describes international environmental regimes through their expressions of human capital, organizational capital, and social capital. This approach is based on the observation stated earlier that in cases when states implement, enforce, and effectuate international environmental law, they do so rarely because of the inevitability of an environmental rule of law, but because of a fortuitous confluence of organizational, physical, human, and social capital assets. Concurrently, this chapter essays to sketch the broad outlines of Central Asia's integration into international environmental regimes. Both of these efforts are a preface to the case studies of Chapter 6, which attempt to capture the impacts of the transition period on stocks of natural capital in Central Asia and the movement of the region towards sustainability.

The story of international environmental law in the new states of Central Asia started in Kazakhstan during the first days of independence. The Central Asian republics set the stage for a strong movement towards both democracy and sustainability through their endorsement of the Alma-Ata Declaration (December 21, 1991), which created the Commonwealth of Independent States. The newly independent states began this Declaration by affirming the need for democratic rule of law and followed by committing themselves to fulfill the international obligations stemming from the treaties and agreements of the former USSR. In 1991, this declaration appeared, in accordance with international law, to set the stage for the succession of each state to the ozone regime, CITES, Ramsar, and many other environmental treaties. Yet, in a violation and confusion of international norms on succession, no treaty secretariat save UNESCO heeded this declaration as one of succession and only some of the states subsequently sent secretariats of only some conventions notes on succession.[12] To this date, no treaty secretariat, no development agency, no established scholar, and only one small international NGO has complained about this negation of the promise and stated rules of international law governing state succession.[13]

The effect of this failure of international organizational capital was to require the states of Central Asia deliberately and explicitly to integrate themselves into (or hold themselves aloof from) the variety of regimes existing for the global environment. Their choices along the way, the behavior of their international partners, and the effects on the environment of this unprecedented type of succession reveal more about prospects for sustainability in the region than would otherwise have been the case.

THE NEW SOVEREIGNTY AND MANAGED COMPLIANCE AS ORGANIZATIONAL AND SOCIAL CAPITAL

The kind of analysis suggested above requires viewing the world of environmental treaties and institutions as a world of environmental regimes. Since such a viewpoint is a requirement, I must define more narrowly what I mean by regime.

Taken alone, the texts of treaties or the charters of organizations invariably mislead. The treaties themselves are significant of but not wholly dispositive of their eponymous regimes, since not all provisions of conventions are implemented or enforced equally and since a great number of issues and practices develop outside the convention text. Similarly, international institutions do not always faithfully pursue the goals and objectives for which they were (ostensibly) created, nor does their authority or their power remain static.

Accordingly, by "regime" I mean a governance system that is keyed to a specific issue. In turn, governance in this context is the "establishment and operation of a set of rules of conduct that define practices, assign roles, and guide interaction so as to grapple with collective problems."[14] Therefore, an international environmental regime is the sum of the operative rules deployed in the international arena around a specific environmental concern. These rules concern both normative aspects of behavior (the objectives of the regime) and actual rules of how shortfalls in compliance with the normative rules are addressed (enforcement). While some of these rules are explicit, and here the texts of treaties are particularly relevant, others operate as unstated norms or are borrowed from other instruments and institutions, and both change over time. An appreciation of the complex and sometimes contradictory nature of a regime usually requires a more ambitious effort than is possible by concentrating on one treaty or one international organization.

So, the sources of regime rules and changes in regime rules are pluralistic and usually involve some combination of international law, the preferences of hegemonic states, the availability of funding, the activities of subsidiary scientific and compliance bodies, and pressures from non-governmental forces (both businesses and NGOs). For example, a full accounting of the history and present-state of the ozone regime would include, *inter alia*, the relevant treaties,[15] changing rules of international trade in light of the World Trade Organization, the efforts of the GEF to expand its mandate to ozone depleting substances, the reactions of the subsidiary bodies to smuggling and non-compliance, and the pressures brought to bear over the years by Dupont and Greenpeace.

While the normative content of an international environmental regime is founded in a variety of sources, the mechanisms and practices of enforcement are similarly hard to find identified in any one document. It is through this regime lens that the gulf between the ideal of strong rule of law and the bricolage of existing environmental law becomes visible. Whether and which international environmental rules of law are enforced and how depends strongly on an array of economic, political, geopolitical, security, and private interests.

Nevertheless, in some contrast to how enforcement does or does not operate in other international regimes such as human rights, trade, or arms control, a distinct mode of general enforcement exists within environmental regimes. To date, violations of environmental treaties have little history of sparking serious international tensions, at least many that spill outside the regime in question. Violators are as likely to receive assistance in the form of capacity building funds, extended deadlines, or simple looks-the-other-way as they are to endure sustained scrutiny of their actions or lack of actions. So, while Turkmenistan was harshly scolded in 1999 for its lack of good-faith effort to meet its obligations under the ozone regime, it and all former Soviet republics have also benefited from millions of dollars in new aid from the GEF in response to their general inability to meet deadlines. It is this kind of management of non-compliance that is described generally by Chayes and Chayes in *The New Sovereignty*[16] and that has been catalogued by more recent scholars interested specifically in environmental regimes.[17]

The viability of managed compliance as a meaningful strategy is closely linked to the idea of "the new sovereignty." Classical interpretations of sovereignty suggest that states bind themselves to international regimes only when they have something to gain, specifically when the results of that regime have something to offer them directly to compensate them for their loss of latitude and independence. Therefore states have a presumption against acceding to treaties. The new sovereignty, in contrast, argues that many states, especially developing states, bind themselves to treaties not only when the treaty is in their direct interest, but also because they are driven to seek recognition of their sovereign status through such accessions. Thus, new sovereignty suggests that, for many states, there exists a presumption in favor of acceding to treaties. As Chayes and Chayes posit:

> Sovereignty, in the end, is status—the vindication of the state's existence as a member of the international system. In today's setting, the only way most states can realize and express their sovereignty is through participation in the various regimes that regulate and order the international system. Isolation from the pervasive and rich international context means that the state's potential for economic growth and political influence will not be realized. Connection

to the rest of the world and the political ability to be an actor within it are more important than any tangible benefits in explaining compliance with international regulatory agreements.[18]

Within Central Asia, the new sovereignty has quickly established itself as a constant presence in the environmental sector. I have never seen an official analysis of an environmental treaty ratification in the local press that did not comment on the ratification's "affirmation" of that state's sovereign status. Nor in my interviews with finance, environment, justice, and foreign affairs ministry staff did I uncover more than a handful of individuals, out of several dozen, who did not list such "affirmation" in the first or second place in a list of explanations of why a ratification occurred.

Just as the new sovereignty challenges the stark and two dimensional cost–benefit narratives of more traditional views, the range of actors in the world of new sovereignty is complex. With increasing status, formerly excluded non-governmental actors are now mediating between regimes, the status they confer, the material rewards of managed compliance, and interested states. While NGOs are now active in virtually every international regime, in environmental regimes they are arguably the most dynamic.[19] Within environmental regimes, NGOs issue independent verification reports, create policy, attend almost all conferences of the parties, and even implement some of the most substantial grants of the GEF. Despite this broad reach, the environmental NGO community remains insular enough to allow it to take on many aspects of a community; its members know each other and have frequent interactions with each other.

In contrast, NGOs have no more than a peripheral place in arms control regimes; they are not allowed access to information or a presence during negotiations. Similarly, while the situation is now beginning to change, the trade regime has formally excluded NGO participation from its earliest days.[20] Consequently, NGOs in such regimes are not confronted with the kind of difficult choices thrust upon NGOs in environmental regimes; they are too far from any decision making to allow their subtle ideological differences to come to the surface.

At the opposite end of the spectrum, human rights NGOs in the developing world share much more programmatically with their developed country peers than do environmental NGOs. However, even despite recent interventions in Yugoslavia and Rwanda, the human rights regime is distinct in that it commands almost no history of enforcement at the global level. Without any enforcement and without the substantial financial resources that make conditionality a potent substitute for enforcement, human rights regimes (not including humanitarian assistance regimes) lack dynamism. In part, this lack of dynamism is reflected by the fact that environmental NGOs are somewhat more deeply invested in issues of economic development, technology, trade, and the future than their human rights peers.

Moreover, human rights regimes have the luxury of offering a "correct" vision of society on states, and they have the curious opportunity of offering several developed states as models of human rights, thereby implying that human rights and development are mutually reinforcing. By contrast, morality is much more contested in the environmental realm; just as many developing world environmental NGOs point to the United States as a model as curse it as the root of the problem. This dynamism has the consequence that prescriptive proposals are more numerous and diverse in the environmental community than is the case with the human rights regime.

Finally, while NGOs are expected to fulfill oversight functions in human rights regimes, in environmental regimes they are also increasingly called upon to play the role of stand-ins for the state; NGOs are frequently the managers of water users associations, pilot environmental projects, and even international environmental institutions. The World Conservation Union, an important and influential international body composed of both state and NGO members has no parallel in other regimes. Their provision of various economic and social services in addition to oversight and educational functions means that NGOs participating in the environmental context display a great diversity of form and ability.

It is this curious mix of formal and informal rules and state and nonstate actors, both embedded in a discrete community,[21] that imparts to the management of international environmental regimes an unusual balance between organizational and social capital. Moreover, the development of these regimes in recent years has depended as much on strengthening formal verification, scientific, and governance bodies as it has on expanding the role of global civil society within these regimes.

Accordingly, the states that are most influential within environmental regimes are very often the ones whose NGOs are the most active, with the important exceptions of China and, to a lesser extent, India. For most other states, large and small, developed and developing, the benefits of these regimes accrue most strongly to those countries active both formally and informally. While small, the Scandinavian states, Denmark, Switzerland, and the Netherlands are among the most active at the formal end of developing international environmental law. For example, they support the core functions of many treaties and protocols such as CITES and the 1998 Aarhus Convention on Access to Information, Public Participation in Decision-Making and Access to Justice in Environmental Matters.[22] They also serve as the headquarters for NGOs such as World Conservation Union and WWF and, through both foundations and governments, as primary sources of funding for NGOs in developing states.

On the other end of the spectrum, both the governments and NGOs of Costa Rica and Pakistan are far more active and influential in these regimes than their size would predict, but their receipt of financial assistance matches their level of activity, not their comparative global environmental importance. States such as Iran, France, and Argentina, in contrast, are more minor players in global environmental regimes, in part because they do not boast as many active international environmental NGOs.

The Central Asian states consistently express the opinion that they can only contribute meaningfully to the resolution of global environmental problems and can only solve their own environmental problems with financial and technical assistance from the West. Accordingly, the current modes of participation of the Central Asian states in these regimes may be important in gauging the success these states will achieve in garnering such support.

In this regard, Central Asia reveals disappointing signs. By 1999, only one Central Asian had achieved visibility within global environmental regimes; Uzbekistan's Victor Ovchinnikov sat on the Scientific Commission of the Convention to Combat Desertification. Almost no Central Asians are currently employed by the secretariats of conventions, in part because the states in question, in stark contrast to actors like Pakistan, do not make a serious effort to nominate candidates. Virtually no Central Asians are sent by their states to participate in any of the meetings of the subsidiary bodies of conventions, the bodies where important decisions are increasingly being made.

When Central Asian state delegates do attend important regime events, such as conferences of the parties, as a rule they, on a good day, sit silently in the conference rooms and, on a bad day, skip all regime events in order to sightsee. Instead of viewing these meetings as important venues in which to further state interests, the states have a rich history of sending employees to these meetings as rewards; quite frequently delegates do not speak English or know the basics of international law. Finally, the Central Asian states are more apt to frustrate the plans of their local NGOs who wish to participate in such events than to facilitate them. To wit, the normal international practice of including national and international NGOs on official state delegations is not yet the norm in Central Asia, although even Russia has adopted the practice.

EPISTEMIC COMMUNITIES AS HUMAN AND SOCIAL CAPITAL

Not only do international environmental regimes strongly privilege NGOs; they also uniquely privilege scientists. Scientists are not core actors in trade or human rights regimes. Within arms control regimes, they act in a limited fashion; they assist policy makers to understand what is possible and to make sense of verification data. Yet, they are not expected to generate solutions. So, while groups such as the Union of Concerned Scientists do have a place within arms control regimes, it is at best peripheral. Moreover, the open negotiations of many environmental regimes are pervaded by a kind of pure scientific uncertainty that is quite different than the technological uncertainty or simple lack of reliable information inherent in arms control settings. A generalization is that scientists involved in environmental regimes are to a greater degree independent voices and more often confront scientific questions than their peers in arms control contexts, where technology and engineering dominate. As a result, largely missing from trade, human rights, and arms control regimes are what regime scholars call epistemic communities.

"An epistemic community is a professional group that believes in the same cause–effect relationships, truth tests to assess them, and shares common values."[23]

In context, epistemic community means relying on scientists as a supranational form of identity that promotes the formation of a solidary group based in bridging social capital. Yet what distinguishes epistemic communities from other sorts of communities is their lack of an organizational or membership component. In most respects, epistemic communities are ad hoc entities, lacking an organizational or leadership framework; accordingly, studies of epistemic communities privilege the role of individuals over the influence of organizations.[24] From the preceding chapter's review of social capital, one implication of solidary groups is that they produce externalities.

In this context, Haas discovered that the states whose positions in MedPlan (the plan to conserve the Mediterranean Sea environment) moved from opposition to support of the regime were those states in which scientists boasted gains in internal political influence and administrative representation over that period.[25] While Haas coined the phrase epistemic community, the insights that ground a reliance on epistemic communities were well developed from the first days of MedPlan under the guidance of one of its UNEP architects and epistemic community leaders, Stjepan Keckes, a Yugoslav oceanographer. Frequently, MedPlan is considered to have achieved its successes by basing much of its policy on scientific foundations and actively including scientists at all stages of the plan's development. Yet, generally speaking, epistemic communities contribute to regimes in two ways beyond merely bequeathing a regime with a scientific foundation for the identification and resolution of environmental problems. In addition, epistemic communities facilitate regimes by altering the negotiating positions of states and by serving as consumers of assistance programs.

In the former case, as adjunct members of negotiating delegations and as state officials, scientists can impact the development of foreign policy within their home states. In both capacities, scientists nudge their states toward negotiating positions congenial to regime building.[26] Scientists take pains to point out beliefs held by state officials that may be unfounded or hinder consensus.[27] Generally, in Central Asia, while scientists and officials who attend international meetings are quiet, within the internal political realm, scientists act in just the fashion described above.

In the latter case, applicable most pertinently to any regime with developing states, regime financial assistance provided to national scientific institutions facilitates consensus in two ways. First, these funds are viewed as victories for developing states and reason to continue participation in a regime. Second, the results of such funding do more than just advance scientific knowledge about the issue to be regulated. In many cases, the results of scientific work so funded do not produce new information. However, they do produce national information, and state officials in many cases are more prone to accept and react to internally generated scientific reports than to reports about problems presented by other, or developed, states.[28] While I do not find strong grounds for the claim that Central Asian governments are not receptive to "non-native" scientific conclusions, the allure of possible funding, even funding of only a few thousand dollars, continues to be a powerful incentive in the region. Such funding is both a major reason for

Central Asian state regime participation and a powerful tool for altering the negotiating positions of these states.

The reason why epistemic communities are of particular relevance to Central Asia is a direct result of the human capital development programs of the USSR; Central Asia claims more scientists and engineers per capita than most European states. Thus, while regional seas programs served as the environmental regimes that highlighted for academics and policymakers the force of epistemic communities, the emerging Caspian Sea regime begs to be analyzed and its success predicted along the lines of epistemic communities. The littoral states of this regime will contain more scientists and scientific institutions than that of any of UNEP's 14 existing regional seas regime except the emerging Black Sea regime, which is also primarily post-Soviet.[29] Moreover, given Soviet norms of education, of those Central Asian state officials involved in international environmental regimes who are not scientists by profession, more than half will have nevertheless received university degrees in the natural or technical sciences.

Yet, that epistemic communities are a pertinent research question for Central Asia does not automatically mean that they are healthy and influential in the region and productive of the benefits regime analysts expect of epistemic communities.

Throughout Central Asia, science's decline tempers enthusiasm about epistemic communities. Figure 5.1 illustrates that this decline was felt early by scientists in the reform period and reflected a loss, continuing today, of influence, funding, and even social standing.

Such a decline may have strong effects on the links between epistemic communities and productive national participation in international environmental regimes. Describing why its epistemic community has been relatively unsuccessful in forcing France to be a more positive player in MedPlan, Haas concludes that epistemic communities are ineffective if their claims are not respected elsewhere in the government.[30] In other words, one should not conflate the static existence of environmental political institutions with the strength of epistemic communities. While the moments of creation of such institutions correlate strongly with an increase in the political influence of scientific advice, the continued existence of such institutions may have no deeper explanation than bureaucratic inertia.

This inertia will be particularly misleading when a state moves away from scientific decision making to emphasize neorealistic calculations of state power.[31] For all the states of Central Asia, geopolitical security and influence are extremely important, and these objectives suffuse and inform a cross-section of state-decision making. For example, Turkmenistan points to its announcement of neutrality as a supposed proof of its commitment to environmental security, and Kazakhstan points to its environmental burdens from the Soviet era as a vague proof of commitment to environmental sustainability. In both cases, such strategic political rhetoric frustrates regime building on scientific grounds,[32] and the continuing effective marginalization of scientists by politicians exacerbates this weakness.

Accordingly, for science as a whole, the post-Soviet era has not seen the advancement of scientific leaders within national governments in Central Asia, although during Soviet times leadership in national academies of science was one

Not long ago our sciences were an object of great pride, but today we are forced to prove to society that fundamental research exists primarily to meet the needs of society....

Our national academies of science have a history of not much more than half a century, but during that period they succeeded in creating many scientific schools of thought that have received deserved recognition from the world scientific community, they have created 'an extensive network of scientific research institutes, and have made notable contributions to the economic development of their republics.

For the first time in the history of our peoples, there exists a national scientific intelligentsia and substantial scientific potential has been created, which is one of the national treasures of each republic and should serve as a foundation for true sovereignty.

Unfortunately, during this socio-economic crisis, the lack of appropriate attention on the part of state agencies to science threatens to destroy science... The lack of funding for the elementary survival of research institutions (transportation, heat, electricity), and the low salaries of scientific employees have led to a sharp decrease in the prestige of scientific labor, a reduction in research, loss of talented youth to government and commercial structures, and a loss of faith in society's need for science....

[I]n such conditions of the breakup of socio-economic relations and the transition to markets, science that is deprived of state support is practically doomed. Such an outcome will inflict irreparable harm to our nations and lead to the de-intellectualization of society, leaving our states completely dependent on developed countries....

FROM THE ACADEMIES OF SCIENCES OF:

Azerbaijan, President E. Yu. Salaev
Kazakhstan, President U. M. Sultangazin
Kyrgyzstan, President I. T. Aitmatov
Tajikistan, President S. Kh. Negmatullaev
Turkmenistan, President A. G. Babaev
Uzbekistan, Acting President M. S. Salakhitdinov
October 16, 1992

Figure 5.1 Appeal to the heads of state and governments of the republics of Central Asia, Kazakhstan, and Azerbaijan.
Source: *Bulletin of the Kazakhstan Academy of Sciences,* 1993.

of the stepping stones to national political power. More parochially, within the environmental community, the region's half dozen living ex-environmental ministers have not moved to other ministerial positions or even deputy minister positions, as is the norm for government ministers, but have invariably receded into obscurity.

Science is clearly on the decline in the former Soviet world. This decline transcends the general financial and institutional crisis in the region; science's problems are deeper than drastic budget cuts and governments with chaotic and ineffective policies. The best and brightest students in the former USSR are no longer headed for math, physics, and chemistry, but instead focus on law, business administration, and English. To wit, while many private and state donors are active in Kazakhstan and Turkmenistan, none of the most influential stress the importance of science in society, and none provide meaningful funds for the preservation of scientific human capital.[33]

If the environmental regimes will last more than one generation in Central Asia, who will take the places of the scientists who have already provided these regimes with a firm scientific foundation? Will local scientists continue to be capable of fueling the regime and monitoring its effectiveness? Likewise, whereas the traditional capacity building elements of environmental regimes in developing countries expect an expansion of scientific potential, perhaps for any such regime in Central Asia, the focus should instead be on strategically protecting and safeguarding portions of what already exists.

Accordingly, the Central Asian states will probably be unable to take full advantage of the opportunities opened to them through international environmental regimes as long as current trends of marginalizing national environmental agencies and eroding the social standing of scientists continue. Without a national community of scientists that continues to attract young scholars, which no state possesses any longer, while future delegates to international meetings may speak English, they will not possess the human capital assets necessary to achieve leadership positions in regimes. As a direct result, no Central Asian state will be seen as a strong player in international environmental issues. Already, the opinion concerning the Central Asian states within regimes, based on my communications with secretariat staff, is that they offer more problems to the regimes than they offer assets valuable to the regimes.

ENVIRONMENTAL ADMINISTRATIVE AGENCIES AS HUMAN AND ORGANIZATIONAL CAPITAL

During the course of the past 30 years, the appearance of new environmental conventions has been complemented by the expansion of existing conventions. Most of the environmental accords in the preceding pages now have well over 100 state parties. Moreover, they boast an increasingly complex array of subsidiary bodies. In the past, the average environmental regime, for example Ramsar, consisted of a secretariat of a half dozen people with an annual budget of tens or hundreds of thousands of dollars, a conference of the parties every 3 years, and some ad hoc committees composed of volunteers from the scientific communities of developed states and convening rarely. The modern environmental regime looks much different.

Each major new environmental regime of recent years, and in response the older regimes are also moving towards this model, boasts a large secretariat and a conference of the parties that meets no less often than once every 2 years. These new regimes also have nearly weekly convenings of larger standing committees and commissions composed of a broad range of state delegates, and several NGOs entrusted with semi-official regime functions. For example, the regime surrounding the biodiversity convention is now organized as follows.[34] The still rapidly expanding CBD secretariat employs more than 50 people but will soon reach 88; its similarly expanding budget now adds up to well more than $10,000,000 annually.[35] Among the more frequent meetings of the regime are those negotiating the Biosafety Protocol, the Subsidiary Body on Scientific, Technical and Technological Advice, a half dozen "liaison groups" on specific issues (*inter alia*, coral reefs, forests, the ecosystem approach, agrobiodiversity, and dryland, Mediterranean, arid, semi-arid, and grassland Savannah ecosystems), an expert panel on access and benefit sharing, intersessional meetings on operation of the convention, a Consultative Working Group of Experts on Biological Diversity Education and Public Awareness, and "technical experts" groups on the same issues as the "liaison groups." This voluminous list does not even include those bodies related to the Clearinghouse Mechanism,[36] which is attempting to bring all wildlife conventions under the umbrella of the CBD.

In addition to the hundreds of people who are involved in the secretariat and these subsidiary bodies (not to mention the thousands who attend the conferences of the parties), the CBD Secretariat essays to convince the regime's roughly 177 state parties to appoint a half dozen focal points each for various biodiversity issues. Complementing (or confusing) this activity, the World Bank, UNEP, and UNDP also have complicated numbers of staff and programs specifically tuned to the biodiversity regime, many hundreds at the country level, not the least since the GEF is the financial mechanism for the Biodiversity Convention. The entire list of subsidiary bodies above does not even include any of the pantheon of funding sources of the regime.

A well-funded Canadian NGO, International Institute for Sustainable Development (IISD), now sends out daily and colorful reports from CBD Conferences of the Parties (COPs) and related events for free to interested parties. Previous to 1999 no such comprehensive source of information existed in easily accessible form; the IISD bulletins are now something of an industry standard.[37] Yet, despite this coverage, whereas the basic maintenance of past environmental conventions could survive on several tens of thousands of dollars a year, and whereas scholars could follow in intimate detail the workings of several conventions simultaneously, no one person could ever hope to follow even the biodiversity regime alone in detail now. Moreover, whereas high levels of funding for regimes in the past almost automatically signified that funds were moving out the doors of secretariats to fund environmental projects in states, today millions of dollars are needed just to keep the administration of regimes functioning. Whether or not this trend is simply bureaucratization in the worst sense of the word or the capacity building needed to effect serious change is open to debate. In the case of the CBD, however, were the regime asked to present a list of accomplishments produced from its secretariat budget, it would be at a loss to point to even a few cases of actual biodiversity protection. It could, at best, point to alleged improvements in the stocks of the regime's human, social, and organizational capital assets; somewhere along the way in the past decade, most regime activities quietly reassigned direct efforts to save natural capital assets to secondary importance.

In connection with this trend, in the last decade a revolution occurred in environmental regimes similar to that which occurred in the United States in the first third of the twentieth century. Most governance and decision making devolved in all but their most symbolic forms from constitutional (treaty) bodies to administrative agencies and expert commissions. While this transition, and its predictable pitfalls, have received virtually no attention in scholarly literature, it has radically changed the normative bases for a state's successful participation in environmental regimes. Broadly, it has changed the mechanisms through which, first, the international regime penetrates the space of the state and, second, the mechanisms through which the state acts at the international level. While these two changes are intimately connected, for purposes of analysis, they can be addressed separately.

This first change means that conferences of the parties and very occasional visits of secretariat staff are no longer the only connection between states and regimes. If formerly almost all information about states, save some NGO information, was carefully crafted by states themselves and presented no more often than once a year, in the present day states have far less control over information. Today, secretariat staff frequently visit states to collect information, conduct trainings, and consult with governments.

However, the more important change concerns funding agencies. World Bank and UNDP, and occasionally UNEP, maintain offices within most developing states. These agencies have done for environmental development what the IMF did for economic development; they standardized it and programmatically homogenized it to reflect the bureaucratic needs of funders.

Really little different in their production from IMF structural adjustment plans, an assortment of "action plans" (for, *inter alia*, biodiversity, climate change, and environmental protection, at the national and regional levels) now constitute mandatory preconditions for states seeking substantial environmental funding through UNDP and the World Bank. Whereas even 5 years ago a sharply conceived project to conserve biodiversity in a discrete area of a Central Asian state could receive funding within 18 months through the GEF, now the fundamental ideas of such a proposal are of only secondary importance.

If an overarching plan does not exist, these agencies insist as a priority that it be created, with most of the funds for this process usually going to local offices of and expatriate staff of UNDP and World Bank. Not surprisingly, the number of such plans increases with each passing year. Whereas once there was only a biodiversity action plan, now there should be biodiversity enabling activities, a national biodiversity action plan, and, for Central Asia, a regional biodiversity action plan. Invariably, this process pushes aside the best discrete local conservation plans or increases their scale to unworkably large proportions. This top–down approach with its predilections for gigantomania and opportunities for corruption are very Soviet in flavor[38] and inefficiency. Thus, their emplacement in a more general effort to assist Central Asia make the transition from social to decentralized free markets is a paradox. Likewise, to the extent that, especially in Turkmenistan and Tajikistan, local UNDP offices have essentially arrogated for themselves the functions of a national environmental ministry, that these efforts are justified as capacity building projects is irony.

Given the declines in Central Asian environmental ministries in the past decade and the spectacular increase in UNDP budgets and offices over the same period, capacity building takes on a meaning in Central Asia different from that held by scholars of environmental regimes. Indeed, UNDP offices in Central Asia now have approximately the number of staff environmental ministries had 7 years ago, and vice versa, illustrating the connection between these agencies' decline and UNDP's growth.

This trend is not surprising if one accepts UNDP as an administrative agency instead of a philanthropic organization. One of the basic habits of administrative agencies is that, whatever their missions, they pursue tactics intended to expand their budgets and protect their privileges. UNDP exhibits these traits strongly, in part because UNEP lacks local offices, and in part because no international environmental NGO like WWF or IUCN maintains a presence in Central Asia; both factors have reduced demands for accountability on UNDP local offices. Therefore, it is a pressing question, given the range of interested actors in the region, whether environmental programs in Central Asia, all of which claim to build capacity, be sustainable, and target environmental needs, are in fact efficient, effective, and further the long-term environmental interests of the region. In this regard, it is curious that UNDP all but ignored environmental issues until environmental development funds appeared in the mid 1990s.

More generally, now that environmental aid is a tangible commodity, the donors most active in democracy and market development are essentially the same as the environmental donors. With this shift, the aspirations of environmental aid also began to shift. While the international community is well aware that the World Bank, IMF, WTO, and (for those states that seek membership) European Union strongly impact government structure in developing states, it is less appreciated that equivalent normative pressures are now increasingly being placed on national environmental agencies. If a national environmental agency or equivalent agency charged with environmental management is not isomorphic with Western forms, environmental regimes managed by UNDP or the World Bank will essay strongly to reshape them. Through this lens, the managers of environmental regimes resemble management consultants in the United States; much of their value arises out of homogenizing sectors of the economy, not just in assisting individual firms.

The second major change in environmental regimes concerns the range of possibilities now open for state representation. In the past, the major form of state representation consisted of state delegations to COPs. However, now, COPs in large regimes merely rubber-stamp decisions; they are no longer the negotiating forums of past years. While important negotiations do occur at COPs, the bulk of decisions are made prior to COPs, as testified by the fact that the vast majority of final documents issued at such events can be obtained as draft decisions many months before a COP. Accordingly, states interested in advancing their interests within regimes increasingly must act during the periods in between COPs and they must act through subsidiary bodies. The single best way to advance such interests is to have your nationals occupy authoritative leadership positions within such bodies.

While a strong state can strong-arm its delegates onto such bodies, it cannot make other members respect its delegates. A review of widely regarded environmental leaders within regimes highlights the extent to which educational achievement in the sciences and status within the scientific community are prerequisites for such authority. Such leaders need not be from developed states or states with strong scientific programs; Egypt has produced two of the most well-known figures active in environmental regimes: Mohamed T. El-Ashry, the GEF CEO and Chairman, and Mostafa Tolba, the former UNEP Executive Director. Two other states, Costa Rica and Pakistan, illustrate the degree to which the example of Egypt can be copied.

Thus, for a state to integrate itself successfully into international environmental regimes, it will almost certainly need to draw on or develop appropriate stocks of organizational and human capital. It will need to study and understand the rules and procedures of international environmental regimes and how to manipulate these rules to its advantage; a core part of such an effort will involve advancing suitable scientifically trained delegates, from both the state and NGO sectors, to subsidiary bodies. Likewise, perhaps of critical importance, developing states will need to develop the ability to resist efforts by international environmental agencies to arrogate funds and responsibilities intended to remain within state hands.

With the partial exception of Kazakhstan, none of the states in the region has made such an effort to understand the organizational foundations of international environmental regimes. While the scientifically trained staff of Kazakhstan's National Environment Center does possess the most developed understanding in the entire region of these processes, the ministries of foreign affairs and environment have made no concerted effort to advance these scientists within subsidiary bodies. Quite the opposite, this National Environment Center is sequestered in Kokshetau, and its staff are low on the pecking order of state officials chosen to attend international events.

Moreover, no Central Asian state has made any serious effort to restrain UNDP's arrogation of environmental authority on the national level. My research suggests strongly that national officials assume that local UNDP offices have a mandate to intrude on national authority as a condition of funding. Yet, UNDP officials in New York resist even the very suggestion that such intrusions are consonant with UNDP's mission. At the same time, UNDP staff in New York admit that they know little about what happens in field offices and that national UNDP mission heads have a great amount of latitude of action.

CONNECTING INTERNATIONAL REGIMES TO NATURAL CAPITAL: COMPLIANCE AND EFFECTIVENESS

Methodologically, analyses of how international environmental regimes relate to their mission of protecting stocks of natural capital depend on differentiating between three stages of these regimes. First, regime formation involves negotiations and drafting that create specific obligations and an instrument of international law. Second, regime implementation involves effecting the latter through national legislation and national enforcement mechanisms. Finally, regime compliance entails the process of fulfilling the specific obligations and activities envisioned by the treaty. Thus, in practice, analysts must examine the activities of and interactions between state agencies, NGOs, and scientists as treaties are drafted and later revised, as national laws are drafted and responsibilities are allocated between stakeholders, and as domestic projects and strategies are carried out in furtherance of (or in spite of) the treaty goals.

Where a regime is well founded and exhibits high levels of compliance, the regime will likely also be effective; effectiveness refers to the impact of the regime on stocks of natural capital. If a regime is founded on false premises, watered-down, or timed inopportunely, even high levels of compliance may not result in effectiveness. Likewise, for the same reasons, a high non-compliance regime may be effective.[39] Thus, while compliance and effectiveness are often mistakenly conflated, compliance refers merely to the organizational capital aspects of a regime, while effectiveness refers primarily to natural capital.

Thus, an analysis of the transition period in Central Asia through the lens of environmental regimes tracks these three stages of environmental regimes, and evaluates effectiveness as a separate question. Tracking these three stages of regimes involves intersections with the region's array of social, physical, human, and organizational capital assets, assets that are pertinent to a great many other issues, such as the democratic transition, the role of religion, and educational systems.

While such information should not displace the insights of anthropology, sociology, or traditional political science, it does promise to challenge these other approaches by opening up a new arena of inquiry, especially since many actors display unexpected behavior when released from a purely domestic context and when the specter of international comparisons is imminent. For certain issues, such as the strength of Central Asian scientists in general, purely domestic research falls short of providing the kinds of insights available when such scientists interact with their peers from other parts of the world.

As part of a general overview of these three stages of regime participation in Central Asia, to date the governments of the region have been largely uninvolved in multilateral environmental negotiations. Where they have had strong opportunities for such involvement, such as for the 1997 UN Convention on the Law of Non-Navigable Uses of International Watercourses or the Kyoto Protocol, they have simply remained on the sidelines. Where they have been encouraged by the international community to engage in such negotiations for the sake of solving their own regional problems, they have shown no effort beyond that needed to make statements

Nukus Declaration (September 20: 1995):
- Concludes Aral Crisis conference.
- "Affirms" duty of basin states to cooperate to resolve problem and calls on donors for assistance.
- Announces region's commitment to sustainable development as guiding principle, including "not allowing" deterioration of quality of life while ensuring for needs of future generations.
- Cites necessity of creation of regional system of environmental management.
- Commits states to "unswerving" adherence to all previous (i.e. Soviet) water use agreements and regimes.
- Call for creation of a *Convention for the Sustainable Development of the Aral Sea Basin.*
- Contains no "binding" language.

Almaty Declaration (February 28, 1997):
- Reiterates all Aral Sea reform policies.
- Announces 1998 as Central Asian Year of Environmental Protection.
- Calls Central Asia a Non-Nuclear Zone.
- Contains no "binding" language.

Figure 5.2 Central Asia subregional cooperation: recent declarations of heads of state (excluding AZ).

at conferences. The shortfalls between the promises contained in the 1995 Nukus Declaration and the 1997 Almaty Declaration (Figure 5.2) and the reality that no state even penned a draft treaty for the Aral Sea highlights this lack of effort.

The region's accession to international environmental agreements is, however, more impressive, as documented in Table 5.1 following this chapter. Most of the Central Asian states have now acceded to most of the major global environmental accords, and each state has plans to expand its membership in such environmental regimes. However, some of these accessions and ratifications have occurred in contravention of constitutional law, especially Uzbekistan's accession to the climate change convention through a unilateral "approval" from Uzbekistan's Minister of Foreign Affairs to the United Nations Secretary-General and Kazakhstan's ratification of CBD through an equally unilateral resolution of Kazakhstan's executive branch.[40] Both accessions are presumably valid under international law, and both fail to observe the legislative foundations of both lawmaking and constitutional separation of powers.

Moreover, no state in the region has displayed a substantial effort to implement these conventions; in part this lack of effort is connected to the immense expense that such an effort would entail. Also, since each state grants primacy to international law over national law, implementation could be merely a formality. Yet, implementation is not merely a formality considering three active trends in the region. The texts are not widely published; courts resist applying provisions of such conventions;[41] and since new environmental legislation continues to pass in the region in disregard of the provisions of treaties, implementation is still important and its absence clearly frustrates the integration of these states into environmental regimes. Moreover, state practice in the region allows foreign companies to operate outside the realm of environmental law; by contract several foreign companies have received exemptions from national (and international) environmental law. The most well-known example concerned the leak in 1999 that revealed that Karachaganak Petroleum Operating Company is contractually exempt from payment of environmental fines.[42] Since many transnational corporations operating in Central Asia have guarantees from state governments[43] that they will not be subject to changes in environmental law (either by adoption of new legislation or by treaty accession), the region faces severe limitations on its ability to participate in a number of environmental regimes.

Table 5.1 also provides an overview of the record of compliance of the Central Asian states in international environmental regimes, a record that shows great diversity between states, but on the whole attests to a generally low level of compliance. On a subjective level, I note no decline in wildlife smuggling in the region, poaching, or industrial emissions as a result of the region's participation in environmental regimes. Not only are states failing to increase the efficacy of interventions to protect the environment through their involvement in such regimes, they are also largely failing to comply with their administrative responsibilities under these regimes. Most of the membership dues and most of the reports that the Central Asian states are required to submit to secretariats and subsidiary bodies are submitted at least a year late, if at all. In March 2000, faced with dues in excess of $21 million and suspension of its membership in many international organizations, Kazakhstan announced that it would only meet its obligations in 21 per cent of the treaty regimes to which it had acceded,[44] leaving it in stark noncompliance for almost all of its environmental dues.

In the case of Central Asia, non-compliance with treaties does lead to a failure to meet the natural capital goals of environmental regimes. The Central Asian environment is in no appreciable manner better protected or less degraded than it was a decade ago. The major improvements (lower levels of industrial pollutants, lowered rates of application of agricultural chemicals, and the closure of the region's nuclear, chemical, and biological weapons facilities[45]) have scant connection to the activities or programs of environmental regimes. Despite this grim reality, states continue to suggest in public statements that the region is moving towards sustainable development, and donors are equivalently vocal in advertising purported successes in this direction. Recognizing the political self-interest of these claims, I distinguish this pervasive practice and its attendant exuberance from true environmental effectiveness.

Whether the governments of the region are to blame for development failures or whether donors have been irresponsible and gullible is not yet clear. What is clear is that both sets of institutions operate free of much oversight or substantive democratic accountability. Put differently, both donors and Central Asian governments can pretty much say whatever they want and do whatever they want *in Central Asia* without much concern (at least as long as constituents continue to accept their statements as dispositive of reality) for the veracity, legality, or consequences of their actions. In this regard, the lack of democracy within Central Asia and the lack of democracy in environmental regimes both resemble the state of the global trade regime prior to the 2000 Seattle protests.

Claims of development and success should be evaluated critically and skeptically. Otherwise, an accounting 10 years from now of environmental development in Central Asia will probably advertise the kind of impressive, glowing, and Orwellian discourse of battles won as was boasted by the post-Soviet market developers until 1998 erected sobriety and reality as barriers to such doublespeak.

In operative terms, the Alma-Ata Declaration of 1991 was a failure on all fronts. Domestically, new republican governments failed to pay much, if any, attention to international environmental conventions. Internationally, the world community and its host of organizations refused to acknowledge this declaration as sufficient to establish membership in the various international environmental regimes then in existence. In retrospect, the world's disregard of the actual provisions of the Alma-Ata Declaration was Central Asia's introduction to the fact that international environmental law and international environmental politics constitute an arcane, complex, and highly manipulable world.

Table 5.1 Status of international environmental accords in Central Asia[1]

Compliance measured on a rating scale of (1) to (6) for each regime from virtual non-involvement in regime or gross violation of regime to very high compliance or performance beyond requirements of regime.	Includes information related to **notable state compliance**, *notable state non-compliance*, AND ERRORS STEMMING FROM SECRETARIATS AND INTERNATIONAL AGENCIES. Normal discrepancies between dates of accession or ratification expressed as date of national act followed by [date of receipt by secretariat/depository]
Kazakhstan	
Aarhus Convention on Access to Information, Public Participation in Decision-Making and Access to Justice in Environmental Matters (3)	Signed 25/6/98;[2] Ratified 23/10/00,[3] **Focal Point Named and Active in Ensuring NGO access to information,**[4] *Kazakhstan focal point and ECE listed focal point not the same. No enabling legislation, limited access to courts*

Notes
1 Current to November 2000 and compiled as author's contribution to Law and Environment Eurasia Partnership, "Global Accords and Ecological Human Rights: Advocacy for Rule of Law and Environmental Reform in Central Asia" (Unpublished Project Report to John D. and Catherine T. MacArthur Foundation, 2000).
2 United Nations Economic Council for Europe, "Multilateral treaties deposited with the Secretary-General-TREATY I–XXVII" (undated), available at http://www.unece.org/env/pp/ctreaty.htm.
3 Zakon Respubliki Kazakhstan ot 23 oktyabrya 2000 g. N 92-II O ratifikatsii Konventsii o dostupe k informatsii, uchastiyu obschestvennosti v protsesse prinyatiya reshenii i dostupe k pravosudiyu po voprosam, kasayuschimsya okruzhayuschei sredy.
4 Focal point is Tatyana Adamovna Shakirovna. For examples of efforts to provide information to NGOs, *see* most issues of *KazEcoPravda*, available at http://www.ecostan.org/vestniki.html.

Agenda 21 Reporting Requirements	*Noncompliance:* In 1997 submitted a few vague paragraphs.[5] Rio + 5 report largely sufficient;[6] currently effort under way to submit full report[7]
(3)	
Convention on Biological Diversity (CBD)	Signed 9/6/92,[8] *Government acceptance 19/8/94*[9] [Ratification 6/9/94[10]]. *Violation of provisions of Constitution related to treaties,* POSSIBLY UNDERTAKEN IN RELIANCE ON INVALID ADVICE FROM REPRESENTATIVE OF BIODIVERSITY SECRETARIAT. *As of 8/98 dues 4 years in arrears: $64,000, Late submission of National Report*
(2)	
Convention on International Trade in Endangered Species (CITES)	Acceded 6/4/99,[11] Note of accession sent only on 14/12/99 [20/1/00[12]]; Entered into force 19/4/00. Active international smuggling of, *inter alia,* argali and sturgeon
(2)	
Convention on Law of Non-Navigable Uses of International Watercourses	Voted to adopt in 21/5/97 GA vote.[13] *Failed to sign and failed to apply provisions to potentially favorable leverage in disputes over Syrdarya, Ili, and Irtysh rivers*
(2)	
Convention on Long-Range Transboundary Air Pollution	Acceded 23/10/00[14]
(3)	
Convention on the Protection and Use of Transboundary Watercourses and International Lakes	Acceded 23/10/00,[15] *Fails to apply provisions to potentially favorable leverage in disputes over Syrdarya, Ili, and Irtysh rivers*
(2)	
Convention on the Transboundary Effects of Industrial Accidents	Acceded 23/10/00[16]
(4)	
Convention on Transboundary Environmental Impact Assessments	Acceded 23/10/00[17]
(3)	

5 United Nations Commission on Sustainable Development, "Information on Kazakhstan" (undated), available at http://www.un.org/esa/agenda21/natlinfo/countr/kazakh/index.htm.

6 Kazakhstan, "Country Profile: Implementation of Agenda 21: Review of Progress Made since the United Nations Conference on Environment and Development, 1992." (1997), http://www.un.org/esa/earthsummit/kazak-cp.htm.

7 Resolution 12-8/3869 of the Government of the Republic of Kazakhstan (requiring ministries to assist efforts of Agenda 21 Working Group).

8 Convention on Biological Diversity, "Ratification" (August 14, 2000), available at http://www.biodiv.org/conv/pdf/ratification-alpha.pdf.

9 Postanovlenie N. 918 ot 19 avgusta 1994 Kabineta Ministrov Respubliki Kazakhstan.

10 Convention on Biological Diversity, "Ratification."

11 Zakon Respubliki Kazakhstan ot 6 aprelya 1999 goda N 372-1 O prisoedinenii Respubliki Kazakhstan k Konventsii o mezhdunarodnoi torgovle vidami dikoi fauny i flory, nakhodyaschimisya pod ugrozoi ischeznoveniya.

12 Convention on International Trade in Endangered Species of Wild Fauna and Flora, "List of Parties" (undated), available at http://www.wcmc.org.uk/CITES/common/parties/alphabet.shtml.

13 United Nations General Assembly, "General Assembly Adopts Convention on Law of Non-Navigational Uses of International Watercourses," Press Release GA/9248 (May 21, 1997).

14 Zakon Respubliki Kazakhstan ot 23 oktyabrya 2000 g. N 89-II O prisoedinenii Respubliki Kazakhstan k Konventsii o transgranichnom zagryaznenii vozdukha na bolshie rasstoyaniya.

15 Zakon Respubliki Kazakhstan ot 23 oktyabrya 2000 g. N 94-II O prisoedinenii Respubliki Kazakhstan k Konventsii ob okhrane i ispolzovanii transgranichnykh vodotokov i mezhdunarodnykh ozer.

16 Zakon Respubliki Kazakhstan ot 23 oktyabrya 2000 g. N 91-II O prisoedinenii Respubliki Kazakhstan k Konventsii o transgranichnom vozdeistvii promyshlennykh avarii.

17 Zakon Respubliki Kazakhstan ot 23 oktyabrya 2000g. N 86-II O prisoedinenii Respubliki Kazakhstan k Konventsii ob otsenke vozdeistviya na okruzhayuschuyu sredu v transgranichnom kontekste.

Table 5.1 (Continued)

Convention on Migratory Species (CMS)	Internal government agreement on accession. **Signed Memorandum of Understanding concerning Conservation Measures for the Siberian Crane 13/12/98**[18] **Signed Memorandum of Understanding concerning Conservation measures for**
(2)	**Slender-billed Curlew 2/12/94**[19]
Convention to Combat Desertification (CCD) (4)	Signed 14/10/94.[20] Ratified 7/7/97[21] [9/7/97[22]]; entry into force 7/10/97
Framework Convention on Climate Change	Signed 8/6/92. Ratified 4/5/95[23] [17/5/95[24]]; Entry into Force 15/8/95 *As of 8/98 dues three years in arrears: $44,500,* **Focal Point Named, Submitted National Communication Early (11/5/98), 98 COP Announced Voluntary Reductions (only COP non-host state to do so) and attempted to join Annex 1.**[25]
Kyoto Protocol (6)	Signed 3/12/99[26]
Global Environment Facility Rule Compliance	Participant since 30/3/98,[27] *Failed to notify GEF of change of focal points Failed to join Constituency on GEF Council even after November 2000 GEF Council when other Central*
(2)	*Asian states chose constituency.*[28]

18 Convention on Migratory Species, "Agreement Summary Sheet: Memorandum of Understanding concerning Conservation Measures for the Siberian Crane," (February 19, 1999), available at http://wcmc.org.uk/cms/sib_summ.htm.

19 Convention on Migratory Species, "Agreement Summary Sheet: Memorandum of Understanding concerning Conservation Measures for the Slender-billed Curlew. *Numenius tenuirostris*," (July 1, 1998), available at http://wcmc.org.uk/cms/sbc_summ.htm.

20 UNCCD, "Status of Ratification and Entry into Force of the UNCCD," (October 11, 2000), available at http://www.unccd.int/convention/ratif/doeif.php.

21 Zakon Respubliki Kazakhstan ot 7 iyulya 1997 goda N 149-1 O ratifikatsii Konventsii Organizatsii Obyeninennykh Natsii po borbe s opustynivaniem.

22 UNCCD, "Status of Ratification and Entry into Force of the UNCCD."

23 Ukaz Prezidenta Respubliki Kazakhstan ot 4 maya 1995 goda N 2260 O ratifikatsii Ramochnoi Konventsii Organizatsii Obyedinennykh Natsii ob izmenenii klimata.

24 Framework Convention on Climate Change-Secretariat, "Update on Ratification of the Convention," (September 7, 2000), available at http://www.unfccc.de/resource/conv/ratlist.pdf .

25 *See* United Nations, Framework Convention on Climate Change FCCC/CP/1999/2 (May 28, 1999).

26 Ukaz Prezidenta Respubliki Kazakhstan ot 12 marta 1999 goda 84 O podpisanii Respubliki Kazakhstan Kiotskogo protokola k Ramochnoi Konventsii Organizatsii Obyedinennykh Natsii ob izmenenii klimata.

27 Global Environment Facility, "List of States Participating in the Restructured GEF, " (October 1, 1999), available at http://www.gefweb.org/participants/Members_Countries/members_countries. html.

28 Global Environment Facility, "New Participants in Constituencies," GEF/C.16/11 (October 11, 2000), available at http://www.gefweb.org/Documents/Council_Documents/GEF_C16/GEF_C.16 11.pdf.

Ramsar Convention on Wetlands of International Importance	Not a party, but internal government resolution to accede exists, although government support declining; BUT *LIST OF WETLANDS OF INTERNATIONAL IMPORTANCE* INCLUDES (1) KURGALJIN/TENGIZ LAKES, AND (2) LOWER TURGAI AND IRGIZ LAKES[29] AND INCLUDES (2) ON THE MONTREUX RECORD.[30]
Vienna Convention on Ozone	Acceded 30/10/97[31] [26/8/98[32]], Entry into force 24/11/98[33]
Montreal Protocol	Acceded 31/10/97[34] [26/8/98[35]], Entry into force 24/11/98;[36] *By MOP 11 (11/99) had not provided 1986 Baseline Data for Annex A substances (over two years overdue);[37] Only Non-Article five State party (and one of only nine state parties) that had never provided any ODS date to Secretariat by MOP 11[38]*
London Amendments	Failed to Accede; SECRETARIAT MISTAKENLY CLAIMS KZ MORE THAN TWO YEARS OVERDUE TO REPORT 1989 BASELINE HCFCs, BUT KZ NOT A PARTY TO LONDON AMENDMENTS[39]
Copenhagen Amendments	Failed to accede
World Heritage Convention	Sec. reports "acceptance" 29/4/94[40] Kazakhstan reports 29/7/94, *Possible violation of Constitution. As of 8/98, dues four years in arrears: $29, 700; only paid on March 19, 1999. Environmental Ministry not informed of composition of KZ Committee for World Heritage, in which president's daughter included*

29 Ramsar Bureau, "The List of Wetlands of International Importance," (November 7, 2000), available at http://www.ramsar.org/sitelist.pdf.

30 Ramsar Bureau, "The Montreux Record," (November 5, 2000), available at http://www.ramsar.org/key_montreux_record.htm.

31 Zakon Respubliki Kazakhstan ot 30 oktyabrya 1997 goda N 177-1 O prisoedinenii Respubliki Kazakhstan k Venskoi Konventsii ob okhrane ozonovogo sloya.

32 The Ozone Secretariat, "Status of Ratification," (September 28, 2000), available at http://www.unep.org/ozone/ratif.htm.

33 Global Environment Facility, "Kazakhstan: Programme for Phasing Out Ozone Depleting Substances," (2000), p. 20, available at http://www.gefweb.org/wprogram/Feb00/undp/Kazakhstan/Part%20I.doc.

34 Zakon Respubliki Kazakhstan ot 30 oktyabrya 1997 goda N 176-1 O prisoedinenii Respubliki Kazakhstan k Monrealskomu Protokolu po veschestvam, razrushayuschim ozonovyi sloi.

35 The Ozone Secretariat, "Status of Ratification."

36 Global Environment Facility, "Kazakhstan: Programme for Phasing Out Ozone Depleting Substances," p. 20.

37 United Nations Environment Programme, "Eleventh Meeting of the Parties to the Montreal protocol on Substances that Depleted the Ozone Layer: Report of the Secretariat on Information provided by the Parties in Accordance with Articles 7 and 9 of the Montreal Protocol," (October 5, 1999), UNEP/OzL.Pro.11/6, p. 2, available at http://www.unep.ch/ozone/pdf/11mop-6-en.pdf .

38 Ibid., p. 4.

39 Ibid., p. 3.

40 United Nations Educational, "Scientific and Cultural Organization, Convention concerning the Protection of the World Cultural and Natural Heritage," (October 1, 2000), available at https://www.unesco.org/whc/wldrat.htm#debut.

Table 5.1 (Continued)

Kyrgyzstan

Aarhus Convention on Access to Information, Public Participation in Decision-Making and Access to Justice in Environmental Matters **(4)**	Failed to Accede
Agenda 21 Reporting Requirements **(1)**	Noncompliance[41]
Basel Convention on Transboundary Movements of Hazardous Wastes **(4)**	Ratified 18/1/96[42] [Acceded 13/8/96[43]]
Convention on Biological Diversity (CBD) **(2)**	Ratified 26/7/96 [Acceded 6/8/96[44]], *Never Provided a National Report*
Convention on Law of Non-Navigable Uses of International Watercourses **(1)**	KG recorded as neither for, against, abstaining, or absent for 21/5/97 GA vote[45]
Convention on Long-Range Transboundary Air Pollution **(5)**	Acceded 14/1/00[46] [25/5/00[47]]
Convention to Combat Desertification (CCD) **(4)**	Acceded 21/7/99;[48] [ACCESSION 19/9/97[49]]; SECRETARIAT CONSIDERED KG STATE PARTY WITHOUT ACCESSION BY KG TO REGIME
Global Environment Facility Rule Compliance **(2)**	Participant since 9/1/97,[50] Failed to notify GEF of change of focal points, *Failed to join Constituency on GEF council until 2000 (Switzerland)*[51]
Framework Convention on Climate Change **(5)**	Acceded 14/1/00[52] [25/5/00[53]]
Ramsar Convention on Wetlands of International Importance **(2)**	Nonparty. But *List of Wetlands of International Importance* includes Lake Issyk-kul[54] and also includes site on the Montreux Record[55]

41 United Nations Commission on Sustainable Development, "Information on Kyrgyzstan," (undated), available at http://www.un.org/esa/agenda21/natlinfo/countr/kyrgyz/index.htm.
42 Postanovlenie N. 304-1 ot 18 yanvarya 1996 Zakonodatelnogo sobraniya Jogorku Kenesha Kyrgyzskoi Respubliki O ratifikatsii Kyrgyzskoi Respubliki Bazelskoi Konventsii o kontrole za transgranichnoi perevozkoi opasnykh otkhodov i ikh udaleniem.
43 UNEP, "Status of Ratifications of the Basel Convention" (October 9, 2000), available at http://www.unep.ch/basel/ratif/ratif.html.
44 Convention on Biological Diversity, "Ratification."
45 United Nations General Assembly, "General Assembly Adopts Convention on Law of Non-Navigational Uses of International Watercourses."
46 Zakon Kyrgyzskoi Respubliki ot 14 yanvarya 2000 goda N 11 O prisoedinenii Kyrgyzskoi Respubliki k Ramochnoi Konventsii OON ob izmenenii klimata i Konventsii EEK OON po transgranichnomu zagryazneniyu vozdukha na bolshie rasstoyaniya.
47 UNECE, Convention on Long-range Transboundary Air Pollution, "Status of Ratification," (July 3, 2000), available at http://www.unece.org/env/lrtap/conv/lrtap_st.htm.
48 Zakon Kyrgyzskoi Respubliki ot 21 iyulya 1999 goda N 85 O prisoedinenii Kyrgyzskoi Respubliki k Konventsii po borbe s opustynivaniem v stranakh, kotorye ispytyvayut seryeznuyu zasukhu i/ili opustynivanie, osobenno v Afrike.
49 UNCCD, "Status of Ratification and Entry into Force of the UNCCD."
50 Global Environment Facility, "List of States Participating in the Restructured GEF."
51 Global Environment Facility, "New Participants in Constituencies."
52 Zakon Kyrgyzskoi Respubliki ot 14 yanvarya 2000 goda N 11 O prisoedinenii Kyrgyzskoi Respubliki k Ramochnoi Konventsii OON ob izmenenii klimata i Konventsii EEK OON po transgranichnomu zagryazneniyu vozdukha na bolshie rasstoyaniya.
53 Framework Convention on Climate Change-Secretariat, "Update on Ratification of the Convention."
54 Ramsar Bureau, "The List of Wetlands of International Importance."
55 Ramsar Bureau, "The Montreux Record."

Rotterdam Convention on the Prior Informed Consent Procedure for Certain Hazardous Chemicals and Pesticides in International Trade (6)	Signed 11/8/99;[56] Ratified (promulgated; law signed January 15) 26/1/00.[57] [25/5/00[58]], **One of first three states in the world to ratify**
Vienna Convention on Ozone	Acceded 15/1/00 [31/5/00[59]]
Montreal Protocol	Acceded 15/1/00 [31/5/00[60]]; Only Central Asian state to be an Art. 5 developing country, as of 2000[61]
London Amendments	Failed to Accede
Copenhagen Amendments (5)	Failed to Accede
World Heritage Convention (2)	Acceded 10/6/95;[62] [3/7/95[63]]

Tajikistan

Aarhus Convention on Access to Information, Public Participation in Decision-Making and Access to Justice in Environmental Matters (2)	Failed to accede
Agenda 21 Reporting Requirements (1)	Noncompliance
Convention on Biological Diversity (CBD)	Ratified 15/5/97;[64] [RATIFICATION 29/1/98 AND ACCESSION 29/10/97[65]], *Focal Point Named by Secretariat, but unknown to Tajikistan,* NO CHM FOCAL POINT ALTHOUGH LETTER SENT 21/4/98 TO CBD SECRETARIAT NAMING MINISTRY OF NATURE PROTECTION; *Never Provided a National Report*
(2)	
Convention on Law of Non-Navigable Uses of International Watercourses (2)	Absent from 21/5/97 vote[66]
Convention to Combat Desertification (CCD)	Ratified 12/8/97. *However, Prime Minister Azizov sent letter of accession 1/7/97.*[67] [ACCESSION 12/8/97[68] AND 16/7/97[69]] CONSIDERED TJ A PARTY IN CONTRAVENTION OF TJ LAW; Entry into force 14/10/97
(3)	

56 Interim Secretariat of the Rotterdam Convention on the Prior Informed Consent (PIC) Procedure for Certain Hazardous Chemicals and Pesticides in International Trade, "Status of Signature and Ratification, Acceptance, Approval, and Accession," (October 31, 2000), available at http://www.chem.unep.ch/Rotterdam/status_of_signature_and_ratifica.htm.

57 Zakon Kyrgyzskoi Respubliki ot 15 yanvarya 2000 goda N 15 O ratifikatsii Rottersamskoi konventsii OON o protsedure predvaritelnogo obosnovannogo soglasiya v otnoshenii otdelnykh opasnykh khimicheskikh veschestv i pestitsidov v mezhdunarodnoi torgovle.

58 Interim Secretariat of the Rotterdam Convention on the Prior Informed Consent (PIC) Procedure for Certain Hazardous Chemicals and Pesticides in International Trade, "Status of Signature and Ratification, Acceptance, Approval, and Accession."

59 The Ozone Secretariat, "Status of Ratification."

60 The Ozone Secretariat, "Status of Ratification."

61 Decision adopted at Twelfth Meeting of the Parties, December 2000. *See Earth Negotiations Bulletin* (December 15, 2000), p. 7.

62 Postanovlenie N. 98-1 ot 10 iyunya 1995 Soveta narodnykh predstavitelei Jogorku Kenesha Kyrgyzskoi Respubliki O prisoedinenii Kyrgyzskoi Respubliki k Konventsii ob okhrane vsemirnogo kulturnogo i prirodnogo naslediya.

63 United Nations Educational, "Scientific and Cultural Organization, Convention concerning the Protection of the World Cultural and Natural Heritage."

64 Postanovlenie N. 882 ot 10 marta 1997 goda Majlisi Oli Respubliki Tajikistan O prisoedinenii Respubliki Tajikistan k Konventsii OON o biologicheskom raznoobrazii.

65 Convention on Biological Diversity, "Ratification."

66 United Nations General Assembly, "General Assembly Adopts Convention on Law of Non-Navigational Uses of International Watercourses."

67 Note 18/2-51 of July 1, 1997 from Prime Minister of the Republic of Tajikistan Y. Azimov.

68 UN Representative Alimov fax of 18/8/97, paragraph 4.

69 UNCCD, "Status of Ratification and Entry into Force of the UNCCD."

Table 5.1 (Continued)

Framework Convention on Climate Change		Accession 28/8/97[70] [7/1/98[71]], Entry into force 7/4/98, *No Focal Point*
Kyoto Protocol	(3)	
Global Environment Facility Rule Compliance		Participant since 1/10/99;[72] *GEF incorrectly lists 2 political focal points,* Helped engineer accession of Central Asian states to Switzerland constituency (first and only constituency of developed state representing developing or transition states)[73]
	(3)	
Ramsar Convention on Wetlands of International Importance	(3)	Deposited Declaration of Succession Likely accession in 2000
Rotterdam Convention on the Prior Informed Consent Procedure for Certain Hazardous Chemicals and Pesticides in International Trade	(3)	Signed 28/9/98[74]
Vienna Convention on Ozone		Acceded 4/11/95[75] [6/5/96[76]]; Entered into force 4/8/96
Montreal Protocol		Acceded 13/12/97[77] [7/1/98[78]]; Entered into force 7/4/98[79]]; *By MOP 11 (11/99) had not provided 1986 Baseline Data for Annex A substances (over 2 years overdue);*[80] *Did Not Report 1998 Data by 11th MOP (12/99)*
London Amendments		Acceded 13/12/97[81] [7/1/98[82]]; *By MOP 11 (11/99) had not provided 1989 Baseline Data for Annex B substances or HCFCs (over 2 years overdue)*[83]
Copenhagen Amendments	(2)	Failed to Accede

70 Postanovlenie N. 1152 ot 28 avgusta 1997 goda Majlisi Oli Respubliki Tajikistan O prisoedinenii Respubliki Tajikistan k Ramochnoi Konventsii OON ob izmenenii klimata.
71 Framework Convention on Climate Change-Secretariat, "Update on Ratification of the Convention."
72 Global Environment Facility, "List of States Participating in the Restructured GEF."
73 Global Environment Facility, "New Participants in Constituencies."
74 Interim Secretariat of the Rotterdam Convention on the Prior Informed Consent (PIC) Procedure for Certain Hazardous Chemicals and Pesticides in International Trade, "Status of Signature and Ratification, Acceptance, Approval, and Accession."
75 Postanovlenie N. 188 ot 4 noyabrya 1995 goda Majlisi Oli Respubliki Tajikistan O prisoedinenii Respubliki Tajikistan k Venskoi Konventsii ob okhrane ozonovogo sloya.
76 The Ozone Secretariat, "Status of Ratification."
77 Postanovlenie N. 538 ot 13 dekabrya 1997 goda Majlisi Oli Respubliki Tajikistan O prisoedinenii Respubliki Tajikistan k Monrealskomu Protokolu po veschestvam, razrushayuschim ozonovyi sloi i Londonskoi Popravke.
78 The Ozone Secretariat, "Status of Ratification."
79 The Ozone Secretariat, "Status of Ratification."
80 United Nations Environment Programme, "Eleventh Meeting of the Parties to the Montreal protocol on Substances that Depleted the Ozone Layer: Report of the Secretariat on Information provided by the Parties in Accordance with Articles 7 and 9 of the Montreal Protocol," p. 2.
81 Postanovlenie N. 538 ot 13 dekabrya 1997 Majisi Oli Respubliki Tajikistan O prisoedinenii Respubliki Tajikistan k Monrealskomu Protokolu po veschestvam, razrushayuschim ozonovyi sloi i Londonskoi Popravke.
82 The Ozone Secretariat, "Status of Ratification."
83 United Nations Environment Programme, "Eleventh Meeting of the Parties to the Montreal protocol on Substances that Depleted the Ozone Layer: Report of the Secretariat on Information provided by the Parties in Accordance with Articles 7 and 9 of the Montreal Protocol," pp. 2–3.

World Heritage Convention (3)	SEC. REPORTS THAT TJ SUCCEEDED TO CONVENTION 28/8/92,[84] although TJ does not consider itself a party

Turkmenistan

Aarhus Convention on Access to Information, Public Participation in Decision-Making and Access To Justice in Environmental Matters (1)	Acceded 30/4/99[85] [Ratified 25/6/99[86]], *but no credible movements to implement*
Agenda 21 Reporting Requirements (1)	Noncompliance
Basel Convention on Transboundary Movements of Hazardous Wastes (3)	Ratified 18/6/96 [Acceded 25/9/96[87]], *Failed to name focal point*
Convention on Biological Diversity (CBD) (2)	Ratified 14/6/96 [Accession 18/9/96[88]], *Never Provided a National Report; Did not pay 1997–1999 Dues to CBD Trust Fund; as of 1/20 6453 \$US in Arrears*[89]
Convention on Law of Non-Navigable Uses of International Watercourses (1)	Absent from 21/5/97 vote[90]
Convention on Migratory Species (CMS) (4)	**Signatory of Memorandum of Understanding Concerning Conservation Measures for the Siberian Crane 13/12/98**[91]
Convention to Combat Desertification (CCD) (4)	Signed 27/3/95.[92] Ratified 14/6/96 [18/9/96[93]]; Entry into force 26/12/96
Global Environment Facility Rule Compliance (2)	Participant since 29/5/97[94] *Failed to join Constituency on GEF Council until 2000 (Switzerland),*[95] UNEP–GEF FAILED TO FORWARD APPOINTMENT OF FOCAL POINT TO SECRETARIAT IN 1997.[96]
Framework Convention on Climate Change (4)	Accession 1996, [ACCESSION 5/6/95[97]]; Entry into Force 3/9/95, **Focal Point Appointed**, *No National Communication by Deadline*

84 United Nations Educational, "Scientific and Cultural Organization, Convention concerning the Protection of the World Cultural and Natural Heritage."

85 Postanovlenie ot 30 aprelya 1999 goda Mejlisa Turkmenistana O prisoedinenii k Konventsii o dostupe k informatsii, uchastii obschestvennosti v protsesse prinyatiya reshenii i dostupe k pravosudiyu po voprosam, kasayuschimsya okruzhayuschei sredy, promulgated in *Neitralnyi Turkmenistan*, May 5, 1999, p. 2.

86 United Nations Economic Council for Europe, "Multilateral treaties deposited with the Secretary-General-TREATY I–XXVII."

87 UNEP, "Status of Ratifications of the Basel Convention."

88 Convention on Biological Diversity, "Ratification."

89 United Nations Office at Nairobi, Invoice No. Fund 5080 TUK (May 20, 1999).

90 United Nations General Assembly, "General Assembly Adopts Convention on Law of Non-Navigational Uses of International Watercourses."

91 Convention on Migratory Species, "Agreement Summary Sheet: Memorandum of Understanding concerning Conservation Measures for the Siberian Crane."

92 UNCCD, "Status of Ratification and Entry into Force of the UNCCD."

93 UNCCD, "Status of Ratification and Entry into Force of the UNCCD."

94 Global Environment Facility, "List of States Participating in the Restructured GEF." *See also* Letter 4-299 of May 29, 1997 from Deputy Chairman of the Council of Ministers of Turkmenistan Ilaman Shikhiyev to GEF CEO.

95 Global Environment Facility, "New Participants in Constituencies."

96 Letter of March 15, 1997 from Minister of Nature Use and Environmental Protection of Turkmenistan P. Kurbanov to Ahmed Djoghlaf, appointing Deputy Minister Khabibulla Atamuradov.

97 Framework Convention on Climate Change-Secretariat, "Update on Ratification of the Convention."

Table 5.1 (Continued)

Kyoto Protocol	(4)	Signed 25/9/98 [28/9/98[98]]; Ratified 1/11/99
Ramsar Convention on Wetlands of International Importance		Turkmenistan not a party, *but environmental ministry believed state to be a party until 1998;* BUT LIST OF WETLANDS OF INTERNATIONAL IMPORTANCE INCLUDES KRASNOVODSK AND NORTH-CHELEKEN BAYS SITE[99]
	(4)	
Vienna Convention on Ozone		Accession 3/8/93[100] [18/11/93[101]]
Montreal Protocol		Accession 3/8/93[102] [18/11/93[103]]: *Dues to MLF 96–99 in Arrears (235,757 $US[104]); By MOP 11 (11/99) had not provided 1986 Baseline Data for Annex A substances (over 2 years overdue);*[105] *Submitted no 1997 ODS report;*[106] *Did Not Report 1998 Data by 11th MOP (12/99); Draft 11 MOP Resolution (XI/25)*[107] *Notes that Turkmenistan 1996 Ods Use not for Permitted Purposes-TM "WARNED" for NONCOMPLIANCE for Articles 2A–2E of Protocol; 11th MOP resolved to allow TM to substitute GEF project timetable to 2003*
London Amendments		Accession 15/3/94;[108] *by MOP 11 (11/99) had not provided 1989 Baseline Data for Annex B substances or HCFCs (over 2 years overdue)*[109]
Copenhagen Amendments	(1)	Failed to Accede
World Heritage Convention		SEC. REPORTS THAT TM SUCCEEDED TO CONVENTION 30/9/94,[110] although TM did not consider itself a party until recently, when it
	(1)	successfully nominated Merv as first site

98 UNFCCC, "Kyoto Protocol: Status of Ratification," (September 28, 2000), available at http://www.unfccc.de/resource/kpstats.pdf.

99 Ramsar Bureau, "The List of Wetlands of International Importance."

100 Postanovlenie Prezidenta Turkmenistana No. 1424 ot 3 avgusta 1993 g. O prisoedinenii Turkmenistana k Venskoi Konventsii po okhrane ozonovogo sloya, Monrealskomu Protokolu po veschestvam, razrushayuschim ozonovyi sloi, i Popravki k Monrealskomu protokolu po veschestvam, razrushayuschim ozonovyi sloi.

101 The Ozone Secretariat, "Status of Ratification."

102 Postanovlenie Prezidenta Turkmenistana No. 1424 ot 3 avgusta 1993 g. O prisoedinenii Turkmenistana k Venskoi Konventsii po okhrane ozonovogo sloya, Monrealskomu Protokolu po veschestvam, razrushayuschim ozonovyi sloi, i Popravki k Monrealskomu protokolu po veschestvam, razrushayuschim ozonovyi sloi.

103 The Ozone Secretariat, "Status of Ratification."

104 The Ozone Secretariat, "Status of Ratification."

105 United Nations Environment Programme, "Eleventh Meeting of the Parties to the Montreal protocol on Substances that Depleted the Ozone Layer: Report of the Secretariat on Information provided by the Parties in Accordance with Articles 7 and 9 of the Montreal Protocol," p. 2.

106 Ibid., p. 5.

107 Contained in UNEP/OzL.Pro.11/L.2, pp. 20–22 (November 30, 1999).

108 The Ozone Secretariat, "Status of Ratification."

109 United Nations Environment Programme, "Eleventh Meeting of the Parties to the Montreal protocol on Substances that Depleted the Ozone Layer: Report of the Secretariat on Information provided by the Parties in Accordance with Articles 7 and 9 of the Montreal Protocol," pp. 2–3.

110 United Nations Educational, "Scientific and Cultural Organization, Convention concerning the Protection of the World Cultural and Natural Heritage."

Uzbekistan

Aarhus Convention on Access to Information, Public Participation in Decision-Making and Access to Justice in Environmental Matters (2)	Likely to sign, **Focal Point Named**
Agenda 21 Reporting Requirements (4)	**Compliance with both original**[111] **and +5**[112] **reporting requirements**
Basel Convention on Transboundary Movements of Hazardous Wastes (6)	Acceded 22/12/95,[113] Note of ratification sent to Depository 12/1/96[114], [Acceded 7/2/96[115]] 7/5/96 Entry into Force
Convention on Biological Diversity (CBD) (6)	Acceded 6/5/95;[116] Notice sent 27/6/95[117] [19/7/95[118]]; Entered into force 17/10/95.[119] **Provided National Report**
Convention on International Trade in Endangered Species (CITES) (6)	Acceded 25/4/97[120] [10/7/97][121] (diplomatic note of 27/6/97[122]), Entered into force 8/10/97[123]
Convention on Law of Non-Navigable Uses of International Watercourses (2)	Co-Sponsored resolution, but abstained in 21/5/97 GA vote[124]

111 United Nations Commission on Sustainable Development, "Information on Republic of Uzbekistan," (undated), available at http://www.un.org/esa/agenda21/natlinfo/countr/uzbek/index.htm.
112 Republic of Uzbekistan, "Country Profile: Implementation of Agenda 21: Review of Progress Made since the United Nations Conference on Environment and Development, 1992."
113 Postanovlenie N. 188-1 ot 22 dekabrya 1995 g. Olii Majlisa Respubliki Uzbekistan O prisoedinenii k Bazelskoi konventsii o kontrole za transgranichnoi perevozkoi opasnykh otkhodov i ikh udaleniem.
114 Note sent January 12, 1996 from Minister of Foreign Affairs of the Republic of Uzbekistan A. Kamilov to Butros Butros-Gali.
115 UNEP, "Status of Ratifications of the Basel Convention." Under LA 41 TR/221/1 (27-3) of March 12, 1996 UN Legal Advisor accepted instrument of ratification as ratification not accession.
116 Postanovlenie 82-1 ot 6 maya 1995 Olii Majlisa Respubliki Uzbekistan O prisoedinenii Respubliki Uzbekistan k Konventsii o biologicheskom raznoobrazii, podpisannoi v Rio-de-Janeiro v 1992 godu.
117 Letter 05/6054 of June 25, 1995 from Minister of Foreign Affairs of the Republic of Uzbekistan A. Komilov to Butros Butros-Gali.
118 Convention on Biological Diversity, "Ratification."
119 Note LA 41 TR/221/1 (27-8) of September 11, 1995 from The United Nations Legal Counsel Hans Corell to Uzbekistan Permanent Representative to the United Nations Fatikh Teshabaev.
120 Postanovlenie N. 433-1 ot 25 aprelya 1997 g. Olii Majlisa Respubliki Uzbekistan O prisoedinenii k Konventsii o mezhdunarodnoi torgovle vidami dikoi fauny i flory, nakhodyaschimsya pod ugrozoi ischeznoveniya.
121 Convention on International Trade in Endangered Species of Wild Fauna and Flora, "List of Parties."
122 Letter of June 27, 1997 of Minister of Foreign Affairs of the Republic of Uzbekistan A. Kamilov.
123 Notification aux Etats signataires et adherents a la Convention sur le commerce international des especes de faune et de flore sauvages menacees d extinction (CITES), conclue a Washington le 3 mars 1973, Departement Federal des Affaires Etrangers, P.242.45 (undated).
124 United Nations General Assembly, "General Assembly Adopts Convention on Law of Non-Navigational Uses of International Watercourses."

Table 5.1 (Continued)

Convention on Migratory Species (CMS)	Ratified 1/5/98,[125] Notice of accession sent to depository 26/5/98[126] [1/9/98[127]]. **Memorandum of Understanding Concerning Conservation Measures for the Slender-billed Curlew Signed and in Force 10/9/94,**[128] **Memorandum of Understanding Concerning Conservation Measures for the Siberian Crane Signed and in force 13/12/98.**[129] **Final Act of Agreement on the Conservation of African–Eurasian Migratory Waterbirds Signed**[130]
(2)	
Convention to Combat Desertification (CCD)	Signed 7/12/94.[131] Ratified 31/8/95;[132] [31/10/95[133]]; Entry into force 26/12/96, **13th State to Ratify, Uzbekistani served as vice-chair of Scientific Panel**
(6)	
Global Environment Facility Rule Compliance	Participant since 5/4/95,[134] *Failed to join Constituency on GEF Council until 2000 (Switzerland)*[135]
(2)	
Framework Convention on Climate Change	Approved 20/6/93[136] [ACCEDED 20/6/93[137]], Entry into Force 21/3/94. *Violation of Article 78.21 of Constitution of Uzbekistan,* **Focal Point Named,**[138] *No National Communication by Deadline (due 3/21/97),* submitted 22/10/99[139]
(3)	

125 Postanovlenie N. 631-1 ot 1 maya 1998 g. Olii Majlisa Respubliki Uzbekistan O prisoedinenii k Konventsii po sokhraneniyu migriruyuschikh vidov dikikh zhivotnykh.

126 Note sent May 26, 1998 from Minister of Foreign Affairs of the Republic of Uzbekistan A. Komilov to German Foreign Minister Klaus Kinkel.

127 Convention on Migratory Species, "Parties to the Convention on the Conservation of Migratory Species of Wild Animals," (October 1, 2000), available at http://wcmc.org.uk/cms/partlst.htm.

128 Convention on Migratory Species, "Agreement Summary Sheet: Memorandum of Understanding concerning Conservation Measures for the Slender-billed Curlew. *Numenius tenuirostris.*"

129 Convention on Migratory Species, "Agreement Summary Sheet: Memorandum of Understanding concerning Conservation Measures for the Siberian Crane."

130 Convention on Migratory Species, "Agreement Summary Sheet: Agreement on the Conservation of African–Eurasian Migratory Waterbirds (AEWA)" (July 1, 1998), available at http://wcmc.org.uk/cms/aew-summ. htm.

131 UNCCD, "Status of Ratification and Entry into Force of the UNCCD."

132 Postanovlenie N. 125-1 ot 31 avgusta 1995 g. Olii Majlisa Respubliki Uzbekistan O ratifikatsii Konventsii OON po borbe s opustynivaniem v tekh stranakh, kotorye ispytyvayut seryeznuyu zasukhu i/ili opustynivanie, osobenno v Afrike.

133 UNCCD, "Status of Ratification and Entry into Force of the UNCCD."

134 Global Environment Facility, "List of States Participating in the Restructured GEF."

135 Global Environment Facility, "New Participants in Constituencies."

136 Letter 02/2814 of May 14, 1993 from Minister of Foreign Affairs of the Republic of Uzbekistan Sadyk Safaev to Butros Butros-Gali.

137 Framework Convention on Climate Change-Secretariat, "Update on Ratification of the Convention."

138 October 18, 1999 Letter No. 6-4/10-38 from Deputy Prime Minister B. S. Khamidov to UNFCCC Executive Secretary Cutajar.

139 Main Administration of Hydrometeorology, *Initial Communication of the Republic of Uzbekistan Under the United Nations Framework Convention on Climate Change* (Tashkent: Main Administration of Hydrometeorology, 1999), available at http://www.unfccc.de/resource/docs/natc/uzbnc1.pdf.

Kyoto Protocol **(3)**	Signed 20/11/98; Ratified 20/8/99[140] [12/10/99[141]]
Ramsar Convention on Wetlands of International Importance **(3)**	Not a party, *but environmental committee believed state to be a party until 1998*
Vienna Convention on Ozone	Succeeded through note of 10/5/93[142] [ACCEDED 18/5/93[143]]
Montreal Protocol	Succeeded through note of 18/5/93[144] [ACCEDED 18/5/93[145]], entered into force 16/10/97; **In FULL COMPLIANCE with all Montreal, London, and Copenhagen reporting requirements as of MOP 11 (11/99);** *Did Not Report 1998 Data by 11th MOP (12/99);* **97% Reduction in All ODS as compared to Baseline as of 1997; 86% as of 1996.**
London Amendments	Ratification 1/5/98[146] [Accession 10/6/98[147]]; 8/9/98 Entry into force
Copenhagen Amendments **(6)**	Ratification 1/5/98[148] [Accession 10/6/98[149]]; 8/9/98 Entry into force
World Heritage Convention **(3)**	Acceded 22/12/95,[150] ALTHOUGH SEC. REPORTS UZ A PARTY BY LETTER OF SUCCESSION 13/1/93[151]

140 Postanovlenie N. 834-1 ot 20 avgusta 1999 g. Olii Majlisa Respubliki Uzbekistan ratifikatsii Kiotskogo Protokola k Ramochnoi konventsii Organizatsii Obyedinennykh Natsii ob izmenenii klimata.

141 UNFCCC, "Kyoto Protocol: Status of Ratification."

142 Letter 11/2734 of May 10, 1993 from Minister of Foreign Affairs of the Republic of Uzbekistan Sadyk Safaev to Butros Butros-Gali.

143 The Ozone Secretariat, "Status of Ratification."

144 Letter 11/2734 of May 10, 1993 from Minister of Foreign Affairs of the Republic of Uzbekistan Sadyk Safaev to Butros Butros-Gali.

145 The Ozone Secretariat, "Status of Ratification."

146 Postanovlenie N. 627-1 ot 1 maya 1998 g Olii Majlisa Respubliki Uzbekistan O ratifikatsii Londonskoi popravki k Monrealskomu protokolu po veschestvam, razrushayuschim ozonovyi sloi.

147 The Ozone Secretariat, "Status of Ratification." Under Letter LA 41 TR/221/1 (27-2 (b) and (c)) of June 25, 1998, UN Legal Advisor explains that instruments of ratification accepted as instruments of accession.

148 Postanovlenie N. 628-1 ot 1 maya 1998 g Olii Majlisa Respubliki Uzbekistan O ratifikatsii Kopengagenskoi popravki k Monrealskomu protokolu po veschestvam, razrushayuschim ozonovyi sloi.

149 The Ozone Secretariat, "Status of Ratification." Under Letter LA 41 TR/221/1 (27-2 (b) and (c)) of June 25, 1998, UN Legal Advisor explains that instruments of ratification accepted as instruments of accession.

150 Postanovlenie N. 182-1 ot 22 dekabrya 1995 g. Olii Majlisa Respubliki Uzbekistan O ratifikatsii Konventsii ob okhrane vsemirnogo kulturnogo i prirodnogo naslediya ot 1972 goda.

151 United Nations Educational, "Scientific and Cultural Organization, Convention concerning the Protection of the World Cultural and Natural Heritage."

6 Case studies: internationalizing the Central Asian environment

> The more closely we become acquainted with these [donors], the more evident it becomes that many of them work in an extremely ineffective manner. [W]e have noticed that where one person worked last year, now 4–7 people do the job of this one person. [We were incorrect in] viewing recent political changes as erasing a bureaucratic system which held paper as a god and had an unlimited number of forms and documents. [R]escued from the grasp of the Soviet bureaucratic system, we have been delivered not into a fresh current of enlightened work and stimulating initiative, but into a painfully familiar world of bureaucrats. . . . [D]onors began to demand that work hours be accounted for in [time sheets]. They require the workdays in the chart to be marked with eights. Just as under the Soviet era, we can fill in our eights; they don't necessarily mean anything though, nor can they suggest to us how to more efficiently organize our work. . . . Nevertheless, they teach us how to fill in our eights.[1]

At the dawn of independence, international institutions enjoyed both popular legitimacy and substantial influence in Central Asia. This legitimacy and influence reflected both the USSR's strong iterative respect for the United Nations and international law,[2] as well as a mood swing away from Soviet symbols towards international, "normal," and "successful" institutional modalities and models.[3] After 3 years of direct contact with the actual staffs and projects of the United Nations and other international donor and development agencies, as opposed to their promotional literature, most local environmental professionals come to adopt the view that Western organizations suffer from the same pathologies as their now defunct Soviet counterparts. Moreover, a large number of local professionals further conclude that the human capital assets of the West are in some areas weaker than their Soviet counterparts, especially in some technical fields.[4]

The erosion of this general presumption of the efficacy and moral authority of international organizations coincides with expansion by the Central Asian states of their participation in international environmental regimes. Environmental protection within Central Asia, even for environmental issues that are not considered transboundary in nature, is increasingly tied to international regimes, institutions, and donors. Almost no environmental programs or efforts within Central Asia are any longer purely national in character; those environmental agency staff without international connections and those environmental programs not funded by foreign donors are the most discontent and weakest in the entire region. Any particular lack of internationalization within environmental affairs in Central Asia is now simply dispositive of someone's failure to succeed in making international connections. However, as mentioned above, this embrace of internationalization coincides with a lessening level of faith, respect, and awe of international institutions; the embrace is, unfortunately, one increasingly of monetary resources alone.

The Central Asian states all actively request funding from foreign investors and donors to support state environmental agencies, the environmental sciences, and specific environmental protection programs. Not all of these funds come through such major donors as GEF, the European Union's Program on Technical Assistance to the Commonwealth of Independent States (TACIS), UNDP, the World Bank, UNEP, or targeted donors such as the secretariats of conventions. Some funds come from transnational corporations. These efforts have met with mixed, but not necessarily disappointing, results. Chevron helped the Kazakhstan Zoological Society publish a new edition of the Kazakhstan Red Data Book on Endangered Species,[5] and TengizChevroil is perhaps Kazakhstan's most active charitable donor.[6]

Some funds have also come through multilateral lenders not originally associated with the GEF. Asian Development Bank has implemented a program for the Institutional Support for Sustainable Agricultural Development in Uzbekistan,[7] and IUCN has coordinated biodiversity activists and environmental lawyers throughout the region.[8] Some of the funds have come from private philanthropic foundations. The John D. and Catherine T. MacArthur Foundation provided a grant to Dashkhovuz Ecological Guardians (TM) to create a professional association of Central Asian environmental scientists,[9] and local Soros foundations make grants to more than a dozen environmental NGOs in the region. Some of the funds have come from bilateral donors. Germany assists Kazakhstan in water conservation in urban areas, and Switzerland provides funds to improve the state forestry service of Kyrgyzstan.[10]

All told, more than 1000 discrete internationally funded environmental projects have arisen in Central Asia since 1991, ranging in size from the several hundred dollar grants to Turkmenistan and Uzbekistan environmental education NGOs provided by Minnesota's Cottonwood Foundation[11] to loans of tens of millions of dollars provided by the World Bank for Aral Sea agriculture and sewage remediation projects. Despite a great diversity of funders, recipients, sizes, repayment obligations, and expectations, every single project in the region hoped to, directly or indirectly, improve the state of the environment in Central Asia.

Figure 6.1[12] shows how almost all environmental donors approached and still approach their efforts in Central Asia. While ambitious foreign donors are still putting the cart before the horse, in 2001 it will be difficult to find any local expert in Central Asia willing to believe that by 2005 the region will have "implemented basic institutional infrastructure, completed essential economic reforms, and averted immediate environmental health risks." Quite the opposite impression flows from the empirical evidence of the past 10 years. In the last decade, the region made modest progress in building basic institutions, little progress in building healthy economies, some progress in establishing or re-establishing

> **Long-term priorities, 2005 and beyond**
>
> Once the newly independent states have implemented basic institutional infrastructure, completed essential economic reforms, and averted immediate environmental health risks, attention can shift toward achieving the ambitious long-term goal of achieving Europe-wide convergence in environmental policies and conditions. This will require increased efforts and investments in expanding the coverage and quality of water supply in rural and urban areas and of sewarage in urban areas, managing air pollution from the growing number of vehicles in urban areas, and introducing sustainable land use practices into sector policies.

Figure 6.1 Example of World Bank environmental planning.

non-sustainable economies, and simply no aggregate progress in ensuring environmental health. Indeed, the survey below of Central Asia's explicit connections to international environmental regimes suggests that there exist scant grounds to claim that internationalization of the Central Asian environment yields environmental benefits or that, whatever the effects of disparate individual projects, the region is moving towards sustainable development.

AGENDA 21, OPENING STATES, AND THE NEW ERA OF SUSTAINABLE DEVELOPMENT

In an international sphere where state coordination is critical and information limited, the first step towards resolving most issues is to initiate dialogue. Accordingly, for those interested in bringing the states of the world together to work in concert to avert global environmental collapse and to pioneer and implement new strategies of sustainable development, chances to initiate, develop, and expand dialogue have always contained elemental importance. The role of dialogue, or negotiation, is to share information and build the awareness needed to develop consensus about the gravity of an issue, to marshal the resources needed to develop data needed for a full analysis of the issue, and to foster the cooperation and integrated understandings needed to address an issue.

Efforts that focus primarily on dialogue and cooperation, instead of primarily on changing specific practices, are called "soft law." Examples of "hard law" in the international environmental sphere come almost exclusive from regimes concerning the atmosphere or trade. For example, the ozone regime definitively requires states, by certain dates, to cease trade in and production of ozone depleting substances. The Kyoto Protocol of the Climate Change Convention will bind developed states to restrictions on emissions of greenhouse gases as compared to

1990 levels. CITES generally restricts trade in endangered species. In these cases, international environmental law comes close to resembling the core of a general conception of "law": a clear proscription on certain kinds of behavior. Should they fail to punish or otherwise react to state parties who flagrantly fail to abide by these proscriptions, these regimes will risk losing their authority and legitimacy within the international community and under international law.

Yet, clear "environmental laws" are infrequent in environmental regimes. There is no equivalent "law" requiring states to prevent loss of biodiversity, prevent desertification, or refrain from pollution of internal waterways. Rather, regimes in these fields impose on states a set of obligations of a less dramatic and more negotiated character. Often these obligations consist of little more than filing reports with secretariats, participating in activities intended over time to yield legal statements, conducting inventories, paying membership dues, and refraining from the pursuit of activities that would flagrantly undermine the goals of the eponymous convention. Occasionally such agreements also anticipate binding arbitration between states in cases of disputes. States and scholars have little problem accepting such obligations as "law," albeit under a definition that already diverges far from the colloquial meaning of the term and converges upon what most people would term morality.

Thus, it is a fair description that international efforts for environmental protection contain not only directed efforts to build environmental law, but also efforts to use legal machinery to achieve dialogue, awareness, and cooperation, and then to label the outcomes of such efforts "law." For example, the 1992 Earth Summit, like the 1972 Stockholm Convention, focused world attention on environmental issues. The 1972 Report of the United Nations Conference on the Human Environment (the Stockholm Declaration) and the 1992 Agenda 21,[13] which was the primary document resulting from the Earth Summit, are nothing less than textbooks on global environmental problems and possible solutions, but they are simultaneously at the core of international environmental law. Although Agenda 21 adds little to the knowledge base of humanity, it does offer itself as a blueprint for the future, ground its authority in its authorship by diverse environmental and legal experts, and essay to make its contents a fundamental text of modern human society. Passages contained within Agenda 21 about the need for states to bind themselves to principles of sustainable development, the precautionary principle, and intergenerational equity express at best, in a legal sense, a rough estimate of the content of future binding environmental laws.

Invariably, meetings and documents in the soft law vein envision follow-up meetings, reports, and assessments to continue and build dialogue. Since such meetings and documents often require little of states other than that they show up and participate, critics of soft law complain that these efforts do not go far enough. It would be essentially nonsensical under international law to claim that Kazakhstan violated Agenda 21 because it did not follow the precautionary principle in its environmental legislation; Kazakhstan assumed no such obligation to do so when it signed this document in Rio de Janeiro.[14] Critics of soft law commonly fail to consider that such "soft" efforts will nevertheless be critical for any efforts, which may or may not appear in the future, that do go "far enough."

Soft law provides low stakes fora for state diplomats to negotiate, share information, and otherwise build the social capital that enables later ambitious organizational capital breakthroughs.[15] Prominent examples in the present day include the Committee on Environmental Policy of the UNECE,[16] the United Nations Commission on Sustainable Development (which sponsors Agenda 21/Rio+ meetings), and the UNESCO-sponsored Earth Charter meetings.[17] Thus, for states at the margins of international environmental regimes, soft law fora provide an invaluable opportunity to facilitate integration into environmental regimes, improve national reputations, seek funding, and build general capacity.

Given this rough outline of soft law regimes, such regimes may be analyzed along much the same lines as other environmental regimes. Thus, the number of states that endorse Agenda 21 or that showed up at the Earth Summit are metrics that are popular, but not significant. Rather, the impacts of soft law regimes should be sought in the intersection between international dialogue and state action. Whether states meet deadlines in the submission of and submit thorough national reports, whether they build capacity through these regimes, whether new national legislation reflects Agenda 21, whether school curricula change, and whether the principles of Agenda 21 begin to suffuse national dialogues are all more revealing, albeit more difficult to measure, criteria. What an analysis of these factors in Central Asia reveals is ambiguous; while state efforts around Agenda 21 do not inspire, grassroots reactions produce more hope.

The participation of the Central Asian states in the Agenda 21 regime illustrates the degree to which the region fails to capitalize on the external opportunities open to it. Two main avenues for Agenda 21 participation exist: submission of national reports and attendance at Agenda 21 meetings at United Nations Headquarters.

National reports on sustainable development are arguably the only requirement of Agenda 21 signatories, and at that they are technically only recommended.[18] Yet, because the Commission on Sustainable Development has decided to publish these reports and otherwise draw attention to them as the central component of Agenda 21 implementation,[19] they are as close to a requirement of regime participation as exists. No Central Asian state, with the partial exception of Uzbekistan, has taken advantage of the opportunities accorded by this reporting system, and no state has invested any effort to engage meaningfully in the actual meetings of the Commission on Sustainable Development.

The basic reports should have been submitted before 1997, at which point states began to submit Rio+5 reports. Only Uzbekistan submitted a basic report that could be considered adequate; although it provided basic information, it failed to use the report as an opportunity to argue for its needs or exhibits strengths. As for the Rio+5 reports, heavily funded by the United Nations to do so, Kazakhstan's National Environment Center did submit such a report;[20] yet, like Uzbekistan three years earlier, Kazakhstan failed to exhibit strengths or argue well for its needs.

In fact, Kazakhstan's report contains three glaring failures beyond its lack of information. First, it lists millions of dollars of environmental aid provided to Kazakhstan, but provides little evidence of any result of this aid. Second, it suggests that Kazakhstan has signed several, but ratified no, environmental conventions. Finally, it contains repeated assurances that Kazakhstan witnesses great progresses in exactly those instances in which the state should have declared defeat and requested aid. For instance, despite the crash in the scientific community in human and financial terms, the report assures readers that the "Scientific community has already established ways in which to address the general public and deal with sustainable development."[21]

In contrast, in its 1997 report, Uzbekistan provides far more complete information, suggests that half its scientific potential has been wiped out, and praises international assistance while giving itself only adequate marks for progress in sustainable development.[22] Tajikistan failed to submit any kind of report. Kyrgyzstan and Turkmenistan not only did not submit a report; the Commission on Sustainable Development also fails to even include them in its list of world states.

Fortunately, the national aspects of Agenda 21 in Central Asia paint a more hopeful picture. While there has been almost no effort to create Agenda 21 commitments at the municipal level, most new environmental legislation does explicitly draw attention to Agenda 21 as a source of environmental legal consensus and borrows, at least at a general level, from Agenda 21. Ironically, those new laws most impacted by foreign legal assistance are, contrary to what one would expect, the ones least connected to Agenda 21. Foreign environmental lawyers employed as advisors to the Central Asian states, especially those from the United States, command little awareness of international environmental law. As a consequence, they undermine the global ambitions of Agenda 21 by denying it a role in their own influential drafts and recommendations submitted to the states, sometimes even explicitly frustrating efforts by local NGOs and ministries to make textual connections to Agenda 21.

Finally, the Central Asian states deserve recognition for the degree to which Agenda 21 has become part of the core awareness of both the environmental community and environmental education curricula. Undoubtedly the most impressive aspect of Agenda 21 impact on the Central Asian states, the general consensus and mood of cooperation among NGOs, experienced activists, dedicated teachers, and ministries of education to expand environmental education and incorporate Agenda 21 into all curricula are hampered only by lack of resources in the post-Soviet era. It is partly on this general public interest in Agenda 21 that Kazakhstan based its hopes to produce in 2000 an Agenda 21 report of much better quality than its predecessors.[23]

Accordingly, "soft" international environmental law in Central Asia analyzed through Agenda 21 is largely a success at the grassroots level, a noticeable influence on the national level, and largely a failure at the highest levels of state and foreign affairs. Other aspects of soft international environmental law in Central Asia have unfolded in largely similar fashion.

Beyond Agenda 21, several other soft law environmental regimes also impact Central Asia. Some of these, such as UNESCO's Earth Charter essentially parallel Agenda 21, and it is open to argument whether they complement other efforts or frustrate them by crowding consciousness and demanding scarce resources. However, there also exist a set of soft law efforts that aim not at building shared environmental awareness and consensus regarding future laws, but at spreading the normative institutions of sustainable development as these impact state structure. Specifically, two regimes exist to spread environmental civil society and environmental planning.

The 1998 UNECE Convention on Access to Information, Public Participation in Decision-Making and Access to Justice in Environmental Matters (Aarhus Convention) seeks to move states towards guaranteeing certain rights for private actors. These rights are essentially those currently enjoyed by the publics of North America and, more recently, Europe. Over the past decade, the only environmental convention that has received equivalent attention in Central Asia has been CCD; just as euphoria over CCD began to subside in 1999, the Aarhus Convention moved into the void. 2000 saw numerous well-funded regional and national conferences and trainings that expended considerable funds to bring together NGOs, state officials, and Aarhus Convention European donors. This support for the Aarhus Convention, however, is in itself proof of Central Asia's failures.

European donors, like OSCE, actively push the Aarhus Convention because its appearance coincided with their general realization that, despite their funding, democracy and rule of law are on the decline in Central Asia. The Aarhus Convention operates now, as a result of this realization of development failure, often as more of a synecdoche for the need for Westernization than as a vehicle for sustainable development. In other words, the environmental content of the Aarhus Convention is not at all what drives its external support in the region. Rather, the Aarhus Convention is primarily a stand-in for other possible vehicles through which to criticize the Central Asian states for their failures to conduct free and fair elections, observe human rights, and be accountable to their own citizens. To date, it has not been invoked by Western actors with analogous vigor to criticize the Central Asian states for failures that stem directly from the convention itself, such as failures to effect environmental reforms, allow private parties access to courts, or pass implementing legislation for the convention itself.

Against the background of this co-optation of the Aarhus regime by state interests not overly concerned with the environment, the second structural soft law regime is more clearly related to sustainable development. The narrow focus of this second regime, at the center of which there is no discrete convention, is the establishment of effective institutions for environmental management. Within the Central Asian context, this normative aspiration, since environmental committees or ministries already existed in every republic, has focused primarily on environmental action plans.

World Bank, UNDP, and TACIS fund a variety of efforts in every republic to create national and regional environmental actions plans for general environmental protection and for specific environmental problems. A ubiquitous aspect of this funding is the creation of a special and very well furnished office for the national environmental action plan (NEAP), a kind of office that stands in stark contrast to anything that the Central Asian states could support on their own for their environmental state agencies. Kazakhstan's NEAP began in 1995, Kyrgyzstan's in 1994, Turkmenistan's in 1996, and Uzbekistan's in 1997. As an offshoot emblematic of manifestations in other republics, in 1999, Turkmenistan formed a National Commission for the Implementation of United Nations Environmental Conventions and Programmes.[24]

UNDP has been the most active in the NEAP process, and the United States has been almost entirely absent. Accordingly, NEAPs are best understood as part of UNDP's agenda within the region, and should be understood within the framework of the comments of the next section. However, it should be noted that part of the appeal of NEAPs within the region is that they are plans. They require both no action beyond assembling paper, and they resurrect and re-valorize modalities and rhetorical triggers of the planned economy that are familiar to bureaucrats in the region. No NEAP has yet been meaningfully implemented anywhere in the region. Instead, "successful" NEAPs are those that produce not action for environmental protection, but a permanent bureaucracy. In April 1998, the Kazakhstan NEAP became the National Environment Center for Sustainable Development, an organization meant not to produce a plan, but to be a core environmental agency in Kazakhstan.

Thus, the most interesting aspect of NEAPs is not their tendency to divert attention away from local problems and non-standard approaches or their alienation of those environmental agencies that do not directly receive their exuberant funding. Rather, the most interesting aspects of NEAPs are that they are plan-based (as opposed to market-based, reaction-based, or action-based), avowedly hierarchical, and beholden to the idea that foreign subsidies will enable implementation. To date, no one has seemed to notice that these fundamental assumptions, all of which are endorsed by UNDP staff, inherently and flatly contradict the stated meta-goal of all Western donors to assist the Central Asian states to move away from the planned economy, pioneer meaningful decentralization, and embrace the market economy. UNDP and related UN staff, flying in from the proverbial Miami Beach to the sloping mountains way down in the south of Eurasia, are bringing back the USSR.

INTO THE OPENING: GEF AND THE GEF IMPLEMENTORS

The Global Environment Facility was created in 1991, and by mid-1999 had received $2.4 billion in contributions from donor states, with the United States the only developed state that failed to contribute its pledged contribution.[25] GEF is the only donor in Central Asia that concentrates its funding attention exclusively on projects of a global nature (Table 6.1).

Bilateral donors, like Finland, Germany, Switzerland, and the Netherlands, complement GEF projects with additional funding, sometimes at levels exceeding those of GEF itself. For example, TACIS funds a several million dollar river ecology program in Azerbaijan that is part of the GEF-funded Caspian Environment Programme. By its mandate, GEF may only fund the "incremental costs" of environmental projects that have an impact on the global environment.[26] This

Table 6.1 Funded preparation projects in GEF pipeline at end of 1999
(*Enabling Activities, PDF A, PDF B funding*)*

Name	States
Wind Power	KZ
Migratory Bird Habitat	KZ
Mountain Agrobiodiversity	KZ
Biodiversity Strategy	KZ
Biodiversity Strategy	UZ
Wetland Biodiversity	UZ
Biodiversity EA	KG
Biodiversity EA	UZ
Southern Biodiversity	KG
Mountain Biodiversity	KG
Energy Efficiency: Hot Water/Heat Supply	KZ
Energy Efficiency: Hot Water/Heat Supply	UZ
Montreal Protocol	UZ, TM
Montreal Protocol	AZ
Climate Change Study	UZ
Climate Change EA	TM
Climate Change EA	UZ
Climate Change EA	AZ
Nuratau Reserve	UZ
Ozone Compliance	TJ, UZ, TM
FCCC Reporting	TM

Note
* Derived from various GEF sources, including Global Environment Facility,
Operational Report on GEF Programs.

restriction on GEF funding makes the institution unique, and it is what requires additional inputs such as those by TACIS described above.

Because incremental costs remain widely misunderstood, they deserve explication. Incremental costs are part of a two stage cost/benefit sharing and analysis that the GEF Council uses to make decisions on funding. In the first part of the incremental cost analysis, national benefits are distinguished from global benefits. Only those costs of a conservation initiative that exceed the conservation expenditures that a state would undertake anyway (baseline costs) are eligible to be incremental costs. Furthermore, such costs are discounted to the extent that they provide national benefits. The remaining dollar amount is what constitutes, theoretically, a request to GEF. If the dollar amount is negative (indicating a profit), the project should seek a loan (such as from the World Bank) instead of a GEF grant.

The second part of the incremental cost analysis examines the environmental benefit per dollar. In practice, this approach is feasible for climate change projects (since carbon emission reductions are quantifiable), easy for ozone depleting substances projects (for similar reasons), a stretch for international waters and desertification (where metrics exist, but means of comparison are vague), and sophistic for biodiversity (since a discrete metric is unavailable).[27]

GEF's founding logic involves a complementary relationship among its implementing agencies' comparative advantages:[28] UNEP's environmental experience, UNDP's expertize in capacity building and local partnerships, and World Bank's technical expertize in complex infrastructure projects. UNEP's role has, to date, been understated; GEF projects in Central Asia are either UNDP or World Bank, with the three largest projects in Table 6.2 belonging to World Bank and most of Table's 6.1 projects under the supervision of UNDP. Only with Kazakhstan's three million dollar wind power project and six million dollar ozone project in early 2000 did any large UNDP–GEF projects in Central Asia appear.

UNDP generally pursues smaller projects developed through close contact with epistemic communities placed on the UNDP payroll directly or indirectly, and it relies heavily on the continued loyalty (bonding social capital) of these experts. World Bank, in contrast, uses money as a leverage to win compliance from ministry level institutions (organizational capital) and places less emphasis on personal relations. In both cases, it is a myth that either agency is an indifferent but professional part of the GEF structure committed primarily to facilitating efforts by governments, NGOs, and local communities in Central Asia. As a preface to this Chapter's review of specific projects, neither UNDP nor World Bank operates without problems, and both are among the least indifferent actors in the entire region when it comes to the design, content, and priorities of GEF proposals.

UNDP projects ubiquitously employ expensive foreign consultants, who are regularly 40 times as expensive as equivalently, or better, qualified local experts.[29] Moreover, despite original GEF emphases on specific actions for the environment, over time UNDP projects have come to contain fewer and fewer such actions and more and more public education, public outreach, and similar endeavors whose efficacy is questionable, but whose demand for more intimate UNDP involvement is undeniable.

Traditionally, UNDP has taken 13 per cent of the funding of a project for its own budgets in its development work.[30] However, that figure has appeared

Table 6.2 GEF-funded large and medium sized projects in Central Asia at end of 1999*

Name	States involved	Rounded millions (with cofinancing)
Tian Shan Biodiversity	KZ, KG, UZ	10 (14)
Aral Sea Program	KZ, KG, TM, TJ, UZ	12 (72)
Caspian Environment	AZ, KZ, TM	8 (18–163)
Small Grants	KZ	1
Ozone	UZ	3
Ozone	AZ	7
Ozone	TM	1

Note
* Derived from various GEF sources, including Global Environment Facility, *Operational Report on GEF Programs* (December 31, 1999).

excessive within the framework of GEF, and so UNDP has operated within the GEF through a set of financial procedures differing from those of its usual agency support cost arrangements. However, UNDP has in the past decade made no serious efforts to reveal what its take of GEF projects in fact actually is, which is curious for an agency that releases in minute financial detail all other aspects of projects. For the Small Grants Program 1998 Proposal, 6 per cent of the $31.6 million award went to UNDP partner UNOPS (United Nations Office for Project Services[31]) as the executing agency for vague "support," a euphemism for an unrestricted award. Almost $4 million was allocated for UNDP to hire staff for the program under local employment contracts with the local UNDP mission.[32]

Both of these figures contrast starkly with the 1 per cent take by UNDP that UNDP Kazakhstan's senior environmental officer, Zharas Takenov, claims publicly is the extent of UNDP's take under the Small Grants Program, and the 3 per cent taken for all other GEF-financed projects.[33] Takenov's modest estimates of UNDP's intrusion into GEF funds meant by definition for the benefit of developing states (and not UN agencies) are widely echoed by most other UNDP employees in the region. In fact, Takenov and his colleagues, who are all far from New York, may not be aware that their employer's interest in every GEF project is much deeper. Indeed, the actual scale of GEF funds siphoned off by UNDP is dramatically greater.

For example, UNDP's Mission in Uzbekistan expects to get well over a million dollars a year for the foreseeable future from GEF projects, which UNDP itself calls "sustainable development funds."[34] Since the core annual budget allocated to each UNDP office in Central Asia is roughly $700,000 ($1.1 million for Kazakhstan),[35] even though GEF administrative funds do not exceed 10 per cent of the total UNDP budget, they increase by 20–100 per cent the internal capacity of UNDP offices in Central Asia.[36] GEF's billions of dollars have effected, effect, and will continue to effect the building of UNDP capacity worldwide, dramatically.

To read the dozens of books and booklets issued each year by the GEF implementors is to assume that these agencies have assumed a thankless task. The Corporate Business Plans for both FY00–02 and FY02–04 discuss Implementing Agency fees and a "fee-based structure," but without any information on what these fees might be in dollar or percentage terms.[37] The lack of any dollar figures is a notable departure from the norm of GEF documents, which deluge readers in figures.

Despite its professed commitment to "total transparency,"[38] GEF buries its actual disclosure of the take of the Implementing Agencies in its annual reports, and almost nowhere else. As of mid-1999, the Implementing Agencies and similar UN agencies, in addition to roughly 5 per cent taken directly in many proposals, such as in the Small Grants Program noted above, had taken 21.4 per cent of all disbursements from the GEF Trust Fund, or $220 million.[39] The 1999 Annual Report also reveals that an oft-mentioned and never defined "fee-based system" innovation is nothing other than, at its start, a 1999 $71 million bonus to the unsatiated Implementing Agencies,[40] in addition to the $220 million already mentioned, bringing the total cut to the Implementing Agencies to roughly 30 per cent of all GEF funds. By comparison, when former Soviet governments tweak their books and expenses to siphon off smaller percentages of World Bank loans and IMF tranches, the rest of the world has little problem complaining of corruption on the part of entrenched interests. In its continuance, this fee-based system means that, as of the November 2000 GEF Council meeting, UNDP takes a flat fee equivalent to roughly 20 per cent of project awards for medium-sized projects.[41]

As disappointing as these figures are, actual project accountability is little better. GEF's own targets are to increase its measurable impact, country ownership of programs, the commitment of its implementing agencies to the global environment, its partnership with a wide range of organizations, and its institutional effectiveness.[42] Yet, some of its practices cannot be reconciled with these ambitions. For example, it is not staff from the CBD Secretariat that evaluates GEF biodiversity projects. Rather, the fox is minding the henhouse. UNDP staff and/or the GEF Secretariat's Management and Evaluation Team (in its annual Project Implementation Review) are primarily responsible for assuring the regime of its own effectiveness. Compounding these problems, a 2001 GEF-sponsored NGO "global assessment" of GEF projects fails to include any Central Asian projects in its list of 81 projects to review.

Moreover, problems of accountability are magnified in Central Asia, where nepotism and other non-UNDP forms of corruption, language barriers, and insulation from the frontlines of scrutiny also regularly challenge the integrity of development programs. For example, when UNDP–GEF celebrated the success of its Small Grants Program in 1998 by sharing country reports of each of the 18 states where the small grants program operated, it subtly essayed to hide the fact that its report was really only about 14 states;[43] UNDP–GEF's Kazakhstan staff failed to submit a report to UNDP.

This same Kazakhstan staff (falsely) told local NGOs such as the Karaganda EcoCenter that they could only apply for medium-sized grants after they had successfully completed a small grant,[44] and (illegally) refused to accept or forward on this NGO's medium-sized project proposals. Even worse, in 1998, a coalition of Tajikistan environmental NGOs submitted a medium-sized project proposal to, since there was no World Bank presence in Dushanbe, the UNDP mission in Tajikistan. The local UNDP (falsely) told the NGOs that they could not leave the project with UNDP and that the local UNDP mission had nothing to do with the GEF, belying UNDP Headquarters claims to have developed GEF expertise in its missions worldwide,[45] claims trumpeted extensively during the October 1998 GEF Council Meeting[46] that coincided with these events in Tajikistan. The local NGOs (accurately) informed the local UNDP mission of its responsibilities and this time insisted on leaving their project. Yet, instead of responding within the fourteen day deadline that all GEF documents agree are an essential part of the proposal process, UNDP simply never responded.

Still not capitulating, the Tajikistan NGOs contacted UNDP Headquarters in New York, and Headquarters immediately promised to get the process back on track. Yet, after several months, UNDP–GEF and the local UNDP mission had both failed to respond. The fourteen day deadline was missed several times over. Under GEF rules, if an Implementing Agency fails to respond to such a submission, it must include that proposal automatically in the GEF Pipeline of Projects Under Review.[47] UNDP failed to do that as well.

Finally, on November 8, 1999 UNDP–GEF responded. UNDP Coordinator for Europe and the CIS, Christopher Briggs wrote that the proposal would be suitable for GEF funding if indeed the biodiversity of the Southern Hissar Range was truly endangered and of global significance.[48] As requested, the NGOs quickly assembled a detailed reply to Briggs confirming the global significance of the endangered biodiversity of the Southern Hissars. They heard nothing more for more than 6 months.

In summer 2000, the UNDP–GEF representative in Tajikistan told the project proposers that the proposal was on the verge of being funded. But, in September 2000, a UNDP biodiversity consultant, 9 months late, finally arrived in Tajikistan. He told the NGO coalition that the project was unsuitable for GEF funding because it involved not the Shirkent Reserve itself, but a border area of the reserve and because it did not pursue merely biodiversity conservation. According to this consultant, since the project would also reduce emissions of greenhouse gases and provide for improvements in local standards of living,[49] it was more aptly described as an effort at sustainable development.[50] The GEF, the consultant concluded, does not fund sustainable development, and so the consultant saw no need to evaluate the incremental cost analysis of the project, even for its biodiversity benefits.

Ironically, that consultant's home UNDP office in Uzbekistan calls GEF funds "sustainable development" funds, and exactly concurrent to the release of the consultant's conclusion, GEF stated that "much of the GEF portfolio has been in protected areas, but the time is ripe for supporting broader government and community sustainable development efforts in surrounding areas."[51] The project, still in contravention of GEF rules, was still not included in the Pipeline.[52]

This project history illustrates the norm within Central Asia for projects that do not arise out of UNDP's own "pocket" epistemic communities in NEAPs; thus UNDP has unilaterally effected a revision of the term "country-driven" to narrow the definition of country to those citizens of a host country already employed by or beholden to UNDP.

In stark contrast, World Bank GEF efforts in Central Asia exhibit agency disconcern for the financial aspects of GEF projects. On the World Bank scale, GEF funding is miniscule. However, GEF funding exceeds by an order of magnitude the amount the World Bank possesses in grant funds. Eager to improve its reputation in the environmental sphere, World Bank seeks the public relations, instead of the financial, rewards from GEF projects. Nevertheless, all three World Bank-facilitated GEF projects in Central Asia located their genesis in Washington, D.C. meeting rooms, and all three were suggested to the states in question long after the projects were already well-formulated. All they needed, in order to be funded, was legitimization in the form of local voices.

BIODIVERSITY: EMBRACING CBD DOLLARS AND AVOIDING CITES DUTIES

While the Central Asia Transboundary Biodiversity Project[53] (CATBP) only in 1999 received approval for full GEF funding, for the preceding 3 years it received preparatory funding from GEF and other donors. The preparation heavily involved Flora and Fauna International, a United Kingdom NGO. By all local accounts, this participation absorbed undue funding, and foreign experts contributed little except translation and coordination burdens considering the high level of scientific talent already in the region. For geopolitical reasons, the World Bank did not endorse early local appeals to include experts from Russia, in this and many other projects, instead of consultants from Europe.

CATBP is a bellwether for biodiversity projects in the region because of its explicit connection to other GEF biodiversity projects (NEAPs and Enabling Activities), other UNDP environmental activities (i.e. Agenda 21 implementation), and other state donors, especially Germany, Switzerland, and Denmark. These related projects involve funding in excess of CATBP funding, but CATBP is clearly the showcase, central, and model project for the region.

The purpose of the project is to support the protection of vulnerable and unique biological communities within the Western Tien-Shan Range, which hosts 170 endemic species,[54] and to assist the three countries to strengthen and co-ordinate national polices, regulations and institutional arrangements for biodiversity protection.[55]

However, Tajikistan was excluded from this project, which involves only Kazakhstan, Kyrgyzstan, and Uzbekistan. Nominally, World Bank consultants excluded Tajikistan because it had not ratified CBD, but that explanation is disingenuous. The planners included Kyrgyzstan, despite the fact that it, too, was not a CBD signatory, and they successfully encouraged Kyrgyzstan to ratify CBD in 1996. Tajikistan independently ratified in 1997, could easily have ratified sooner if a carrot had existed, and could have been included prior to project submission. In fact, World Bank and the other three Tien-Shan states excluded Tajikistan simply because none of them desired to burden themselves with what they projected would be the difficulties of including Tajikistan, which was still engulfed in civil war. Thus, CATBP stands as a nadir in regional cooperation even though it includes cooperation between three states.

Yet, it also is the best example of transboundary biodiversity protection in the region since it actively embraces the goal of creating habitat corridors between four roughly adjacent nature reserves: Aksu-Dzhabagly (KZ), Besh-Aral and Sary-Chelek (KG), and Chatkal (UZ). Coming years will test the important questions of how well the three participating states can cooperate, whether expectations for economic benefits will be realized, and whether this project will indeed have positive spillover effects on government practices and programs.

Worldwide, 25 per cent of mammal species and 11 per cent of bird species are at risk of extinction.[56] Figure 6.2 reveals that, over the past decade, hopes within development agencies to preserve biodiversity have, in the face of scientific

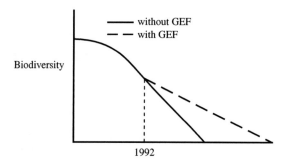

Figure 6.2 Actual graphic used in powerpoint trainings by UNDP–GEF in Central Asia.

data, evolved into less heroic, but more realistic, attempts to mitigate losses of biodiversity.

In this regard, whatever hopes may exist for CABTP, biodiversity protection in Central Asia at the present date is in shambles. In thousands of pages of reports and project updates, no donor has yet to claim any tangible progress in preserving biodiversity in the region. Rather, the outcomes of expensive projects are typically documents, such as the Uzbekistan National Biodiversity Action Plan.[57] Donors gloss the lack of biodiversity content in biodiversity projects by celebrating the participation of NGOs, state agencies, and epistemic communities in the formulation of such reports – a substitution of human organizational diversity for species diversity.

This unmitigated lack of substantive progress contrasts sharply with the mixed record of Soviet success in protecting biodiversity. Whereas the Soviet Union witnessed steady declines in biodiversity, it nevertheless also boasted more than a few success stories. For example, in the late Soviet period, Turkmenistan's reserve system painstakingly worked with local communities and law enforcement agencies to increase populations of subspecies of urial (*Ovis vignei*; wild goats) and kulan (*Equus hemionus onager*, wild asses).

Both have now been decimated. Urial populations have declined generally by one-third to two-thirds.[58] Worse, until August 2000, the Turkmenistan Ministry of Nature Use and Environmental Protection believed that the kulan population had risen from less than 2000 to more than 5000 head since the early 1980s. In August 2000, a WWF sponsored census revealed that only 200 kulan remain in Turkmenistan.[59] In the face of such decimation, at least for Central Asia, Figure 6.3 presents a better view of reality than Figure 6.2.

Edible plants and animals, especially sport species, have been ravaged in the post-Soviet period. Many of these species are taken not just for local subsistence, but for export. To the extent that export of endangered species contributes to loss of critical biodiversity, CITES exists as a mechanism to introduce protections for wildlife. While CITES does complicate exports of critical biodiversity from

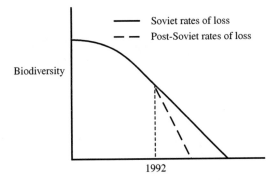

Figure 6.3 Graphic that will not be used in powerpoint trainings by UNDP–GEF in Central Asia.

Central Asia (partially because in the CITES regime, exporters need both export and import permits), it in no way precludes local extirpation due to trade.

When the Soviet Union disassembled in 1991, the Central Asian states pledged to comply with their CITES obligations even though not officially state parties. In this regard, they authorized the CITES Management Authority of the Russian Federation to process relevant import and export permits. Accordingly, someone wishing to export a protected species from Tajikistan should not have been allowed into, say, France, without an export permit from the Russian Management Authority.

However, almost as soon as independence dawned in Central Asia, reports started to appear about massive hunting and export of endangered tortoises, sheep, snow leopards, sturgeon, raptors, and butterflies by and for Europeans, Arabs, and Americans. These reports came from wildlife biologists who saw their study populations disappear, from concerned NGOs, and from whistleblowers in environmental and customs agencies. However, the validity of these reports came into question precisely because of how CITES works. Over-export from one state should be traceable through import records of other states. In this regard, no importing states raised any flags.

The fact that they did not do so points directly to the failings of CITES to accomplish its goal, which is to protect endangered species by removing the incentives for their extirpation generated through international trade. Importing states did not raise flags because of the ease with which smuggling occurs. The case study below illustrates the failings of the CITES regime in Central Asia.

Argali sheep (*Ovis ammon*[60]) are included on the CITES lists of species and subspecies to be regulated in international commerce. Argali are also one of the most sought-after sport trophies, and Central Asia provides arguably the most impressive argali hunting in the world. All of the Central Asian states except Turkmenistan contain globally significant populations of argali. Each state has introduced limits on the hunting of argali, in most cases a licensing system that restricts to a few dozen the number of animals that may be taken every year. As opposed to an outright ban on hunting, these licensed hunts present both opportunities and dangers. All the states claim that proceeds from licenses go towards conservation.[61] At the local level observers claim that none of the funds go further than the pockets of corrupt officials; they also claim that local (subsistence) poaching increases dramatically as a result of such hunts since sport hunting destroys incentives for local populations to themselves refrain from hunting. However, this corruption and local subsistence poaching, no matter how deleterious for the national society and environment, are beyond the scope of CITES.

Within the scope of CITES is the simple observation that most of these states actually issue (through Russia until they themselves become CITES parties) more export permits than their national laws allow hunts on argali. By how much they exceed their own quotas is unknown, and perhaps unknowable. From within Central Asia, no more than half of argali sportsmen in any given year are from the United States. Since the United States strictly forbids any argali imports from Kazakhstan,[62] in general more Europeans hunt in Kazakhstan,[62] and more Americans hunt in Kyrgyzstan and Tajikistan. The U.S. prohibition on imports of argali occurred under a determination by the U.S. Fish and Wildlife Service, pursuant to the Endangered Species Act, that argali subspecies in Kyrgyzstan and Tajikistan were less endangered and better protected than in Kazakhstan,[63] a patently fantastic determination.

The hunters' divvying up Central Asia between continents aside, more argali permits have been issued to American alone in Kyrgyzstan and Tajikistan than these countries admit issuing. For 1996, documents received through the Freedom of Information Act[64] establish that American hunters alone received at least 27 permits to hunt argali and attempted to import at least 27 argali trophies. Kyrgyzstan claimed to have issued only 18 permits that year to hunters of all nationalities,[65] in accordance with Kyrgyzstan law, which placed an upper limit on permits of 20 for 1996.[66] Moreover, some of the permit applications contain testimonials that establish convincingly that the hunts in Kyrgyzstan and Tajikistan are on endangered populations and have no connection to conservation.[67]

While there is a ban on imports of argali trophies from Kazakhstan, Americans continue to hunt in Kazakhstan and may be smuggling their trophies into the United States, possibly by using Kyrgyzstan as a transit point. Kyrgyzstan is almost certainly exceeding the number of permits it is allowed to issue by law (20 annually), perhaps in the form of permits for argali killed in Kazakhstan and perhaps in simple contravention of Kyrgyzstan law.

Given the problems of CATBP and failures of CITES, scant grounds exist for enthusiasm about the region's prospects to conserve biodiversity. Yet, one project in the region does point not only to a replicable model for biodiversity preservation, but also to a mode of development assistance to challenge the practices of UNDP, World Bank, USAID, and other donors.

The German Society for Nature Conservation (Naturschutzbund Deutschland–NABU) is active in Kazakhstan, Kyrgyzstan, and Uzbekistan. In each state, it endeavors to create a Biosphere Reserve[68] out of an existing zapovednik and strengthen protection through additional listing of the area as a World Heritage site. These are Tengiz-Kurgalzhin in Kazakhstan, Issyk-Kul in Kyrgyzstan, and Nuratau-Kyzylkum in Uzbekistan. Thus, NABU is the only foreign organization in the entire region that, independent of any GEF funds, from the start approached Central Asian environmental issues from the standpoint of internationalization of the environment.

Moreover, NABU is the only large foreign environmental protection organization in Central Asia that meets the fabled definition of a nonprofit or civil society organization; NABU is largely volunteer, grassroots, and effective. NABU's dozens of in-country staff are mostly graduate students from East Germany who speak far better Russian than even those World Bank and UNDP foreign consultants advertised as fluent Russian speakers. Moreover, these students are truly volunteer; they contrast strongly with representatives of United Nations Volunteers, who almost never in Central Asia speak local languages and who actually earn on average $30,000 tax free during their year of eleemosynary endeavor.[69] NABU staff live on the ground with their local partners, accepting the general living conditions of these partners, a view of partnership that would not be remarkable if any of the major development agencies shared it.

However, since NABU concentrates its efforts in the rural areas in which its projects are situated, it has had little interaction with other organizations in the region, especially with other foreign organizations, which rarely travel outside the major cities. Yet, NABU is now on the verge of informing the mainstream of environmental development in Central Asia through its successful bid for GEF funds. In 1998, NABU officially began to assemble a medium-sized project for Nuratau; in summer 2000 its project was awarded $750,000 from the GEF.[70] This award represents the first NGO medium-sized project in Central Asia. Now, highlighting again the supremacy of the environmental paper chase in Central Asia, NABU will be forced to bid as a subcontractor to UNDP on the very proposal that would not exist but for NABU.

Should NABU maintain control over this project, it stands ideally situated to highlight the deficiencies of UNDP and World Bank programming. NABU will stand poised to prove how much can be done per GEF dollar spent, which will create pressure on the GEF implementors in Central Asia to increase their own efficacy.

THE TRANSBOUNDARY ATMOSPHERE: OZONE, CARBON, AND LRTAP

Without question, efforts by the Central Asian states to reduce their production and use of ozone depleting substances stand out as the most complete and successful contribution of the region to global environmental cooperation. However, in this, Central Asia merely matches the global norm; weaning the industrial economies of ozone depleting substances has proven to be easier than expected. The region's progress towards phasing out ozone depleting substances has been financed almost entirely by GEF. GEF ozone projects are relatively straightforward payments to entice the states away from ODS; these projects do not require the civil society participation or cost-sharing of other GEF projects.

In 1998, the GEF Council reviewed an Uzbekistan ODS proposal (written by UNDP, not Uzbekistan) and awarded Uzbekistan $3.3 million.[71] For the total project, far less than 5 per cent of total funds came from non-GEF sources, which were Uzbekistan itself and a refrigerator factory in Samarkand, not UNDP or UNEP. In 1999, GEF awarded similar grants to Tajikistan[72] and Turkmenistan,[73] and a $5.6 million project for Kazakhstan was awarded in 2000.[74]

In this beneficence, the ozone regime has chosen to ignore extensive smuggling of ODS from Russia to the Central Asian states, despite the fact that evidence of such smuggling is readily apparent. Banned ODS is freely available in Tajikistan markets, since Tajikistan is the republic most dependent on Russia, and is not difficult to find from automotive repair merchants in all the other republics. Moreover, these ODS are not even (or at least rarely) disguised with secondary packaging or false production dates, and no law enforcement efforts within any of these republics target illegal resale of ODS beyond (empirically ineffective or non-existent) customs points of entry clearances in each republic.

By 2050, the ozone layer should recover to pre-1980 conditions.[75] Despite the raw success of the global ozone regime, it has had special problems with Central Asia; the Secretariat has singled out Turkmenistan as one of the least compliant states. Outside of seven small Pacific Island states of no consequence to the ozone regime, Liberia and Kazakhstan are the only significant ozone regime parties that have never submitted any information on their production or use of ozone depleting substances to the Secretariat; Kazakhstan, of course, is exponentially more significant in this regard, both in terms of use of ODS and scientific capacity to report on its use.[76] Kyrgyzstan was one of the last states on earth to join the ozone regime, only joining in 2000. Uzbekistan, by contrast has reduced its consumption of ODS by 97 per cent,[77] one of the best records in the entire regime. Moreover, since smuggling issues involving Central Asia have been ignored, Uzbekistan boasts a near-perfect record of compliance with all aspects of the ozone regime, even if it has not had Kazakhstan's success in winning large amounts of GEF funding.

No regime better illustrates Kazakhstan's favored status within the GEF than climate change. While Kazakhstan's official position is that, "in any transition country, climate change is only a priority to the extent that it is related to the general national conception of the sustainable development and preservation of the environment,"[78] in reality climate change is really a priority since that's where the money is. Throughout the region, most of this money has gone into the generation of paper, such as that used in the lengthy Uzbekistan Country Study on Climate Change[79] or its Kazakhstan counterpart.[80] Most states have also sought funds for stock projects to "remove barriers to energy efficiency in municipal heat and hot water supply."[81] Despite this spreading around of resources, because it is the only state in the region to have received substantial international assistance to facilitate its participation in the climate regime (receiving far more than all other states combined thanks to both USAID and GEF contributions), Kazakhstan serves to illustrate the strengths and weaknesses of the climate regime.

Kazakhstan's contributions to the climate change regime are unique in this survey; it contributes to the scientific development of the regime, to ongoing negotiations, and to national aspects of regime effectiveness. From 1993 to 1997, Kazakhstan's Hydrometeorological Agency coordinated climate change regime activities; in 1997, the Ministry of Ecology and Natural Resources took leadership of an Interagency Commission on UNFCCC.

Applying the basic scientific models of U.S. climate change researchers,[82] researchers from the Kazakhstan Scientific Research Institute to Monitor the Environment and Climate have used data from Kazakhstan's 251 meteorological monitoring stations[83] to develop robust forecasts about climate change in Kazakhstan. In part, they draw on climate data gathered within Kazakhstan since 1894 to establish that the mean temperature in Kazakhstan has increased by 1.3 °C and mean annual precipitation decreased by 17 mm over the past century.[84] Most of their forecasts suggest that climate change will decrease the number of acres of prime agricultural land in Kazakhstan by 6 per cent to 23 per cent over the next half century, leading to a generalized decrease in the spring wheat yield of up to 27 per cent[85] and a loss of up to 70 per cent yield in certain areas.[86] Although general levels of precipitation in Kazakhstan should increase by up to 25 per cent, climate aridity will also increase because of increased temperatures of roughly 5–7 °C.[87] Moreover, 20 per cent to 30 per cent of Kazakhstan's surface water resources could disappear, with the Ishim River the most adversely affected of the state's major watercourses; one-third of the Ishim is expected to, and up to three-quarters in a worst-case scenario may, disappear, and one-tenth to one-quarter of most other major rivers.[88]

In 1990, Kazakhstan emitted the equivalent of 352,000,000 metric tonnes of carbon dioxide.[89] In 1994, Kazakhstan emitted two-thirds that amount, and in 1997 only slightly more than half that amount. As Figure 6.4[90] illustrates, in 1998, Kazakhstan projected that it would not emit 1990 levels of greenhouse gases until 2010–2015, depending on the scale of economic recovery and Kazakhstan's implementation of measures to reduce greenhouse gas emissions.[91] Kazakhstan currently emits slightly more than the carbon equivalent of one metric tonne of coal for every $1000 of its GDP, one of the very worst ratios in the world, and more than 2.5 times more than the OECD average of 0.39 tonne.[92] In 1990, Kazakhstan emitted 15.9 tonnes of greenhouse gases per capita,[93] and only the United States has a larger per capita emission.[94] This lack of efficiency also suggests that Kazakhstan can adapt to the future emissions reductions requirements of the regime in large part through relatively basic implementation of best practices in other parts of the world.

Kazakhstan's proposed efforts to reduce its emissions of greenhouse gases include, *inter alia*, increasing efficiency, constructing dozens of new hydroelectric facilities and wind power stations, passing new legislation to create positive incentives, and, possibly, shifting to reliance on nuclear power. However, the cost of these measures comes to over $5 billion,[95] and Kazakhstan explicitly

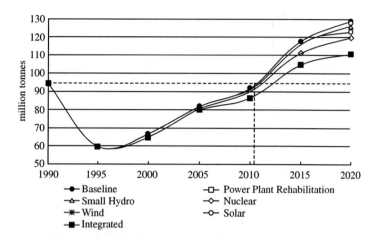

Figure 6.4 Kazakhstan's 1998 projected increase in greenhouse gas emissions for electricity production.

states that it can cover only up to 15 per cent of that cost. Moreover, Figure 6.5 suggests that Kazakhstan's forecasts for its increased carbon emissions may be unfounded; the upswing is always, coincidentally, projected to begin the year after an official report is issued.

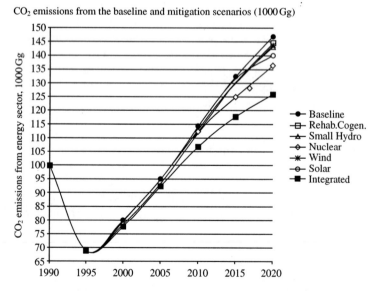

Figure 6.5 Kazakhstan's 1996 projected increase in greenhouse gas emissions for electricity production.

At the fourth COP of UNFCCC in 1998 Kazakhstan announced that it would be willing to assume voluntary reductions in carbon emissions. Flowing from this announcement, on April 24, 1999, Kazakhstan proposed to amend Annex 1 of the Convention to include Kazakhstan.[96] At COP 5, the states did not agree to this amendment. Were Kazakhstan an Annex 1 state, it would be subject to heavy and frequent burdens to submit reports on implementation to the Secretariat. However Annex 1 status would also allow Kazakhstan to engage in the emissions trading and joint implementation that is being restricted to transfers between developed states. The "Clean Development Mechanism" would allow for transfers between developed and developing states, but is also strongly resisted by many parties to the UNFCCC. Accordingly, Kazakhstan reiterated its desire to be included in Annex I at the opening session of COP 6 in November 2000.[97]

While not stated anywhere in materials produced by U.S. development agencies or Kazakhstan's environmental agencies, both sides hope that emissions trading and joint implementation will allow the United States to defray much of this cost in coming decades. At its 1990 baseline, 61 per cent of Kazakhstan's primary energy consumption came from coal.[98] Over the past decade, through the U.S. Country Studies Program and related initiatives, the United States has allocated well over $10,000,000 to Kazakhstan and its internal reporting efforts.

Kazakhstan also recently parlayed its small wind power efforts into a major GEF grant that will likely effect the first tangible climate change reform in the region. Under this three million dollar grant, part of the funds will be used to establish a 5 MW wind farm as a pilot project.[99] Through part of its new $1 billion Climate Change Initiative, the United States expects to expand its experience in Kazakhstan to the rest of Central Asia, and the region in general is both one of the 12 primary foci of this initiative and has baseline emissions that place it on the level of the ten largest states in the world for greenhouse gas emissions.[100]

However the other republics' prospects under UNFCCC are not as propitious as Kazakhstan's. For example, Uzbekistan did not experience the crash of Kazakhstan, and in 1990 was already relying on natural gas as its principal fuel.[101] As a result, neither Uzbekistan nor any of the other republics have the abundant "superheated air"[102] that makes Kazakhstan especially attractive to Western states.

Most tellingly, since Kazakhstan boasts such a bad record in the ozone regime and ratified the UNECE Convention on Long-Range Transboundary Air Pollution only after Kyrgyzstan did so, Kazakhstan's efforts in the climate change regime only reinforce the impression that Kazakhstan has little commitment to international environmental issues. Kazakhstan adequately meets commitments when fulfillment of obligations is tied to financial rewards, and it ignores such commitments otherwise. Consequently, if funds within the climate change regime become endangered, so too will be hopes that Kazakhstan will implement real reforms to lessen climate change.

DESERTIFICATION

The Central Asian states remain interested in the CCD regime and, more generally, in addressing their own problems with desertification. Should desertification and degradation problems become exacerbated within the region, they could lead to an environmental refugee problem for neighboring states. All indicators are that climate change will only accelerate processes of desertification and land degradation within Central Asia.[103] And yet, climate change is only one aspect of desertification and land degradation; Soviet practices of industrial pollution and waste disposal continue to spoil the land on a massive scale. 60,000,000,000 kg of industrial wastes, half of them toxic or radioactive, cover 3300 ha in just the Zhambyl Region of Kazakhstan.[104] Over half of Kazakhstan's industrial enterprises lack any sort of waste treatment,[105] much less effective treatment.

Accordingly, most of the Central Asian states have prepared national action plans to combat desertification,[106] held various roundtables on desertification, and assembled annual reports on desertification.[107] These efforts have involved wider cross-sections of society and been more sincere than efforts connected to other regimes. However, these efforts are not qualitatively different than those extant in other regimes; they are primarily urban and paper efforts.

Thus, despite their interest, the states have yet to implement any strong measures to control desertification beyond issuing reports. At best, these reports merely track the pace of desertification and land degradation in the region. At worst, they do nothing to prevent the enactment of new threats to the land of Central Asia. For example, Turkmenistan in 2000 announced plans to create an immense artificial lake in the Karakum Desert that will almost certainly only exacerbate land degradation conditions in southern Central Asia.[108] While some local communities have pioneered innovative approaches to local control of desertification, in the aggregate no reform since the Soviet period can be claimed. Accordingly, UNDP predicts "continuing declining productivity and extensive land degradation."[109]

REGIONAL ECOSYSTEMS IN THE GLOBAL ENVIRONMENT: THE CASPIAN ENVIRONMENT PROGRAMME[110]

The Caspian may contain the third largest hydrocarbon reserves in the world: ten billion tons of oil and six trillion cubic meters of natural gas.[111] The wider Caspian Sea region also boasts substantial hydrocarbon reserves close to shore, especially in Kazakhstan and Turkmenistan.[112] Disputes aside about the relative importance of Caspian hydrocarbons, the region certainly faces a serious challenge of trying to preserve the sea's ecosystem in the face of certain hydrocarbon development and transportation. Oil is not the only "black gold" of the Caspian; historically and into the present more revenues and greater dispersion of financial rewards have come from sturgeon products than from hydrocarbons. Various voices in the Caspian region argue that caviar could still be more lucrative than oil.

The Caspian Sea actually boasts a comparatively long pedigree as an environmental regime. In order to protect sturgeon, in 1962 the USSR prohibited open-sea fishing,[113] and began to increase regulation of other fisheries.[114] After 1991 some states discontinued the 1962 pelagic fishing ban, and in most states pelagic poaching of sturgeon expanded dramatically and continues today, which accounts for the population crash that has a virtual ban on caviar trade a likely event within the coming 2 years.

Shore populations and the state have historically also relied heavily on seals, nesting migratory bird populations, and other biological resources connected to the sea's ecosystem. In the latest die-off of seals in May 2000, more than 10,000 seal carcasses littered the beaches of Kazakhstan and Russia.[115] The seals primarily inhabit the Northern Caspian shelf, the very shallow but highly biologically productive area shared by Kazakhstan and Russia; it is here that Kazakhstan began drilling for hydrocarbons in 1999. It is also near here that Central Asia's only non-research nuclear power plant is located. This reactor is both obsolescent and has a history of mishaps, including suffering a fire as recently as September 2000.[116]

Several important nature reserves lie on the shores of the Caspian or embrace parts of the sea. These include Kyzylagach Zapovednik (AZ, 88,360 ha), Astrakhan Zapovednik (RU, 634,000 ha), Dagestan Zapovednik (RU 19,061 ha)[117] and Khazar Zapovednik (TM, 262,000 ha). All these reserve serve as important nesting areas for migratory birds and waterfowl, like flamingo, herons, and francolins.

Russia's Volga Delta (800,000 ha) and several Iranian sites (like Anzali Mordab, 15,000 ha) are on Ramsar's *List of Wetlands of International Importance.*[118] In fact, the convention is named after the Iranian Caspian coastal city where the convention was concluded. The *List of Wetlands of International Importance* still lists the Krasnovodsk and Cheleken Bays (TM, 188,700 ha) and the Kirov Bays (AZ, 132,500 ha), although their states did not succeed to and have still not acceded to the Ramsar Convention. The Kirov Bays site and some of the Iranian sites (like Anzali Mordab) are also listed on the convention's Montreux Record of endangered wetlands.[119] The Caspian's biological resources are protected under several additional international regimes, like World Heritage, CBD, the UNESCO Biosphere Reserve Programme, and the Convention for the Safety of Life at Sea.

Whereas in the first years after the dissolution of the USSR, debates centered on the enclosed sea/international lake dichotomy extrapolated from the Law of the Sea, it is now clear that no dispositive scientific or historic evidence will resolve the character of the Caspian.[120]

Even were this situation not true, the sea/lake distinction under the Law of the Sea is also one that is in danger of containing no difference. In a Caspian "Sea," littoral states could have a right to navigate Russia's Volga/Don canal system connecting to the Black Sea, which would be of importance to the land-locked post-Soviet states. But, they can use this system now; "free" navigation would not mean that Russia would be unable to use tariffs and administrative tools to make the canal even less expedient than it is now.

With the exception of Azerbaijan and, recently, Kazakhstan, no state in the region even considers the Caspian its major hydrocarbon source,[121] and no littoral state sees the Caspian seabed as the optimal transportation route. Questions of succession, monism, development, popular sovereignty, and agency within these management regimes are, in fact, more pertinent to the region's contribution to the advancement of international law and are questions that international law scholarship can partially determine or elucidate.

At a 1994 meeting of deputy foreign ministers, Iran proposed the creation of a Caspian Cooperation Organization.[122] In the ensuing 5 years, dozens of meetings at the ministerial, deputy minister, and ministry department level occurred between the littoral states on a variety of issues relevant to management of the Caspian. These meetings, increasingly specialized, addressed the sea's legal status through a variety of proposed treaties, rights to hydrocarbon development, fishing, transportation, and ecology.[123] Of particular note, the states developed several draft conventions, although to date none of these have found support from all five littoral states at the same time.[124]

The Caspian Environment Programme (CEP) constitutes the international response to concerns for sustainable management of the Caspian. The CEP builds on more than a decade of meetings between and plans developed by local scientists and policy makers. In 1995, a joint mission to the Caspian region by World Bank, UNEP, and UNDP brought CEP into existence as a name. Between 1995 and 1998, CEP existed as an informal set of informally connected national efforts financed primarily with funds from the European Union.[125] In 1998, the GEF approved a proposal to address the transboundary aspects of the CEP,[126] transforming CEP into a larger and more truly transnational project, and in May 1998, in Ramsar, the littoral states officially launched CEP. World Bank, UNDP, and UNEP, in coordination with state governments, will implement CEP.

CEP will pursue the "environmentally sustainable development and management of the Caspian environment, including living resources and water quality, so as to obtain the utmost long-term benefits for the human populations of the region, while protecting human health, ecological integrity and the region's sustainability for future generations."[127]

To pursue this goal, CEP's structure includes a Programme Coordination Unit (currently in Azerbaijan), ten Caspian Regional Thematic Centers (CRTCs) and a Steering Committee that convenes once a year. CRTCs include Data and Information Systems (AZ), Pollution Control (AZ), Pollution Monitoring (IR), Coastal Zone Management (IR), Water Level Fluctuations (KZ), Biodiversity (KZ), Legal, Regulatory and Economic Instruments (RU), Fisheries and Commercial Bioresources (RU), Sustainable Human Development (TM), and Desertification (TM), as well as an Emergency Response Center in Iran.[128] Major areas of CEP emphasis include regional cooperation, public awareness, data management, environmental assessment and monitoring, coastal planning, desertification, sustainable human health, regulatory development, and investment policy.

Embedded within these CEP efforts is an initiative, also funded by various sources, but primarily within the purview of UNEP and the legal CRTC, to create a Framework Convention to Protect the Marine Environment of the Caspian Sea (FCCS). Four meetings of state experts resulted in adoption of the final text of the first three articles in March 2000. While projected dates for adoption of a final text of the entire FCCS are repeatedly pushed back, plans now call for the littoral states to sign the FCCS in November 2001.[129]

The context for FCCS is the existing CEP. Only beginning now are CEP research and monitoring efforts beginning to assume a transnational character. During the 1990s, what cooperation existed in the Caspian Basin consisted primarily of sharing results and, later, establishing uniform modes of research and monitoring so as to make national programs complementary. While this nationalization of international cooperation falls short of the ultimate goals of CEP, it is a typical stage in the development of regional seas regimes.[130] Similarly, that FCCS will consume a half decade from conception to adoption of the final text does not of itself hint at problems in regime building; such a time span is typical. The central question to be asked is whether FCCS will facilitate the sustainability of the larger Caspian regional seas program.

Since the later stages of the Caspian regime will likely require states to alter their modes of industry and transportation, as well as their environmental standards, at some point states will need to change the behaviors of their domestic actors, ostensibly through both economic incentives and threats of force. While ad hoc negotiations among states and informal agreements along these lines may go far in facilitating these measures, a formal framework treaty offers the distinct advantages of assuring other parties that each state is serious, that options for backtracking are limited, and that a central and undisputed forum exists for clear and current statements of the requirements of the regime.

The draft FCCS[131] is a sparse framework agreement that anticipates subsequent protocols or agreements. The goal of the FCCS is to protect the marine environment of the Caspian from all sources of pollution and to protect and restore the living resources of the Caspian. In very general terms, the FCCS requires the littoral states to take measures to limit and control pollution (both land-based and other), protect and restore living resources, and cooperate. In these actions, the states are to be guided by both the precautionary principle and the polluter pays principle.

Section III of the FCCS explicitly binds states to work towards a Land-Based Sources Protocol that includes best available technology, point source licensing, and special agriculture rules. Five additional explicitly required protocols include those to regulate uses of the seabed (including for hydrocarbon and other mineral development and transportation), pollution from ships, dumping from planes and ships, cooperative emergency response procedures, and sea-level effects. Three protocols explicitly envisioned (but not mandated) would regulate agriculture, recreational boating, and invasive species. At this stage, the FCCS is silent as to whether the Caspian regime will attempt to regulate pollution entering the Caspian basin from non-littoral states, and is vague about whether these protocols will require separate ratification.

Section IV binds states to pursue conservation programs based on the best available scientific evidence to ensure sustainable human welfare, sustainable yields, prevent incidental catches and extinctions, restore endangered populations, and preserve rare or endangered ecosystems. Section V constrains states to conduct impact assessments for projects that may have a significant impact on the environment, share assessment results with other state parties, and create uniform assessment procedures.[132] Further, states commit to cooperate in environmental monitoring and research, and to expand existing scientific efforts. The parties further agree to create Appendices to the FCCS of toxic substances subject to regulation or prohibition. Finally, Section VI establishes the Caspian Environmental Protection Organization and its administrative secretariat, responsible for monitoring compliance with both FCCS and CEP's Strategic Action Plan.

The FCCS is silent on a number of issues, such as public participatory rights and the degree to which science will be the backbone of administrative agencies (instead of merely being confined to research and monitoring). Yet, the two CEP proposals to the Global Environment Facility (signed by all the littoral states) are authoritative and partially binding statements to questions about regime rules not answered directly by the FCCS. Reading the states' declaration that "links between science and policy are presently weak and should be strengthened by a regional program," looking at the current staff of the CEP Programme Coordination Unit, and considering the professional backgrounds of national focal points, it is clear that the emerging regime is highly dependent on and geared toward epistemic communities. Likewise, the proposals, in particular the envisioned Small Grants Programme and a seat for NGOs on the Steering Committee, constitute a recognition of and reliance on local stakeholders and public participation substantially better than that reserved in the early stages of any other regional seas regime.[133]

Quite unlike the experience of the colonies of European states, the national republics were full partners in the human capital building efforts of the USSR. To a degree unknown in colonial settings, the USSR attempted to level the playing field between its capital and its more remote territories, within and beyond the Russian Federation. From the 1920s on, Soviet policies established national academies of sciences, dozens of institutions of higher education (focused primarily on the technical and natural sciences), and dozens of well-equipped research institutes in each republic. By the end of the Soviet period and not including university and ministry research programs and staff, Kazakhstan claimed 159 research institutes within its Academy of Sciences,[134] and Turkmenistan claimed a dozen.[135]

While this list does not do justice to the range of interests in the region, it does suggest the strength of the Caspian's advantages. In contrast, the Aral Sea Basin project promises little for Kyrgyzstan or Tajikistan, who consider themselves largely unaffected by the crisis. Even the upstream states wonder whether there is any strong economic benefit to an altered water regime, especially considering that the shoreline area of the sea was never a population center in any state and is not near a capital city. Similarly, there are few clear short-term economic and social reasons to protect biodiversity or maintain nature reserves; hopes for ecotourism are understandably slim, despite the prevalence of the term in justifications for protection.

Third, perhaps serendipitously, CEP is by far the most professional of the regimes. Symptomatically, the 1997 project proposal does not contain the spelling errors, poor writing, and weak incremental cost assessments of its subregional peers. Underlying these observations, the scientific data on the sea already makes the Caspian one of the most thoroughly studied bodies of water on the planet.

Thus, CEP may be the environmental regime that casts the most favorable light on Central Asian participation. However, and disappointingly, none of the activities of the regime thus far has had any effect on improving the environmental conditions in the Caspian region. Without such improvements, the states' participation in the region is not actually more than participation for the sake of participation; while such participation may increase chances for effective environmental conservation efforts in the future, at present the regime itself has substantial compliance victories and virtually no victories of effectiveness.

TRANSBOUNDARY WATERCOURSE MANAGEMENT: THE IRTYSH RIVER[136]

In 1998, in breaking the story of diversion of the Irtysh River, Asia's largest and the world's fifth largest,[137] Erik Nurshin accused Kazakhstan's government of placating China and betraying its citizens.[138] Billion-dollar Project 635 anticipates diverting, initially, from 5–15 per cent of the flow of the Irtysh[139] to the needs of the Karamai oil fields and to irrigate 140,000h,[140] and it threatens the millions of people and dozens of ecosystems that line the Irtysh's 5000-plus kilometer length. China may increase its diversion to 50 per cent of the Irtysh,[141] and there are persistent rumors that it also plans to divert the Ili,[142] south of the Irtysh for a total annual diversion of up to 6 km³.[143] The environmental communities in Kazakhstan and Russia believe that this diversion will degrade the river's viability as habitat for important biodiversity and lower water quality levels throughout the river basin, adversely affecting human health. Moreover, Kazakhstan's commercially significant river ports will have difficulty operating, and the large hydroelectric cascade may fail if the water level drops further.

The Irtysh controversy is synonymous with opposition to President Nazarbaev. One of Nazarbaev's rivals, Murat Auezzov, the former Ambassador to China, is now Executive Director of George Soros's Kazakhstan Open Society Institute, and Auezzov leaked the story to Nurshin. Auezzov paints a devastating picture of the Chinese as stonewalling prevaricators and the Kazakhstan government as incompetent collaborators.[144] Auezzov claims that Kazakhstan was aware of suspicious activity on the Irtysh in the early 1990s. His first ambassadorial act in 1992 was to present a proposal to China on "the joint use of border rivers."[145] Expecting an answer within 2 months; despite his pressing, he left China in 1995 with no answer.[146] Lamenting a total lack of political will from Astana and Moscow, Auezzov declares, "the leaders of Kazakhstan and Russia must take forcible measures."[147] From my fieldwork, I believe that most of northern Kazakhstan agrees.

While the Kazakhstan press agitates on the Irtysh issue, and while NGOs actively lend their voices, the government refuses to elevate the issue to a tangible national priority. Instead, it takes pains to focus on the exaggerations of the press and NGOs.[148] On the one hand, more substantive recognition of the issue would entail acknowledging the perspicacity of opposition groups pushing the issue. Yet, on the other hand, despite its sovereignty, Kazakhstan has virtually ignored both the law of sovereign states and the opportunities inherent in international environmental regimes to protest this diversion. Rather than a scholarly conclusion, this assessment implicitly belongs to Auezzov. Nurshin's article, essentially a paraphrasing of Auezzov, of all the dozens of press articles to follow, alone adequately presents the legal aspects of the diversion under international law. "Under international agreements [sic], one party does not have the right...to substantially impair the functioning of a river without [consulting] the other party."[149] This article alone also hints that Kazakhstan can defend its rights through international regimes; Nurshin comments that neither Nazarbaev nor the Foreign Minister had even mentioned the Irtysh during their recent addresses to the UN General Assembly.[150]

China's diversion violates international environmental law, both treaty-based and customary. Nurshin exhibits the general tenor of this law, even though his phrasing is inaccurate. Under both treaty and custom, China cannot interfere with Kazakhstan's use of the Irtysh for navigation. Under custom, since China's diversion is permanent (the water does not cycle back into the Irtysh basin), China has violated international law in failing to provide notice to Kazakhstan and Russia, in failing to consult these states, in failing to conduct an environmental assessment, and in failing to, in good faith, consider the interests of Kazakhstan and Russia.[151] Yet, Kazakhstan has glaringly failed to accuse China of violations of international law.[152]

Kazakhstan pretends to ignore the 1957 USSR–China treaty to which it succeeded that is violated by this diversion's interruption of navigation.[153] Likewise, Kazakhstan has failed to accede to the 1997 Convention on the Law of Non-Navigable Uses of International Watercourses (1997 Treaty), which codifies much existing customary law on international waters. While all Irtysh riparians actively negotiated the 1997 Treaty, none has ratified it, even though Kazakhstan did vote for adoption of the Treaty.[154] China was one of only three states to vote against it.[155]

Under such law, once China manages to move several million people into the affected area, and once these people are dependent on the diversion project for life, the law's preference for "vital human needs," will begin to favor China's peasants over Kazakhstan industry. China's use of the Irtysh to support the modest (by comparison with Kazakhstan and Russia) livelihoods of a "local" population "dependent" on this source of water will be of decisive importance.

Kazakhstan has also failed to protest this diversion on ecological grounds within international environmental regimes, particularly those in which both Kazakhstan and China figure, such as World Heritage, Ramsar, CBD, and CCD. The only current connection between the Irtysh and international environmental regimes comes under the ozone regime. While as a result of poor practices in production of caustic soda at the Pavlodar Chemical Factory, over 900 metric tonnes of mercury is seeping towards the Irtysh,[156] the Pavlodar Chemical Factory is the recipient of foreign aid under the GEF not to address this horrific problem, but to replace CFC-113 as a cleaning agent in oxygen manufacturing equipment.[157]

Yet, international environmental administrative settings actually would allow Kazakhstan several platforms for negative publicity beyond immediately apparent outlets like the media, NGOs, and the United Nations General Assembly. For example, under Article 11(4) of the World Heritage Convention, the World Heritage Committee[158] maintains a List of World Heritage in Danger. Practice shows that states, especially jealously independent and sovereign states like China, find inclusion of any of their territory on this list to be very distasteful. While consultation with the host State is required, sites may be, and since 1991 have been, included on or nominated for inclusion on this List over the objections of the host State.[159] Accordingly, Kazakhstan could nominate the Golden Mountains of Altai site in order to provoke discussion of China's project, even though there appears to be only an attenuated basis for arguing that the Irtysh diversion threatens this site. More particularly, Kazakhstan could attempt to list Lake Zaisan and similar sites along the Irtysh as World Heritage sites.[160] Having done so, it would then be able to call upon China to refrain from actions that would violate the principles of preservation of acknowledged World Heritage Sites and could self-nominate the Zaisan Site for the List of Endangered World Heritage.

Ramsar offers a similar vehicle. While Kazakhstan did not succeed to Ramsar, Kazakhstan has stated repeatedly its intention to accede to Ramsar and maintains close communications with the Ramsar Bureau.[161] Under Ramsar, "parties shall consult with each other about implementing obligations arising from the Convention especially in the case of a wetland extending over the territories of more than one Contracting Party or where a water system is shared by Contracting Parties."[162] This provision gives both Kazakhstan and Russia occasion to argue that China is in violation of Ramsar.

Moreover, under Ramsar, a Montreux Record[163] lists wetlands in danger. Kazakhstan's Lower Turgai and Irgiz Lakes system was placed on this list in 1993, even though Kazakhstan was not even a State Party at that time; such treatment accords Kazakhstan a *de facto* party status. Accordingly, Kazakhstan could attempt both to list Zaisan[164] as a Ramsar and Montreux Record site or propose that Russia's Irtysh wetlands Ramsar site be listed in the Montreux Record. Zaisan, which virtually straddles the border with China where the Irtysh crosses, is, according to the Ramsar Bureau, one of "the most important areas for birds in Western Asia."[165] At 5,500 km^2, Zaisan is also one of the 30 largest lakes in the world and considerably larger than America's Great Salt Lake. The Zaisan area is also important snow leopard habitat. By offering, in these and other venues, the world such a threat to "charismatic megafauna" as a synecdoche for China's activities, Kazakhstan could succeed in maximizing the efficacy of its efforts to embarrass China into backing down.

All the riparian states are also original parties to CBD.[166] CBD obligates states to, "in the case of imminent or grave danger or damage, originating under its jurisdiction or control, to biological diversity within the area under jurisdiction of other States... notify immediately the potentially affected States of such danger or damage, as well as initiate action to prevent or minimize such danger or damage."[167] China's actions arguably constitute "grave or immediate" danger to the widely acknowledged endangered and endemic biodiversity of the Ob-Irtysh Basin. Accordingly, China has apparently violated CBD notification and mitigation requirements. In disputes, CBD requires good faith negotiations followed, if needed, by binding third party dispute resolution.[168]

Finally, Kazakhstan and China both became parties to CCD in 1997. In contrast to World Heritage and CBD, CCD lacks strong language on state obligations. However, CCD's general purpose is to reduce desertification. Russian and Kazakhstan specialists agree that an Irtysh diversion would likely exacerbate serious desertification problems in the Irtysh basins of both states, both directly and due to projected regional warming trends produced by the climate change projected to occur with lowered river flow.[169] Kasym Duskaev of Kazakhstan's Ministry of Environmental Protection predicts that the Irtysh diversion will lead to increased desertification in Kazakhstan and Russia.[170] Thus, even without specific language in the treaty, China's project may give Kazakhstan grounds for protesting the diversion within the CCD regime, perhaps even with resort to CCD's dispute resolution procedures.

Kazakhstan has remained silent in all the regimes listed above, and in all similar regimes. Indeed, instead of reaching out to the international community, Kazakhstan helps China keep this issue out of the international spotlight. Kazakhstan really. only reached out to its closest neighbors, Russia and Kyrgyzstan. It failed to convince Russia to take its side.[171] While the Russian press and NGOs, alerted by Kazakhstan colleagues, voice condemnation of the project,[172] the issue is likely not among the Kremlin's major impending catastrophes. More interestingly, Kazakhstan inquired into whether Kyrgyzstan could threaten China with river diversion; the rivers shared by these two states mostly flow from Kyrgyzstan into China.[173] Despite close ties with Kazakhstan, Kyrgyzstan refrains from such threats.[174]

Failing with these two allies, Kazakhstan ceased its search for international support. Today, most international environmental institutions and most of the scholarly community remain unaware of this issue. The major Irtysh riparians are members of the "Shanghai Five," the Russian term for China and the former Soviet republics bordering China,[175] and it is only, on China's request, within this grouping or in bilateral talks that Kazakhstan voices its concerns. The international community and the English language press either ignore the meetings of the Shanghai Five or fail to report the results of issues put low on the agenda, like the Irtysh.

As for bilateral talks, Kazakhstan began actively to seek such talks only after sustained protests by newspapers and NGOs[176] alleging a dangerous plot to appease China and suppress information. Negotiations began in May 1999 in Beijing, and it was only there that Kazakhstan received information sufficient to fulfill China's requirement of notification.[177] China stated plans to divert

450 million cubic meters in 2000 and to expand this diversion to 1km^3 by 2020.[178] Kazakhstan presented a draft bilateral agreement on the use and conservation of transboundary waters,[179] but China passed. China also assured Kazakhstan that it has no plans to divert the Ili River.[180] The second round of negotiations took place in November 1999 in Almaty. Astana's goals at this round were to secure China's signature on a "framework" agreement and establish a joint Irtysh management authority.[181] It attained neither goal.

However, as a result of the third round of negotiations, held in June 2000 in Beijing, Kazakhstan's government, now under increasing pressure from the public, suggested that China had agreed to a bind itself never to take more than 1km^3 for its diversion.[182] Kazakhstan experts still had difficulty reconciling the immense size of the Irtysh-Karamai Canal with this comparatively modest diversion.[183] During 2000, Kazakhstan's government began increasingly to suggest in public that law would be at the center of all issues concerning its 8700 mile border, including all issues of transboundary watercourses.[184] To the extent that this vague statement hinted that the two states had signed some sort of binding bilateral agreement, on the eve of the fourth round of negotiations, Kazakhstan's Minister of Foreign Affairs, Erlan Idrisov disappointed his constituents. In an interview provocatively entitled *Do We Have an Active Position in Foreign Affairs?* in an opposition newspaper, Idrisov admitted that no such agreement existed.[185]

However, during the fourth round of negotiations in Almaty, even the state newspaper *Kazakhstanskaya Pravda* chimed in with, what only a year ago, were phrases only to be found in the opposition press, such as the contention that if China proceeded with plans to divert 40 per cent of the Irtysh's flow a "global environmental catastrophe" would ensue.[186] The article also states that Kazakhstan cannot allow more than 6 per cent of the Irtysh's flow to be diverted without risking local extirpation of muskrat.[187] Moreover, Kazakhstan reopened allegations of China's plans to divert the Ili, threatening to turn Kazakhstan's Lake Balkhash, one of the largest lakes in the world, into another Aral Sea.[188]

Kazakhstan's dealings with China resemble those of the KazakSSR with the Kremlin during Perestroika; however, at that time, the KazakSSR had inestimably fewer recourses to international law. Yet, while Kazakhstan's options have changed, its leadership and methods remain essentially those of 1989. Straightforward power politics characterize Kazakhstan's view of its range of possibilities. Kazakhstan's lack of faith in legal arguments and methods, while understandable for post-communism, contrasts sharply with its eagerness to appear active in regimes founded on global environmental accords.

BEYOND THINKING GLOBALLY: LOCAL ACTION FOR THE ARAL SEA

The first reaction of the newly sovereign Central Asian states in response to the plight of the Aral Sea was not to band together to address root causes of the Aral crisis, despite the existence of Soviet and UNESCO studies outlining clear policy and management reforms. Instead, no state made any notable reforms within its own borders, and regional cooperation consisted of unanimity in blaming the situation on the Soviet Union and urging Western assistance. Even to this day, resolution of the Aral Sea crisis is not a salient priority in any state; this situation displays how regional harmony can endure despite little progress in the enforcement of environmental laws or adherence to environmental commitments.[189]

In February 1992, the states created an Interstate Commission for Water Coordination (ICWC) to determine annual water allocations. The commission had little funding and no enforcement powers. With active donor participation, especially World Bank and USAID, in March 1993, the states created an Interstate Council on the Aral Sea (ICAS) and folded ICWC into this new body. Concurrently, they created an International Fund for the Aral Sea (IFAS), to which the states were to contribute 1 per cent of their GNP. The council was as politically unremarkable as the fund was poor, both the result of state disregard for these institutions.

World Bank and USAID actively encouraged plans in 1994 for a billion dollar aid program for the Aral Sea, called the Aral Sea Basin Program. In time, these donors began subtly to try to back away from their early commitments to "save the sea." In July 1994, the states continued a clear effort to create symbols of the need to take action by creating a Sustainable Development Commission. In 1997, IFAS swallowed ICAS, and the former is now governed through an Executive Board composed of deputy environment ministers of the five Aral Sea Basin states.

The UNDP Aral Seashore Rehabilitation and Capacity Development Project began in April 1997.[190] It has provided 16,000 residents of Karakalpakstan with safe drinking water[191] and planted thousands of trees unsuited to the local climate that died immediately.[192] Expensive and unsustainable, these UNDP projects are still the most notable successes in the region.

While the Aral crisis generated an unusually large number of World Bank grants, these grants have totaled on average only a couple hundred thousand dollars a year,[193] an order of magnitude less than the amount of grant money made available through GEF. This began to change when the Bank spearheaded the effort to get GEF funding for an Aral Sea project (AralGEF). AralGEF envisions accepting the loss of the sea, but in its place creating small but viable wetlands and fisheries in Uzbekistan and Kazakhstan through restoration of a modest flow to the old seabed. This modest flow is envisioned to be made possible through improvements in the efficiency of irrigation and curtailing out of basin water transfers.

While advertised as an IFAS and GEF project, AralGEF is in fact almost entirely an Uzbekistan and World Bank creation. At the time of AralGEF's submission, only Uzbekistan was a GEF participant. Since each state receives funding under the project, no state has protested to donors (although Uzbekistan taxes grant funds), but as of this writing, the Tajikistan government, including the Tajikistan director of this GEF project, cannot explain how, when, or where Tajikistan agreed to this project. Symptomatically, Uzbekistan alone receives the half of the grant earmarked for a pilot wetlands restoration project in northern Uzbekistan. Under this project, Lake Sudoche will be improved and is slated to become the first Ramsar site in Uzbekistan.

While this ambition appears on its surface to be a laudable and desirable result, even if disproportionately favorable to Uzbekistan, its larger context is that it highlights the deep animosities between World Bank and UNDP in Central Asia. In order for AralGEF to be realized, World Bank envisions that agricultural runoff along the Amudarya will be almost entirely restored to the Amudarya. Much of this water for decades has run into Uzbekistan valleys outside the Amudarya watershed, collected there, and formed immense lakes that now support local agriculture, fisheries, recreation areas, and biodiversity habitat.

Accordingly, UNDP endeavors to nominate one of these lakes,[194] the Dengiz-Kul as Uzbekistan's first Ramsar site since that lake does now constitute important habitat for migratory species that, ostensibly, formerly relied on now inhospitable Aral Sea waters. Under World Bank's plans, Dengiz-Kul, and a number of other large lakes, will virtually disappear.

World Bank views the root causes of the Aral crisis to lie in the fact that irrigation waters from the Amudarya become both heavily polluted and fail to return to the Amudarya. UNDP views the root causes of the Aral crisis to lie in the general unsustainability of both present and past human practices in the region. Which, if either, of these agencies is correct is a different question from that of whether the (attempted) removal of the root, Soviet-era, causes of the Aral crisis could conceivably lead to protection of biodiversity, healthier waterways, better living conditions, and sustainable development within the region.

What World Bank seems to ignore is the fact that the Aral Basin, including the Aral Sea itself, has changed qualitatively in the past 50 years. Given the current pollution of the Aral region and the extirpation of the sea's aquatic species, increased flow of better quality water into the sea might be a very inopportune use of fresh water resources considering as well that the lower reaches of the Amudarya are among the least densely populated regions in Uzbekistan.

The World Bank evidences little concern for the general population of Central Asia or the health of its ecosystems, but a great desire to claim an environmental victory in saving the Aral Sea, even if that victory is hollow and symbolic. A deeper concern touches on the fact that most stakeholders, including the scientific community, do not expect the project to yield tangible results or substantive environmental improvements.

They base these expectations on general instincts about just how difficult it will be to create incentives to alter water use patterns throughout Central Asia. However, recently their expectations became much more difficult to dismiss. In September, Turkmenistan announced plans to construct an artificial lake in the Kara-Kum Desert one-quarter the size of the previous Aral Sea (Figure 6.6). While under AralGEF both Kazakhstan and Uzbekistan would get sizable lakes, Turkmenistan's lake will be substantially larger. Of course, the problem is that the lake is to be filled with water diverted from the Amudarya, which will preclude fulfillment of AralGEF's ambitions. In addition, most models of the effects of climate change suggest that it, too, will reduce the flow of both the Amudarya and Syrdarya.[195]

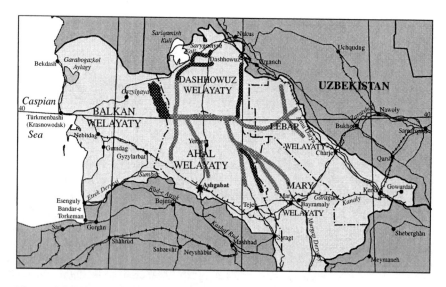

Figure 6.6 Proposed drainage system for Lake of the Golden Century.

These practical snafus in addressing the Aral Sea's environmental problems and the fact that these problems rest in fundamental conflicts between the main agents of reform (the states, World Bank, and UNDP) engender pessimism about the viability of even minor proposals for reform in the Aral Sea basin. This general failure is also mirrored in the Aral Sea's connection to international environmental law itself. In September 1995, the Central Asian heads of state issued the Nukus Declaration in an attempt to draw international donor attention to the Aral Sea. In Article 2 of this Declaration, the heads of state declared it "necessary to create an International Convention for the Sustainable Development of the Aral Sea Basin." After this declaration, no state even prepared a draft convention; money set aside by UNDP for this purpose was never sought by any of the states.

EVALUATING CENTRAL ASIA AND THE INTERNATIONALIZED ENVIRONMENT

When I interviewed dozens of the most key officials for international environmental regimes from environmental, justice, and foreign affairs ministries in all five Central Asian states in 1998, my near-decade of work in the region left me unprepared for the confusion surrounding international environmental regimes that I documented. For the most part, the officials I interviewed enjoyed a solid understanding of and concern for environmental problems, yet they struggled to understand how regimes operated to effect environmental change.

Only one person, Dr Marat Ishankulov, the Chair of the Committee on International Environmental Conventions of the Kazakhstan National Environment Center, provided both thorough and reliable information on his state's integration into international environmental regimes.[196] Ishankulov was not only unusual in his breadth; his reliability was also unusual. The average environmental minister in 1998 (not to mention his deputy minister charged with international affairs) could not state, and possessed no reliable information about, to which conventions his state had acceded. With the exception of Kyrgyzstan, no foreign ministry possessed a clear understanding of issues of succession or the differences between ratification, succession, and accession, much less any staff prepared for environmental diplomacy. Ministries of finance did not know how much and where to wire membership dues.

Justice ministries acknowledged the problem of non-implementation, but rightly explained that until funds and computers became bountiful, they could do nothing. National focal points for specific conventions usually had never read or understood the convention whose regime was under their supervision. A spattering of lower level technical specialists knowledgeable about the technical and vaguely familiar with the legal aspects of regimes were clearly the forces sustaining these states' connections to international regimes. Ironically, non-English speakers usually were more knowledgeable about international environmental regimes than their younger, better-traveled, and heavily internationally trained colleagues, despite the lack of materials on the subject in Russian. Even where, as in Kyrgyzstan, substantial efforts are made to coordinate ministries and monitor compliance, the government reports that result from such efforts are so disappointing that they are not released to the general public.

Yet, over several years, I began to realize that Ishankulov was not necessarily unique in the ways I initially imagined. When Ishankulov himself began to admit over time that he could see some small improvement, but very few solutions, to be gained from international regimes, he also began to voice fears that the gains in organizational capital in environmental agencies in Kazakhstan were probably at least offset by their losses in human capital. Younger staff, proficient in English and Western organizational practices, were equivalently non-proficient in scientific analyses and an intuitive sense of ecological systems.

In time, I began to realize that the confusion around international environmental regimes within Central Asia stemmed as much from a lack of indoctrination as from a lack of knowledge. Environmental leaders within the region wanted to see in international environmental regimes the rational and effective mechanisms for environmental protection that the regime leaders and literature trumpeted, but their own scientific training, fieldwork, and experience erected substantial cognitive barriers. Since the source of this confusion has been cognitive dissonance and not simply lack of information, the dozens of trainings and glut of informational materials now available in the region has created increased ability to work with regime leaders, but no increased faith in the underlying regimes.

The question begging to be asked from this survey of the internationalized environment of Central Asia is whether conditions would have been even worse without international environmental regimes. That is, without such a counterfactual, the worsening environment in Central Asia does not really constitute a denunciation of international environmental regimes. Indeed, it is almost certain that the environment would be even worse in the transition period in the short term were it not for international environmental regimes and their infusion of information and financial support to environmental agencies.

That said, corruption might not have reached its current levels absent such international environmental regimes. Corruption and legitimization of disregard for the context of environmental projects (that is, environmental projects are no longer assessed primarily on their environmental results) do leave open the question of long-term impacts of international environmental bureaucratization on sustainable development. The personalistic bonding social capital world of UNDP, World Bank, and other international agencies creates substantial rent-seeking opportunities that fuel corruption. Moreover, the examples in this Chapter of supposedly august international institutions breaking their own rules and dismissing issues of accountability within their own ranks sends a destructive message to their local partners.

For example, in their efforts to assemble successful projects, World Bank staff violate GEF procedures regularly. GEF proposals require proof of state support before review, and official GEF focal points exist in each state to sign-off on proposals. Instead of proposals to these focal points, World Bank, in every case, has simply asked its primary government contact to sign the proposal, and then claimed that person to be that state's authorized focal point.[197] UNDP has committed numerous similar infractions of GEF protocol with focal points, but at least in its largest projects in the region, most notably the 2000 Kazakhstan wind power project, it has secured the appropriate focal point endorsement.

Even in 2000, Kazakhstan's ozone proposal still lacked approval from the correct operational focal point.[198] The GEF Council, for its part, for 3 years running ignored the fact that proposals submitted from Central Asian states rarely meet the basic formal requirement of endorsement by the authorized focal points. This practice is perhaps the single clearest example of donor disregard for the fundamentals of rule of law in Central Asia; to follow established GEF Procedures would simply burden World Bank, and so Bank staff merely ignore these procedures. As with other donor practices, it merely suggests to post-Soviet officials that Soviet era undemocratic modes are actually acceptable and justifiable in regular day-to-day administration.

Generally, GEF staff actively seek opportunities to expand their role, influence, and sources of funding. In this, they are no different than those of any other administrative apparatus.[199] GEF actively seeks to be named the financial mechanism of any new global environmental accord and announces this intention publicly to architects of such new regimes, such as that forming now around the draft convention on persistent organic pollutants.[200]

The relationship of GEF to democratization and markets is counterintuitive. GEF exists on, and its implementing agencies compete for, exactly the kinds of subsidies that flowed from Moscow to the republics, those foreigners paid (all under non-private sector contracts[201]) to help the region overcome the negative environmental externalities of the Soviet Union and move towards democratic markets now receive better than market rates for their services, exemplifying the deep paradoxes of this system.

While the Soviet Union brandished "democratic centralization," the GEF implementors claim adherence to "country-driven" priorities. Both slogans contain hollow claims to democracy. The USSR never trusted its populace to make correct decisions; in exactly the same way, GEF's managers do not trust developing states to handle GEF funds without supervision. In this, GEF projects foster democracy in no less indirect and paternalistic a manner than does, say, Niyazov (or Karimov, or Nazarbaev) when he claims adherence to democracy in the long term but that the population of his state is, in the short term, "not yet ready for democracy."

Importantly, UNDP missions, unlike their World Bank counterparts, must maintain strong relations with the host government. UNDP Resident Representatives are, arguably, as responsible to UNDP Headquarters as they are to the host government; any local office that soured relations with the host government would be considered a failure. What would keep local UNDP offices clean, honest, and focused on results in such a system?

If the Soviet Union suffered not only because its basic ideology was flawed, but also because claims to adhere to the "correct" ideology do not in themselves create good governance, then the supposed beneficence of UNDP and World Bank efforts deserve critical attention. Such attention, not surprisingly, reveals that the very same problems that flowed from the quasi-legitimate national republic governments under the USSR flow from UNDP and World Bank in-country missions in Central Asia.

Rarely today in Central Asia do internationalized environmental projects immediately impact or improve their target problems. While the internationalized environmental community fosters development of social and organizational capital, the assets it produces within Central Asia are not necessarily consonant with sustainable development. These assets encourage the operation of organizations that are not effective in meeting their administrative goals, but often suffer from agents substituting their personal goals for those of the principal. These assets also encourage quasi-epistemic communities that are insular, ambiguously professional, and revolve around incentives to capture scarce zero-sum resources (like funding) instead of around incentives to share public goods (like information). Thus, to the extent that, in Central Asia, human capital assets relevant to sustainable development are also not increasing, the first post-Soviet decade has been one of both worsening environmental conditions and little or no progress towards building the foundations for sustainable development.

Conclusion: prospects for sustainable development in Central Asia

This book argues that current prospects for sustainable development in Central Asia are less encouraging now than at the dawn of independence, not the least because the last decade eroded the potential of Central Asia and exacerbated many environmental problems. However, the events, trends, and figures presented herein are admittedly not the whole story, but only selective portraits. Some practitioners, both local and foreign, remain optimistic about the directions reform pursues within Central Asia. Especially for such optimists, the data upon which my arguments rely are open to potentially substantive criticism if the "black boxes" of these arguments are opened. Such concerns urge a revisitation of methods.

For example, optimists would argue that I ignore or underemphasize important facts. To wit, development agencies often point to newly drafted laws, actions plans, and concluded seminars as establishing a dynamic and necessary foundation for future reforms. Likewise, donors suffuse reports of their programs with glowing testimonials from stakeholders and participants attesting to the importance and success of programs. As someone formerly enthused by such paper successes (for the three years during which I worked for development agencies) and someone who took pride in glowing reviews of my own programs in the region, I appreciate the force of conviction that such positive reinforcement breeds. However, time spent standing on the proverbial other side of the fence of such projects creates equally strong contradictory impressions. Despite great hope for the implementation of paper successes, the bulk of such paper plans and laws finds very little real world application. Likewise, there are just as many compliments issued to development staff as there are biting allegations issued outside of the earshot of donors, often, ironically, made by the same individuals.

Even high-level successes in the region often do not withstand much scrutiny. For example, Kyrgyzstan announced in several ways in 1997 and 1998 that its government would find all future policies on UNDP's conception of "sustainable human development." In making such an announcement, Kyrgyzstan indeed was more daring than most other states in the world. I myself am still encouraged by Kyrgyzstan's unusual move. However, disappointingly, I find no substantive connection between this discursive reform and any actual reforms for sustainability within Kyrgyzstan. In short, Kyrgyzstan is not, in fact, actually adhering to the ambitions it stated to UNDP. Other policy decisions announced contemporaneously by the Kyrgyzstan government, such as that to reduce wheat production in order to make tobacco its primary export,[1] belie ambitions for sustainability.

Moreover, even where substantive reforms occur, they are usually offset by related disappointments in the same sector. For example, everywhere in Central Asia, new nature reserves have been established. Yet, their benefits have been more than offset by degradation or dissolution of pre-existing reserves.[2] Similarly, where true reforms for sustainability have occurred, state reaction to them can be unambiguously negative. Kazakhstan's population is 10 per cent less now than in 1990. Yet, Kazakhstan (like Russia) considers its declining population (a result of emigration) to be a tragedy instead of an opportunity. Likewise, all the states consider their downturn in industrial pollution levels to be a grossly inadequate reward for lowered levels of industrial production. Thus, in the aggregate, non-discursive non-ambiguous and welcome reforms for sustainability in Central Asia are almost non-existent. It may be that abandonment of Soviet era levels of application of agricultural chemicals is the only major such reform visible through readily available statistical information related to environmental issues. While important, that reform alone will not produce sustainability in Central Asia.

However, the more relevant second concern regarding my methods is that available statistics related to sustainability issues may mislead. To be sure, Soviet-era statistics painted an overly-rosy picture of development success within Central Asia. If a problem of the post-Soviet era in Central Asia is that development agencies incorrectly conflate paper plans with real world impacts, this practice is not unprecedented in the region, but, rather echoes Soviet-era practices of tweaking paper reports for political purposes. Conversely, if independence era statistics, often lacking in reliability, overstate declines in the region, declines may not have been as harsh as I detail or, conversely, my analysis may have missed a reversal of decline in recent years. Indeed, the 10 year period of transition tracked herein marks only the beginning of an ongoing process.

To address this concern, while Soviet statistics were opportunistic, they were not divorced from reality. In other words, they were not so grossly inflated as to allow one to argue credibly that incomes, levels of education, and levels of environmental protection in Central Asia were actually not greater in 1990 than today. However much Western critics may wish argue that they were no better in 1990, even the staunchest local anti-communists and staunchest foreign anti-communists who have spent time in the region in both periods will readily concede this point.

Yet, I cannot as quickly dismiss the possibility that Central Asia is now bounding back from a post-independence depression. UNDP Human Development Reports from the various republics suggest scattered significant increases in incomes, and states claim, across the board, substantial accretions to GDP in 2000.[3] Likewise, although critical of their own initial efforts, World Bank and IMF staff now trumpet that the post-Soviet states have "recovered" to roughly 60 per cent of their previous output.[4] Yet, none of the states claims substantially better schooling, health, or democratic freedoms, but, nevertheless, positive signs should not be dismissed.

Accordingly, while these victories hint at recovery and better conditions for sustainable reforms, they do not alter the fact that the 1990s was a decade of strong decline in Central Asia. I endeavor no hard policy prescriptions for the region, nor any clear predictions of what the future may bring. In the end, my description of the degradation of capital assets in Central Asia during the 1990s is more severe than that anticipated at the beginning of the decade and deeper than generally recognized at the end of the decade. The contours of this decline follow.

TRACKING THE DECLINE IN COMPREHENSIVE CAPITAL

Central Asia's diverse stocks of capital assets degraded both strongly and unevenly during the first decade of independence. The independence era continued Soviet era degradations of natural capital assets, exacerbated Perestroika era declines in human capital, sparked declines in organizational capital, and may have least adversely affected assets of social capital.

Central Asia's endowments of natural capital are considerable. The region possesses what may be the planet's fourth most important reserves of hydrocarbons and large reserves of precious metals and diamonds. Based on these reserves, many Central Asians expected their states to become new Kuwaits. Nowhere did this happen. Outside of these reserves of natural resources, due primarily to Soviet development, Central Asia inherited degraded stocks of the natural capital necessary to a healthy environment for humans. In other words, at independence, the agricultural lands of the region were degraded and salinized, the major watercourses heavily polluted, and residential areas inflicted with high concentrations of industrial pollutants. Moreover, levels of biodiversity in the region declined sharply during the Soviet period.

During the past decade, Caspian fisheries collapsed, the Aral Sea all but disappeared, deserts expanded, and air pollution in major cities increased due to cars. In addition, several more important species neared extinction. On the other hand, with foreign funds, chemical, biological, and nuclear testing facilities have been closed and/or restructured. Moreover, an economic dislocation that has closed factories has also made the post-Soviet period in Central Asia less environmentally unsustainable by reducing levels of industrial effluents, although it has also seen the decay of existing pollution mitigation technology. Yet, this economic dislocation has also stripped the region of its potential to use the momentum of this token movement towards sustainability to effect further reforms for sustainability, which are desperately needed considering growing threats to the viability of the region's lands and the ability of major watercourses to support life, both non-human and human.

The USSR garnered a remarkable track record in building human capital. One-third of the physicians on the planet, at one time, practiced in the USSR.[5] Yet, in the past decade Central Asia's human capital infrastructures crumbled. Hospitals lack even the most basic of supplies. Near epidemics of diseases such as tuberculosis, largely unknown by the end of the Soviet period, are now common. Diseases linked to environmental problems, diseases such as cancers and respiratory problems, increased dramatically in the final decade of the USSR, and have remained at high levels in independence. Life expectancies for both men and women have fallen by several years in the past decade.

These declines in health are matched by educational declines. The region began independence with near universal literacy and an educational system that, at least for grammar schools, was very strong. Literacy is now in decline, and schools cannot hire or keep talented teachers. As for higher education, while the region began independence with large numbers of scientists and engineers, funds for research have largely disappeared, and this cohort has experienced the highest level of emigration. Paralleling these problems, median monthly personal incomes fell from roughly $300 at the beginning of the decade to roughly $60 at the end of the decade, with roughly half the population living below the poverty line in 1999.

In considering these trends, while the USSR did bequeath to Central Asia an array of problems challenging the region's maintenance of high levels of human capital, it also left behind the medical schools, hospitals, norms of nutrition, sports habits, and lifespans upon which any credible effort to maintain or expand the region's human capital would necessarily depend. The speed of Central Asia's degradation of human capital stocks does not only erode the potential of the region to recover, it contains a great deal of suffering as people die at young ages for lack of simple medical supplies or attention, as parents cannot educate their children, and as people abandon professions to seek subsistence employment.

The Soviet Union's track record in building organizational capital is more problematic. The USSR's major mobilizations of organizational capital, especially in the early decades of the regime, were for repression, war, and forced integration. Yet, even from its earliest days, the Soviet state devoted considerable resources to create the infrastructure of a modern state, with schools, housing, courts, and transportation systems. At the end of the Stalin era, repression abated considerably, although efforts to create a modern state continued and achieved success in integrating the diverse areas of the USSR into a shared cultural space. While the USSR, and especially Central Asia, never (and, because of the limits of Soviet economic planning perhaps never could have) reached Western levels of organization, progress over the course of 70 years was impressive considering the region's lack of development at the beginning of the century.

During the Perestroika era in Central Asia, both the state and the populace embarked on efforts to battle corruption, embrace democracy, experiment with decentralized economic decisionmaking, and improve rule of law and civil society. Despite the state origins of Perestroika, the Communist Party continued to resist the implications of such reforms on the continued legitimacy of economic planning, restrictions on free enterprise, and the curtailment of individual liberties. Nevertheless, improvements in all these areas occurred, but they were largely offset by an economic downturn that suffused the 1980s, exacerbated the dislocations produced by Perestroika reforms, and left the Soviet Union ripe for internal disassembly.

Thus, as Central Asia entered independence, ideas such as popular sovereignty, rule of law, civil society, and free enterprise were far more legitimate than 5 years earlier. However, as the USSR's disassembly was peaceful, Central Asia also entered independence with a cadre of political leaders groomed in the communist system and expert in communist modes of career advancement. Throughout the decade, one by one, with the ambiguous exception of war-ravaged Tajikistan, the presidents of the region abandoned democratic reforms in order to maintain power, with the result that levels of democracy and individual rights in the region were lower at the end of the decade than at the beginning.

Moreover, in every republic this nomenklatura turned the economic reform process, especially privatization and international credits, into a mechanism to create personal wealth. Most of the presidents of Central Asia are now widely rumored to be billionaires. The region's experience with privatization reflects deep failures of organizational capital. Privatization, as suggested by Western developers, assumed that the region's organizational capital produced incentives isomorphic with those in Western states. Privatization was envisioned as the best way to inspire restructuring of inefficient firms. Only now are economists beginning to admit that post-Soviet privatization could not have led to such restructurings given actual conditions;[6] in reality it led to asset stripping instead of secondary trading.[7]

While often not considered together, the failures of privatization and the failures of democratic accountable government in Central Asia are symptoms of the same disruption of organizational capital. In both cases, managers have engaged in ultimately rational rent seeking behavior that has depleted the organizational capital assets, as well as other capital assets, of the region.[8] Information about exactly how such asset stripping has occurred is mostly anecdotal; stakes are high enough to keep such information out of public discourse since documentation could lead to criminal cases, re-nationalization, and confiscation.

Finally, social capital remains an understudied aspect of Central Asian capital assets. During Perestroika, the region witnessed a sharp rise in numbers of independent associations suggestive of active stocks of bridging social capital. While numbers of NGOs in the region are still high, popular movements in Central Asia have no victories to boast comparable to pre-independence success in closing weapons test sites, halting state plans to divert northern rivers, and introducing reform legislation. Moreover, through traditional structures such as mahalla residential community associations, the region evidently also contains strong stocks of bonding social capital. Soviet and post-Soviet patterns of communal housing, newspaper readership, carpooling, informal employment, socializing, hobby groups, travel, information exchange, and even norms of downsizing all suggest that social capital survived and even flourished in many parts of the Soviet system, despite the assumptions of theorists like Francis Fukuyama that communism and social capital were mutually exclusive. Nevertheless, while group solidarity appears not to have been eroded strongly in the post-Soviet period, ongoing reforms in Uzbekistan suggest that bonding social capital may also be threatened. Likewise, bridging social capital assets may be less robust now that at the beginning of independence due to the reversion of many people from "modern" lifestyles in the Soviet era to current subsistence lifestyles.

The decline of Central Asia's capital assets catalogued above relies exclusively on measurements within the region, but the increasing implications of globalization for publics around the world impels an examination of Central Asia's capital assets as they relate to global regimes. Theories of comparative advantage and neorealistic international relations, among others, predict contradictory impacts of globalization on developing states, the former, for instance that developing states will experience more income and the latter, that strong states will manipulate affairs so as to divert wealth to themselves. While a full assessment is still many years away, landlocked Central Asia's limited experience with globalization is largely negative. International trade, as yet, has not developed into a more lucrative endeavor than Soviet autarky's guaranteed markets and state subsidies. Although many more years may be needed for international trade to fully develop in Central Asia, especially since only Kyrgyzstan is a WTO member, globalization has more quickly impacted the other two media of globalization: people and capital. Those migrating from Central Asia to Russia and the West disproportionately represent the most educated and wealthy classes. Of similar negative impact on the capital assets of the region, wealthy individuals in the region, do not automatically apply their wealth to domestic investments. Quite frequently, they choose to dismantle physical capital for sale overseas and/or to hold their wealth in foreign banks and firms, where such funds find application, for the most part, in fueling the economies of developed states. Both emigration and unregulated flows of capital challenge claims of comparative advantage theories to improve equitable distributions of wealth under globalization, and, consequently, the net impact of globalization in Central Asia may be to exacerbate post-Soviet declines.

In other words, asset stripping behavior is a partial consequence of globalism and the increasing free trade of goods of services that mainstream proponents of free trade argue furthers both democracy and the prosperity of developing states. Put differently, much of the aspirations of free trade proponents hinge on a conception of comparative advantage that envisions a world in which things move. The soft underside of this theory is a disregard for interest in the movements of non-things, specifically people and money. The glaring hole in the theory is the abundant evidence that flows of people and capital mirror and are exacerbated by flows of trade.[9]

Outside of these overarching theories of globalization,[10] international environmental regimes explicitly aim to facilitate the efforts of developing states to pioneer sustainability. The states of Central Asia receive substantial aid from such regimes, regularly participate in such regimes, and host hundreds of programs and consultants generated through such regimes. Yet, the states fail to maximize the efficacy of their participation in such regimes, and their representatives in such regimes lack the skills to apply the strengths of these regimes to the resolution of Central Asia's environmental problems. In no small part as a result of such weaknesses displayed by Central Asian environmental institutions and professionals, international agencies like UNDP have arrogated many ostensible state duties for environmental development, even in some states displacing environmental ministries.

The two unfortunate results of the failures of the Central Asian states to integrate themselves dynamically into international environmental regimes are undue diversions of resources to international development agencies like UNDP and a lack of discrete interventions to protect the environment. To date, most results of environmental development projects in the region have been limited to the generation of paper plans, draft laws, and completed seminars, even where, as in the cases of the Aral and preventing wildlife poaching, little disagreement existed either at the beginning or at the end of the decade about what kinds of discrete tangible intercessions were required. Moreover, where the Central Asian states encounter environmental challenges not addressed by existing international environmental regimes (such as in the cases of the Caspian, the Aral, and the Irtysh), they have failed to mobilize or respond to conflict resolution mechanisms generated by international law. As a result, while it has been a boon for foreign consultants, the globalization of the international environment has largely failed to date to build capacity within Central Asia or to improve environmental conditions.

Winston Churchill's quip sixty years ago that Soviet Russia was "a riddle wrapped in a mystery inside an enigma" extrapolates in spirit to the bureaucracy surrounding international donor efforts to build sustainable development in Central Asia. These efforts are a strategy wrapped in a program inside a plan. The language and unchallenged ideological platitudes of the international environmental sphere are, especially within the post-Soviet republics, no different and no less rich than Orwellian doublespeak. Practice now demands no more than that projects legitimize their claims for funding and support through discursive claims to be "country-driven," build capacity, "train the trainers," adhere to "project sustainability," draw on all "stakeholders," effect "transition," and further the "plan," usually some sort of national action plan. In mood, these rhetorical tools are deployed by international agencies with zeal equivalent to that which Soviet architects displayed in calling upon the proletariat to effect five-year plans. If yesterday's ideologically confident prescription for socialism was electrification plus Soviet Power, today's ideologically confident prescription for sustainable development is the National Environmental Action Plan plus civil society.

ACCOUNTING FOR DECLINE

Even if decline was not expected in the region, it may have been inevitable given Central Asia's difficult landlocked geopolitical position, the state of the world in the 1990s, and the shortfalls of capital assets inherited from the Soviet Union. Even if this decline was inevitable, it surely has deeper roots than Soviet failings, cultural traits, the actions of dictators, or the mistakes of donor agencies alone.

Of the possible reasons suggested at the beginning of this study, "civilization clash" and that the region's decline is a mere "blip" appear unlikely. Two other possible reasons, globalization and unnecessary dislocations, find more ready application. First, there are structural alterations introduced in the global system by globalization; in short, the tighter commodity markets, increased personal mobility, and the isomorphic institutionalism of the era of globalization put any state that undergoes deep structural changes at the present time at a serious disadvantage. Second, donor policies and pressures from influential states have weakened Central Asia; in particular, failures of international planning institutions have led to needless distortions in local societies and abandonment of the stronger aspects of Central Asia, like emphases on education, community, science, and Perestroika expressions of consensus for substantive democratic reforms. Yet, mitigating this last reason for decline, there is no indication that donor avoidance of the area would have led to a better future for Central Asia, only that the donor community fell far short of its potential.

In the end, the environmental disappointments of the independence period could only have been prevented by massive reorientations of local economies and equivalently unusual capital investments. For example, to save the Aral Sea, the states would have needed to effect an immediate ban on transfers of water outside the basin, an immediate improvement in irrigation technology, and drastic reduction in cotton production. Such reforms, among other things, would have wiped out infusions of foreign capital to the governments of Turkmenistan and Uzbekistan. Neither the financial resources nor the political will existed to embark on this project, and Western states applied little pressure. To save Caspian fisheries (or preserve other commercially valuable biodiversity), the states would have needed to enforce existing anti-poaching laws militantly and allow access to each other's facilities to provide oversight of state fishing monopolies. Here, the loss of control by central governments over local activities and the distrust between state governments prevented effective local law enforcement and precluded a regime of interstate accountability.

To continue, the creation of strong environmental ministries would have required the existence of key officials versed in environmental law, international law, English, and economics, as well as the support of central governments. Unfortunately, competing ministries usually outmaneuver environmental ministries, nepotistic oligarchies preclude appointments of capable individuals to senior environmental positions, and, anyway, the Soviet legacy left not one single person with all these qualifications. Similar shortfalls in critical financial, human, organizational, and social capital assets lay at the heart of other environmental development failures in the region. Similarly complex interactions illustrate the dilemmas that frustrated preservation of scientific institutions, hospitals, democratic elections, and important professional networks.

Consequently, despite the promise felt at the beginning of the decade, Central Asia was probably destined to experience decline in its first decade of independence. Yet, foreign assistance probably exacerbated the severity of this decline, or, at the very least, foreign influence and aid could have been managed so that decline was not as severe as it has been. Ironically, the failures of foreign aid in Central Asia find their roots in the existence within aid agencies of the very qualities that the Western world identified as both "Soviet" and "liabilities." The foreign aid enterprise in Central Asia, although directed towards building the non-state economy, democratic accountability, and a new reliance on effectiveness over jingoism, has itself been almost exclusively state directed, unaccountable, and defiantly managed for ideological and political correctness.

Whereas Eastern Europe benefited from an outpouring of assistance and new enterprises generated through private foundations and European businesses, Central Asia has, by comparison, received almost no private-sector assistance. For example, according to a December 1997 Foundation Center report,[11] in comparison to $40,000,000 provided by US foundations (not including Soros) to Hungary, $40,000 was provided to Uzbekistan. In comparison to $9,000,000 provided by US foundations to Russia, MacArthur's $15,000 to Dashkhovuz Ecological Guardians was the only funding for Turkmenistan. 1000:1 and 600:1 discrepancies such as these make it difficult to overstate the comparative disadvantages that nascent Central Asian democratic and environmental institutions face. Moreover, since the programs of Soros's Open Society Institute in the region are both more cost effective and more effective overall than those of USAID or TACIS, some estimate of the cumulative disadvantage of so much state-sector support for the private sector can be guessed.

However, to the extent that Central Asia certainly needed foreign assistance in order to make its transition to democracy and markets, donor agencies and states had limited choices. Western states could not mandate to private foundations that they work as assiduously and actively in Central Asia as they did in the more developed, more Christian, and less Asian areas of the former communist world. Moreover, the failures of the private foundation world as a community to address Central Asia raise uncomfortable allegations of latent Eurocentrism or racism that do not afflict USAID. Partly to address this problem, USAID and TACIS provided grants and contracts to private foundations and NGOs to administer reform programs in Central Asia. However, importantly, such state donors kept their fundees on short leases and, as the case of the 1995 Kazakhstan Constitution showed, were willing to stifle free speech, ignore violations of the law, and assent to authoritarianism for short term assurances of stability and protection of international investors. To the extent that states like the United States will probably never be willing to relinquish control over U.S. funded development projects, this corruption of development by state interests was inevitable.

A negative view of foreign assistance now reigns among analysts in the former USSR. For example, in response to President-elect Bush's threat to cease aid, Russian Presidential Economic Advisor Illarionov replied that "[t]he rejection of corrupting aid is true assistance."[12] For Illarionov, American assistance to Russia, by opening paths for corruption, has done more harm than good. Sergei Duvanov argues that the same thing occurred in Kazakhstan. He believes that the manner in which the bulk of American assistance was distributed through the ruling oligarchy meant, ironically, that it constituted a subsidy (instead of market assistance) and (since the State Department refused to care much about accountability) was used to enrich the oligarchy, protect oligarchic businesses against private competitors, and kill democracy.[13]

In contrast, donor lack of appreciation for local culture and local practices does not rest in similarly systemic problems of foreign assistance, but merely in poor planning and research. For example, in hindsight, Perestroika dialogues should have been nurtured[14] in the post-independence era. Perestroika dialogues had more in their favor than their gradualism. Indeed, perhaps the disassembly of the Soviet Union and the counterfactual of China's successes suggest that they were not gradual enough. The Perestroika dialogues were as celebratory of democracy, as cognizant of the efficiency of decentralized decisionmaking (for governments and for markets), and as committed to rule of law as any of the Western agencies and reformers who entered the shattered Soviet Union. The Perestroika reforms may not have been committed to the American or European institutional manifestations of rule of law, democracy, and decentralization, but that does not besmirch the ideological strengths that they did exhibit. Likewise, especially given the failures of Western developers and, again, China's recent experience, it was in hindsight a mistake to place too much emphasis on or read too much into the shortfalls between Perestroika aspirations and actual events.

The dialogues of Perestroika showed promise of becoming no less forceful and eloquent foundations for democracy and rule of law in the former Soviet world than the Federalist papers were for the United States of America. To be sure, continental political philosophers deserve credit for penning the best and first general expressions of democracy, constitutionalism, and accountable government in the eighteenth century. In parallel, there can be no doubt that Western economists and constitutional scholars of the twentieth century beat out their post-Soviet counterparts in describing the normative bases of modern secular states. Yet, in the American experience, for the American people, and even for American courts, the Federalist papers read with an authority not possessed by any continental philosopher. Likewise, notwithstanding his erudition or personal ambitions, Jeffrey Sachs should not have hoped to or been allowed to attempt to displace Andrei Sakharov and other authoritative local critical voices. Accordingly, the actions of Western development agencies, especially Americans, in ignoring Perestroika dialogs and advocating what, in effect, was a tabula rasa approach to democracy, rule of law, and civil society, was a terrible mistake that derailed much of the potential for reform in the region.

> As social and organizational capital turns out to be so fragile and like Humpty-Dumpty, "hard to put back together again," one can argue that it is best to start with existing social institutions and try to induce their incremental transformation—rather than trying to eliminate them "root-and-branch" in order to start out with a "a clean sheet of paper."[15]

As this quote from World Bank Vice President Joseph Stiglitz suggests, international institutions now view with suspicion plans to effect radical change in the institutional foundations of states. This caution contrasts starkly with and was in no small part formed by the failed efforts of developers in the former Soviet Union in the past ten years.

IMPLICATIONS OF DECLINE FOR SUSTAINABLE DEVELOPMENT

The full costs of repairing the environment in Central Asia and ensuring that this part of the world does not exacerbate global environmental problems probably exceed the total GDP of the states by several times; even mitigation measures may be well beyond the financial means of these states. The states are all already unable to meet the burdens imposed on their budgets by basic social welfare programs for education, medical care, and poverty alleviation. Environmental problems exacerbate demands for further expenditures for medical care, poverty alleviation, and mitigation, which further weaken these states and reduce revenue coming back into state budgets. Central Asia's confluence of environmental disaster and economic dislocation has launched these states into a positive feedback loop of decline.

How and whether states resolve the environmental challenges facing the world in the twenty-first century are two distinct questions. Not only will states need to develop and coordinate a level of will heretofore not seen in any single state, much less the community of states in the aggregate. Also, successful environmental responses may require adjustments in population, patterns of consumption, and sovereignty unheard of in any peacetime setting.

Moreover, not all states will be able to implement policies to effect these adjustments, no matter how high their level of will. The examples yielded by Central Asia's environmental practices in the post-Soviet decade suggest that these states will be among those probably lacking the capacity to implement such reforms even if the general population supports such reforms. This condition leads to the argument that arm's length assistance may not be enough, especially when such assistance is so often diverted. An aid regime more suffused with accountability and control may be needed; whatever it is called, such a regime would restore elements of colonialism and reduce the sovereignty of affected states. Sovereignty, in the end, may not further the welfare of either the citizens of Central Asia or the global welfare.

Unfortunately, if this assessment is accurate, Central Asia would not be the first region of the world so affected. Africa, particularly Rwanda,[16] yields a compelling, albeit a distasteful argument, that a citizen of a state subject to the human and organizational capital practices of colonialism, as practiced by the English and French, may be better situated than a citizen of a state subject to the human and organizational capital practices of development assistance, as the latter is now practiced by UN agencies, the United States, and the European Union.

Faced with serious environmental and other security problems, humanity may not be able to permit for much longer the coordination quagmires, free riding, and strategic behavior occasioned by the existence of 200 sovereignties, especially the kind of sovereignties now dotting the landscape south of Russia. It is an irony of twentieth century history that the first half of the century generated momentum towards popular revolts against colonialism and an end to colonialism despite the ambitions of developed states. Since free trade now ensures the access formerly enabled through colonialism, but without attending responsibilities, the irony is that the century ends with the developed states now decidedly convinced that colonialism is not in their national interests, while popular will in many developing states would welcome a new colonial order. Indeed, my own general impression from having spent half of the past decade in the region is that the general population of Central Asia would, with each passing year, more warmly welcome the chance to be a European colony, weakly as regards Russia, but strongly as regards any other developed state.

An emerging rule of international environmental law is the principle of "common but differentiated responsibility,"[17] enshrined in, *inter alia*, the ozone and climate change regimes. This principle acknowledges the need for all states to act, but places a greater burden on developed states. While hints of a such a principle in development assistance also exist, they should be formalized to ensure that developed states do not shirk responsibility for humanity, and also do not shirk responsibility for the actions of their agents in developing states.[18] Quite the opposite, for development assistance to be effective, enduring and lasting commitments from donor states to achieve results must at least be as extensive and meaningful as under colonialism.

The general population of Central Asia remains concerned about environmental problems and yearns to live in a democratic rule of law state. Complementing this will, the population of the post-Soviet world remains more educated than the norm for developing states. However, this human capital remains, except for Soros-funded efforts, a rare target of development assistance. More than likely taking their cue in part in reaction to expressions of Western perceptions of priority needs, none of the post-Soviet republics has essayed to maintain human capital.

For example, shortly after it was announced that he won the 2000 Nobel Prize for physics, Russian Duma deputy Zhores Alferov, a communist, complained publicly about just this problem. He complained that, in stark contrast to levels of science funding in the Soviet era, one apartment building being planned for legislators would absorb several times more government funds than all capital investments in science.[19]

Yet, in order to move into the kind of information and service economy that characterizes the developed states, Central Asia will need to draw specifically on this human capital. And in order for that economy to be sustainable, natural capital stocks will need to be safeguarded. Such a sustainable transition will require innovations that the Central Asian republics are increasingly unlikely to make. While command economies stifle innovation,[20] a market economy devoid of scientific and technological capital does not merely stifle innovation; it precludes it. No state in the "failed state" pantheon popularized by Robert Kaplan produces innovations at a scale near that of the Soviet Union.

To date, Western scholars of Central Asia, who tend to see Central Asia as it was long before Soviet development policies took hold, and international development agencies, who want to see Central Asia as like some South American or

African state in which they have experience, underestimate or overlook Central Asia's strongest endowments for development. People, not hydrocarbons, are Central Asia's strongest endowment.

For both sustainable development and development in general, not all aspects of the Soviet past should be dismissed. Educational policies favoring the natural sciences, Perestroika dialogues on rule of law, restrictions against fetishistic consumerism, and disdain for nationalism are all consonant with sustainable development and strongly contrast with Western emphases in the first post-Soviet decade. To truly move beyond the limitations of Cold War defensiveness, it is time for even the strongest proponents of democracy, sustainable development, and individual dignities to admit that, partly due to abandonment of the strengths of the Soviet system, Central Asia is further from these goals today than it was just 10 years ago.

Notes

Introduction: Central Asia in transition – the capital of sustainable development

1 In my discussion, "Central Asia" means the contiguous area covered by five former USSR republics: Kazakhstan (KZ), Kyrgyzstan (KG), Tajikistan (TJ), Turkmenistan (TM), and Uzbekistan (UZ). Occasional references will also be made to the sixth "Islamic" republic of the former Soviet Union, Azerbaijan (AZ).

2 *See* Douglas Saltmarshe, "Civil Society and Sustainable Development in Central Asia", 15 *Central Asian Survey* (1996). Actual assessments of programs, in contrast to scholarly recommendations and donor prospective descriptions of programs, have been rare. The few environmental transition assessments from donor agencies were positive prior to 1998. While assessments are now increasingly critical, many donors still claim environmental and other developmental successes in Central Asia. For example, Asian Development Bank (ADB) describes its projects as of "major environmental importance . . . with direct positive impacts on the environment in Central Asia." Asian Development Bank, *Central Asian Environments in Transition* (Manila: Asian Development Bank, 1998), p. 25. World Bank not only claims that most of its projects, including environmental projects, in the region have been successful, but that they are more successful than the global average. Nagy Hanna *et al.* (1999) *Annual Review of Development Effectiveness* (Washington, D.C.: World Bank Operations Evaluation Department, 1999), p. 43. The United States Agency for International Development (USAID) notes its "significant progress towards the twin objectives of establishing a region-wide energy system and managing transboundary water issues." USAID, *USAID's Assistance Strategy for Central Asia 2001–2005* (Almaty: USAID Regional Mission for Central Asia, 2000), p. 66.

3 Richard N. Frye, *The Heritage of Central Asia* (Princeton: Markus Wiener Publishers, 1996), p. 35.

4 B. G. Gafurov, *Tajiki: Drevneishaya, drevnyaya i srednevekovaya istoriya* (Volume I) (Dushanbe: Irfon, 1989), p. 88.

5 The Uzbeks, as well as the Kazakhs who split from them in the sixteenth century, emerged from the Turko–Mongolian Golden and White Hordes of Siberia that claimed legitimacy through tracing their origins back to Chinggis Khan.

6 Gregory Gleason, *The Central Asian States* (Boulder: Westview Press, 1998), p. 116.

7 *See* Benedict R. Anderson, *Imagined Communities* (New York: Verso, 1991). Cf. Olivier Roy, *La Nouvelle Asie Centrale ou La Fabrication des Nations* (Paris: Seuil, 1997). Roy argues that Anderson's ideas about the development of national identities are applicable to Central Asia. While he acknowledges some important distinctions between Central Asia and Latin America (esp. the kinds of efforts made by intellectuals to spark national identification, pp. 15–16), he also exaggerates the degree to which Central Asians (and other non-Russians) were excluded from USSR and Russian Federation posts (pp. 170–174). For example, while Roy praises Chingiz Aitmatov as Central Asian (p. 16), he appears to be unaware that Aitmatov is now a Russian Ambassador, not a Kyrgyzstan

Ambassador. Likewise, he seems unaware of the consensus that Kazakhstan's Nazarbaev was a likely, at least viable, candidate to succeed Gorbachev. In stark, even shocking contrast to Anderson, Roy relies on weak sources (i.e. no Russian language or Central Asian sources), fails to display any access to the colloquial that vivifies Anderson's work, and casts a very thin net. On this last point, Roy restricts his analysis to formal political leaders, failing to appreciate the symbolic and ideological importance of numerous USSR-level scientists, astronauts, state heroes, army generals, and other very visible persons from Central Asia serving in Moscow, Leningrad and other Russian cities.

8 International agencies are incurring a long list of apparent violations of international norms in treating these states on an ad hoc basis. *See* Akbar Rasulov, "Pravopreemstvo i Tsentralnaya Aziya," in Eric W. Sievers *et al.* (eds), *Mezhdunarodnoe ekologicheskoe pravo i Tsentralnaya Azia* (Almaty: XXIv, 2001), pp. 146–164.

9 Samuel P. Huntington, *The Clash of Civilizations: Remaking of World Order* (New York: Simon and Schuster, 1996).

10 *See* Saskia Sassen, *Globalization and its Discontents* (New York: The New Press, 1998).

11 *See* Robert Kaplan, "The Coming Anarchy," *The Atlantic Monthly* (February, 1994), p. 44 and Robert D. Kaplan, *The Ends of the Earth: A Journey at the Dawn of the 21st Century* (New York: Random House, 1996).

12 Notably, this argument is now ridiculed. *See* Joseph E. Stiglitz, "Whither Reform: Ten Years of the Transition" Paper presented April 28, 1999 at Annual Bank Conference on Development Economics (Washington, D.C.: The World Bank, 1999), p. 21. Available at: http://www.worldbank.org/research/abcde/washington_11/pdfs/stiglitz.pdf.

13 *See* Robert D. Putnam, *Making Democracy Work* (Princeton: Princeton University Press, 1993) and Robert Putnam, *Bowling Alone* (New York: Simon and Schuster, 2000).

14 *See* Eugene B. Skolnikoff, *The Elusive Transformation* (Princeton: Princeton University Press, 1993).

15 Paul W. Kahn, *The Cultural Study of Law* (Chicago: University of Chicago Press, 1999), p. 40.

16 Stephen Kurkjian, "Officials of Harvard Program that Aided Russia are Probed," *The Boston Globe* (Jan. 15, 1999), p. A1.

17 Steve Levine, "Probe Begun of U.S. Fund in Central Asia," *Wall Street Journal* (December 27, 2000), p. 8.

18 China recognizes the threat from climate change, but argues (justifiably) that to the extent atmospheric carbon concentrations are the result of Western development, the West must cut its emissions drastically and allow developing states the opportunity even to increase their emissions. For China's ambiguous position on international environmental policies, *see* Elizabeth Economy, "Chinese Policy-Making and Global Climate Change: Two-Front Diplomacy and the International Community," in Miranda A. Schreurs and Elizabeth C. Economy (eds), *The Internationalization of Environmental Protection* (Cambridge: Cambridge University Press, 1997), p. 19.

19 World Commission on Environment and Development, *Our Common Future* (1987), p. 43.

20 All of these forms of capital are described in detail below.

21 Robert Goodland and Herman Daly, "Environmental Sustainability: Universal and Non-Negotiable," *Ecological Applications* 6 (1996), p. 1002. *See also,* Eric Sievers, "Ustoichivoe razvitie: Proklyatiye ili spaseniye?" *Vestnik "Zelenoe spaseniye"* 1 (1995), pp. 55–64.

22 Cf. Fukuyama claims that social capital replenishment requires centuries, if it can happen at all. Francis Fukuyama, *Trust: The Social Virtues and the Creation of Prosperity* (New York: Simon & Schuster, 1995), p. 321. However, in this conclusion, Fukuyama contradicts himself in many ways. He claims that ideas can change quickly, but cultures cannot; yet he also claims that East Germans, as a result of communism, now have more in common with Bulgarians and Russians (Ibid).

23 "Enough" will here mean a level heretofore not seen in any development or peace-keeping interventions. Europe and the United States have the capacity to simply buy off Sierra Leone's residents with huge cash subsidies (to overcome the critical problem of generating internal support for their efforts) and station troops (who would not be withdrawn after an incident of violence). That the West will not expend a billion dollars or thousands of human lives in order to save Sierra Leone is not relevant to a consideration of whether it has the capacity to do so. In fact, Sierra Leone would only marginally impact the reserves of capital of the West.

24 In part relying on such concerns, in exploring the implications of diverse forms of capital on definitions of sustainable development, economists Robert Goodland and Herman Daly refine the term to emphasize natural capital: "sustainable development is development without growth in throughput of matter and energy beyond regenerative and absorptive capacities." Goodland and Daly, "Environmental Sustainability: Universal and Non-Negotiable."

25 *See generally*, Stiglitz, "Whither Reform: Ten Years of the Transition."

26 Whether this decline is Soviet or post-Soviet depends on context. Whereas declines in other forms of capital rapidly register in economic balance sheets, or at most require a generation to register, only losses of natural capital can require, potentially, decades or centuries to manifest in monetary terms.

27 This assumption may be false. One current of development economics posits that low stocks of natural capital are preferable in the global service economy. However, this argument embraces only a quantitative conception of natural capital (i.e. it would not argue in favor of the benefits of air pollution) and states not that natural capital is bad, but that a particular reliance on natural resource exports is bad. More recently, some comparative evaluations of transition suggest that among the "adverse initial conditions" for transition states is a "high degree of industrialization," such as possessed by the CIS but not by China. Accordingly, transition states heavily reliant on agriculture faced better "initial conditions" for transition than their industrialized peers. IMF Staff, *Transition Economies: An IMF Perspective on Progress and Prospects* (Issue Brief 00/08, November, 2000).

28 To wit, in the former Soviet Union, the wealth held by billionaires means little since it is held in Swiss banks or invested largely in the West. Similarly, "good" government is what I mean by "high" stocks of organizational capital.

29 Goodland and Daly, "Environmental Sustainability: Universal and Non-Negotiable," p. 1004.

30 This is roughly equivalent to what Goodland and Daly call "strong sustainability." Ibid., p. 1005.

31 Examples include all of the recent work of Francis Fukuyama and much of the recent work of Samuel Huntington. Both authors employ a discursive strategy of describing other parts of the world in order to create a platform for their ultimate goal, namely to make policy points relevant to United States society. Yet, in the process, both authors tend towards opportunistic descriptions of other countries and cultures, descriptions that draw almost exclusively on English sources, on sources often eschewed by more careful scholars. Consequently, Huntington's and Fukuyama's ostensibly neutral factual descriptions of other states find very little support among regional specialists. For example, while I find both authors' descriptions of the Soviet Union and post-Soviet events misleading and factually troubled, Middle Eastern, Chinese, and other area scholars point overwhelmingly to similar flaws in the ways in which these authors treat their areas. While I leave it to other authors to reveal the myths and errors that Huntington and Fukuyama propagate about other areas of the world, an objective of later chapters in this work is to suggest that their theories about culture clash, trust, and social capital have great relevance for Central Asia, but only when viewed in the context of a balanced analysis of the region's history and culture. In other words, by abandoning these authors' political agendas and thin scholarship, I endeavor to evaluate

the strengths of their theoretical work. Put to the test of Central Asia, Fukuyama's general ideas fare far better than Huntington's.

32 During the first years of independence, perhaps the bulk of reform project focused on trainings, both within Central Asia and as components of trips to Western states. All local USAID staff and contractors were involved in candidate selection for trainings. Thus, I was frequently contacted about candidate nominations and selections for environmental, democracy, law, and NGO training programs, programs that I estimate involved more than 1000 Central Asians. In each case (the situation may have changed) USAID summarily threw out applications of any applicants over 40 on the explicit assumption that they were "too set in their ways," no matter a person's accomplishments or dissident activities. Such individuals were only selected when USAID or its trainings coordinator, Academy for Educational Development, was lobbied intensively. Thus, for a human rights program, USAID would prefer a 20-year old student with no discernible commitment to a 45-year old dissident who had continued human rights work in the Soviet era despite repression.

33 For example, in the fields of democracy and environment, Gregory Gleason, Kathleen Braden, Nancy Lubin, and Michael Glantz are some of the senior scholars in U.S. institutions with substantial experience in Central Asia whose thoughtful criticism of early USAID development programs (both through direct participation and through scholarly works) was, unfortunately, more often ignored than considered.

34 While only a minority of development professionals ground themselves in the discipline of economics, those wielding the most influence over general development strategies speak economics as a lingua franca. While economics is a dynamic discipline, ever open to new ideas, it is also exceedingly insular. Until ideas are expressed in its own language, the ideas will be meaningless to economics and, as far as the world of development is concerned, not exist. Accordingly, for me it is axiomatic that those who would wish to communicate fruitfully with economists are well-advised to do so in their own language.

35 For example, reflecting one of these extreme statistical discrepancies even among relatively conservative sources, a 1998 Asian Development Bank source posits Kazakhstan's 1994–1996 per-capita GDP to have been $410. Asian Development Bank, *Central Asian Environments in Transition*, p. 35. Despite the economic travails of intervening years, UNDP in 2000 posits that 1998 per-capita GDP in Kazakhstan was $4378. UNDP, *Human Development Report 2000*, p. 158. For the period covered by the ADB report, UNDP reported per-capita GDP in Kazakhstan of $3284. UNDP, *Human Development Report* (UNDP: New York, 1997).

36 *See* Putnam, *Making Democracy Work*.

37 Walter D. Connor, "Class, Social Structure, Nationality," in Alexander J. Motyl (ed.), *The Post-Soviet Nations* (New York: Columbia University Press, 1991), pp. 276–278.

38 Gurgen, "Central Asia: Achievements and Prospects", p. 42. While Gurgen's numbers are quite conservative, moderately conservative estimates are 6–10 per cent per year. UNDP, *Human Development Report 2000*, pp. 203–204; Grzegorz W. Kolodko, "Ten Years of Postsocialist Transition: the Lessons for Policy Reforms" (Washington, D.C.: The World Bank Development Economics Research Group, 1998), p. 3.

39 While Soviet era statistics should be used with caution, and while I note that Soviet statistical agencies inflated many statistics for political reasons, I do not directly address these shortcomings in later chapters in the belief that were more accurate statistics available they would reduce in scale but would not change the general contours of decline that I track.

40 Goodland and Daly, "Environmental Sustainability: Universal and Non-Negotiable," p. 1005.

41 Not analyzed here, time discounting exacerbates this relationship by making intercessions to safeguard natural capital appear irrational under all but an unusually low discount rate, or unless generational discounting is used. *See* Jerome Rothenberg,

"Economic Perspective on Time Comparisons: Evaluation of Time Discounting," in Nazli Choucri (ed.), *Global Accord: Environmental Challenges and International Responses* (Cambridge: MIT Press, 1993), p. 333.

42 John A. Dixon and Kirk Hamilton, "Expanding the Measure of Wealth," *Finance & Development* 33 (December 1996), p. 16. *See generally* The World Bank, *Expanding the Measure of Wealth: Indicators of Environmentally Sustainable Development* (Washington, D.C.: The World Bank, 1997); *see also* The World Bank, *Monitoring Environmental Progress: A Report on Work in Progress* (Washington, D.C.: The World Bank, 1995).

43 Patricia Annez and Alfred Friendly, "Cities in the Developing World: Agenda for Action Following Habitat II" *Finance & Development* 33 (December, 1996), p. 13.

44 Dixon and Hamilton, "Expanding the Measure of Wealth," p. 15.

45 Robert C. Ellickson, "Property in Land," *Yale Law Journal* 102 (1993), p. 1353.

46 *See generally*, Eugene B. Skolnikoff, *The Elusive Transformation* (Princeton: Princeton University Press, 1993), pp. 112–128.

47 John J. Donahue III and Steven D. Levitt, "Legalized Abortion and Crime," *Quarterly Journal of Economics* (forthcoming).

48 Explicitly ignored in this analysis are armies. Armies (and national defense in general) pose a major challenge to the premises of my analysis (which assumes international allocations through markets and not through force) and are simply beyond the scope of the present work. While in my analysis size of population is of ambiguous importance, in a more traditional political economy, for national defense reasons, size of population is of key importance. A more mature account of development, or an actual development intervention, could not ignore armies and national defense, both to the extent that they may be necessary and to the extent that they produce major domestic negative externalities. *See* any publication of IMF, *World Economic Outlook* (Washington, D.C.: International Monetary Fund, 1993–present).

49 For example, Aristotle and Tolstoy. *See* Paul W. Kahn, *The Cultural Study of Law*.

50 For the theoretical argument, *see* Eric A. Posner, "The Regulation of Groups: The Influence of Legal and Nonlegal Sanctions on Collective Action," *University of Chicago Law Review* 63 (1996), p. 133. For the empirical argument, *see* Eric W. Sievers, "Uzbekistan's Mahalla: From Soviet to Absolutist Residential Community Associations," Unpublished paper presented September 29, 2000 at Central Eurasia Studies Conference, University of Wisconsin.

51 Accordingly, I posit that definitions of corruption such as "use of public office for private gain" fail on all counts. Cheryl W. Gray and Daniel Kaufman, "Corruption and Development" *Finance & Development* 35 (March 1998), p. 7. Such a definition limits corruption to state offices and limits its externalities to negative externalities. A better and broader definition would define corruption as transgression of a rule (formal or informal) against appropriation of a specific consumer surplus as a rent. Such a definition also highlights the fact that not all "offices" encourage corruption, but only those that intersect with (or, often, create) consumer surplus in the form of a rent. While his analysis also precludes private corruption, a similar definition ("corruption can occur where rents exist...and public officials have discretion in allocating them") is contained in Paulo Mauro, "Corruption: Causes, Consequences, and Agenda for Further Research," *Finance and Development* 35 (March 1998), p. 11.

52 For a historical perspective, *see* Harold James, "From Grandmotherliness to Governance," *Finance & Development* 35 (December, 1998) p. 44.

53 Francis Fukuyama, "Social Capital and Civil Society," *IMF Working Paper* WP/00/74 (April, 2000).

54 Francis Fukuyama recently provided a roughly similar definition, but his definition lacks internal consistency. Despite attempting to define social capital through the argot of economics, he ultimately contradicts this attempt by conflating the term with his previous work on trust, expanding the term to encompass absolutely all social norms, and ignoring the non-trust externalities of social capital (i.e. information). *See* Ibid. Moreover,

Fukuyama fails to produce a symmetrically valid definition of social capital; he defines it as "an instantiated norm that promotes cooperation between two or more individuals." This definition fails to appreciate the clear evidence that some social capital frustrates cooperation and it fails to identify a social capital asset. Fukuyama criticizes others for substituting a manifestation of social capital for a definition, he does just that as well.

55 "[C]onsider social facts as things." Emile Durkheim, *The Rules of Sociological Method* (New York: Free Press, 1964), p. 14.

56 *See generally*, Robert C. Ellickson, *Order Without Law: How Neighbors Settle Disputes* (Cambridge: Harvard University Press, 1994), pp. 64–66.

57 I borrow the terms "bonding" and "bridging" from Robert Putnam, although he does not employ these terms in this economic context. *See* Putnam, *Bowling Alone*, pp. 22–24.

58 The lack of bonding social capital may also be a severe handicap, which is why I explicitly disagree that the task of development is to replace bonding with bridging social capital. Scholarship has yet to inquire into the consequences of overly low bonding social capital, but does appreciate the consequences of overly high bonding social capital. It would be a mistake of logic to extrapolate from the conclusion that high levels of bonding social capital produce negative externalities that returns from reduction of bonding social capital would remain positive as bonding social capital approached zero. Bonding social capital is vital to healthy child psychology, to informal insurance mechanisms, and to a variety of other human needs. For an empirical investigation of bonding social capital and insurance in Uzbekistan residential associations, *see* Sievers, "Uzbekistan's Mahalla: From Soviet to Absolutist Residential Community Associations."

1 Natural capital: the Central Asian human and natural environment

1 G. K. Melnikova *et al.*, "A four state crisis: the Sarezsky Lake" *Ecostan News* 10 (November, 1997), pp. 2–3.

2 V. P. Charsky and N. M. Tishkova, "Tsekh No. 7," *Adam zhana Gera* 9 (May–June, 1998), pp. 13–15.

3 Kazakhstan Ministry of Natural Resources and Environmental Protection, "Ekologicheskaya obstanovka v Respublike Kazakhstan," *Ekologicheskii byulleten'* 1 (1999), pp. 5–44.

4 Republic of Kazakhstan, *Initial National Communication of the Republic of Kazakhstan under the United Nations Framework Convention on Climate Change* (Almaty: KazNIIMOSK, 1998). Available at: http://www.unfccc.de/resource/docs/natc/kaznc1.pdf

5 Michael Thurman, "A photographic tour of irrigation in Uzbekistan," 1999. Available at: http://homepages.infoseek.com/~mirablik/atraf-muhit/photo.html.

6 International Fund for the Aral Sea, "Water and Environmental Management in the Aral Sea Basin," *GEF Project Proposal* 1997. Available at: http://www.gefweb.org/wprogram/JULY97/ARALSEA.DOC.

7 Marjukka Hiltunen, *Environmental Development Co-operation Opportunities: Kazakstan, Kyrgyz Republic, Turkmenistan, Uzbekistan* (Helsinki: Finnish Environment Institute, 1998), p. 6.

8 Oleg Tsaruk, "Big water flows to the Kyzylkum or is the Aral dying?" *Ecostan News* 3 (April, 1995), pp. 2–3.

9 Niyaz Ataev, "The Turkmenbashi-Aral Sea," *Ecostan News* 7 (July, 2000), p. 8.

10 Richard Stone, "Coming to grips with the Aral Sea's grim legacy," *Science* 284/5411 (April, 1999), pp. 30–33.

11 Food and Agriculture Organization, "Contaminated water devastates health across the Aral Sea region," 1997. Available at: http://www.fao.org/NEWS/1997/970104-e.htm.

12 Eric Sievers, "China Set to Divert World's Fifth Largest River" *Ecostan News* 7 (July 2000), p. 2.

13 *See,* e.g. Asian Development Bank, *Central Asian Environments in Transition,* pp. 61, 136.

14 United Nations Development Programme, *Kazakhstan Human Development Report* (Almaty: UNDP, 1996).

15 P. Kurbanov (ed.), *Sostoyaniye okruzhayuschei sredy v Turkmenistane* (Ashgabad: Ministry of Nature Use and Environmental Protection, unpublished), p. 153.

16 Kh. Atamuradov, Kh., *Environmental Information Systems in Turkmenistan* (Arendal: UNEP GRID, 1998).

17 V. K. Yesekin *et al., Sostoyanie okruzhayuschei sredy v Respublike Kazakhstan,* undated. Available at: http://www.grida.no/prog/cee/enrin/htmls/kazahst/soe/start.htm.

18 M. B. Baratov *et al.,* "Osnovnye napravleniya zemledeliya v Respublike Tajikistan i ikh vliyaniye na strukturu i sostoyaniye zemel' v usloviyakh perekhodnogo perioda" Paper presented 16 April at National Seminar on Implementation in the Republic of Tajikistan of the United Nations Convention to Combat Desertification (Dushanbe, 1998).

19 D. M. Makhsudov, "Oroshaemoe zemledeliye i problemy opustynivaniya zemel' v Tajikistane" Paper presented 16 April at National Seminar on Implementation in the Republic of Tajikistan of the United Nations Convention to Combat Desertification (Dushanbe, unpublished, 1998).

20 Kh. M. Akhmadov, "Opustynivaniye i bor'ba s nim v razlichnykh prirodo-lesokhozyaistvennykh zonakh Tajikistana" Paper presented 16 April at National Seminar on Implementation in the Republic of Tajikistan of the United Nations Convention to Combat Desertification (Dushanbe, unpublished, 1998).

21 Sixty-five per cent of Africa's croplands are degraded. The World Bank, *Toward an Environment Strategy for the World Bank* (April, 2000 Progress Report/Discussion Draft), p. 12.

22 V. I. Nifadiev *et al.,* "Sostoyaniye okruzhayuschei sredy Kyrgyzstana" (undated). Available at: http://www.grida.no/prog/cee/enrin/htmls/kyrghiz/soe/indexr.htm.

23 Galina Kamakhina, "An alternative approach to saving Turkmenistan's biodiversity" *Ecostan News* 5 (September, 1997): 2–4. *See also* Anonymous, *Tajikistan State of the Environment,* 1998. Available at: http://www.grida.no/prog/cee/enrin/htmls/tadjik/soe/index.htm.

24 Elena Mukhina, "Soaproot Poaching" *Ecostan News* 3 (May, 1995), pp. 6–7.

25 Vladimir Krever *et al.* (eds), *Biodiversity Conservation in Central Asia* (Moscow: World Wide Fund for Nature, 1998), p. 9.

26 Ibid., p. 12.

27 Sievers *et al.,* "National Parks, Snow Leopards, and Poppy Plantations: The Development and Degradation of Central Asia's Preserved Lands."

28 Ibid.

29 N. Safarov (ed.), *Ekologiya i okhrana prirody* (Dushanbe: Ministry of Nature Protection of the Republic of Tajikistan, 1998).

30 A. Kovshar and A. Zatoka, "Printsipy razmeshcheniia i infrastruktura osobo okhraniaemykh prirodnykh territorii v aridnoi zone SSSR," *Problemy osvoeniia pustyn'* 3–4 (1991), pp. 155–160.

31 Ruben A. Manatsakanian, *Environmental Legacy of the Former Soviet Republics* (Edinburgh: University of Edinburgh Press, 1992), p. 82.

32 Sergei Elkin, "Kazakhstan and international greenhouse gas emissions trading," Unpublished talk presented April 30, 1999 at Harvard Institute for International Development.

33 United States Department of Energy Information Administration, "Kazakhstan" (April 2000), http://www.eia.doe.gov/emeu/cabs/kazak.html.

34 Ibid.

35 Asian Development Bank, *Central Asian Environments in Transition,* p. 44.

36 Kyrgyz Press, "Na yuge Ferganskoi doliny ekologi obnaruzhili rtut' dazhe v grudnom moloke u zhenschin" (June 28, 2000 wire report).

37 Kurbanov, *Sostoyaniye okruzhayuschei sredy v Turkmenistane*, pp. 37–38.
38 Tatyana Kostina (ed.), *Gorod XXI veka* (Almaty: Greenwomen, 1999), p. 72.
39 Ibid., pp. 58–59.
40 Irina Matveenko, "Kyrgyzstan NGOs fight paper mill" *Ecostan News* 6 (March 1998), pp. 2–5.
41 Vladimir Kotov and Elena Nikitina, "Implementation and Effectiveness of the Acid rain Regime in Russia," in David G. Victor *et al.* (eds), *The Implementation and Effectiveness of International Environmental Commitments* (Cambridge: MIT Press, 1998), pp. 519–547. *See also* Tatyana Kostina (ed.), *Gorod XXI veka*, p. 57.
42 United States Department of Energy Information Administration, "Kazakhstan."
43 Michael H. Glantz, "Global environmental problems in the Caspian region" Unpublished paper presented at March 15, 1999 NATO Advanced Research Workshop on the Caspian Sea in Venice.
44 Igor S. Zonn, "Ecological Consequences of Oil and Gas Development," in William Ascher and Natalia Mirovitskaya (eds), *The Caspian Sea: A Quest for Environmental Security* (Amsterdam: Kluwer Academic Publishers, 2000), p. 67.
45 I. S. Zonn, *Kaspiiskii memorandum* (Moscow: Korkis, 1997), p. 137.
46 Ibid, p. 145.
47 TRAFFIC Europe Russia, "Vylov osetrovykh v Rossii i torgovlya imi" (unpublished, 1999).
48 Law and Environment Eurasia Partnership, "Review of existing fisheries management measures for Sturgeon in the Caspian Sea, Danube and Amur River basins range states: Kazakhstan and Turkmenistan" (unpublished, 2000).
49 "Prikaspiiskie strany sokratyat vylov osetrovykh" *Panorama* (January 21, 2000), http://www.panorama.kz. Quotas on smaller fish were also reduced.
50 M. R. Mansimov, "Kolebanie urovnya i zatoplenie pribrezhnoi zony Kaspiiskogo morya" Unpublished paper presented March 15, 1999 at NATO Advanced Research Workshop on the Caspian Sea in Venice.
51 Timur Berkeliev, "Radiation Wastes and Pollution in Turkmenistan" *Ecostan News* 5 (June, 1997), pp. 2–4.
52 Liz Fuller, "Kazakhstan to Close Nuclear Power Plant" *RFE/RL Newsline* 169 (September 1, 2000).
53 L. A. Kustareva, "Dorogoi moi Issyk-kul" *Adam zhana Gera* 9 (May–June, 1998), p. 11.
54 Irina Matveenko, "Issyk-kul" *Ecostan News* 6 (June–August, 1998), pp. 2–5.
55 K. J. Bokonbaev *et al.*, "Barskoon. Mai, 1998. Chto bylo i chego ne bylo" (Unpublished report of former Minister of Environment).
56 Dr Yuri Alekseevich Rubezhansky, "Atbasar," *Ecostan News* 2 (February, 1994), pp. 5–6.
57 Bella Sewall, "Caspian Seal Tragedy," *Ecostan News* 7 (July 2000), pp. 9–10.
58 Kyrgyz Press, "Na yuge Ferganskoi doliny ekologi obnaruzhili rtut' dazhe v grudnom moloke u zhenschin."
59 Asian Development Bank, *Central Asian Environments in Transition*, p. 44.
60 *See* Eric W. Sievers, "Beyond Ecocide: Cats and Ecology," *Central Asia Monitor* 5 (1997), pp. 18–26.
61 Donald R. Hill, *Islamic Science and Engineering* (Edinburgh: Edinburgh University Press, 1993), p. 175.
62 D. J. Peterson, *Troubled Lands: The Legacy of Soviet Environmental Destruction* (Boulder: Westview Press, 1993), p. 109.
63 Ibid., p. 66.
64 *See* World Health Organization, *The World Health Report 1999: Making a Difference* (Geneva: World Health Organization, 1999).
65 Food and Agriculture Organization, "Contaminated water devastates health across the Aral Sea region."
66 *See*, e.g. Ayse Kudat *et al.*, *Needs Assessment for the Proposed Uzbekistan Water Supply, Sanitation and Health Project* (Tashkent: World Bank, 1995).

67 *See generally* Murray Feshbach and Alfred Friendly, Jr, *Ecocide in the USSR* (New York: Basic Books, 1992); Manatsakanian, *Environmental Legacy of the Former Soviet Republics*; and Peterson, *Troubled Lands: The Legacy of Soviet Environmental Destruction.*

2 Human capital: health, education, and science in Central Asia

1 A. A. Akaev, "July 29, 1997 Report to the Security Council of the Kyrgyz Republic," in K. J. Bokonbaev *et al.* (eds), *Ekologicheskaya bezopasnost' Kyrgyzstana* (Bishkek: Salam, 1998), p. 13.

2 *See,* e.g. Massimo Livi-Bacci, *Population and Nutrition: An Essay on European Demographic History* (New York: Cambridge University Press, 1991).

3 *See,* e.g. Yu. Zhukov (ed.), *Narodnoe khozyaistvo Kirgizskoi SSR v 1989 godu* (Frunze: Kyrgyzstan, 1991); I. Gribnev (ed.), *Narodnoe khozyaistvo Tadzhikskoi SSR v 1987 godu* (Dushanbe: Irfon, 1988); and *Narodnoe khozhyaistvo Uzbekskoi SSR 1987* (Tashkent: Fan, 1988).

4 Dmitri Chebotarev, "Problems of Gerontology and Health of the Population," in Sergei Burenkov (ed.), *Medicine and Health Care in the USSR* (New York: International Universities Press, 1985), p. 230.

5 Criteria described at WHO, *The World Health Report 2000: Health Systems*, p. 144.

6 For comparative tables showing the region's 1980–1990 advances over Pakistan, *see* T. Koichuev *et al.* (eds), *Istoriya Kyrgyzov i Kyrgyzstana*, pp. 281–282.

7 The 30 per cent of humanity that has access to no medical care is virtually all contained in the world's poorest states. Kaplan, *The Ends of the Earth: A Journey at the Dawn of the 21st Century,* p. 434.

8 Eighty per cent of diseases in the developing world are caused by contaminated water. Deborah Moore and Leonard Sklar, "Reforming the World Bank's Lending for Water: The Process and Outcome of Developing a Water Resources Management Policy," in Jonathan A. Fox and L. David Brown (eds), *The Struggle for Accountability: The World Bank, NGOs and Grassroots Movements* (Cambridge: MIT Press, 1998), p. 345.

9 The World Bank, *Toward an Environment Strategy for the World Bank,* p. 10.

10 K. J. Bokonbaev, "July 29, 1997 Report to the Security Council of the Kyrgyz Republic," in Bokonbaev *et al.* (eds), *Ekologicheskaya bezopasnost' Kyrgyzstana,* p. 23.

11 *See* WHO, *World Health Report 1999,* WHO, *World Health Report 2000,* and UNDP *World Development Indicators.*

12 UNDP, *1998 Human Development Report: Uzbekistan* (Tashkent: UNDP, 1998), p. 17.

13 *See* The World Bank, *Sector Strategy: Health, Nutrition, & Population* (Washington, D.C.: The World Bank, 1999).

14 Two per cent in Uzbekistan in 1897 and 8 per cent in Kazakhstan in 1917. A. V. Koltsov, *Rol' Akademii nauk v organizatsii regionalnykh nauchnykh tsentrov SSSR* (Leningrad: Nauka, 1988), p. 12.

15 While rates by 1970 were nearly 100 per cent, even by 1939 they were roughly 80 per cent, some parts of the region surpassing Belorussia's rates. Ibid., p. 49.

16 Koichuev *et al.* (eds), *Istoriya Kyrgyzov i Kyrgyzstana,* p. 302.

17 While Russia was by all measures more advanced than Central Asia, at the time of the October Revolution, it had a literacy rate of only 27 per cent. Koltsov, *Rol' Akademii nauk v organizatsii regionalnykh nauchnykh tsentrov SSSR* 1988, p. 12.

18 *See* Enric Fernandez and Paulo Mauro, "The Role of Human Capital in Economic Growth: The Case of Spain," *International Monetary Fund Working Paper* WP/00/8 (Washington, D.C.: International Monetary Fund, 2000). Their data includes panel education figures for many European countries. By their economic model and mathematical formulas, Central Asia should have per capita GNPs of over $30,000.

19 Sanjeev Gupta *et al.*, "Public Spending on Human Development," *Finance & Development* 35 (September, 1998), p. 10.
20 UNDP, *1998 Human Development Report: Uzbekistan*, p. 15.
21 "Idet priem dokumentov v vuzy strany," *Neitralnyi Turkmenistan*, August 2, 2000, p. 1.
22 A. S. Sadykov *et al.* (eds), *Akademiya nauk Uzbekskoi SSR* (Tashkent: Fan, 1983), p. 54.
23 *See, generally,* Hill, *Islamic Science and Engineering. See also* Ahmad Y. al-Hassan and Donald R. Hill, *Islamic Technology* (Cambridge: Cambridge University Press, 1994). Also *see* A. S. Sadykov *et al.* (eds), *Abu Ali ibn Sina i estestvennye nauki* (Tashkent: Fan, 1981) and Richard N. Frye, *The Heritage of Central Asia* (Princeton: Markus Wiener Publishers, 1996).
24 *See, generally,* Robert D. McChesney, *Waqf in Central Asia* (Princeton: Princeton University Press, 1991).
25 *See, generally,* Edward Allworth, *The Uzbeks* (Palo Alto: Hoover Institution Press, 1990) and Edward Allworth (ed.), *Central Asia* (Durham: Duke University Press, 1994).
26 K. Karaveev, *Akademiya nauk Kirgizskoi SSR* (Frunze: Ilim, 1974), pp. 24–25.
27 E. A. Belyaev and N. S. Pyshkova, *Formirovanie i razvitie seti nauchnykh uchrezhdenii SSSR* (Moscow: Nauka, 1979), p. 174.
28 Koltsov, *Rol' Akademii nauk v organizatsii regionalnykh nauchnykh tsentrov SSSR*, p. 83.
29 Ibid, p. 84.
30 Ibid, p. 88.
31 Ibid, p. 185.
32 Ibid, pp. 92–93.
33 Ibid, p. 138.
34 For example, in Tajikistan in the 1980s, physics/math and engineering were always in the top three places among all scientists, while physics/math, biology, engineering, and medicine were the four most populous graduate programs in 1987. Gribnev (ed.), *Narodnoe khozyaistvo Tadzhikskoi SSR v 1987 godu*. This trend dates back to the earliest days; in statistics for 1950, well over half of all students at Tajikistan State University were in just two science departments. *Narodnoe khozyaistvo Tadzhikskoi SSR 1968* (Dushanbe: Irfon, 1969).
35 For example, even though numbers slightly declined from 1980–1989, three of the four most populous graduate subjects in Kyrgyzstan (often three of the three most populous) were always engineering, physics/math, and medicine. Biology and chemistry were not far behind. Zhukov (ed.), *Narodnoe khozyaistvo Kirgizskoi SSR v 1989 godu*.
36 Indeed, Japanese scientists in general recognize that Soviet scientific education provided more theory than in Japan and a much greater concentration on the natural sciences. Similarly, students from Central Asia comment frequently that, especially in math and physics, American undergraduate and graduate students are inferior on average to their Central Asian colleagues (of the pre-independence period). The later lack of access to funding, international contacts (i.e. the globally dominant English language scientific community, which remained ignorant of many advances in the Russian-speaking world), and equipment of course limited the abilities of the research efforts of Central Asian scientists. Yet, since this book's topic concerns potential, these latter factors are not relevant.
37 Loren R. Graham, "Preface," in Loren R. Graham (ed.), *Science and the Soviet Social Order* (Cambridge: Harvard University Press, 1990), p. xii.
38 *See Vestnik Akademii nauk Respubliki Kazakhstana* 5 (1996). Issue dedicated to history of the academy.
39 A. M. Kunaev, *Akademiya nauk Kazakhskoi SSR* (Alma-Ata: Nauka, 1978).
40 Loren Graham, *Science in Russia and the Soviet Union* (Cambridge: Cambridge University Press, 1993), p. 232.
41 *See* Kunaev, *Akademiya nauk Kazakhskoi SSR.*
42 Kunaev, *Akademiya nauk Kazakhskoi SSR*, pp. 81–82.
43 S. T. Tabyshaliev *et al.* (eds), *25 let Akademii nauk Kirgizskoi SSR* (Frunze: Ilim, 1980).

44 N. I. Akhunbaeva *et al.*, *Khirurg Akhunbaev* (Frunze: Kyrgyzstan, 1983), pp. 40–41.
45 Koltsov, *Rol' Akademii nauk v organizatsii regionalnykh nauchnykh tsentrov SSSR*, p. 140.
46 Kh. M. Saidmuradov *et al.* (eds), *Akademiya nauk Tadzhikskoi SSR* (Dushanbe: Donish, 1979).
47 Alexander Vucinich, *Empire of Knowledge: The Academy of Sciences of the USSR (1917–1970)* (Berkeley: University of California Press, 1984), p. 183.
48 Saidmuradov *et al.*, *Akademiya nauk Tadzhikskoi SSR*.
49 Sources disagree on the year of formation. Some claim 1924 as the year of formation. See Koltsov, *Rol' Akademii nauk v organizatsii regionalnykh nauchnykh tsentrov SSSR*, p. 34.
50 Ibid, p. 148.
51 Ibid, p. 150.
52 Sadykov *et al.* (eds), *Akademiya nauk Uzbekskoi SSR*, p. 8.
53 *See* Gribnev (ed.), *Narodnoe khozyaistvo Tadzhikskoi SSR v 1987 godu*.
54 *See* http://www.nsf.gov/sbe/srs/databrf/tb297305.gif
55 National Research Council, "Women Scientists and Engineers Employed in Industry: Why So Few?" Available at: http://www.cwru.edu/affil/wwwethics/ecsel/abstracts/women-indust.html
56 *See Narodnoe khozhyaistvo Kazakhstana za 60 let.*
57 Ibid.
58 *Narodnoe khozyaistvo Kirgizskoi SSR v 1978 godu*; *Narodnoe khozyaistvo Kirgizskoi SSR v 1982 godu*, and *Narodnoe khozyaistvo v Kirgizskoi SSR za gody Sovetskoi vlasti* (Frunze: Kyrgyzstan, 1987).
59 *Narodnoe khozyaistvo Tadzhikskoi SSR v 1968 godu* (Dushanbe: Irfon, 1969); *Narodnoe khozyaistvo Tadzhikskoi SSR v 1980 godu* (Dushanbe: Irfon, 1982); and Gribnev (ed.), *Narodnoe khozyaistvo Tadzhikskoi SSR v 1987 gody.*
60 *Narodnoe khozyaistvo Tadzhikskoi SSR v 1980 godu* and Gribnev (ed.), *Narodnoe khozyaistvo Tadzhikskoi SSR v 1987 gody.*
61 *Turkmenistan za 50 let; Turkmenistan v tsifrakh 1986*; and *Narodnoe khozyaistvo Turkmenskoi SSR v 1988* (Ashgabad: Turkmenistan, 1989).
62 *Narodnoe khozhyaistvo Uzbekskoi SSR 1987.*
63 *Turkmenistan za 50 let; Turkmenistan v tsifrakh 1986; Narodnoe khozyaistvo Turkmenskoi SSR v 1988*; and *Narodnoe khozhyaistvo Uzbekskoi SSR 1987.*
64 D. V. Nalivkin. *Nashi pervye zhenschiny-geologi* (Leningrad: Nauka, 1979).
65 UNDP, *1996 Kazakstan UNDP Human Development Report*, (New York: UNDP, 1997).
66 Republic of Kazakhstan, "Ob osnovnykh itogakh fundamentalnykh i prikladnykh issledovanii v Respublike Kazakhstan v 1996–1997 gg." Available at: http://www.president.kz/Science
67 Uzbekistan, in accord with the growth rates of Figure 2.3 of this Chapter claimed forty-six thousand research scientists in 1992, but only twenty-seven thousand in 1995. Republic of Uzbekistan, "Country Profile: Implementation of Agenda 21: Review of Progress Made since the United Nations Conference on Environment and Development, 1992" (1997), http://www.un.org/esa/earthsummit/uzbek-cp.htm. Likewise, it admitted to budget cuts of 70 per cent for research over the same period. Ibid.
68 A. Poladov. "Kto pravil sovetskoi sistemoi" *Turkmenskaya iskra* (June 26, 1998), p. 2.
69 "Postanovleniye Prezidenta Turkmenistana o deyatelnosti Akademii nauk Turkmenistana," *Turkmenskaya iskra* (June 27, 1998), p. 1.
70 Republic of Kazakhstan, "Strategicheskie tseli i prioritety razvytiya nauki do 2030 g." Available at http://www.president.kz/Science
71 "Ob organizatsii Zapadno-Kazakhstanskogo otdeleniya Akaademii nauk Respubliki Kazakhstana," *Vestnik Akaademii nauk Respubliki Kazakhstana* 7 (1992), pp. 3–5.

72 Meaning with an office in and annual expenditures of no less than five million dollars.
73 While this term is used in a variety of contexts, only the general context of develop-
    ment as practiced by the development community is here implied.
74 *See* Kendall E. Bailes, *Science and Russian Culture in an Age of Revolutions*
    (Bloomington: Indiana University Press, 1990), for the story of why V. I. Vernadsky
    chose not to enroll in a university humanities program in the Tsarist era. This trend
    held true not only for many scientists, but also for others who eventually returned to
    the arts. For example, Yevgeny Zamyatin's consistent literary interests and later literary
    career; Zamyatin was trained as an engineer and designed the Soviet Union's first
    icebreaker.
75 *Statisticheskii yezhegodnik Kazakhstana 1994* (Almaty: Goskomstat, 1995) and *Statis-
    ticheskii yezhegodnik Kazakhstana 1996* (Almaty: Almatstatagenstvo, 1997).
76 Author's personal correspondence with Ariana and Catena, June and July 2000.
77 *See, generally,* Saskia Sassen, *Globalization and Its Discontents.*
78 William J. Carrington and Enrica Detragiache, "How Extensive is the Brain Drain?"
    Finance & Development 36 (June, 1999) p. 46. "Immigration flows of individuals with
    no more than a primary education are quite small." Ibid. The authors also suggest that
    numerous developing states lose upwards of 30 per cent of their college educated
    population to emigration to developed states.
79 A. Dianne Schmidley and Campbell Gibson, *Profile of the Foreign-Born Population
    in the United States: 1997* (Washington, D.C.: U.S. Government Printing Office,
    1999), p. 6. I predict that the 2000 census will show unusual success among the
    400,000 recent emigrants from the former Soviet Union and that the 2010 census will
    reveal that this group earns more than native-born Americans, a challenge to current
    conceptions about mediocre Soviet educations and the strengths of the U.S. educa-
    tional system.
80 *See* UNDP, *Human Development Report 2000,* p. 252. Not only is Kazakhstan's
    suicide rate equivalent to Russia's, but it is highest in the areas of the country that are
    most environmentally devastated. Asian Development Bank, *Central Asia Environments
    in Transition,* p. 91.
81 *See,* e.g. United Nations Development Programme, *Making Things Happen: Getting it
    Done* (New York: UNDP Regional Bureau for Europe and CIS, 1998).
82 Derived from WHO, *The World Health Report 2000,* pp. 158–162. Birthrates dropped
    from 18–21 per cent in each republic, a very uniform decrease.
83 Stephen Dalziel, "London's Russians," *BBC World Service On Assignment* (July 10, 2000).
84 *See, generally,* Saskia Sassen, *Globalization and Its Discontents.*
85 In this effect, Central Asia matches precedents from other areas, regardless of
    whether recipient states were declining or growing. "The worldwide evidence shows
    rather clearly that there is considerable patterning in the geography of migrations, and
    that the major receiving countries tend to get immigrants from their zones of
    influence. This holds for countries as diverse as the United States, France, or Japan.
    Immigration is at least partly an outcome of the actions of the governments and major
    private economic actors in receiving countries." Sassen, *Globalization and Its Dis-
    contents,* p. 8.
86 Nursultan Abishevich Nazarbaev, "Respublika v bratskoi sem'e." *Narodnoe
    khozyaistvo Kazakhstana* 2 (1982), p. 2. Nazarbaev was then a republican party second
    tier leader speaking at an academy function.
87 Gro Harlem Brundtland, "Message from the Director General," in *The World Health
    Report 1999,* p. viii.
88 Jeffrey Sachs, "A New Map of the World," *The Economist* (June 24, 2000).
89 Cf. "Uzbekistan has everything to put into action: new innovative models of develop-
    ment founded on the expanded and effective use of scientific and technical possibil-
    ities, wide implementation of the achievements in fundamental and applied sciences,
    scientifically capacious technologies, increase of the number of highly qualified and

gifted scientific experts. This serves as the main requisite and a reliable basis of the country's break through to the rank of economically and industrially developed countries of the world." Islam Karimov, *Uzbekistan on the Threshold of the Twenty-First Century* (Tashkent: Uzbekiston, 1997), p. 223. While Karimov insists that this situation still holds, I argue that as a politician and head of state he feels it expedient to continue to say this although it is no longer true.

3 Formal organizational capital: governments and markets

1 Kolodko, "Ten Years of Postsocialist Transition: the Lessons for Policy Reforms," pp. 8, 16.
2 The previous Chapter's assertion that most wealth creation stems from human capital, not natural or physical capital, assumed only three kinds of capital. Injecting a fourth kind of capital, organizational, reduces the absolute contribution of human capital and explains how the former USSR can have exuberant human capital and yet be in decline. Together, human and organizational capital constitute the source of the bulk of the world's wealth creation.
3 Black boxes represent, for cyberneticians, complex feedback relationships and networks. In the place of such relationships or networks, engineers and scientists "draw a little box about which they need to know nothing but its input and output." Bruno Latour, *Science in Action: How to Follow Scientists and Engineers Through Society* (Cambridge: Harvard University Press, 1987), p. 3. *See also* Brian Greene, *The Elegant Universe: Superstrings, Hidden Dimensions, and the Quest for the Ultimate Theory* (New York: Vintage Books, 1999), p. 57.
4 Beyond ideological difference between proponents labeling themselves identically, this divergence is also due to the fact that organizations need not be the products of intentional design, but may evolve.
5 In March 1991, a USSR-wide referendum was held on whether to keep the USSR intact. Over 3/4 of voters cast their ballots in support of "preserving the union," and the author's firsthand experience in Kazakhstan and Russia during the week of voting confirms that on that day the mood of voters was indeed in favor of keeping the union. Moreover, voters in Central Asia constituted the single most avowedly pro-union region. *See* Gleason, *The Central Asian States*, pp. 74–75. Thus, not only was the demise of the USSR (as opposed to the mere secession of some republics) a violation of national and international law, it was also a violation of democratic principles.
6 Not courts applying positive law (*lex*), but the turns toward natural law (*jus*) witnessed in post-Nazi Germany, among other places. H. L. A. Hart, *The Concept of Law* (New York: Oxford University Press, 1998), p. 208.
7 In sociological terms, this definition would fall within behavioralist or utilitarian schools, the appeal of both of which has been reduced through arguments similar to those voiced below.
8 This does not, of course, imply or assume that all human behavior is rational, nor does it need go as far as some economic and anthropological analyses in the functionalist vein. While an analysis of the meaning of rationalism for the social sciences is beyond the scope of this analysis, *see generally* Martin Hollis and Steven Lukes (eds), *Rationality and Relativism* (Cambridge: MIT Press, 1982). Also significantly, my analysis ellides the epistemology of incentives, a set of questions examined most prominently in contemporary scholarship by neo-functionalist law and economic scholars. *See* Ellickson, *Order Without Law: How Neighbors Settle Disputes* and Richard A. Posner, *The Economics of Justice* (Cambridge: Harvard University Press, 1990).
9 Cf. Theory of action sociologists would argue that unreflexive responses invalidate the rational-actor model. *See* Lynne G. Zucker, "The Role of Institutionalization in Cultural Persistence," *American Sociological Review* 42 (1977), pp. 726–743. Yet, the law

and economics (organization economics) response to such alleged irrationality would be that it is often less costly, and so more efficient, to pursue habitual (unreflexive, black box) responses than to expend the resources needed to make an intentional, rational decision. The unproved meta-assertion of law and economics is that, if over a sufficient time period the losses incurred from such unreflexive activity outweigh the gains from economizing on costs of decisionmaking, then the unreflexive response will break down and yield to either a new unreflexive response or intentional decision-making. Similarly, "irrational" organizations, even those the product of careful human design, may persist even when they become suboptimal. Cf. Lynne G. Zucker, "Production of Trust: Institutional Sources of Economic Structure, 1840–1920," *Research in Organizational Behavior* 8 (1986), pp. 53–111.

10 For an overview of the context of nationality in this regard, *see* Ronald L. Jepperson and John W. Meyer, "The Public Order and the Construction of Formal Organizations," in Walter W. Powell and Paul J. DiMaggio (eds), *The New Institutionalism in Organizational Analysis* (Chicago: University of Chicago Press, 1991), pp. 204–231.

11 One regime scholar has acknowledged this feedback through the insight that organizations "do not merely reflect the preferences and power of the units constituting them; the [organizations] themselves shape those preferences and that power." Robert O. Keohane, "International Institutions: Two Research Programs," *International Studies Quarterly* 32: (1988), pp. 379–396.

12 For arguments for relativism in the social sciences, *see* Hollis and Lukes (eds), *Rationality and Relativism*.

13 Because pure Pigouvian and pure Coasian administrative solutions to externalities are impractical in real world situations, complex compromises between the two capture the majority of efforts of and immensity of the task set before modern governments. *See* Ugo Mattei, *Comparative Law and Economics* (Ann Arbor: University of Michigan Press, 1998), pp. 63–70.

14 Amartya Sen, *Poverty and Famines: An Essay on Entitlement and Deprivation* (New York: Oxford University Press, 1981).

15 Ibid., p. 7.

16 Stemming back to the introduction of the term comparative advantage in the 19th century by Ricardo. *See* David Ricardo, *Principles of Political Economy and Taxation* (Amherst, New York: Prometheus Books, 1996).

17 *See* Francis Fukuyama, *Trust: The Social Virtues and the Creation of Prosperity* (New York: The Free Press, 1995). *Also see* Fukuyama, *Social Capital and Civil Society.*

18 For Nash equilibria, *see* Martin J. Osborne and Ariel Rubinstein, *A Course in Game Theory* (Cambridge: MIT Press, 1994), pp. 14–15. For the application of related concepts to good government, *see* Jerry L. Mashaw, *Greed, Chaos & Governance: Using Public Choice to Improve Public Law* (New Haven: Yale University Press, 1999), pp. 185–195.

19 *See* Douglass C. North, *Institutions, Institutional Change and Economic Performance* (New York: Cambridge University Press, 1990).

20 David Christian, *Imperial and Soviet Russia* (New York: St. Martin's Press, 1997), pp. 372–373.

21 Herman E. Daly, "Problems with Free Trade: Neoclassical and Steady-state Perspectives," in Durwood Zaelke *et al.* (eds), *Trade and the Environment: Law, Economics and Policy* (Washington, D.C.: Island Press, 1993), p. 157.

22 While the Kazakhstan opposition cites *Financial Times* and *Guardian* articles from recent years as proof that Nazarbaev is worth several billion dollars, in fact neither publication ever included Nazarbaev in lists of the world's richest people. Despite this folk myth, Nazarbaev is very wealthy and he personally has extensive foreign holdings.

23 For instance, Uzbekistan resisted packages of economic reform pushed by the IMF in the last decade, and in response was widely condemned. Specifically, Uzbekistan was almost daily criticized for not being more like Kyrgyzstan. With the collapse of the

economies in Russia and Kyrgyzstan, who were among the most compliant with respect to World Bank and IMF lending programs, ironically, multilateral lenders now discuss the normative advantages of the "Uzbekistan model of development." Jeromin Zettelmeyer, "The Uzbek Growth Puzzle," *IMF Staff Papers* 46(3) (1999), pp. 274–292

24 United Nations General Assembly, "United Nations Millennium Declaration," UNGA A/55/L.2 (September 6, 2000), art. 24.

25 Bruce Ackerman, *We The People: Foundations* (Cambridge: Harvard University Press, 1991).

26 This analysis, for purposes of space, ignores the issue of local governments and their role as checks on the national government. This elision is possible only because local governments in all republics are headed by presidential appointees, and in no republic has the legislature or judiciary emerged as the power broker. While local government is a crucial factor in balancing key coalitions and fueling patronage systems in every republic, only in Tajikistan could one argue that regions have really been a transparent check on national power, and in that republic those tensions (serving as a proxy for regional oligarchic economic interests) were the primary reason for the civil war.

27 Gleason, *The Central Asian States*, p. 85.

28 Constitution of Turkmenistan (May, 1992); Constitution of the Republic of Uzbekistan (December, 1992); Constitution of the Kyrgyz Republic (May, 1993); and Constitution of the Republic of Tajikistan (November, 1994).

29 This referendum's results were legally invalid because the referendum failed to attract enough voters; 50 per cent of eligible voters must have voted in order for referendum results to have had legal force. 1995 Presidential Decree Having the Force of a Constitutional Law On Republican Referenda, art. 32. The government, drawing on Soviet practice, fudged the results to make the results appear valid. Assertion based on author's observations during the referendum. Likewise, the last act of the legislature in 1995, giving Nazarbaev the power to adopt decrees with the force of law explicitly violated the 1993 Constitution's nondelegatory vesting of lawmaking power in the legislature. 1993 Kazakhstan Constitution, Preamble (stating that state power is based on the separation of legislative and executive branches) and art. 62 (stating that the legislature is the "only legislative" body in the Republic of Kazakhstan).

30 The United States was the most aggressive such state. Barnabas Johnson, "The Role of the United States in the Erosion and Collapse of Constitutional Governance in Kazakhstan," *Central Asia Monitor* 6 (1995), pp. 14–19.

31 For a more wide-ranging review of the phenomenal organizational capital inviability of USAID programs in Kazakhstan, *see* Matt Bivens, "Aboard the Gravy Train: In Kazakstan, the Farce that is U.S. Foreign Aid," *Harper's Magazine* (August, 1997), pp. 69–76.

32 Gleason, the most influential Western writer on this subject, is misleading about the source of this illegality. He asserts that "Akaev's constitutional referendum itself was patently illegal since Kyrgyzstan's constitution only empowered the parliament, not the president, to call referenda." Gleason, *The Central Asian States*, p. 100. However, under the original 1993 Kyrgyzstan Constitution, art. 46.5, the President was entitled to call referenda on questions of "state life;" the legal meaning of "state life" is constrained to a sphere of issues separate from "state structure," which would be the appropriate legal term for a constitutional change. To wit, art. 96 explicitly stated that the constitution could be amended only by the legislature, not by direct popular vote. Thus, a popular referendum to amend the constitution was illegal, although in general the President could call referenda.

33 Gleason, *The Central Asian States*, p. 100.

34 The People's Council consists of the president, government ministers, regional governors, people's advisors (allegedly democratically elected), the legislature, and the chairpersons of high courts of law. Constitution of Turkmenistan, Chapter 2.

35 Constitution of Tajikistan, art. 65. Since the 1994 Constitution was adopted concurrent to the 1994 presidential election, the argument can (incredulously) be made that Rakhmonov has been elected only once for the purposes of this constitution's two term limit.

36 Aleksandr Melekhov, "Sostav pravitelstva ne tolko obnovilsya, no i sokratilsya," *Kabar News Agency Analytical Brief* (January 9, 2001); http://www.kabar.gov.kg/russian/gazet/2001/01/9htm.

37 *See, generally,* Gleason, *The Central Asian States.*

38 Oleh Havrylyshyn and John Odling-Smee, "Political Economy of Stalled Reforms," *Finance & Development* 37 (September, 2000), p. 8.

39 Ibid.

40 Beyond the zero-sum implications of corruption, economists identify another important implication of corruption applicable to Central Asia, especially to the region's interesting history of mega-projects, such as Kazakhstan's new capital in Astana, Kyrgyzstan's Manas celebrations, Tajikistan's monument to Oli Somon, Turkmenistan's "Lake of the Golden Century," and Uzbekistan's noticeable Washington, D.C. embassy. "One specific channel through which corruption may harm economic performance is by distorting the composition of government expenditure.... Corrupt politicians [are] more inclined to spend on fighter aircraft and large-scale investment projects than on textbooks and teachers' salaries." Mauro, "Corruption: Causes, Consequences, and Agenda for Further Research," p. 12.

41 Stanley Fischer and Ratna Sahay, "Economies in Transition: Taking Stock," *Finance & Development* 37 (September, 2000), pp. 2–6.

42 To complement this picture, only in September 2000 were the replica of Boston's "Make Way for Ducklings" bronze statues that also charm Moscow's children restored in Moscow. The statues, donated by Barbara Bush in 1991 were stolen for scrap, sawed off at the legs, in 1999. Anna Dolgov, "Stolen duck statues restored in Moscow," *Boston Globe* (September 18, 2000).

43 A third basic goal should be to effect sustainable scale, but this goal is only slowly gaining support among mainstream economists. *See* Daly, "Problems with Free Trade: Neoclassical and Steady-state Perspectives," p. 156.

44 *See* Peter Elkind, "The Pirate of Prague: The Incredible Half-Billion-Dollar Azerbaijani Oil Swindle," *Fortune* 141 (March 6, 2000), p. 106; King Banaian, *The Ukrainian Economy Since Independence* (Northampton, MA: Edward Elgar, 1999); and Andrei Shleifer and Daniel Treisman, *Without a Map: Political Tactics and Economic Reform in Russia* (Cambridge: MIT Press, 2000). IMF and World Bank sources hint at failures of privatization in Central Asia, but offer no details. *But see* Jeanne Whalen, "Kazakhstan: Foreigners Feel the Pain," *Financial Times* (July 1, 1999), p. 4.

45 For example, Aristotle and Tolstoy. *See* Kahn, *The Cultural Study of Law.*

46 *See, generally,* Jeffrey D. Sachs and Katharina Pistor (eds), *The Rule of Law and Economic Reform in Russia* (Boulder: Westview Press, 1998). In their introduction, the editors exemplify this commitment to an implicit belief that there exists a Rosetta Stone to development.

47 *See* W.E. Butler, "Perestroika and the Rule of Law," in W.E. Butler (ed.), *Russian Legal Theory* (New York: New York University Press, 1996), pp. 417–431. Moreover, this concern with rule of law was not new in Russia. The "liberal intellectual tradition in pre-revolutionary Russia was [strong and]...the main concern of Russia's liberal thinkers was the problem of the rule of law." Andrzej Walicki, *Legal Philosophies of Russian Liberalism* (Notre Dame: University of Notre Dame Press, 1992), p. 1.

48 For example, laws on social associations, on cooperatives, on environmental protection, and on religion; in many cases these laws were better enforced and more liberal than their donor funded post-Soviet replacements.

49 For example, Kazakhstan's Green Salvation sued Alma-Ata's mayor for negligent homicide in an environmental suit. Eric W. Sievers, "The Caspian, Regional Seas, and the Case for a Cultural Study of Law," *Georgetown International Environmental Law Journal* 13 (2001), pp. 397–98.

50 Eric W. Sievers, "Caspian Environment Programme: Prospects for Regime Formation and Effectiveness," in William Ascher and Natalia Mirovitskaya (eds), *The Caspian Sea: A Quest for Environmental Security*, (Amsterdam: Kluwer Academic Publishers, 2000), pp. 338–339.

51 *See* Robert Cooter and Thomas Ulen, *Law & Economics* (New York: Addison-Wesley, 1999), p. 70; James Q. Whitman, "Ancient Rights and Wrongs: At the Origins of Law and the State: Supervision of Violence, Mutilation of Bodies, or Setting of Prices?" *Chicago Kent Law Review* 71 (1995), p. 41.

52 For an illustrative example of the connection between defeat and belief systems, *see* Paul Forman, "Weimar culture, causality, and quantum theory, 1918–1927: Adaptation by German physicists and mathematicians to a hostile intellectual environment," *Historical Studies in the Physical Sciences* 3 (1991), pp. 1–115.

53 Fischer and Sahay, "Economies in Transition: Taking Stock," p. 2.

4 Social capital: civil society and solidarity

1 To complement the preceding chapter's views on rule of law, the concept of rule of law is not contained in one axis of organizational capital, but depends upon the interaction between the formal content of laws, formal organizational enforcement of law, informal norms of lawfulness, and impacts of informal actors on incentives to obey the law.

2 Alejandro Portes and Patricia Landolt, "The Downside of Social Capital," *The American Prospect* 26 (May–June 1996), pp. 18–21. *Also see* Giles Mohan and Kristian Stokke, "Participatory Development and Empowerment: The Dangers of Localism," *Third World Quarterly* 21 (2000), pp. 247–268.

3 *See* World Bank Group, "Social Capital for Development," http://www.worldbank. org/poverty/scapital /index.htm. "Social capital is defined as the norms and social relations embedded in the social structures of societies that enable people to coordinate action to achieve desired goals." Ibid.

4 *See* Francis Fukuyama, "Social Capital and Civil Society." Concurrently, Fukuyama defines social capital as "society's stock of shared values" and "a set of informal values or norms shared among members of a group that permits cooperation among them." Francis Fukuyama, *The Great Disruption: Human Nature and the Reconstitution of Social Order* (New York: Simon & Schuster, 2000), pp. 14, 16.

5 *See generally*, Ellickson, *Order Without Law: How Neighbors Settle Disputes*, pp. 64–66.

6 *See* Putnam, *Bowling Alone*, pp. 22–24.

7 As a consequence, social capital is not a "public good;" it can be created and enjoyed by individuals. Some social capital scholars erroneously treat social capital as a public good underproduced by markets. For a general refutation, *see* Fukuyama, *The Great Disruption: Human Nature and the Reconstitution of Social Order*, pp. 255–257.

8 Putnam, *Bowling Alone*. Fukuyama's *The Great Disruption: Human Nature and the Reconstitution of Social Order* attempts to survey social capital in the entire developed world, but lacks Putnam's general depth, any appropriate local sources, and breadth.

9 This fieldwork, conducted 1997–2000, drew primarily upon two methodologies: multi-point ethnography and sociological survey. My research was supported by Switzer Foundation, the USEPA, National Research Council, Coca-Cola World Fund, and a Boren Fellowship.

10 *See* James S. Coleman, "The Creation and Destruction of Social Capital: Implications for the Law," *Journal of Law, Ethics, and Public Policy* 3 (1988), pp. 375–404.

11 Fukuyama, *The Great Disruption: Human Nature and the Reconstitution of Social Order*, p. 30.
12 *See* Kaplan, *The Ends of the Earth: A Journey at the Dawn of the 21st Century.*
13 Fukuyama misses this point, conflating the lack of an independent Soviet civil society with a total absence of both social capital and secondary associations. Fukuyama, *Trust: The Social Virtues and the Creation of Prosperity*, pp. 54–55, *passim*. To read Fukuyama is to imagine the USSR as a place where people went to work and then came home to (conniving) families, nothing more; in between the individual and state there were "virtually no social groups whatsoever." Ibid., p. 55. Excluded from Fukuyama's view are the facts that Soviets socialized outside the family in informal secondary associations. *See*, description of "spontaneous socializing" in Ibid. They also prized family, participated in many formal secondary associations (which while state-run were still secondary), and had potentially greater access to several forms of association (ballet schools, civil aviation clubs, etc.) than Western counterparts.
14 Adele Lindenmeyr, *Poverty is Not A Vice: Charity, Society, and the State in Imperial Russia* (Princeton: Princeton University Press, 1996), pp. 101–102.
15 Ibid., p. 237.
16 Thomas Owen, *The Corporation under Russian Law, 1800–1917* (Cambridge: Cambridge University Press, 1991), p. 48.
17 Ibid., p. 107.
18 Vucinich, *Science in Russian Culture 1861–1917*, p. 83.
19 For information on these science-oriented NGOs, *see* Graham, *Science in Russia and the Soviet Union* and Vucinich, *Science in Russian Culture 1861–1917.*
20 Ibid., pp. 229–231.
21 Christian, *Imperial and Soviet Russia*, pp. 141–143.
22 I. A. Isaev, *Istoriya gosudarstva i prava Rossii* (Moscow: Yurist, 1996), p. 313.
23 Richard Lorenz, "Economic Bases of the Basmachi Movement in the Farghana Valley," in Edward Allworth (ed.), *Muslim Communities Reemerge* (Durham: Duke University Press, 1994), p. 277.
24 *See* Sukhareva, *Kvartalnaya obschina pozdnefeodalnogo goroda Bukhary.*
25 Helene Carrere d'Encausse, "The Stirring of National Feeling," in Edward Allworth (ed.), *Central Asia* (Durham: Duke University Press, 1994), p. 172. *References omitted.* History repeats itself; a Kazakhstan deputy minister of internal affairs issued a letter to regional departments of internal affairs on 22 October 1997 warning them that NGOs were really revolutionary societies. Anonymous, "Kazakstan Government Threatens Human Rights," *Ecostan News* 6 (1994), pp. 2–4.
26 d'Encausse, "The Stirring of National Feeling," p. 196.
27 Ibid., p. 198.
28 Ibid., p. 191.
29 *See* Ibid.
30 *See* Galina Kudryavtseva, *Materialnaya osnova deyatelnosti obschestvennykh organizatsii na sovremennom etape* (Moscow: Nauka, 1988). *See also* Aron Isaakovich Schiglik, *Zakonomernosti stanovleniya i razvitiya obschestvennykh organizatsii v SSSR* (Moscow: Nauka, 1977), pp. 3–4. SSGOs are the subject of the next Section.
31 This terminology differs from that used in Soviet texts, but accurately conveys the conceptions in these texts.
32 According to the standard Soviet legal account, only bourgeois democracies required separation of powers given their intrinsic lack of a state purpose. In contrast, the USSR was imagined to have a clear purpose (in the Hegelian sense) and its agents to have undivided loyalties.
33 Soviet political scientists, economists, and legal scholars envisaged social and environmental problems as resulting from the rent-seeking of private actors. Since all relevant actors in the Soviet economy (factories, planners, state agencies) were supposed to be agents of the state and people, rent-seeking was *a priori* precluded.

34 Conflicts between nonstate and state agencies were similarly theoretically precluded by the confluence of fiduciary duties. While nonstate agencies could claim to overcome certain transaction costs (particularly in information and monitoring costs), they could not reasonably be imagined to be in conflict with the state. Beginning in the Constitution of the USSR in 1936, and continuing until a February 1990 removal of the clause, Article 6 (art. 126 in the 1936 Constitution) defined the climate in which social associations operated: "The Communist Party of the Soviet Union is the leading and guiding force of Soviet society and the nucleus of its political system and of state agencies and social associations. The CPSU exists for the people and serves the people ...." USSR art. 6 (1976).

35 Since the values of nonstate organizations were merely in their subsidiarity (both in terms of issue disaggregation and in terms of geographic particularity), it would be wasteful for the Soviet state or people to have two clubs for radio enthusiasts, two environmental organizations, or two women's councils. Accordingly, Soviet civil society was diverse in a corporatist, but not a pluralistic, sense.

36 Putnam implicates television as perhaps the major culprit in the decline of social capital in the United States. Putnam notes that television "privatizes" personal lives, an interesting observation considering privatization of state assets throughout the former Soviet Union. Robert D. Putnam, "Tuning In, Tuning Out: The Strange Disappearance of Social Capital in America" (Unpublished speech delivered as the 1995 Ithiel de Sola Pool Lecture of the American Political Science Association).

37 Vitalii Ponomarev, *Obschestvennye organizatsii v Kazakhstane i Kyrgyzstane 1987–1991* (Alma-Ata: Glagol, 1991), p. 6. For the earliest coherent English language report on NGOs in Kazakhstan *see* Bess Brown, "Informal Groups in Kazakhstan," *Radio Liberty Research Report, RL 549/88* (December 1, 1988). For a more current general theoretical investigation of NGOs in Central Asia *see* Saltmarshe, "Civil Society and Sustainable Development in Central Asia."

38 Ponomarev, *Obschestvennye organizatsii v Kazakhstane i Kyrgyzstane 1987–1991*, p. 82.

39 For Ponomarev, "political" does not mean partisan, but engagement in any activity that could have an eventual political character. Thus, this includes almost all environmental, ethnic, publication, and even discussion NGOs.

40 Ingvar Svanberg, "Kazakhs," in Graham Smith (ed.), *The Nationalities Question in the Soviet Union* (New York: Longman, 1990), p. 208.

41 Ponomarev, *Obschestvennye organizatsii v Kazakhstane i Kyrgyzstane 1987–1991*, p. 7.

42 Ibid., p. 82.

43 Ibid.

44 "Razbuzhennoi initsiative- politicheskuyu zrelost i sozidatelnost," *Kazakhstanskaya Pravda* (November 27, 1988), pp. 1–2.

45 Ponomarev, *Obschestvennye organizatsii v Kazakhstane i Kyrgyzstane 1987–1991*, p. 11.

46 S. Kuratov and A. Salin, "Gotovtes, katastrofa zaplanirovana," *Panorama* (October 18, 1990), p. 4.

47 Ponomarev, "Sostoyaniye i tendentsiya razvitiye dobrovol'cheskogo sektora v Kazakhstane", p. 65.

48 Ponomarev, *Obschestvennye organizatsii v Kazakhstane i Kyrgyzstane 1987–1991*, pp. 7, 82. *Also see* Ponomarev, "Sostoyaniye i tendentsiya razvitiye dobrovol'cheskogo sektora v Kazakhstane" and Svanberg, "Kazaks."

49 Sergei Kuratov, "The Kazakstan Green Movement" (Unpublished 1993 Report commissioned by the HIVOS Foundation).

50 Gregory Gleason, "The 'National Factor' and the Logic of Sovietology," in Alexander J. Motyl (ed.), *The Post-Soviet Nations* (New York: Columbia University Press, 1992), pp. 1–29.

51 Roughly one tenth of the entire area of Kazakhstan, much of it degraded through testings, was under the jurisdiction of the Soviet military. Thus, the case of Moscow's problems suddenly becoming Almaty's problems was much larger than simply the one

Semipalatinsk testing ground. *See* Ponomarev, "Sostoyaniye i tendentsiya razvitiye dobrovol'cheskogo sektora v Kazakhstane."

52 Executive Board of the United Nations Development Programme and of the United Nations Population Fund, "Second Country Cooperation Framework for Uzbekistan (2000–2004)" (July 17, 2000); DP/CCF/UZB/2, p. 3.

53 N. Ilolov, "A chto ob ekoobrazovanii na Pamire?" *Tabiat* 13 (1996).

54 The content of this section comes from Sievers, "Uzbekistan's Mahalla: From Soviet to Absolutist Residential Associations." The full article contains much more extensive historical and ethnographic analyses.

55 V. I. Chekharina, "Organy obschestvennoi samodeyatelnosti v sfere kultury i narodnogo obrazovaniya," in Aron Isaakovich Schiglik (ed.), *Organy obschestvennoi samodeyatelnosti kak forma sotsialisticheskoi demokratii* (Moscow: Nauka, 1988), pp. 76–113.

56 V. I. Kriger, "Organy obschestvennoi samodeyatelnosti v sfere okhrany pravoporyadka," in Schiglik (ed.), *Organy obschestvennoi samodeyatelnosti kak forma sotsialisticheskoi demokratii*, pp. 150–208.

57 For general descriptions of the powers and activities of all types of women's councils and residential committees, *see* O. V. Orlova, "Territorialnye organy obschestvennoi samodeyatelnosti," in Schiglik (ed.), *Organy obschestvennoi samodeyatelnosti kak forma sotsialisticheskoi demokratii*, pp. 25–75.

58 Uzbekistan law currently differentiates mahalla on the basis of administrative subordination. All urban mahalla are the same under the law, while a separate legal regime exists for town, village, and settlement mahalla. Zakon Respubliki Uzbekistan Ob organakh samoupravleniya grazhdan (September 2, 1993, revised on April 14, 1999), Olii Majlis Resolution 758-1, arts. 10–11.

59 Sukhareva, *Kvartalnaya obschina pozdnefeodalnogo goroda Bukhary*, p. 13. In U.S. urban sociology and property scholarship, the term face-block means only two sides of one street. Albert J. Hunter and Gerald D. Suttles, "The Expanding Community of Limited Liability," in Gerald D. Suttles (ed.), *The Social Construction of Community* (Chicago: University of Chicago Press, 1972), pp. 44–81, 55–57. In the context used here, it means two sides of a main street, as well as the more minor streets and alleys that branch off along this length.

60 David M. Abramson, "Traditionalizing Modernities and Modernizing Traditions: The Forming and Reforming of Ideologies in Post-Soviet Uzbekistan" (Unpublished paper presented at 1997 American Anthropological Meeting in Washington, DC).

61 Sukhareva, *Kvartalnaya obschina pozdnefeodalnogo goroda Bukhary*, p. 19.

62 For the pre-Soviet era, Sukhareva has outlined many of the mechanisms that existed to channel this influence. For instance, in selection of aksaqal, the wealthy often expressed their preferences to the imam of the local mosque, who was in charge of nominating candidates. Ibid., p. 33.

63 A *sunnat toi* celebrates circumcision while a *beshik toi* (cradle celebration) occurs 40 days after birth.

64 Prayers are used to mark events of importance not of national importance (yedi). Yedi include such celebrations as Kurban-yedi (thanksgiving), in which food is distributed to relatives and the poor.

65 Marking the 7th, 12th, and 14th days after death, as well as the first anniversary after death. Funeral ceremonies are usually celebrated as *ertalabki osh* (morning pilau).

66 *Novruz* is the Islamic New Year and *Mustakillik* is Independence Day.

67 Sharing similarities with rotating credit institutions the world over, participants contribute funds to a common pot, which is then handed over to a participant to hold (with a small part of the receipts) at a male only or female only evening *gap* ("discussion," an occasion for ebullient feasting, song, and drinking) that usually precedes that participant's outlays to organize a wedding or funeral event. This mix of mutual benefit and charity contributions is both important, and not really charitable in a larger context, since *gap* is not really anonymous. In a rare empirical demonstration of Ellickson's

"even-up" strategy for maintaining equity and social order in a close-knit group, individual members keep detailed records of to whom, when, and for what such contributions are made, so as to provide a basis for each successive bilateral contribution. *See* Ellickson, *Order Without Law: How Neighbors Settle Disputes*, pp. 225–229.

68 Because of *gap*, the events that concentrate attention of funds to purchase expensive presents instead of on funds to feed hundreds of people often still do have a community-gathering component.

69 In the post-Soviet period, with increased mobility, many wealthy mahalla residents are moving out of home mahalla to certain more fashionable new mahalla to avoid this pressure.

70 Sukhareva, *Kvartalnaya obschina pozdnefeodalnogo goroda Bukhary*, pp. 21–22.

71 The government, in fact, notarized the appointment of an aksaqal on the petition of elders of the mahalla. Aksaqal were also charged with preventing, through mediation, court cases between residents of various mahalla. Ibid., p. 35.

72 Accordingly, social norms almost certainly lie behind many institutions that previous scholarship could only imagine to be the product of a coercive and attentive state. Increasingly, social coordination is replacing coercion in historical narratives, but the implications of this shift for social theory have yet to be fully appreciated.

73 Koroteyeva and Makarova, The Assertion of Uzbek National Identity: Nativisation or State-Building Process? (Unpublished paper presented August 24, 1995 at the Fifth European Seminar on Central Asian Studies, Copenhagen University) Copy on file with author.

74 In the post-Soviet system, a resident whose house is taken (i.e. for a new apartment complex) may exercise one of three options. He may demand a free apartment in the new building; he may demand that the taking agency construct a house on a new plot of land; or he may demand compensation for the house and all improvements made to the land. Law of the Republic of Uzbekistan On Privatization of the State Housing Supply (May 7, 1993), art. 8.

75 Koroteyeva and Makarova, "The Assertion of Uzbek National Identity: Nativisation or State-Building Process?"

76 Cf. "The Soviet state was content to leave the mahalla to its traditional functions as long as it maintained the ideological appearance of a Soviet institution." Ibid.

77 1999 Mahalla Law, art. 7.

78 Koroteyeva and Makarova, "The Assertion of Uzbek National Identity: Nativisation or State-Building Process?"

79 Actual investigation of these questions is still premature. Most mahalla interactions occur without reference to the law. More pertinently, the findings presented here reflect conditions prior to the passage of the 1999 Mahalla Law. Even though provisions of this law (like state salaries for mahalla leaders) had been implemented in practice prior to passage of the law, it is still too early to determine what effect this law will have on mahalla dynamics.

80 Unreported survey data on file with author. The author took no part in this research.

81 Forms of real property are defined in art. 83 of the 1996 Civil Code.

82 We chose these three cities based on the regional differences highlighted in the original survey, the cities are in the Fergana Valley (Andijan), Tashkent, and the Zeravshan Valley (Samarkand).

83 Asked to rank 10 factors for their importance in influencing purchasing decisions, price was most important for 33 of 83 respondents (mean = 1.7), and presence of relatives within a mahalla was most important for 23 (mean = 2.2). All other factors were also important; no factor was never named most important. In a Kruskal-Wallis test, there is no significant difference between city and relatives (chi-squared = 1.5 with two degrees of freedom), but for ranking of price, there is a chi-squared value of 23.

84 The proxy here is whether or not home buyers turned to non-family to a meaningful degree for advice before purchasing. Non-family advisors primarily included friends.

Whether or not an individual turns to non-family for advice on home purchases is predicted strongly ($z = 2.4$, significant at 0.01 level) by which area of Uzbekistan he or she inhabits, again reinforcing the suggestion that there are significant regional differences.

85 The survey was restricted to those who purchased in the past 5 years.

86 Cf. Less than 1 per cent of rural mahalla residents ignore community rituals in general, while nearly 15 per cent of urban residents ignore such rituals. Generally, richer families and more well-educated individuals are far more likely to abstain from community rituals.

87 It is this lack of checks and balances, both within mahalla and within the political system of Uzbekistan itself, that precludes characterization of mahalla as comparable to American condominium associations or more innovative models of urban residential/development associations, such as the Neighborhood Improvement Districts advocated by Ellickson. *See* Ellickson, "New Institutions for Old Neighborhoods." Notwithstanding observations about the unsuitability of courts in Uzbekistan, some effective mechanisms for oversight and accountability is needed.

88 Ibid., p. 100.

89 "Thus, despite attempts to distribute aid through mahalla networks, this focus on mahalla may well strengthen bureaucratic means at the expense of less formal and decentralized ones." Abramson, *"Constructing Corruption: Foreign Aid, Bureaucratization, and Uzbek Social Networks"* (Unpublished paper presented March 20, 2000 at Harvard University).

90 Koroteyeva and Makarova report that this new function gives rise to much mahalla conflict. Koroteyeva and Makarova, "The Assertion of Uzbek National Identity: Nativisation or State-Building Process?" A mitigating component of this system is that aid should not be distributed until a family submits a formal application that outlines family assets, income, and employment and/or until the mahalla committee directly documents the assets of a family. Coudouel and Marnie, "The Mahalla System of Allocating Social Assistance in Uzbekistan." Yet, such disclosures can also work to increasing the leverage of rais and other kengash members within the community.

91 Fukuyama, *The Great Disruption: Human Nature and the Reconstitution of Social Order*, p. 31.

92 Karl A. Wittfogel, Oriental Despotism: A Comparative Study of Total Power (New Haven: Yale University Press, 1957). Indeed, the trend among Western economists, political scientists, and legal scholars of Central Asia is to ignore any social theory that is not statist, and the hydraulic theory is virtually unchallenged still in these communities. For the best recent example, *see* Gregory Gleason, *The Central Asian States*, pp. 37–39 (offering titillating lore about despotism, such as that unsuccessful candidates for office of watermaster were, by rule, executed).

93 For Central Asia, the principle such histories include the work of Wilhelm Barthold, Robert McChesney, and Olga Sukhareva, among others.

94 Hiltunen, *Environmental Development Co-Operation Opportunities*, p. 50.

95 Portes and Landolt, "The Downside of Social Capital."

96 Fukuyama, *The Great Disruption: Human Nature and the Reconstitution of Social Order*, pp. 28–31.

97 Ibid., p. 29.

98 Fukuyama, *Trust: The Social Virtues and the Creation of Prosperity*, pp. 7–9.

99 Ibid., pp. 28, *passim*.

100 Ibid., pp. 140–141.

101 Since Fukuyama's claim that China lacked these things is probably not correct in the first place (pers. communication with Peter Perdue January 30, 2001), my point here is not to use Fukuyama to describe China in any way, but merely to point out the range of deficiencies in Fukuyama's data, and the implications of these deficiencies.

102 Fukuyama, *The Great Disruption: Human Nature and the Reconstitution of Social Order*, pp. 143–144.

103 *See* Fukuyama, *Trust: The Social Virtues and the Creation of Prosperity.*

104 This is the natural corollary to his earlier conclusion that "a nation's well being, as well as its ability to compete, is conditioned by a single, pervasive cultural characteristic: the level of trust inherent in the society." Fukuyama, *Trust: The Social Virtues and the Creation of Prosperity*, p. 7.

105 *See* Robert Cooter, "Law from Order: Economic Development and the Jurisprudence of Social Norms," John M. Olin Working Papers in Law, Economics, and Institutions 96/97-4 (1997). *See also* Robert Cooter, "Inventing Market Property: The Land Courts of Papua New Guinea." *Law and Society Review* 25 (1991), p. 759.

106 *See* Eric A. Posner, "The Regulation of Groups: The Influence of Legal and Nonlegal Sanctions on Collective Action," *University of Chicago Law Review* 63 (1996), p. 133.

5 International environmental regimes and international environmental law

1 Even as early as 1992, there were at least 900 international environmental agreements. Harold K. Jacobson and Edith Brown Weiss, "A Framework for Analysis," in Edith Brown Weiss and Harold K. Jacobson (eds), *Engaging Countries: Strengthening Compliance with International Environmental Accords* (Cambridge: MIT Press, 1998), pp. 1–18.

2 For purposes of conserving natural capital, democratic rule of law is not a necessity. While an environmental autocracy could preserve the global environment (at the expense of other interests), this possibility is largely irrelevant at present since dominant sentiments abhor such a solution and since no such autocrat exists.

3 This norm is reflected in the Constitution of Kazakhstan (art. 3), the Constitution of the Kyrgyz Republic (art. 1), the Constitution of Tajikistan (art. 6), the Constitution of Turkmenistan (art. 2), and the Constitution of Uzbekistan (art. 7).

4 The rule for determining custom is that state practice must conform to the proposed content of that custom, and that conforming behavior must have arisen from a belief among states that they had no choice but to so behave without violating international law (*opinio juris*). Since this test is circular and tries to pass off a subjective test as objective, its determinations are always open to contention. Likewise, the existence of regional customs, layers of customary law (regular customary law and *jus cogens* customs), and varying kinds of jurisdiction (normal jurisdictional rules and *erga omnes* norms) all contradict the validity of referring to an international legislature.

5 *See* Chapter VII, Charter of the United Nations (1945).

6 Under art. 37(2) of the Charter of the United Nations, states can assent to the mandatory jurisdiction of the ICJ; reservations contained in such assents and the withdrawal by key international actors of such assent (such as the United States' withdrawal in 1984) mean that the ICJ has constrained jurisdiction.

7 *See, generally*, Robert G. Darst, "The Internationalization of Environmental Protection in the USSR and its Successor States," in Schreurs and Economy (eds), *The Internationalization of Environmental Protection*, pp. 97–133.

8 However, the 1989 Basel Convention on the Control of Transboundary Movements of Hazardous Wastes and their Disposal was not ratified by the time of the USSR's disassembly.

9 *See, generally*, Paul Wapner, *Environmental Activism and World Civic Politics* (Albany: SUNY Press, 1996).

10 In practice, this approach attempts to reconcile the differences between international relations and comparative politics. *See* Elizabeth Economy and Miranda A. Schreurs, "Domestic and International Linkages in Environmental Politics," in

Schreurs and Economy (eds), *The Internationalization of Environmental Protection*, pp. 1–18.

11 Interestingly enough, the keystone effort by Turkmenistan to pursue isolationism occurred in the most global of venues. *See* United Nations General Assembly Resolution A/RES/50/80 (December 12, 1995). Turkmenistan declared itself a neutral state in the United Nations General Assembly in an effort to insulate itself from scrutiny and in order to create an internationally acceptable policy cover for its efforts to restrain pluralism internally.

12 For a fuller explanation of how these events cannot be reconciled with any dominant theory of international law, *see* Rasulov, "Pravopreemstvo i Tsentralnaya Aziya."

13 *See Central Asia Compliance Monitor* 2 (2000); available at: http://www.ecostan.org/monitor/cacm2.pdf

14 Olav Shram Stokke, "Regimes as Governance Systems," in Oran R. Young (ed.), *Global Governance* (Cambridge: MIT Press, 1997), pp. 27–63.

15 Specifically, the Vienna Convention, the Montreal Protocol, and the numerous amendments to the Montreal Protocol.

16 Abram Chayes and Antonia Handler Chayes, *The New Sovereignty: Compliance with International Regulatory Agreements* (Cambridge: Harvard University Press, 1995). Chayes and Chayes contrast the pitfalls of "coercion" (sanctions and other punishments) with the advantage of "management of compliance" since "the principal source of noncompliance is not willful disobedience but the lack of capability or clarity or priority." Ibid., p. 22.

17 *See, generally,* David G. Victor *et al.* (eds), *The Implementation and Effectiveness of International Environmental Commitments* (Cambridge: MIT Press, 1998).

18 Chayes and Chayes, *The New Sovereignty: Compliance with International Regulatory Agreements*, p. 27.

19 In contrast to this dominant viewpoint, *see* Kal Raustiala and David G. Victor, "Conclusions," in Victor *et al.* (eds), *The Implementation and Effectiveness of International Environmental Commitments*, pp. 667–668.

20 For example, GATT Panels were prohibited from considering non-state *amicus curie* briefs in their adjudication of trade disputes.

21 For a sense of the insularity of the community, *see* Mostafa K. Tolba, *Global Environmental Diplomacy: Negotiating Environmental Agreements for the World, 1973–1992* (Cambridge: MIT Press, 1998).

22 Switzerland is the depository for CITES, and Denmark supported the entire process leading up to the signing of the Aarhus Convention in Aarhus, Denmark.

23 Peter M. Haas, *Saving the Mediterranean: The Politics of International Environmental Cooperation* (New York: Columbia University Press, 1992), p. 55.

24 Young (ed.), *Global Governance.*

25 Haas, *Saving the Mediterranean: The Politics of International Environmental Cooperation*, pp. 155–164.

26 This conception does not deny that many scientists view environmental problems through Marxist, geopolitical, or other lenses. Rather, the argument is that scientists aggregately tend to mitigate the impact of ideologies in negotiations, and they tend to agree on descriptions and prescriptions if they possess the same body of data.

27 Haas points out that scientists involved in MedPlan recognized that foreign affairs diplomats mistakenly assumed that pollutants were carried by currents throughout the entire Mediterranean. Yet, because of slow currents, pollution was essentially localized. Scientists chose to allow diplomats to work under their misconception rather than share knowledge about the reality of pollution, since they assumed that an environmental agreement would be frustrated were this knowledge known by diplomats. Haas, *Saving the Mediterranean: The Politics of International Environmental Cooperation*, pp. 70–71.

28 Moreover, since research institutions in developing countries are often ill-funded, funding from secretariats can make national scientists more dependent on the regime

than on their own governments for funding, and their loyalties can shift accordingly. Ibid., p. 80.

29 Ignoring Iran (which has a large number of scientific institutions for water and the Caspian), the scientific capital brought to the regime by the post-Soviet states is stunning. During the Soviet period, a "Seas of the USSR" program (including the Caspian) existed that framed research on a scale that the Mediterranean only achieved relatively recently under MedPlan. In fact, the USSR offered to conduct MedPlan's open water monitoring, but was rebuffed. Ibid., p. 82. For purposes of comparison, Kazakhstan currently has 13 scientific institutions that are involved in Caspian Sea research and no fewer than two dozen doctoral level researchers. That is, adjusted for population, lower than France's MedPlan capacity, but higher than Spain's. Ibid., p. 212.

30 Ibid., p. 162.

31 Ibid.

32 Not examined here is the fact that post-Soviet scientists are dialectical materialists. Dialectical materialism is a theory of the natural world and natural laws. A form of traditional philosophical materialism, it (ignoring for a moment its variety of incarnations) is not radically different from the worldviews held by many Western scientists. Dialectical materialism can be most concisely described as non-reductionist and non-vitalist materialism that presupposes the existence of different laws on each level of nature (physical, biological, social). For overviews of dialectical materialism, *see* Loren R. Graham. *What Have We Learned About Science and Technology from the Russian Experience?* (Stanford: Stanford University Press), pp. 6–17; Vucinich, *Empire of Knowledge: The Academy of Sciences of the USSR (1917–1970).* What is the effect, then, of a situation in which in an emerging regional seas regime UN scientific experts subscribe to a different worldview than local experts, especially if four-fifths of such a regime subscribes to that different worldview? Dialectical materialism's very existence as a "scientific" philosophy challenges the idea of epistemic communities. Where a divergence of policy recommendations occurs, an epistemic community will not form. Cf. Other regional seas regimes, especially MedPlan, have faced no less uncertain possibilities for epistemic community formation due to religious and racial differences.

33 In this regard, articles describing the post-Soviet period using the word "modern" are suspicious since late Soviet society was modern and industrial, but post-Soviet reorientations toward religion, nationalism, and rejection of science constitute a rejection of modernism towards pre-modernism instead of post-modernism.

34 *See* http://www.biodiv.org.

35 http://www.biodiv.org/conv/QReport09-2000-6.htm.

36 These include an informal advisory committee, meetings of national focal points, regional committees, meetings of technical experts.

37 *See* http://www.iisd.ca. The *Earth Negotiations Bulletin* is in its ninth year, but only recently secured the funding, staff, and technology to make itself a better source of information than newspapers and related standard news media.

38 But, of course, in the present context, experts are no longer from Moscow and the emphasis is no longer on the Russian language, but the underlying structure is essentially identical.

39 For example, the Y2K regime, while not environmental, illustrates some of the conditions of a high non-compliance, high effectiveness regime. The mission of that regime was to prevent chaos on January 1, 2000.

40 *See* Letter 11/2734 of May 10, 1993 from Minister of Foreign Affairs of the Republic of Uzbekistan Sadyk Safaev to Butros Butros-Gali and Postanovlenie N. 918 ot 19 Avgusta 1994 Kabineta Ministrov Respubliki Kazakhstan.

41 Courts in the region operate under a set of instructions regarding sources. While constitutions suggest that courts should apply treaties directly, these instructions, at least the ones I have been able to collect, universally fail to list such international sources of law as admissible as sources of law in judicial review.

42 Y. R., "Predstaviteli NPO Kaspiiskogo regiona namerevayutsya usilit svoe vliyanie na transnatsionalnye korporatsii v voprosakh ekologii," *Panorama* (September 15, 2000); www.panorama.kz. Karachaganak Petroleum is a consortium primarily comprised of Agip, British Gas, and Texaco.

43 More recent laws allowing grandfathering of environmental regulations, for example in Kazakhstan, do not run afoul of this legal dilemma since they are legislative grants, not executive exemptions.

44 Oleg Khe, "Kazakhstan iz-za neuplaty chlenskikh vznosov peresmatrivaet svoe uchastie v mezhdunarodnykh organizatsiyakh," *Panorama* (March 21, 2000), p. 1.

45 Indeed, these closures have often only come about thanks to offers of conditionalized or substantial bilateral foreign aid connected to military interests. For a case study of Kazakhstan's biological weapons dismantling and attempted conversion to biotechnology, *see* Aizhan Madikhojaeva, "Chisto bakteriologicheski my uzhe ne opasny" *Ekspress K* (August 5, 2000), p. 3.

6 Case studies: internationalizing the Central Asian environment

1 Sergei Kuratov and Sergei Solyanik, "The Glare and Glimmer of Cooperation" *Ecostan News* 8 (1995), http://www.ecostan.org/Ecostan/Ecostan308.html.

2 *See* Eric W. Sievers, "Ekologicheskaya reforma, pravovoe gosudarstvo i suverenitet," in Sievers *et al.* (eds), *Mezhdunarodnoe ekologicheskoe pravo i Tsentralnaya Azia*, p. 1.

3 In this regard, in the popular mind, no substantial difference existed between American, European, or United Nations organizational capital assets; all were democratic, rule of law, and efficient – the things that, in the 1990s popular mind, Soviet assets were not.

4 *See* Andrei Aranbaev, "TACIS in Turkmenistan: A Technical Assistance Embarrassment," *Ecostan News* 10 (1995), http://www.ecostan.org/Ecostan/Ecostan310.html.

5 Sergei Kuratov, "Reform of Ecological Legislation in Kazakhstan" (Unpublished 1997 Brandeis University M.A. thesis in sustainable development). Available at: http://www.ecostan.org/Laws/sk.html

6 *See*, i.e. Executive Board of the United Nations Development Programme and of the United Nations Population Fund, "UNDP: Financial, Budgetary and Administrative Matters" (July 26, 2000), DP/2000/39/Add.1 (Annual Review of the Financial Situation), p. 77.

7 ADB project UZB 30502-01. Available at http://www.adb.org/Documents/ADBBO/AOTA/30502012.ASP.

8 IUCN maintains global networks under the Species Survival Commission and Environmental Law Commission. Both boast numerous Central Asian members. At its October 2000 World Conservation Congress, IUCN also resolved to further increase its presence in Central Asia. *See* http://www.iisd.ca/sd/iucn/wcc2/sdvol39no3e.html.

9 The John D. and Catherine T. MacArthur Foundation, *Report on Activities 1995* (Chicago: The John D. and Catherine T. MacArthur Foundation, 1996), p. 18. In addition, much of the data in this book arose in part through a 1999 grant from MacArthur Foundation to Law and Environment Eurasia Partnership. *See* Table 5.1.

10 Hiltunen, *Environmental Development Co-operation Opportunities: Kazakstan, Kyrgyz Republic, Turkmenistan, Uzbekistan*, pp. 19, 30. Hiltunen provides extensive data on bilateral environmental projects in Central Asia funded by the United States, Denmark, Germany, France, Finland, Norway, and other states.

11 *See, generally,* http://www.pressenter.com/~cottonwd.

12 The World Bank, "Environmentally and Socially Sustainable Development" at http://www-esd.worldbank.org/ecssd/aarhus/S7long.html (1998).

13 By Agenda 21, I mean to include the pantheon of 1992 nonbinding Earth Summit agreements: Agenda 21, the Rio Declaration on Environment and Development, and the Statement of Principles for the Sustainable Management of Forests. These all issued

from the United Nations Conference on Environment and Development of June 1992. *See* http://www.un.org/esa/sustdev/agenda21text.htm

14 Unfortunately, in more than half the circumstances in which environmental NGOs in Central Asia accuse their governments of violations of international environmental law, they refer specifically to Agenda 21 as the "law" violated.

15 I argue that this sentence captures what two seminal books in environmental diplomacy are all about. *See* Richard Elliot Benedick, *Ozone Diplomacy* (Cambridge: Harvard University Press, 1995) and Tolba, *Global Environmental Diplomacy: Negotiating Environmental Agreements for the World, 1973–1992.*

16 *See* http://www.unece.org/env/cep

17 *See* http://www.earthcharter.org/welcome

18 *See* Agenda 21, art. 38.38: "...States could consider the preparation of national reports. In this context, the organs of the United Nations system should, upon request, assist countries, in particular developing countries. Countries could also consider the preparation of national action plans for the implementation of Agenda 21."

19 *See* http://www.un.org/esa/agenda21/natlinfo

20 *See* Kazakstan, "Country Profile: Implementation of Agenda 21: Review of Progress Made since the United Nations Conference on Environment and Development, 1992."

21 Ibid.

22 *See* discussion in Chapter 3 and Republic of Uzbekistan, "Country Profile: Implementation of Agenda 21: Review of Progress Made since the United Nations Conference on Environment and Development, 1992."

23 *See* 1999 Resolution 12-8/3869 of the Government of the Republic of Kazakhstan (requiring ministries to assist efforts of Agenda 21 Working Group).

24 Postanovlenie Prezidenta Turkmenistana ot 01/03/1999 goda No. 4091 Ob obrazovanii Gosudarstvennoi komissii po obespecheniyu vypolneniya obyazatelstv Turkmenistana, vytekayuschikh iz Konventsii i programm OON po okruzhayuschei srede.

25 *See* Global Environment Facility, *1999 Annual Report: Volume II* (Washington, D.C.: Global Environment Facility, 1999), pp. 2–3.

26 Global Environment Facility, "Instrument for the Establishment of the Restructured Global Environment Facility" (1994), http://gefweb.org/public/instrume/instrum1.htm, Arts 1.1–1.2.

27 Cf. David G. Aubrey *et al.*, "Incremental Cost Country Experience Case Study: Black Sea and Caspian Sea," Unpublished report presented at May 1999 GEF Council.

28 "The initial commitment of the Implementing Agencies to the GEF had been in developing their GEF activities in areas of their institutional comparative advantage, as provided for in the Instrument." Global Environment Facility, "Corporate Business Plan FY02-FY04," p. 14. "UNDP's niche is defined by its network of 133 field offices and the many years of experience with capacity building programmes in developing countries." Jeff Griffen, *Biodiversity, International Waters and the GEF* (Gland, Switzerland: The World Conservation Union, 1997), p. 3.

29 For every week UNDP, UNEP, or World Bank contributes a staff person to a GEF project, it receives:

Expense category	UNDP	UNEP	WB	Average staff year cost ($)
Salaries	140,400	124,900	113,676	126,325
Mission travel	33,000	20,520	40,000	31,173
General operating costs	43,300	68,368	70,000	60,556
Institutional and fixed costs	20,300	33,428	16,000	23,243
Total	237,000	247,216	239,676	241,297
Average staffweek cost	5,512	5,749	5,574	5,612

Global Environment Facility, "Proposal for a Fee-Based System for Funding GEF Project Implementation" (April 29, 1999), GEF C.13/11, p. 13. Most of the staff in question hold B.A. or M.A. equivalents, not Ph.D.s. For an examination of this trend in general Central Asian development projects, *see* Bivens, "Aboard the Gravy Train: In Kazakstan, the Farce that is U.S. Foreign Aid."

30 UNDP, "Overview of Agency Support Cost Arrangements" (undated), http://www.undp.org/drpc/guidelns/suptcost/ovranx01.htm.

31 UNOPS and UNDP have a continuing partnership in effect since 1997, and the two agencies are indistinguishable from local eyes. *See* http://www.unops.org/aboutunops/unopsandunsys.html.

32 Global Environment Facility, "Project Proposals Submitted for Council Approval: Volume IV" (September 10, 1998), GEF/C.12/3, E-16, p. 15.

33 "Razbor poletov: Programma razvitiya OON ne soglasna s kritikoi v svoi adres," *NPO: Teoriya i Praktika* 10 (2000), p. 4.

34 $5,710,000 from 2000–2004. Executive Board of the United Nations Development Programme and of the United Nations Population Fund, "Second country cooperation framework for Uzbekistan (2000–2004)," p. 5.

35 Executive Board of the United Nations Development Programme and of the United Nations Population Fund, "UNDP: Financial, Budgetary and Administrative Matters" (Annual Review of the Financial Situation), pp. 31, 41–43. GEF project funds are similarly on parity with total other local UNDP project funds. Ibid.

36 On the low side is Turkmenistan. *See* Executive Board of the United Nations Development Programme and of the United Nations Population Fund, "Second country cooperation framework for Turkmenistan (2000–2004)," (May 16, 2000), DP/CCF/TUK/2, p. 9.

37 *See* Global Environment Facility, "GEF Corporate Business Plan FY00-FY02" (September 11, 1998), GEF/C.12/11, pp. 25–29; Global Environment Facility, "Corporate Business Plan FY02-FY04," pp. 17–19.

38 References to "principles of accountability" and to transparency suffuse GEF documents. For example, "Consistent with provisions in the Instrument, there should be transparency in the preparation, conduct, reporting, and evaluation of public involvement activities in all projects." Global Environment Facility, "Public Involvement in GEF-Financed Projects," (June, 1996), http://www.gefweb.org/Operational_Policies/Public_Involvement/public_involvement.html.

39 Global Environment Facility, *1999 Annual Report: Volume II*, p. 4.

40 Ibid., p. 4, 16.

41 That is, UNDP takes $146,000 for any medium-sized project. Assuming that most such projects are roughly $750,000 (and cannot be more than one million), UNDP's fee is slightly under 20 per cent. For projects under $750,000, UNDP's take would still be $146,000, but would constitute a higher percentage in relation to the project as a whole. Figures taken from financial appendices to GEF Council 16 Documents at http://www.gefweb.org/Documents/Council_Documents/GEF_C16/Annexes_A_to_F_final.xls.

42 Global Environment Facility, "Corporate Business Plan FY02-FY04," pp. 3–4.

43 *See* Global Environment Facility, "Report on Progress Made in Implementing the GEF Small Grants Programme" (November 5, 1999), GEF/C.14/Inf.8 (Annex VII-Ia: Summary of Replies from GEF/SGP National Coordinators).

44 Personal correspondence with and interviews of Karaganda EcoCenter staff 1997–1999. The group's proposal was for conservation of Karaganda Argali, an endemic endangered species of *Ovis ammon* with CITES Appendix status.

45 For example, "At the country level, most UNDP Country Offices have a professional staff member in charge of handling GEF projects. This individual accepts submissions of project concepts and provides a wide range of assistance to project proponents including assistance securing governmental endorsement, information on the UNDP Country Programme, and access to a variety of technical experts and stakeholders." UNDP, "Guidebook UNDP–GEF," available at http://www.undp.org/gef/guide/

main.htm#introduction. By the October 1998 Council Meeting, UNDP listed UNDP–GEF contact points in both Kazakhstan and Tajikistan.

46 Observation based on author's observations while in attendance.

47 "A project enters the pipeline [when] an Implementing Agency has received from an eligible country an endorsed request and...the Implementing Agency has not responded to the operational focal point within 2 weeks of receiving their request." Global Environment Facility, "GEF Pipelines of the Implementing Agencies" (April 29, 1999), GEF/C.13/Inf.7, p. 1.

48 Letter of November 8, 1999 from Dr Christopher Briggs to the project proposers of Nursing Back Biodiversity in the Southern Hissar Range. In author's files.

49 The project anticipated establishing a nursery of juniper, walnut, and poplar, extensive restoration of the degraded Hissar slopes in the populated areas outside the Shirkent National Park, and eventual installation of small hydroelectric facilities to replace reliance on wood and coal.

50 Moreover, his comments were essentially prepared by mid-February, 2000 and simply never forwarded to the Tajikistan NGOs. *See* Letter from Jeffrey Griffin, Senior UNDP–GEF Consultant to Chris Briggs, Regional Coordinator for Europe and the CIS, UNDP–GEF, "Recommendations w/respect to the draft proposal entitled 'Nursing Back Biodiversity in the Southern Hissar Range,'" (February 15, 2000).

51 Global Environment Facility, "Corporate Business Plan FY02-FY04," p. 6.

52 The consultant's conclusion has no bearing on the Pipeline issue. "Entry into the pipeline does not necessarily imply concurrence by the GEF Secretariat that the project proposal is consistent with GEF strategy, programs, and policies." Global Environment Facility, "GEF Pipelines of the Implementing Agencies," p. 2.

53 World Bank, "The Central Asia Transboundary Biodiversity Project: Kyrgyz Republic, Kazakstan and Uzbekistan" (1997). Available at: http://www.gefweb.org/wprogram/nov97/capcd4.doc

54 Hiltunen, *Environmental Development Co-Operation Opportunities*, p. 67.

55 World Bank, "The Central Asia Transboundary Biodiversity Project: Kyrgyz Republic, Kazakstan and Uzbekistan."

56 Global Environment Facility, "Corporate Business Plan FY02-FY04," p. 3.

57 The Republic of Uzbekistan, *Biodiversity Conservation: National Strategy and Action Plan* (Tashkent:1997), available at http://www.biodiv.org/natrep/Uzbekistan/Uzbekistan.pdf.

58 Victor S. Lukarevsky, "The Plight of Urials in Turkmenistan," *Ecostan News* 7 (March 2000), pp. 2–6.

59 Unpublished data received directly from ministry in August 2000 on the day information submitted.

60 Five subspecies of argali inhabit Central Asia. These are Altai argali (*O. a. ammon*; KZ), Kazakhstan argali (*O. a. collium*; KZ), Tien Shan argali (*O. a. karelini*; KZ, KG), Kara Tau argali (*O. a. nigrimontana*; KZ), and Marco Polo argali (*O. a. polii*; KZ, TJ, KG).

61 Thirty per cent in Kyrgyzstan should go to conservation measures. Letter from T. Kulumbaev, Chief Inspector of the Kyrgyzstan State Nature Protection Committee to Doug Yajko of Safari Club (March 11, 1994). FOIA Documents, *see infra* note 64. Twenty-five per cent in Kyrgyzstan should go to local communities. "Kelishim, At-Bashi aiyly...." Contract of June 24, 1993 between Naryn Regional Inspectorate and At-Bashi District Governor. Ibid. The State Department relied on (utterly unsupported) information from Safari Outfitters that 100 per cent of argali revenues in Tajikistan go to conservation and serve as the only source of state conservation funds. Ibid. Letter from Gretchen Stark, Safari Outfitters to Mike Carpenter, USFWS (July 23, 1996).

62 From 1990–1996, 2/3 (49 of 73) of hunters of argali in Central Kazakhstan were Europeans. North Americans, led by American citizens, made up the remaining 1/3. Derived from I. V. Kalmykov, "Karagandinskii argali: okhrana i ratsionalnoe

ispolzovanie" (unpublished 1996 report of Chief Inspector of the Karaganda Regional Animal Conservation Inspectorate).

63 Public Employees for Environmental Responsibility, in a report penned by USFWS whistleblowers, alleges that the entire process was corrupt, illegal, and controlled by the Safari Club. Public Employees for Environmental Responsibility, *Tarnished Trophies* (Washington, D.C.: PEER, 1996). PEER incorrectly states that the European Union bans trophy imports, since such individual trophies for which the importer holds a CITES export permit (with the sole exception of Kara-Tau argali) are permissible as "personal effects" under European Union Regulation 338/97 "On the protection of species of wild fauna and flora by regulating trade therein" (December 9, 1996). Information on Kara-Tau argali from personal correspondence in 1998 with Dr Ute Grimm of Germany's CITES Scientific Authority.

64 These documents, hereinafter "FOIA Documents," include most import permit applications filed with USFWS over the years in question.

65 Letter 23G-419 from Kyrgyzstan Minister of Environmental Protection K. J. Bokonbaev to Beagle Association *et al.* (April 17, 1998).

66 *See* Resolution 159 of the Kyrgyz Republic Cabinet of Ministers (April 19, 1992).

67 I.e. "[W]e were taken into an area which we did not have a permit for . . . A number if [sic] incidences of illegal hunting were observed . . . On another occasion the game control agent that was guiding us shot a Medium sized ram in the guts, walked over and looked at it and walked away, when I asked him why he had done that he just waved me off." 1996 Application of T. M. Lavelle to import one Marco Polo argali into the United States, FOIA Documents.

68 Biosphere Reserves, like World Heritage sites, exist under the aegis of UNESCO. Biosphere reserves are intended simultaneously to further conservation, development, and research. *See* UNESCO, "The Man and the Biosphere Programme," http://www.unesco.org/mab. To date, the only Biosphere Reserves in Central Asia are Sary-Chelek (KG), Repetek (TM), and Chatkal, all listed in 1978. *See* UNESCO, "List of Biosphere Reserves," http://www.unesco.org/mab/brlist.htm. Since the Man and the Biosphere Program is not a separate treaty regime, but part of UNESCO, the status of these sites did not change with the disassembly of the USSR.

69 For the "entitlements" of "non-salaried" United Nations Volunteers, *see* http://www.unv.org/unvols/isentitl.htm

70 *See* UNDP Uzbekistan, "Establishment of the Nuratau-Kyzylkum Biosphere Reserve as a model for Biodiversity Conservation in Uzbekistan," June 22, 2000, available at http://www.gefweb.org/Documents/Medium-Sized_Project_Proposals/MSP_Proposals/Uzbekistan.pdf

71 "Uzbekistan: Programme for phasing out Ozone Depleting Substances," in *Project Proposals Submitted for Council Approval, Vol. III* (GEF/C.12/3), D-15 (September 10, 1998).

72 Global Environment Facility, "Tajikistan: Programme for Phasing Out Ozone Depleting Substances" (1999), available at http://www.gefweb.org/meetings/GEF_C14/Tajikistan/tajozo.pdf

73 Project in Author's Files. This project also failed to secure authorization from the operational focal point, but was reviewed anyway. The project anticipates complete disuse of ODS by 2005.

74 Global Environment Facility, "Kazakhstan: Programme for Phasing Out Ozone Depleting Substances."

75 United Nations Environment Programme, *Global Environmental Outlook 2000* (London: United Nations Environment Programme, 1999), p. 4.

76 United Nations Environment Programme, "Eleventh Meeting of the Parties to the Montreal protocol on Substances that Depleted the Ozone Layer: Report of the Secretariat on Information provided by the Parties in Accordance with Articles 7 and 9 of the Montreal Protocol," p. 4.

77 Ibid., p. 28.

78 Republic of Kazakhstan, *Initial National Communication of the Republic of Kazakhstan under the United Nations Framework Convention on Climate Change*, p. 52.

79 United Nations Office in the Republic of Uzbekistan, UZB/95/G31/C/1G/99 (January 1, 1999).

80 Republic of Kazakhstan, *Initial National Communication of the Republic of Kazakhstan under the United Nations Framework Convention on Climate Change*. The preparation of this report was underwritten by the Netherlands, and Kazakhstan's general climate change inventories were supported by the United States from 1994–1998. Ibid., p. 7. For information on the United States Country Studies Program under the Department of Energy, *see* http://www.gcrio.org/CSP. No other Central Asian state received assistance under this program.

81 *See* United Nations Office in the Republic of Uzbekistan, UZB/98/G42 (January 1, 1999) and Table 6.1.

82 Within the United States, the government allocates close to two billion dollars annually to national climate change research. *See* Subcommittee on Global Change Research, Committee on Environment and Natural Resources of the National Science and Technology Council, *Our Changing Planet: The FY 2001 U.S. Global Change Research Program* (Washington, D.C.: National Science and Technology Council, 2000), p. 4.

83 Republic of Kazakhstan, *Initial National Communication of the Republic of Kazakhstan under the United Nations Framework Convention on Climate Change*, p. 31.

84 Ibid., pp. 32–33.

85 Ibid., p. 9. However, from 2010–2030, the yields may actually increase.

86 Ibid., p. 37.

87 Ibid., p. 34–35.

88 Ibid. p. 37–38.

89 Global Environment Facility, "Kazakhstan: Wind Power Market Development Initiative," (2000), http://www.gefweb.org/COUNCIL/GEF_C15/WP/Kazakhstan_Wind.doc. This figure is understated, since it ignored oil and gas production emissions, but it is the "baseline" for Kazakhstan under the FCCC. Republic of Kazakhstan, *Initial National Communication of the Republic of Kazakhstan under the United Nations Framework Convention on Climate Change*, p. 11. For comparison, Uzbekistan emitted 115 million metric tonnes of carbon dioxide (163 million total tonnes of greenhouse gases) in 1990 and 102 million (156 million) in 1997, a much less substantial reduction. *See Initial Communication of the Republic of Uzbekistan Under the United Nations Framework Convention on Climate Change*, p. 36.

90 Republic of Kazakhstan, *Initial National Communication of the Republic of Kazakhstan under the United Nations Framework Convention on Climate Change*, p. 57.

91 Ibid., p. 28.

92 Ibid., p. 55.

93 The Main Administration for Hydrometeorology of the Republic of Kazakhstan, *U.S. Country Studies Program Support for National Action Plan (SNAP) for the Republic of Kazakhstan Final Report* (Almaty: 1999), available at http://www.gcrio.org/CSP/pdf/kazakhstan_snap.pdf, p. 8.

94 United States Agency for International Development, *Climate Change Initiative 1998–2002* (Washington, D.C.: USAID, 1998), available at http://www.dec.org/pdf_docs/PNACC866.pdf, pp. 53–54.

95 Republic of Kazakhstan, *Initial National Communication of the Republic of Kazakhstan under the United Nations Framework Convention on Climate Change*, p. 57.

96 *See* United Nations, Framework Convention on Climate Change FCCC/CP/1999/2 (May 28, 1999).

97 *Earth Negotiations Bulletin* 163, November 13, 2000, p. 2.

98 The Main Administration for Hydrometeorology of the Republic of Kazakhstan, *U.S. Country Studies Program Support for National Action Plan (SNAP) for the Republic of Kazakhstan Final Report*, p. 24.

99 Global Environment Facility, "Kazakhstan: Wind Power Market Development Initiative."

100 United States Agency for International Development, *Climate Change Initiative 1998–2002*, pp. 12, 44. At 1990 levels, Central Asia would have been the seventh largest emitter, occupying the spot in between Germany and the United Kingdom, perhaps even exceeding German levels. By 1995, it had fallen out of the top ten to the level of Mexico. Ibid., p. 12.

101 Main Administration of Hydrometeorology, *Initial Communication of the Republic of Uzbekistan Under the United Nations Framework Convention on Climate Change*, p. 8.

102 A climate change euphemism for levels of emissions so substantially below 1990 levels that under emissions trading other states could purchase considerable additional capacity for themselves. Likewise, Kazakhstan's coal inefficiency creates a similarly rich opportunity under joint implementation.

103 Republic of Kazakhstan, *Initial National Communication of the Republic of Kazakhstan under the United Nations Framework Convention on Climate Change*, p. 36.

104 P. Aitymbetov, "Otkhody: zlo i blago" *Ekokuryer* (July 28, 2000), p. 2.

105 Hiltunen, *Environmental Development Co-Operation Opportunities*, p. 10.

106 *See* United Nations Office in the Republic of Uzbekistan, National Action Plan, UZB/98/X19 (Jan. 1, 1999).

107 *See*, i.e. Turkmenistan Ministry of Nature Protection, *Doklad po osuschestvleniyu Natsionalnoi programmy deistvii po borbe s opustynivaniem v Turkmenistane* (Ashgabad: National Institute of Deserts, Flora and Fauna, 2000). This report could offer as anti-desertification efforts only one pilot project on eight hectares, the distribution of "CCD" t-shirts to raise awareness, and the planting of three million conifer seedlings (most of which are now dead) in the capital.

108 Niyaz Ataev, "The Lake of the Golden Century," *Ecostan News* 10 (2000), pp. 6–9; http://www.ecostan.org/Ecostan/Ecostan710 e.pdf

109 Executive Board of the United Nations Development Programme and of the United Nations Population Fund, "Second country cooperation framework for Uzbekistan (2000–2004)," p. 2.

110 This Section largely derives from Sievers, "The Caspian, Regional Seas, and the Case for a Cultural Study of Law."

111 Arthur P. Mizzi, "Caspian Sea Oil, Turmoil, and Caviar: Can They Provide a Basis for an Economic Union of the Caspian States?" *Colorado Journal of International Environmental Law & Policy* 7 (1996), p. 483.

112 More than 10 billion barrels of recoverable oil and more than 30 trillion m^3 of natural gas. Sarah J. Lloyd, "Land-locked Central Asia: Implications for the Future," in Dick Hodder *et al.* (eds), *Land-locked States of Asia and Africa*, pp. 97, 115 (London: Frank Cass Publishers, 1997).

113 Despite this ban (which applied to all fishing except for industrial sprat catches and scientific research), made for conservation purposes and in an attempt to generate greater export possibilities for caviar (sturgeon spawn in rivers not the sea), poaching was rampant and sturgeon products widely available to coastal populations. Poachers, faced with felony charges for one fish or for 1000 fish, had no incentive to work on a small scale. For a discussion of poaching and Caspian politics in the 1960s and 1970s, *see* Emil Agaev, "Osetr dlya brakonyera," in S. Ganiev and V. Maksimov (eds), *V sudbe prirody-nasha sudba*, pp. 4–39 (Moscow: Khudozhestvennaya literatura, 1990).

114 The most important of which are shad, herring, carp, salmon, sprat, and mullet.

115 Bella Sewall, "Caspian Seal Tragedy," *Ecostan News* (July, 2000), p. 9; http://www.ecostan.org/Ecostan/Ecostan707e.pdf.

116 Liz Fuller, "Fire Extinguished at Nuclear Power Plant in Kazakhstan," RFE/RL Newsline (September 11, 2000).

117 "Strict Nature Reserves (zapovedniki) of Russia", http://syseco.pgu.serpukhov.su/nreserve.

118 Ramsar Bureau, "List of Wetlands of International Importance" (November 8, 1999) at http://www.ramsar.org.

119 Ramsar Bureau, "The Montreux Record" (September 30, 1999) at http://www.ramsar.org/key_montreux_record.htm.

120 The states appear to be moving toward a regime of national delineation for some resources, while relegating navigation, fisheries, and seabed ownership to special regimes. While principles gleaned from the Law of the Sea will be applied to resolving the legal status of the Caspian, international law's normative influence on the resolution of the remaining discrepancies between the state will clearly be highly subordinate to state interests.

121 *See* for example Jean-Christoph Peuch, "The Privatization of International Affairs," *Fletcher Forum for World Affairs* 22 (1998), pp. 29–30 (positing that Russia does not even consider Caspian hydrocarbon reserves as a possible source of revenues).

122 Vyacheslav Gizzatov, "Statement at the Seminar on Caspian problems at the International Institute of Caspian Studies" (unpublished paper distributed by Kazakhstan ambassador at meeting in Tehran in June 1999; http://www.caspianstudies.com/seminars/19990615.htm). For a much more detailed and excellent overview of the pre-1994 diplomatic developments concerning the Caspian, *see* Sergei V. Vinogradov, "Toward Regional Cooperation in the Caspian: A Legal Perspective," in Michael H. Glantz and Igor S. Zonn (eds), *Scientific, Environmental, and Political Issues in the Circum-Caspian Region* (Amsterdam: Kluwer Academic Publishers, 1996), pp. 53–66.

123 *See* Gizzatov, "Statement at the Seminar on Caspian problems at the International Institute of Caspian Studies."

124 Vinogradov, "Toward Regional Cooperation in the Caspian: A Legal Perspective," p. 59.

125 Other funds were contributed by a wide variety of bilateral and international donors, with the glaring exception of the United States; however, the EU's contribution and commitments of more than five million ECU by the end of the century are by far the largest non-GEF contribution. Caspian Environment Programme website, http://www.caspianenvironment.org

126 Caspian Environment Programme, "Project Brief: Addressing Transboundary Environmental Issues in the Caspian Environment Programme" (undated), http://www.gefweb.org/wprogram/Oct98/WP_Sum.htm. The GEF Council awarded more than eight million dollars to this project. Ibid.

127 CEP website.

128 Ibid.

129 Caspian Environment Programme, "Project Proposal: Addressing Transboundary Environmental Issues in the Caspian Environment Programme (CEP) – Strengthened Institutional, Legal, Regulatory and Economic Frameworks for SAP Implementation" (February, 2000), http://www.gefweb.org/Endorsement/Endorsements/Endorsements.htm. AZ hints that it will be the holdout state in terms of resisting FCCS.

130 Likewise, for the first half-decade of MedPlan, all research was national. Haas, *Saving the Mediterranean: The Politics of International Environmental Cooperation*, p. 100.

131 All references are to the March 2000 final text of the FCCS.

132 Russia and TM, as parties to the Aarhus Convention would be required to make assessments public.

133 Cf. Despite this textual exuberance about NGOs and public participation, to date the CEP has a miserable track record of responding to information requests from the public.

134 Koltsov, *Rol' Akademii nauk v organizatsii regionalnykh nauchnykh tsentrov SSSR*, pp. 56, 222.

135 Babaev *et al.* (eds), *Akademiya nauk Turkmenskoi SSR*, p. 10.

136 This section derives from Eric W. Sievers, "Transboundary Jurisdiction and Watercourse Law: China, Kazakhstan, and the Irtysh", Texas International Law Journal (2002), pp. 1–42.

137 Depending on criteria, the Irtysh is listed as high as three and as low as 20 on lists of the world's largest rivers. In terms of drainage basin, the Irtysh, at 3,000,000 km², occupies the fifth spot, behind the Amazon, Nile, Mississippi, and Congo. Joyce L. Vedral *et al.* (eds), *World Resources 1998–1999* (New York: Oxford University Press, 1998), p. 309. Arising in a border region of Mongolia and China, the Irtysh forms KZ's industrial heartland before crosses into Russia, joins the Ob River, and empties into the Arctic Ocean.

138 Erik Nurshin, "Eto li tsena suvereniteta?!" *XXI Vek* (October 15, 1998), http://eurasia.org.ru/archives/october/Kit0021.htm.

139 Vladimir Turov, "Kak Rossiyu ostavlyayut za 'vodo-zaborom'," *Nezavismiaya Gazeta* (May 12, 1999), http://news.eastview.com/99/NGA/05/data/n083-41.htm

140 Aleksei Baliev and Arkadii Medvedev "Reki sami ne umirayut. Ikh ubivayut," *Rossiiskaya gazeta* (February 12, 1999), http://news.eastview.com/99/RGA/02/data/rg021258.html.

141 Guesses vary from 10 per cent to more than 50 per cent as both KZ and Russian journalists clearly expect the worst from China. One journalist cites 25–40 per cent as the initial diversion. Boris Kuzmenko, "Druzhba druzhboi, a vodichka vroz. Paradoksy sosedskikh vzaimootnoshenii," *Iterfaks AIF* (May 14, 1999), http://news.eastview.com/pp/IAI/05/data/i020_011.html. Almost 10 km³ flows yearly across China's border, which, many experts contend, constitutes the bulk of the Irtysh's flow. Ibid.

142 In the 1970s, the Chinese diverted part of the flow of the Ili River, and the consequences for the residents on the Soviet side of the border were unpleasant. Turov, "Kak Rossiyu ostavlyayut za 'vodo-zaborom'."

143 Turov, "Kak Rossiyu ostavlyayut za 'vodo-zaborom'."

144 Russian journalists are more to the point, suggesting that Kazakhstan politicians allow Chinese expansionism because the Chinese "sweeten the pill" through personal bribes. Aleksei Gulyaev, "Kitai-Kazakhstan: Pogranichnyi spor prodolzhaetsya," *Izvestiya* (April 30, 1999), http://news.eastview.com/99/IZV/04/data/i078-23.html.

145 Erik Nurshin, "Eto li tsena suvereniteta?!" XXI Vek (October 15, 1998), http://eurasia.org.ru/archives/october/Kit0021.htm.

146 Based on an interview with Auezzov, in Sergei Borisov, "Kitaitsy mogut vypit Irtysh," *Obschaya Gazeta* (October 28, 1999) http://news.eastview.com/99/OGA/10/data/043-20.html.

147 Ibid.

148 *See*, Makhambet Auezzov, Debyut Ministra," *Delovaya Nedelya* (November, 1999), http://www.asdc.kz/~rikki/arch/1999/44-99/peace07.htm (Foreign Minister Idrisov contending that KZ contributes 80 per cent of the Irtysh's water, refuting the common refrain that 60 per cent of the Irtysh's flow originates in China).

149 Nurshin, "Eto li tsena suvereniteta?!"

150 Ibid.

151 Ibid.

152 In the closest thing to an accusation, one that falls far short of the scope of China's violation, a representative of the KZ Prime Minister stated, "The Irtysh is a transboundary river and a state through which a transboundary river flows has the right to use such water resources to the extent that such use does not cause harm to the wateruse needs of another state." Turov, "Kak Rossiyu ostavlyayut za 'vodo-zaborom'." More typical is the damning statement of Ambassador Amangaliev, the chief negotiator: "There are international conventions drawn up to settle such issues. In line with them, the sides undertake not to inflict any losses on each other. If something like that happens the sides will have to compensate. But now neither we nor China are signatories to such a convention." BBC Worldwide Monitoring report of Kazakh Television Channel One broadcast, May 17, 1999.

153 Soglashenie mezhdu Pravitelstvom Soyuza Sovetskikh Sotsialisticheskikh Respublik i Pravitelstvom Kitaiskoi Narodnoi Respubliki o rezhime torgovogo sudokhodstva na

pogranichnykh i smezhnykh s nimi rekakh i ozere (December 21, 1957), 305 U.N.T.S. 211. For a detailed explication *see* Sievers, "Transboundary Jurisdiction and Watercourse Law: China, Kazakhstan, and the Irtysh."

154 Aaron Schwabach, "The United Nations Convention on the Law of Non-navigational Uses of International Watercourses: Customary International Law, and the Interests of Developing Upper Riparians," *Texas Journal of International Law* 33 (1998), p. 257.

155 While 103 states voted to adopt the 1997 Treaty, only Burundi, China, and Turkey voted against it. Ibid.

156 Gennadi Benditsky, "Pavlodartsy edva ne prevratilis' v afrikantsev: Chernyi mogilnik," *Vremya* (August 10, 2000). Available at http://kztime.virtualave.net/ Archive2000/08-10-00/strana32.htm

157 The factory will receive $106,000. Global Environment Facility, "Kazakhstan: Programme for Phasing Out Ozone Depleting Substances," p. 9.

158 UNESCO, "World Heritage Committee," http://www.unesco.org/whc/committ.htm. China has been on the committee since 1991 and is very proactive. Michael Oksenberg and Elizabeth Economy, "China: Implementation Under Economic growth and Market Reform," in Weiss and Jacobson (eds), *Engaging Countries: Strengthening Compliance with International Environmental Accords*, pp. 375–376.

159 Edith Brown Weiss, "The Five International Treaties: A Living History," in Weiss and Jacobson (eds), *Engaging Countries: Strengthening Compliance with International Environmental Accords*, p. 98.

160 While China could attempt to block any such listings, that would equally well facilitate efforts of KZ to draw the attention of the world community to its plight.

161 Personal communications with staff at KZ National Ecological Center and at the Ramsar Bureau 1997–1999.

162 Ramsar, art. 5.

163 Ramsar Bureau, "The Montreux Record," (May 10, 2000), http://www.ramsar.org/ key_montreux_record.htm.

164 Even before the Irtysh diversion plans came to light, KZ intended to list Lake Zaisan as one of its first Ramsar sites. Personal communication with KZ environmental officials and unpublished environmental ministry documents on Ramsar implementation.

165 Mirabzadeh A. Parastu, "Wetlands in Western Asia," http://www.ramsar.org/ about_western_asia_bkgd.htm.

166 Convention on Biological Diversity, "Ratification," (February 14, 2000), http://www. biodiv.org/conv/pdf/ratification-alpha.pdf.

167 CBD, art. 14(d).

168 Ibid, art. 27, Annex II(1)(1).

169 L. I. Agafonov, "Vodnost Obi i klimat planety tesno svyazany," *Voda Rossii* 87 (1999), p. 8.

170 Baliev and Medvedev, "Reki sami ne umirayut. Ikh ubivayut."

171 Turov, "Kak Rossiyu ostavlyayut za 'vodo-zaborom'."

172 For example, in 1999, 200 NGOs from KZ, Russia, and Europe appealed to the states to hold trilateral talks (with NGOs) and follow the 1992 UNECE Convention on the Protection and Use of Transboundary Watercourses and International Lakes. "Obraschenie uchastnikov Mezhdunarodnoi konferentsii 'Dni Volgi-99' o stroitelstve kanala 'Chernyi Irtysh-Karamai'," http://uchnom.botik.ru:8103/educ/PUSTYN/ecovolga/ kamray.ru.html.

173 KG is the upper riparian for 3 of the 12 major rivers that flow into China, including the second and fourth largest, which transport over $5 \, km^3$ annually. KZ is an upper riparian for two, the Haba and Tekes, with a combined annual flow of over $2.3 \, km^3$. The Haba is the third largest river flowing into China. "China," United Nations Food and Agriculture Organization, *Aquastat*, http://www.fao.org/waicent/faoinfo/agricult/agl/ aglw/aquastat/china/chin-rfr.htm.

174 Cf. One article argues that in 1998 the foreign ministries of Russia, KZ, and KG sent unanswered diplomatic notes to Beijing asking for clarifications of the project. Baliev and Medvedev, "Reki sami ne umirayut. Ikh ubivayut."

175 *See*, Aleksandr Sukhotin, "Bishkek–delo tonkoe," *Obschaia Gazeta* (August 26, 1999), http://news.eastview.com/pp/OGA/08/data/034-11.htm

176 *See* "Obraschenie k Pravitelstvu i Parlamentu Respubliki Kazakhstan," *EcoEkho*, (February 1999), http://www.sys-pro.com/~ecocenter/news/ee2_99/obraschen2.html. The NGOs call on KZ to reveal its planned response measures since a diversion of even 6 per cent of the Irtysh would result in "irreversible consequences." Ibid.

177 Of course, neither side assessed the information in these terms.

178 "V Alma-Ate prokhodit vtoroi raund Kazakhstansko-Kitaiskikh peregovorov po problemam transgranichnykh rek," *Ekspress K* (November 24, 1999), http://www.alatau.ru/scripts/web.exe/doc?id=100718&cp=win&scale=1. The initial diversion will remove roughly 5 per cent of the flow of the Irtysh. Ibid.

179 Ibid. Kazakhstan proposed a similar agreement with China in 1992, and the Chinese response up until the Irtysh diversion became known 2 years ago was that it was "studying the issue." Nurshin, "Eto li tsena suvereniteta?!"

180 "V Alma-Ate prokhodit vtoroi raund Kazakhstansko-Kitaiskikh peregovorov po problemam transgranichnykh rek."

181 Ibid.

182 Vladimir Chernyshev, "Kak podelyat Chernyi Irtysh: Vdol ili poperok?" *Transkaspiiskii proekt*, June 7, 2000, available at http://www.transcaspian.ru/cgi-bin/web.exe/rus/835.html.

183 Ibid.

184 Statement of Ministry of Foreign Affairs representative Bigali Turarbekov, quoted in Aman Kusainov, "Eto sladkoe slovo- granitsa," *Transkaspiiskii proekt*, October 4, 2000, available at http://www.transcaspian.ru/cgi-bin/web.exe/rus/prn00006263.html

185 Evgenii Kosenko, "Aktivno li nasha pozitsiya vo vneshnikh otnosheniyakh?" *Vremya*, October 26, 2000, p. 11.

186 Kseniya Kaspari, "Po obe storony reki: Problemu sovmestnogo ispolzovaniya vodnykh resursov reshayut Kazakhstan i Kitai," *Kazakhstanstanskaya Pravda*, November 5, 2000, available at http://www.kazpravda.kz. The pro-government newspaper *Panorama* carried a similar article, but also detailed the composition of the negotiating delegations for the November 1 to 7 negotiations and stated that China planned to divert 20 per cent of the Irtysh. *See* Kuat Ibraev, "Kazakhstan i Kitai reshayut problemu transgranichnykh rek," *Panorama*, November 3, 2000, available at http://www.panorama.kz/info/index.asp?yearfolder=2000&num=43&NumArticle=19.

187 Kaspari, "Po obe storony reki: Problemu sovmestnogo ispolzovaniya vodnykh resursov reshayut Kazakhstan i Kitai."

188 Ibraev, "Kazakhstan i Kitai reshayut problemu transgranichnykh rek."

189 International Fund for the Aral Sea, "Water and environmental management in the Aral Sea basin."

190 United Nations Office in the Republic of Uzbekistan, UZB/96/005 (January 1, 1999). Despite its name, the half million dollars for this project was almost exclusively for foreign consultants.

191 Executive Board of the United Nations Development Programme and of the United Nations Population Fund, "Second country cooperation framework for Uzbekistan (2000–2004)," p. 5. The Nukus Green Shelterbelt Project can be found at United Nations Office in the Republic of Uzbekistan, UZB/96/006 (January 1, 1996).

192 Ibid.

193 *See* Hiltunen, *Environmental Development Co-Operation Opportunities*, pp. 57–58.

194 *See* United Nations Office in the Republic of Uzbekistan, "GEF PDFA for Project Proposal 'Demonstrating Wetland Biodiversity Conservation in Uzbekistan,' " UZB/99/G43/A/1G/99 (April 1, 1999).

195 Main Administration of Hydrometeorology, *Initial Communication of the Republic of Uzbekistan Under the United Nations Framework Convention on Climate Change*, p. 11.

196 *See also* Komitet po Mezhdunarodnym ekologicheskim konventsiyam, *Uchastie Kazakhstana v Mezhdunarodnykh ekologicheskikh konventsiyakh i soglasheniyakh* (Almaty: National Environmental Center for Sustainable Development of the Republic of Kazakhstan, 1998).

197 For example, in CEP, World Bank claimed that Minister Daukeev (KZ) and Deputy Minister Atamuradov (TM) were authorized focal points; neither was. It never bothered to get any focal point authorizations for Aral-GEF.

198 The proposal was endorsed by Bulat Esekin from the National Environmental Center, while Deputy Minister Murat Musataev from the Ministry of Natural Resources is the actual operational focal point.

199 For a review of the types of behavior and agency costs of the administrative state, *see* Jerry L. Mashaw *et al.*, *Administrative Law* (St. Paul: West Publishing Co., 1998), pp. 36–55.

200 Global Environment Facility, "Corporate Business Plan FY02–FY04" (October 4, 2000), GEF/C.16/8, p. 2.

201 Within Central Asia, such $500/day salaries (even ignoring lush benefit programs) are so fabulously and exponentially beyond, to borrow GEF terminology, "country-driven" markets as to mock any claims these agencies may have to further the Central Asian states' transition to a market economy. For GEF salary information, *see* Global Environment Facility, "Proposal for a Fee-Based System for Funding GEF Project Implementation."

Conclusion: prospects for sustainable development in Central Asia

1 Akaev, "July 29, 1997 Report to the Security Council of the Kyrgyz Republic," p. 13.

2 Sievers *et al.*, "National Parks, Snow Leopards, and Poppy Plantations: The Development and Degradation of Central Asia's Preserved Lands," pp. 17–26.

3 Kazakhstan claimed a 14.6 per cent industrial output rise. Liz Fuller, "Kazakhstan Posts Solid Rise in Industrial Output," *RFE/RL Newsline* (January 16, 2001). Tajikistan claimed an 8.3 per cent GDP increase. Liz Fuller, "Tajik Economy Continues to Recover," *RFE/RL Newsline* (January 18, 2001). Turkmenistan claimed a 17.6 per cent increase in GDP, and added that it had the highest rate of growth in the world. Mikhail Pereplesnin and Yegor Yashin, "Ispytataelnyi srok dlya chinovnikov," *Nezavisimaya gazeta* (January 19, 2001), http://www.ng.ru/cis/2001-01-19/5srok.html.

4 Fischer and Sahay, "Economies in Transition: Taking Stock," p. 2.

5 Novosti Press Agency, "Public Health in the USSR: The Personnel and Their Salaries," in Burenkov (ed.), *Medicine and Health Care in the USSR*, p. 17.

6 John Nellis, "Time to Rethink Privatization in Transition Economies?" *Finance & Development* 36 (June, 1999), p. 16.

7 For a review of the linkage between the development of market institutions and incentives for corruption, *see* Harry G. Broadman and Francesca Rescatini, "Seeds of Corruption: Do Market Institutions Matter?" *World Bank Working Paper* (Washington, D.C.: The World Bank, 2000).

8 While arrogation of political power for personal gains is a well-accepted possibility, the equivalent economic practice has not been as readily accepted until recently, despite work in economics showing that rent-seeking can be more profitable in emerging economies than devoting assets to productive activities. Anne Krueger, "The Political Economy of a Rent-Seeking Society," *American Economic Review* 64 (1974), pp. 291–303. Paraphrased for the transition context, capitalists maximize profits, not the competitiveness of markets. Havrylyshyn and Odling-Smee, "Political Economy of Stalled Reforms," pp. 7–10.

9 *See, generally,* Saskia Sassen, *Globalization and Its Discontents.*

10 An argument not addressed here is that, in the sustainable development context, unregulated global trade cannot be a panacea. First, free trade will only increase resource throughput and, second, free trade cannot alter Liebig's Law. Referring back to the Introduction, Liebig's Law states that ecological carrying capacity is always determined by one limiting factor. If that limiting factor in Central Asia is water, free trade is meaningless for sustainable development, since water will not be imported into the region.

11 Foundation Center, *Grants for Foreign and International Programs* (The Foundation Center: New York, 1997).

12 Paul Goble, "Still More Reaction to Bush Interview," *RFE/RL Newsline* (January 18, 2001).

13 Sergei Duvanov, "Demokratiya po-amerikanski?" (January 16, 2001), http://eurasia. org.ru/2001/analitica/ 01_16_anamer.html.

14 "Reformers who recognize that real transformation requires participation and involvement would have welcomed this reform momentum and would have helped it push all the way to full privatization. Yet, the western-oriented reformers took the opposite course. In Russia, the leasing movement was stopped dead in its tracks in favor of voucher privatization." Ibid. p. 25.

15 Stiglitz, "Whither Reform: Ten Years of the Transition," p. 24.

16 *See* Regine Andersen, "How Multilateral Development Assistance Triggered the Conflict in Rwanda," *Third World Quarterly* 21(3) (2000), pp. 441–456.

17 As stated in the Rio Declaration: "In view of the different contributions to global environmental degradation, States have common but differentiated responsibilities. The developed countries acknowledge the responsibility that they bear in the international pursuit of sustainable development in view of the pressures their societies place on the global environment and of the technologies and financial resources they command."

18 In this regard, the fact that HIID was forced to close its doors because of, among other things, the indiscretions of its Moscow staff under USAID contracts is relevant. Instead of assuming responsibility for either these indiscretions or the general failure of HIID programs, HIID leadership merely opened a new body, the Center for International Development. The explicitly stated focus of CID is sustainable development: "CID has been established with one overriding conceptual notion: the need for cross-disciplinary approaches to challenges of sustainable development." Center for International Development, "Center for International Development at Harvard University," undated, http://www2.cid.harvard.edu/cidpapers/cidbrochure.pdf. In its actions, however, it is still HIID.

19 Julie A. Corwin, "New Nobel Laureate Pleads for More Cash for Science," *RFE/RL Newsline* (October 12, 2000).

20 *See* Skolnikoff, *The Elusive Transformation.*

Index